"*Leaves of Grass* is the first, and perhaps still the only true epic poem in our literature; upon the date of its hundredth anniversary, the fact is clear . . . Whitman was a great primitive poet, a founder of modern verse, a fountainhead of ideas, attitudes, techniques in twentieth-century prose and poetry alike."

SEE INTRODUCTION BY MAXWELL GEISMAR

On the 100th anniversary of the publication of the first edition of *Leaves of Grass*, Pocket Books, Inc. is honored to publish *The Whitman Reader*. Containing the best of Walt Whitman's poetry and prose, superbly edited by one of America's most noted literary figures, Maxwell Geismar, it is a volume that will both reinforce and inspire the reader's faith in the greatness of American letters and the fullness of American life.

The photograph that appears on the front cover of *The Whitman Reader* was taken on Walt Whitman's fiftieth birthday by Spieler. It was reproduced in The Century Magazine in 1893.

THE
WHITMAN
READER

Edited, with an Introduction, by

MAXWELL GEISMAR

POCKET BOOKS, INC. • NEW YORK

This original Cardinal Giant edition, prepared especially for Pocket Books, Inc., is printed from brand-new
plates made from newly set, clear, easy-to-read type.

The Whitman Reader

CARDINAL GIANT edition published March, 1955
1st printing......................January, 1955

L

Contents

LEAVES OF GRASS: SELECTIONS

Contents

PROSE

Contents

Contents

THE
WHITMAN
READER

"The messenger there arous'd, the fire,
the sweet hell within,
The unknown want, the destiny of me."

Introduction

THE SENSE OF AMUSEMENT is the bane of small spirits. Only the great can afford to be ludicrous, and to share in the laughter on which experience floats. In the middle of life we begin to see that things would be unbearable if they were not so comic. In Walt Whitman's verse, too, we must learn to accept the ridiculous as well as the sublime, and to cherish the note of absurdity as the mark of genius.

Leaves of Grass is the first, and perhaps still the only true epic poem in our literature; upon the date of its hundredth anniversary, the fact is clear. Yet it is quite typical of Whitman that among his early lines we should come upon

> "Me imperturbe, standing at ease in Nature,
>   Master of all, or mistress of all, aplomb in the
>   midst of irrational things"

—and that the master, aplomb and imperturbed, should then wish to confront all forms of adversity—night, storms, hunger, ridicule, accidents, rebuffs—as the trees and animals do. For this was a great primitive poet, a founder of modern verse, a fountainhead of ideas, attitudes, techniques in twentieth-century prose and poetry alike. And part of his charm lies directly in an odd mixture of the baroque and the gothic, as it were, until finally we come to enjoy just that part of the poet which is so outrageous to mere sophistication. Another typical line of Whitman's—"how plenteous! how spiritual! how resumé!"—achieves a kind of splendor through its singularity.

He viewed himself as a national bard—of a nation that, dilating from a liberated colony, had little use for poets or for him—and he was not averse to using the rhetoric of the Inde-

pendence Day celebrations. One notices the "red-flushed
cheeks" of lovers in "Proud Music of the Storm." He addressed
the earth as "O, vast rondure"; the sun as "thou orb aloft
full-dazzling"; and the Lord Himself as "thou moral, spiritual
fountain . . . thou reservoir." He delighted in describing the
scientific discoveries and commercial achievements which
Emerson suggested were not the songs of a nation, but its
inventories.

The list of Whitmanisms include such other famous verbal
hybrids as Allons! Camerado, Our Old Feuillage. "What am
I after all but a child, pleased with the sound of my own
name," he said, and very often it was the sound of these
words that got him into trouble; or that, on the other hand,
he may have deliberately invoked to heighten the wild, barbaric yawp of the New World's Muse.

His style was a strange mixture of the turgid, the banal, the
outré, and of brilliant, piercing phrases. (There is also the
quiet line, the orphic utterance, the homely twist and salty
tang of common speech.) Like Beethoven, who missed so
many chances to end his symphonies, Whitman usually has a
series of inscriptions and invocations to his beautiful vistas; a
long row of conclusions, summaries and farewells, to his great
verses. He is a poet who tries to say over again what he has
already said beyond compare. His best things may be hidden
away in an exasperating verbiage, from which they shine
suddenly to dazzle and enchant us, like hidden pools of sunlight in the forest. For long stretches his poetry may seem
commonplace. Then there is the moment of marvelous exhilaration and excitement. And we must accept it, I think,
just as we accept our own experience: in its totality.

2

THESE CONTRADICTIONS in the texture of the poet's art point
the way to other paradoxes in his personality. As in the case
of any major literary figure, there are as many interpretations
of Whitman as there are interpreters. Each man has found
his own image here, and perhaps Whitman is the mirror of

his critics. The cultural historian Vernon Parrington viewed him as the Child of the Enlightenment and the poet of democratic aspirations. The philosopher Santayana saw him, in contrast, as the poet of lost causes—of a primitive and amorphous state of democracy before it took on a mature and fatal shape. One of Whitman's recent editors, Malcolm Cowley, stresses the public mask of the poet, a combination, roughly, of Barnum and the Bowery tough. A second editor, Mark Van Doren, describes the morbid undertones in Whitman the stranger, the alienated individual who lurked behind the apostle of the masses.

If these impressions sometimes contradict each other, so did the poet, as he was proud to admit. Nature contained multitudes. A third recent editor of Whitman's work, Louis Untermeyer, has brought together an excellent compendium of Whitman criticism, and these diverse interpretations have extended from the original publication of *Leaves of Grass*, in 1855. The book was "A great primitive poem,—an alarum or trumpet-note ringing through the American camp," as Thoreau correctly said. But Emerson in turn, with his genuine impulses and inhibited responses, was at first all enthusiasm and then suddenly abashed. Whitman was also a touchstone for his critics. Henry James found his work to be "an offense against art" that slighted the intellect and outraged the taste, or at least his taste. Later he offered some grudging praise for a collection of Whitman's letters as descriptive of "patient, homely American life," and the "enormities of the common," and the "dreary amusements of average life."

If I mention such phrases it is because they are still echoed by the modern disciples of Henry James, who is usually superior to his cult, or by the disciples of T. S. Eliot, who sometimes isn't. But Whitman in his own time was also under attack from the common quarter, just where he felt he had addressed the whole weight of his literary work. The tradition of censorship and suppression has a prominent if not honorable place in our national letters. Perhaps it is even the mark of the masters in both wings of our literature: from the sudden silence which fell over Herman Melville's career after

Moby Dick and *Pierre*—a silence as of black night—to the European exile of Henry James himself, and the ostracism which shadowed the history of Theodore Dreiser. Much of the "critical reception" of Whitman's verse was in fact couched in phrases of calumny almost identical to those which were again hurled at the whole school of New Realists—the makers of modern prose—in the 1900's.

The capacity for invective on the part of those defending the status quo appears to be as limited in our literary as it has been in our societal battles. Perhaps the technique of the "big lie" itself was developed from our infantile human dependence upon repetition and incantation, instead of reason and imagination. Anyhow, we meet such phrases as "the slop-bucket of Walt Whitman" in the popular journalism of his time. His verse was called "entirely bestial," or an example of "gross materialism," on the part of this most idealistic and maybe even too ethereal of poets. He was accused of "indecent exposure"—of the human heart no doubt.

The Philadelphia Society for the Suppression of Vice called *Leaves of Grass* obscene. In New York, the authoritative Anthony Comstock, prototype of the puritan conscience in the livery of the robber barons, declared the book beyond the pale of the post office. In Quebec, in 1948, more than fifty years after Whitman's death, when anger should have ebbed, this acknowledged masterpiece of American literature was still characterized as "subversive." Who is to say, in the contemporary revival of fear and bigotry, that the present edition of Whitman's work will not meet a similar fate in some moral backwater of the Republic? The vitality of Whitman's work endures, and these are its mementos.

3

BECAUSE OF his poetry, Whitman himself had been dismissed from his government post after the Civil War. Writing to friends, in the seventies, he mentioned the general attitude of "denial and sneering" in respect to his work and himself. *Democratic Vistas*, he said, remained "quite unread, uncalled for, here in America." *Leaves of Grass* was contemptuously ignored by all the recognized literary organs. No American publisher would publish it; many of the bookstores refused to stock it; though, as Whitman added, his book had been written in the sun, and with a gay heart.

Thus democracy's prime poet was not only ignored by his own audience, but condemned by the prevailing social institutions of his period. The point, of course, is that he had broken a primary sexual taboo very early in his work. And he continued to stretch the range of his observation and feeling into a second, almost as dangerous area of social criticism.

Today the homosexuality in Whitman's verse is as commonly accepted by scholars as is that in Shakespeare's sonnets. But this was not Whitman's greatest offense. He advocated the value of *all* instinctual responses in human behavior: the complete equality of the body with the spirit.

Melville had hinted darkly at this obvious truth. The Transcendentalists, even Thoreau, who stressed all the homely truths of life, except this one, had transcended the issue through an ecstatic sublimation with the spirit of the universe. In Edgar Allan Poe the living world of human desire was transmuted into a shadow world of chilling pathological fantasies, incestuous, necrophilic. It remained for Whitman, the stubborn, vulgar, half-educated journeyman printer, with the Quaker dissent bred into his bones, to supply the great link between the "black and white" universe of New England letters (in Van Wyck Brooks' phrase) and the famous "revolt of the flesh" through which modern American writing gained the stature and compass of a world literature.

Through this view of Whitman, we can resolve some of the curious strains in his temperament which clustered around or attached themselves to the central sexual impulse in his work. "Myself effusing and fluid, a phantom curiously floating," he said. And he was in truth an oddly ethereal poetic specter who, bringing American poety at least half way down to earth, had remained himself suspended in the esthetic orb. (This was partly in the mode of English roman-

tic verse; but it was also deeply personal.) Transfixed as
Whitman was by the scenes and surfaces of the life around
him, by the *texture* of things, or at best the moods of the
isolated individual, he seemed almost indifferent to the other
meanings of life which are contained in human relationships
and the whole world of human relatedness. His approach to
experience was primarily tactile; and Vachel Lindsay was
correct when he complained about the lack of "gossip" in
Whitman's work. What he lacked in fact was not only the
novelist's concern with all types of people, but even the
poet's concern with his own poetic types. He often appears to
be such a completely unique individual as to dispense with
all ordinary human attributes.

Thus Whitman talks about his grandfather, the Major, as
being "jovial, red, stout, with sonorous voice and characteristic physiognomy." On his family life he notes again in
Specimen Days for 1855: "Lost my dear father this year by
death. Commenced putting *Leaves of Grass* to press for
good . . ." The most confessional of poets also tells us almost
nothing about the mother to whom he wrote such commonplace letters during the Civil War; or about the other members of his family; or about a later series of masculine friendships where, in his verse, we do discern the elements of deep
personal affection. Whitman's odd obsession to identify himself with all the forms and shapes he saw around him, and
to be one with everything: this gross, overwhelming and uni-
versally aspiring egoism, often so effective in his poetry, was
derived from a personal egoism that was itself curiously fluid
and formless. It was an ego that was all ego and yet no ego.

Whitman's statement that he was really interested in only
two things, poetry and democracy, confirms his indifference
to many other phases of the "materialism" which he defended
so warmly. But one realizes that the prevailing view of life in
his poetry is very close to a form of primitive egoism, or pan-
theism, which contends and deeply believes that all things
really are similar to itself, or extensions of itself, or part of
itself. The universal "I" which Whitman used so naturally
and instinctively to describe the role of the democratic seer

who had been everywhere, and shared in every experience, was, in reality, the mystic symbol of an ancient poetic personality who descended from the ecstatic books of the East and from biblical literature. This omnipotent "I" of early poetry was invoked as the witness of all men's affairs, and as the word of God.

It was even more, and was historically more ancient than this, as Robert Graves has recently demonstrated. It was the prevailing mystic sign of those pre-historical and pre-biblical bards who, before the coming of the religious patriarchy, had devoted themselves to the mysteries and magic of the ancient Earth Goddess. It was She, who in her triple guise of birth, love, and death, had dominated all the ancient cultures. She had taken the shape of Isis, Rhea, Astarte, Aphrodite and a thousand other local names, and had ruled supreme with her cults and rites of fertility. And it was to the secrets of the White Goddess that Whitman had instinctively dedicated his earlier verse, in content as well as in its special form, renewing the poet's ancient and indispensable tie with the earth; and desiring to restore the status and the enhancement of the natural life in America. Perhaps this is why the hostility to Whitman's work was so intense and bitter and, as it seems to us today, unreasonable. A later poet, Gerard Manley Hopkins, was quite correct in describing Whitman's verse as "prose bewitched."

4

IN ANOTHER essay on Whitman, D. H. Lawrence has pointed out the tragic sequence between the poet's outspoken hymns to "virile love" and his swift elegies to "death, death, death." The Whitman of the "Adam" and "Calamus" poems was indeed quite suddenly converted from an innocent and rosy vision of the universe—and a sort of intolerable euphoria in the early "Songs"—to a dark and suicidal despair.

These early love poems are of greater value as history than as poetry. They are too close to the poet, and are at best only a form of confessional. One notices soon enough the notes of anguish which are the price of passion; and are always recorded by the writers who have elected to follow their temperaments. If Whitman, in his forty-first year, was determined to tell us the secrets of his nights and days, he recorded also that the "blossoms of his blood" were not pure happiness. "You are often more bitter than I can bear, you burn and sting me." Yet he had long enough stifled and choked, and he was resolved to unbare his breast. In "Out of the Cradle Endlessly Rocking," still contemplating the fire, the sweet hell within, "the unknown want, the destiny of me," he could nevertheless cry: "O if I am to have so much, let me have more!"

It was by means of this syndrome of sexual feeling that Whitman achieved his breakthrough as a poet. His determination to be faithful to his instincts—an act of boldness and perhaps ruthlessness which marks the psychic release of the major artist—urged him forward to his solitary, rebellious and germinal verses. The opening stanzas in "Song of Myself" record also the mystic moments of Whitman's emotional liberation: moments of ecstasy and rapture which are transposed into a great paean to love and life.

> "Earth of the vitreous pour of the full moon just tinged with blue!
> Earth of shine and dark mottling the tide of the river!
> Earth of the limpid gray of clouds brighter and clearer for my sake!
> Far-swooping elbow'd earth—rich apple-blossom'd earth!
> Smile, for your lover comes."

"Prodigal, you have given me love," Whitman added—"Therefore I to you give love! / O unspeakable passionate love." In the litter of the grunting sow, the brood of the turkey hen, and the mother with the half-spread wings—in them and in himself, "the same old law." On all sides he felt those "prurient provokers," stiffening his limbs through means of that villain touch. The sentries had deserted every other part of him, and left him helpless. Given up by traitors, he could only cry: "I talk wildly, I have lost my wits, I and nobody else am the greatest traitor."

Nothing could be clearer, or more magnificent, than this apostrophe to the sexual rapture which pervades Nature. And if the note of personal loss, of dark despair, and of death followed so soon after the moment of ecstasy, that, too, was the inexorable law of the White Goddess. The point was that through this central experience Whitman had already liberated himself from the empty conventions and customs of his time. (It is never really a question of "sublimation" but of the *conversion* of experience into art.) Having experienced his own passion, Whitman could then write of those who, "smartly attired, countenance smiling, form upright," had suffered a different form of death under the breast-bone:

"Under the broadcloth and gloves, under the ribbons and
    artificial flowers,
  Keeping fair with the customs, speaking not a syllable of
    itself,
  Speaking of anything else but never of itself."

Inside of dresses and ornaments, he said—"Inside of those wash'd and trimm'd faces, / Behold a secret silent loathing and despair."

This particular mode of speech was to be picked up later by T. S. Eliot among the modern poets. But we must understand that it was first expressed here within a quite different frame of reference. Instead of the later emphasis on resignation and compliance, or on salvation through ceremonial, Whitman still demanded that every human soul express its own needs, whatever and however. "My call is the call of battle. I nourish active rebellion." In "Song of the Open Road," it was this Whitman who could say

"Listen! I will be honest with you,
  I do not offer the old smooth prizes, but offer rough
    new prizes."

—who demanded freedom from the formulas of the "bat-eyed and materialistic priests"; and who pictured the universe itself as a road, "as many roads, as roads for traveling souls."

It was excellent advice, if mainly ignored by an America barely released from Calvin's purgatory and about to plunge into the inferno of finance. It was a mode of prophecy that still applies, in our own day, to a society which is outwardly more comfortable, perhaps, but inwardly no less cramped.

5

ON THE PERSONAL SIDE, there was no doubt an element of guilt behind the images of love and death in Whitman's verse. The Civil War was in part a perfect resolution for the poet's dilemma. Ministering to the wounded and dying young American soldiers as a male nurse, he could freely loose his feeling, and find in the scene around him everywhere the necessary retribution. More important, however, the war was another turning point for his art. Whitman was fortunate; or to put it more accurately, he knew and sought out, in whatever peculiar guise, his point of realization. Earlier, knowing very little about the "divine average" which he apotheosized, he had been curiously abstract as spokesman for the masses. He had even envisioned a working democracy of manly kisses and rough embraces: an "adhesive proletariat," as it were, or a sort of affectional Marxism which was surely among the oddest of all the odd utopias.

The war poetry in *Drum-Taps* was chauvinistic and rhetorical at the start. But not for long—

"(Arous'd and angry, I'd thought to beat the alarum, and
    urge relentless war,
But soon my fingers fail'd me, my face droop'd and I re-
    sign'd myself,
To sit by the wounded and soothe them, or silently watch
    the dead;)"

And not in the great Civil War poetry. Instead, as Whitman brooded over the underlying issues of the conflict, the masses of men involved on both sides of the battle, the individual cases of suffering and of fortitude which he had known, came the haunting and beautiful elegies in memory of President Lincoln. From this source came Whitman's most mature statement of his social beliefs in "By Blue Ontario's Shore". Written originally in 1856, and revised afterwards, this poem was notable for the undertones of despair and frustration which now attended the gleaming saga of democracy. What had happened since "the haughty defiance of the Year One" and the forming of the Constitution?

The war had indeed ended the epoch of Emerson, Thoreau and Longfellow, among the sages, and opened the epoch of the Vanderbilts and Rockefellers among the titans. Whitman found himself in a familiar posture of suspense, but this time between a past he had found incomplete, and a future he distrusted. Now he was hovering over the chasm of his hopes. In Parrington's phrase he became "the poet and prophet of a democracy that the America of the Gilded Age was daily betraying." What the historian called "the exalted abandon of egoistic experience" had been in reality, in Whitman's true inner development, the universal and immemorial cult of the savage love-goddess. But there was no doubt, at least, that the most deeply religious soul of the post-war epoch was flung into outer darkness by the rude arbiters of a money society.

The distinction was of course between Whitman's "materialism of the flesh"—of individual experience and self fulfilment—and the new materialism of wealth, power and worldly success. And then what acrid, disheartened and prophetic intimations issued from the erstwhile apostle of euphoria! The present age in America, he said, was an age tyrannically regulated with reference to the manufacturer, the financier, the politician. The democratic masses included "our materialistic, self-assertive, money-worshipping Anglo-Saxon race." He could not avoid the "morbid facts" of American life—which appeared everywhere in his later years as a "general malaria of bogs and vapors." What in fact was left of moral power and ethical sanity in that "huge inflammation call'd society" after the advent of the great American fortunes;

and what remedy was there for "the real inmost disease of our times"?

The latter statements were included in his piece on the Quaker preacher Elias Hicks, written in 1888. In the notes of "Collect" he had been even more specific about the "limitless aperture" of mere show, luxury and money-making towards which the American nation was rushing *en-masse.* What had happened here to his earlier concept of a glorious new race of mechanics, farmers and tradesmen who would bulk so large in a divine commonalty? In "Who Gets the Plunder?" he noted the "glittering delusions of great money" which were actually based on the exploitation of the poor. The profits went altogether to a few score select persons—"who by favors of Congress, State legislatures, the banks, and other special advantages, are forming a vulgar aristocracy, full as bad as anything in the British or European castes, of blood, or the dynasties there of the past."

Now this was striking at Whitman's central vision of democracy supplanting the whole idea of dynasties, castes, and privileged social classes. In "Democratic Vistas" he had lamented the glamour which surrounded the crimes of the feudal and dynastic world of the past. "But the People are ungrammatical, untidy, and their sins gaunt and ill-bred." Yet to this Whitman a man was still a summons and a challenge. And time was ample. "Let the victors come after us."

It was in this exultant mood that he had demanded new races of orbic bards with uncompromising sway. "Come forth, sweet democratic despots of the west!" But now he commented on the armies of tramps who swarmed through the States towards the end of the nineteenth century. He wrote about strikes and labor wars and all the other manifestations of a savage new industrial system. And he took a more limited view of things. "I can conceive of no better service in the United States henceforth by democrats of thorough and heartfelt faith, than boldly exposing the weaknesses, liabilities and infinite corruptions of democracy."

Very shortly after Whitman himself had sung the light and splendor of the democratic dawn in the history of the

race, he could have said that again his country awaited the
coming of its bards in silence and in twilight. In his black
moods, as in "Reversals", he had sometimes felt that all his
primary assumptions about life in America could be over-
turned—

> "Let that which stood in front go behind,
>   Let that which was behind advance to the front,
>   Let bigots, fools, unclean persons, offer new propositions,
>   Let the old propositions be postponed,
>   Let a man seek pleasure everywhere except in himself,
>   Let a woman seek happiness everywhere except in her-
>   self."

In the years before the Civil War he had suggested, in the
same vein, that the reformers descend from the stands where
they were forever bawling; that the judges and criminals be
transposed; that those who distrusted birth and death should
lead the rest. Once again, towards the close of his life, he saw
"bats and night-dogs" in his country's capitol, and scum floating on top of the waters. He had learned all too well to
chant "the cold dirges of the baffled, and sullen hymns of defeat," while only matter, triumphant, continued onward.

6

IN HIS OWN VOICE, of course, the aging Whitman was still a
summons and a challenge to his readers. This outwardly
vague, misty, musing spirit came to represent, rather like
Tolstoy in Russia, the true conscience of his country. The
outraged, eloquent and radical Whitman was the recording
angel of the Gilded Age. Just as he had been the chief link
between Herman Melville and Theodore Dreiser in the subterranean biological revolution against a proscriptive Puri-
tanism, so, after the deaths of the New England sages, he
carried forward their spiritual heritage to the opening years
of the twentieth century. Having defied the etherealism of
the Transcendentalists, belonging to the modern world in his

stress on the flesh and the passions in art, he still represented the earlier age in his belief that existence must have a moral center. (And isn't there a certain connection, not yet fully realized, between seeking a fulfilment of individual experience on the psycho-biological level, and insisting upon justice for all men?) "Of Equality"—Whitman said—"As if it harm'd me, giving others the same chances and rights as myself—as if it were not indispensable to my own rights that others possess the same."

But meanwhile he stood in the void—a neglected solitary rebellious figure—between the old agrarian republic and the new economic Empire which, having firmly established itself at home by the 1900's, began to look abroad and to sniff at being a world power. During these years, Whitman described himself as being much like "some hard-cased dilapidated grim ancient shell-fish or time-bang'd conch." Without the use of his legs, utterly "non-locomotive," there was nothing left, as he said, but to behave himself quiet, and to discover what still could be salvaged from those primal buoyant center-pulses down there deep within his gray-blurred old shell. There was also the more famous description of "Me, old, alone, sick, weak-down, melted-worn with sweat." And there are still other magical lines which shine at us from the final period of his writing.

Few American writers have known how to grow old. The trick, said Whitman in *Specimen Days,* was to tone down your wants and tastes low enough, "and make much of negatives." And this poet could still look up at the skies which he had delighted in, to add:

"Old, poor, and paralyzed, I thank Thee!"

He had turned back in age to the Quaker customs and beliefs of his youth (as F.A.O. Matthiessen has noticed), and something of an older faith and loving-kindness shines through these final passages. "I have the most devoted and ardent of friends . . . and of enemies I really make no account." There is the humor of self-perception in these sad and touching little chants of farewell:

> "Soon to be lost of aye in the darkness—loth, O so loth to depart!
> Garrulous to the very last."

His songs of parting did indeed constitute a triumphant farewell to the life which Whitman had celebrated so fully. Still he could lag and pause "and crouch extended with un-shut mouth," as he had said earlier, wondering if there was a single final farewell. In his "last saved items from a vast batch left to oblivion," he could mourn: "How difficult it is to add anything more to literature—and how unsatisfactory for any earnest spirit to serve merely the amusement of the multitude!" He had wanted to show, he said, how a Person in America in the last half of the 19th century would appear in honest type. "Haven't I given specimen clues, if no more? At any rate I have written enough to weary myself—and I will dispatch it to the printers, and cease. But how much—how many topics, of the greatest point and cogency, I am leaving untouch'd!"

Such were the closing lines of the Deathbed Edition of his works which he had arranged: still hungry for life, still curious, still deeply involved, and wanting to say more. A little earlier he had compared all his writing to the peep-hole through which the actors of his period used to survey the "house" before the opening of the show. He was content if through him the future might cast "one brief honest living glance" at the life of his time. But if Whitman's work en-ables us to do just that today, it is because of the "freedom of the masters" which he always applauded in others, and which was the personal mark of the poet himself. This is the aspect of Whitman which continues to enchant and to sus-tain us one hundred years after his book.

Today, too, when we perceive only evil around us, in na-ture's schemes and the systems of society alike, it is useful to recall that Whitman's grand innocence wasn't, in the final analysis, a refusal to see the bad but a wish to transcend it. Like the Quaker Saints whom he came to resemble, like the Thoreau who after witnessing the tortures of natural selection could still cry that no wounds were fatal; like Melville in the final note of *Moby Dick*, Whitman presents a view of life which accommodates and combines those two perhaps merely provincial poles of good and evil. He participated in a universe whose intentions went beyond the cognizance of animals and men; but where the animals had learned to bear their trials with fortitude, and where men should not willingly increase their own.

—MAXWELL GEISMAR

Harrison, Westchester.
1955

Come, said my Soul,
Such verses for my Body let us write, (for we are one,)
That should I after death invisibly return,
Or, long, long hence, in other spheres,
There to some group of mates the chants resuming,
(Tallying Earth's soil, trees, winds, tumultuous waves,)
Ever with pleas'd smile I may keep on,
Ever and ever yet the verses owning—as, first, I here and now,
Signing for Soul and Body, set to them my name,

Walt Whitman

Leaves of Grass

ONE'S-SELF I SING

One's-Self I sing, a simple separate person,
Yet utter the word Democratic, the word En-Masse.

Of physiology from top to toe I sing,
Not physiognomy alone nor brain alone is worthy for the Muse,
    I say the Form complete is worthier far,
The Female equally with the Male I sing.

Of Life immense in passion, pulse, and power,
Cheerful, for freest action form'd under the laws divine,
The Modern Man I sing.

IN CABIN'D SHIPS AT SEA

In cabin'd ships at sea,
The boundless blue on every side expanding,
With whistling winds and music of the waves, the large im-
    perious waves,

Or some lone bark buoy'd on the dense marine,
Where joyous full of faith, spreading white sails,
She cleaves the ether mid the sparkle and the foam of day, or
      under many a star at night,
By sailors young and old haply will I, a reminiscence of the
      land, be read,
In full rapport at last.

Here are our thoughts, voyagers' thoughts,
Here not the land, firm land, alone appears, may then by them
      be said,
The sky o'erarches here, we feel the undulating deck beneath
      our feet,
We feel the long pulsation, ebb and flow of endless motion,
The tones of unseen mystery, the vague and vast suggestions
      of the briny world, the liquid-flowing syllables,
The perfume, the faint creaking of the cordage, the melan-
      choly rhythm,
The boundless vista and the horizon far and dim are all here,
And this is ocean's poem.

Then falter not O book, fulfil your destiny,
You not a reminiscence of the land alone,
You too as a lone bark cleaving the ether, purpos'd I know
      not whither, yet ever full of faith,
Consort to every ship that sails, sail you!
Bear forth to them folded my love, (dear mariners, for you I
      fold it here in every leaf;)
Speed on my book! spread your white sails my little bark
      athwart the imperious waves,
Chant on, sail on, bear o'er the boundless blue from me to
      every sea,
This song for mariners and all their ships.

TO THEE OLD CAUSE

To thee old cause!
Thou peerless, passionate, good cause,
Thou stern, remorseless, sweet idea,
Deathless throughout the ages, races, lands,
After a strange sad war, great war for thee,
(I think all war through time was really fought, and ever will
        be really fought, for thee,)
These chants for thee, the eternal march of thee.

(A war, O soldiers not for itself alone,
Far, far more stood silently waiting behind, now to advance
        in this book.)

Thou orb of many orbs!
Thou seething principle! thou well-kept, latent germ! thou
        centre!
Around the idea of thee the war revolving,
With all its angry and vehement play of causes,
(With vast results to come for thrice a thousand years,)
These recitatives for thee,—my book and the war are one,
Merged in its spirit I and mine, as the contest hinged on thee,
As a wheel on its axis turns, this book unwitting to itself,
Around the idea of thee.

BEGINNING MY STUDIES

Beginning my studies the first step pleas'd me so much,
The mere fact consciousness, these forms, the power of motion,
The least insect or animal, the senses, eyesight, love,
The first step I say awed me and pleas'd me so much,
I have hardly gone and hardly wish'd to go any farther,
But stop and loiter all the time to sing it in ecstatic songs.

BEGINNERS

How they are provided for upon the earth, (appearing at intervals,)
How dear and dreadful they are to the earth,
How they inure to themselves as much as to any—what a paradox appears their age,
How people respond to them, yet know them not,
How there is something relentless in their fate all times,
How all times mischoose the objects of their adulation and reward,
And how the same inexorable price must still be paid for the same great purchase.

TO THE STATES

To the States or any one of them, or any city of the States,
Resist much, obey little,
Once unquestioning obedience, once fully enslaved,
Once fully enslaved, no nation, state, city of this earth, ever afterward resumes its liberty.

TO A CERTAIN CANTATRICE

Here, take this gift,
I was reserving it for some hero, speaker, or general,
One who should serve the good old cause, the great idea, the progress and freedom of the race,
Some brave confronter of despots, some daring rebel;
But I see that what I was reserving belongs to you just as much as to any.

ME IMPERTURBE

Me imperturbe, standing at ease in Nature,
Master of all or mistress of all, aplomb in the midst of irra-
      tional things,
Imbued as they, passive, receptive, silent as they,
Finding my occupation, poverty, notoriety, foibles, crimes, less
      important than I thought,
Me toward the Mexican sea, or in the Mannahatta or the
      Tennessee, or far north or inland,
A river man, or a man of the woods or of any farm-life of
      these States or of the coast, or the lakes or Kanada,
Me wherever my life is lived, O to be self-balanced for con-
      tingencies,
To confront night, storms, hunger, ridicule, accidents, rebuffs,
      as the trees and animals do.

I HEAR AMERICA SINGING

I hear America singing, the varied carols I hear,
Those of mechanics, each one singing his as it should be
      blithe and strong,
The carpenter singing his as he measures his plank or beam,
The mason singing his as he makes ready for work, or leaves
      off work,
The boatman singing what belongs to him in his boat, the
      deckhand singing on the steamboat deck,
The shoemaker singing as he sits on his bench, the hatter
      singing as he stands,
The wood-cutter's song, the ploughboy's on his way in the
      morning, or at noon intermission or at sundown,
The delicious singing of the mother, or of the young wife at
      work, or of the girl sewing or washing,
Each singing what belongs to him or her and to none else,
The day what belongs to the day—at night the party of young
      fellows, robust, friendly,
Singing with open mouths their strong melodious songs.

WHAT PLACE IS BESIEGED?

What place is besieged, and vainly tries to raise the siege?
Lo, I send to that place a commander, swift, brave, immortal,
And with him horse and foot, and parks of artillery,
And artillery-men, the deadliest that ever fired gun.

SHUT NOT YOUR DOORS

Shut not your doors to me proud libraries,
For that which was lacking on all your well-fill'd shelves, yet
     needed most, I bring,
Forth from the war emerging, a book I have made,
The words of my book nothing, the drift of it every thing,
A book separate, not link'd with the rest nor felt by the in-
     tellect,
But you ye untold latencies will thrill to every page.

POETS TO COME

Poets to come! orators, singers, musicians to come!
Not to-day is to justify me and answer what I am for,
But you, a new brood, native, athletic, continental, greater
     than before known,
Arouse! for you must justify me.

I myself but write one or two indicative words for the future,
I but advance a moment only to wheel and hurry back in the
     darkness.

I am a man who, sauntering along without fully stopping,
     turns a casual look upon you and then averts his face,
Leaving it to you to prove and define it,
Expecting the main things from you.

STILL THOUGH THE ONE I SING

Still though the one I sing,
(One, yet of contradictions made,) I dedicate to Nationality,
I leave in him revolt, (O latent right of insurrection! O quench-
    less, indispensable fire!)

TO YOU

Stranger, if you passing meet me and desire to speak to me,
    why should you not speak to me?
And why should I not speak to you?

THOU READER

Thou reader throbbest life and pride and love the same as I,
Therefore for thee the following chants.

STARTING from PAUMANOK

1

Starting from fish-shape Paumanok where I was born,
Well-begotten, and rais'd by a perfect mother,
After roaming many lands, lover of populous pavements,
Dweller in Mannahatta my city, or on southern savannas,
Or a soldier camp'd or carrying my knapsack and gun, or a
    miner in California,
Or rude in my home in Dakota's woods, my diet meat, my
    drink from the spring,

Or withdrawn to muse and meditate in some deep recess,
Far from the clank of crowds intervals passing rapt and happy,
Aware of the fresh free giver the flowing Missouri, aware of
    mighty Niagara,
Aware of the buffalo herds grazing the plains, the hirsute and
    strong-breasted bull,
Of earth, rocks, Fifth-month flowers experienced, stars, rain,
    snow, my amaze,
Having studied the mocking-bird's tones and the flight of the
    mountain-hawk,
And heard at dawn the unrivall'd one, the hermit thrush from
    the swamp-cedars,
Solitary, singing in the West, I strike up for a New World.

2

Victory, union, faith, identity, time,
The indissoluble compacts, riches, mystery,
Eternal progress, the kosmos, and the modern reports.
This then is life,
Here is what has come to the surface after so many throes and
    convulsions.

How curious! how real!
Underfoot the divine soil, overhead the sun.

See revolving the globe,
The ancestor-continents away group'd together,
The present and future continents north and south, with the
    isthmus between.

See, vast trackless spaces,
As in a dream they change, they swiftly fill,
Countless masses debouch upon them,
They are now cover'd with the foremost people, arts, institu-
    tions, known.

See, projected through time,
For me an audience interminable.

With firm and regular step they wend, they never stop,
Successions of men, Americanos, a hundred millions,
One generation playing its part and passing on,
Another generation playing its part and passing on in its turn,
With faces turn'd sideways or backward towards me to listen,
With eyes retrospective towards me.

3

Americanos! conquerors! marches humanitarian!
Foremost, century marches! Libertad! masses!
For you a programme of chants.

Chants of the prairies,
Chants of the long-running Mississippi, and down to the
        Mexican sea,
Chants of Ohio, Indiana, Illinois, Iowa, Wisconsin and Min-
        nesota,
Chants going forth from the centre from Kansas, and thence
        equidistant,
Shooting in pulses of fire ceaseless to vivify all.

4

Take my leaves America, take them South and take them
        North,
Make welcome for them everywhere, for they are your own
        offspring,
Surround them East and West, for they would surround you,
And you precedents, connect lovingly with them, for they con-
        nect lovingly with you.

I conn'd old times,
I sat studying at the feet of the great masters,
Now if eligible O that the great masters might return and
        study me.

In the name of these States shall I scorn the antique?
Why these are the children of the antique to justify it.

5

Dead poets, philosophs, priests,
Martyrs, artists, inventors, governments long since,
Language-shapers on other shores,
Nations once powerful, now reduced, withdrawn, or desolate,
I dare not proceed till I respectfully credit what you have left
　　　wafted hither,
I have perused it, own it is admirable, (moving awhile
　　　among it,)
Think nothing can ever be greater, nothing can ever deserve
　　　more than it deserves,
Regarding it all intently a long while, then dismissing it,
I stand in my place with my own day here.

Here lands female and male,
Here the heir-ship and heiress-ship of the world, here the
　　　flame of materials,
Here spirituality the translatress, the openly-avow'd,
The ever-tending, the finalè of visible forms,
The satisfier, after due long-waiting now advancing,
Yes here comes my mistress the soul.

6

The soul,
Forever and forever—longer than soil is brown and solid—
　　　longer than water ebbs and flows.
I will make the poems of materials, for I think they are to be
　　　the most spiritual poems,
And I will make the poems of my body and of mortality,
For I think I shall then supply myself with the poems of my
　　　soul and of immortality.

I will make a song for these States that no one State may un-
　　　der any circumstances be subjected to another State,

And I will make a song that there shall be comity by day and
      by night between all the States, and between any two
      of them,
And I will make a song for the ears of the President, full of
      weapons with menacing points,
And behind the weapons countless dissatisfied faces;
And a song make I of the One form'd out of all,
The fang'd and glittering One whose head is over all,
Resolute warlike One including and over all,
(However high the head of any else that head is over all.)

I will acknowledge contemporary lands,
I will trail the whole geography of the globe and salute
      courteously every city large and small,
And employments! I will put in my poems that with you is
      heroism upon land and sea,
And I will report all heroism from an American point of view.

I will sing the song of companionship,
I will show what alone must finally compact these,
I believe these are to found their own ideal of manly love,
      indicating it in me,
I will therefore let flame from me the burning fires that were
      threatening to consume me,
I will lift what has too long kept down those smouldering
      fires,
I will give them complete abandonment,
I will write the evangel-poem of comrades and of love,
For who but I should understand love with all its sorrow and
      joy?
And who but I should be the poet of comrades?

7

I am the credulous man of qualities, ages, races,
I advance from the people in their own spirit,
Here is what sings unrestricted faith.
Omnes! omnes! let others ignore what they may,

I make the poem of evil also, I commemorate that part also,
I am myself just as much evil as good, and my nation is—and
    I say there is in fact no evil,
(Or if there is I say it is just as important to you, to the land
    or to me, as any thing else.)

I too, following many and follow'd by many, inaugurate a re-
    ligion, I descend into the arena,
(It may be I am destin'd to utter the loudest cries there, the
    winner's pealing shouts,
Who knows? they may rise from me yet, and soar above every
    thing.)

Each is not for its own sake,
I say the whole earth and all the stars in the sky are for re-
    ligion's sake.

I say no man has ever yet been half devout enough,
None has ever yet adored or worship'd half enough,
None has begun to think how divine he himself is, and how
    certain the future is.

I say that the real and permanent grandeur of these States
    must be their religion,
Otherwise there is no real and permanent grandeur;
(Nor character nor life worthy the name without religion,
Nor land nor man or woman without religion.)

8

What are you doing young man?
Are you so earnest, so given up to literature, science, art,
    amours?
These ostensible realities, politics, points?
Your ambition or business whatever it may be?

It is well—against such I say not a word, I am their poet also,
But behold! such swiftly subside, burnt up for religion's sake,

For not all matter is fuel to heat, impalpable flame, the essential life of the earth,
Any more than such are to religion.

9

What do you seek so pensive and silent?
What do you need camerado?
Dear son do you think it is love?

Listen dear son—listen America, daughter or son,
It is a painful thing to love a man or woman to excess, and yet it satisfies, it is great,
But there is something else very great, it makes the whole coincide,
It, magnificent, beyond materials, with continuous hands sweeps and provides for all.

10

Know you, solely to drop in the earth the germs of a greater religion,
The following chants each for its kind I sing.

My comrade!
For you to share with me two greatnesses, and a third one rising inclusive and more resplendent,
The greatness of Love and Democracy, and the greatness of Religion.

Melange mine own, the unseen and the seen,
Mysterious ocean where the streams empty,
Prophetic spirit of materials shifting and flickering around me,
Living beings, identities now doubtless near us in the air that we know not of,
Contact daily and hourly that will not release me,
These selecting, these in hints demanded of me.

Not he with a daily kiss onward from childhood kissing me,
Has winded and twisted around me that which holds me to
      him,
Any more than I am held to the heavens and all the spiritual
      world,
After what they have done to me, suggesting themes.

O such themes—equalities! O divine average!
Warblings under the sun, usher'd as now, or at noon, or
      setting,
Strains musical flowing through ages, now reaching hither,
I take to your reckless and composite chords, add to them,
      and cheerfully pass them forward.

11

As I have walk'd in Alabama my morning walk,
I have seen where the she-bird the mocking-bird sat on her
      nest in the briers hatching her brood.

I have seen the he-bird also,
I have paus'd to hear him near at hand inflating his throat
      and joyfully singing.

And while I paus'd it came to me that what he really sang for
      was not there only,
Nor for his mate nor himself only, nor all sent back by the
      echoes,
But subtle, clandestine, away beyond,
A charge transmitted and gift occult for those being born.

12

Democracy! near at hand to you a throat is now inflating itself
      and joyfully singing.

Ma femme! for the brood beyond us and of us,
For those who belong here and those to come,

I exultant to be ready for them will not shake out carols
　　stronger and haughtier than have ever yet been heard
　　upon earth.

I will make the songs of passion to give them their way,
And your songs outlaw'd offenders, for I scan you with
　　kindred eyes, and carry you with me the same as any.

I will make the true poem of riches,
To earn for the body and the mind whatever adheres and
　　goes forward and is not dropt by death;
I will effuse egotism and show it underlying all, and I will
　　be the bard of personality,
And I will show of male and female that either is but the
　　equal of the other,
And sexual organs and acts! do you concentrate in me, for I
　　am determin'd to tell you with courageous clear voice
　　to prove you illustrious,
And I will show that there is no imperfection in the present,
　　and can be none in the future,
And I will show that whatever happens to anybody it may be
　　turn'd to beautiful results,
And I will show that nothing can happen more beautiful than
　　death,
And I will thread a thread through my poems that time and
　　events are compact,
And that all the things of the universe are perfect miracles,
　　each as profound as any.

I will not make poems with reference to parts,
But I will make poems, songs, thoughts, with reference to
　　ensemble,
And I will not sing with reference to a day, but with reference
　　to all days,
And I will not make a poem nor the least part of a poem but
　　has reference to the soul,
Because having look'd at the objects of the universe, I find
　　there is no one nor any particle of one but has reference
　　to the soul.

13

Was somebody asking to see the soul?
See, your own shape and countenance, persons, substances,
        beasts, the trees, the running rivers, the rocks and sands.

All hold spiritual joys and afterwards loosen them;
How can the real body ever die and be buried?

Of your real body and any man's or woman's real body,
Item for item it will elude the hands of the corpse-cleaners
        and pass to fitting spheres,
Carrying what has accrued to it from the moment of birth to
        the moment of death.

Not the types set up by the printer return their impression,
        the meaning, the main concern,
Any more than a man's substance and life or a woman's
        substance and life return in the body and the soul,
Indifferently before death and after death.

Behold, the body includes and is the meaning, the main con-
        cern, and includes and is the soul;
Whoever you are, how superb and how divine is your body,
        or any part of it!

14

Whoever you are, to you endless announcements!

Daughter of the lands did you wait for your poet?
Did you wait for one with a flowing mouth and indicative
        hand?
Toward the male of the States, and toward the female of the
        States,
Exulting words, words to Democracy's lands.

Interlink'd, food-yielding lands!

Land of coal and iron! land of gold! land of cotton, sugar, rice!

Land of wheat, beef, pork! land of wool and hemp! land of the apple and the grape!

Land of the pastoral plains, the grass-fields of the world! land of those sweet-air'd interminable plateaus!

Land of the herd, the garden, the healthy house of adobie!

Lands where the north-west Columbia winds, and where the south-west Colorado winds!

Land of the eastern Chesapeake! land of the Delaware!

Land of Ontario, Erie, Huron, Michigan!

Land of the Old Thirteen! Massachusetts land! land of Vermont and Connecticut!

Land of the ocean shores! land of sierras and peaks!

Land of boatmen and sailors! fishermen's land!

Inextricable lands! the clutch'd together! the passionate ones!

The side by side! the elder and younger brothers! the bony-limb'd!

The great women's land! the feminine! the experienced sisters and the inexperienced sisters!

Far breath'd land! Arctic braced! Mexican breez'd! the diverse! the compact!

The Pennsylvanian! the Virginian! the double Carolinian!

O all and each well-loved by me! my intrepid nations! O I at any rate include you all with perfect love!

I cannot be discharged from you! not from one any sooner than another!

O death! O for all that, I am yet of you unseen this hour with irrepressible love,

Walking New England, a friend, a traveler,

Splashing my bare feet in the edge of the summer ripples on Paumanok's sands,

Crossing the prairies, dwelling again in Chicago, dwelling in every town,

Observing shows, births, improvements, structures, arts,

Listening to orators and oratresses in public halls,

Of and through the States as during life, each man and woman my neighbor,

The Louisianian, the Georgian, as near to me, and I as near
    to him and her,
The Mississippian and Arkansian yet with me, and I yet with
    any of them,
Yet upon the plains west of the spinal river, yet in my house
    of adobie,
Yet returning eastward, yet in the Seaside State or in Mary-
    land,
Yet Kanadian cheerily braving the winter, the snow and ice
    welcome to me,
Yet a true son either of Maine or of the Granite State, or the
    Narragansett Bay State, or the Empire State,
Yet sailing to other shores to annex the same, yet welcoming
    every new brother,
Hereby applying these leaves to the new ones from the hour
    they unite with the old ones,
Coming among the new ones myself to be their companion
    and equal, coming personally to you now,
Enjoining you to acts, characters, spectacles, with me.

15

With me with firm holding, yet haste, haste on.

For your life adhere to me,
(I may have to be persuaded many times before I consent to
    give myself really to you, but what of that?
Must not Nature be persuaded many times?)

No dainty dolce affettuoso I,
Bearded, sun-burnt, gray-neck'd, forbidding, I have arrived,
To be wrestled with as I pass for the solid prizes of the uni-
    verse.
For such I afford whoever can persevere to win them.

16

On my way a moment I pause,
Here for you! and here for America!
Still the present I raise aloft, still the future of the States I
    harbinge glad and sublime,
And for the past I pronounce what the air holds of the red
    aborigines.
The red aborigines,
Leaving natural breaths, sounds of rain and winds, calls as of
    birds and animals in the woods, syllabled to us for
    names,
Okonee, Koosa, Ottawa, Monongahela, Sauk, Natchez, Chatta-
    hoochee, Kaqueta, Oronoco,
Wabash, Miami, Saginaw, Chippewa, Oshkosh, Walla-Walla,
Leaving such to the States they melt, they depart, charging
    the water and the land with names.

17

Expanding and swift, henceforth,
Elements, breeds, adjustments, turbulent, quick and audacious,
A world primal again, vistas of glory incessant and branching,
A new race dominating previous ones and grander far, with
    new contests,
New politics, new literatures and religions, new inventions
    and arts.

These, my voice announcing—I will sleep no more but arise,
You oceans that have been calm within me! how I feel you,
    fathomless, stirring, preparing unprecedented waves
    and storms.

18

See, steamers steaming through my poems,
See, in my poems immigrants continually coming and landing,
See, in arriere, the wigwam, the trail, the hunter's hut, the
    flat-boat, the maize-leaf, the claim, the rude fence, and
    the backwoods village,

See, on the one side the Western Sea and on the other the
    Eastern Sea, how they advance and retreat upon my
    poems as upon their own shores,
See, pastures and forests in my poems—see, animals wild and
    tame—see, beyond the Kaw, countless herds of buffalo
    feeding on short curly grass,
See, in my poems, cities, solid, vast, inland, with paved streets,
    with iron and stone edifices, ceaseless vehicles, and com-
    merce,
See, the many-cylinder'd steam printing-press—see, the electric
    telegraph stretching across the continent,
See, through Atlantica's depths pulses American Europe reach-
    ing, pulses of Europe duly return'd,
See, the strong and quick locomotive as it departs, panting,
    blowing the steam-whistle,
See, ploughmen ploughing farms—see, miners digging mines
    —see, the numberless factories,
See, mechanics busy at their benches with tools—see from
    among them superior judges, philosophs, Presidents,
    emerge, drest in working dresses,
See, lounging through the shops and fields of the States, me
    well-belov'd, close-held by day and night,
Hear the loud echoes of my songs there—read the hints come
    at last.

19

O camerado close! O you and me at last, and us two only.
O a word to clear one's path ahead endlessly!
O something ecstatic and undemonstrable! O music wild!
O now I triumph—and you shall also;
O hand in hand—O wholesome pleasure—O one more de-
    sirer and lover!
O to haste firm holding—to haste, haste on with me.

SONG of MYSELF

1

I celebrate myself, and sing myself,
And what I assume you shall assume,
For every atom belonging to me as good belongs to you.

I loafe and invite my soul,
I lean and loafe at my ease observing a spear of summer grass.

My tongue, every atom of my blood, form'd from this soil,
      this air,
Born here of parents born here from parents the same, and
      their parents the same,
I, now thirty-seven years old in perfect health begin,
Hoping to cease not till death.

Creeds and schools in abeyance,
Retiring back a while sufficed at what they are, but never for-
      gotten,
I harbor for good or bad, I permit to speak at every hazard,
Nature without check with original energy.

2

Houses and rooms are full of perfumes, the shelves are
      crowded with perfumes,
I breathe the fragrance myself and know it and like it,
The distillation would intoxicate me also, but I shall not let it.

The atmosphere is not a perfume, it has no taste of the dis-
tillation, it is odorless,
It is for my mouth forever, I am in love with it,
I will go to the bank by the wood and become undisguised
and naked,
I am mad for it to be in contact with me.

The smoke of my own breath,
Echoes, ripples, buzz'd whispers, love-root, silk-thread, crotch
and vine,
My respiration and inspiration, the beating of my heart, the
passing of blood and air through my lungs,
The sniff of green leaves and dry leaves, and of the shore and
dark-color'd sea-rocks, and of hay in the barn,
The sound of the belch'd words of my voice loos'd to the
eddies of the wind,
A few light kisses, a few embraces, a reaching around of arms,
The play of shine and shade on the trees as the supple boughs
wag,
The delight alone or in the rush of the streets, or along the
fields and hill-sides,
The feeling of health, the full-noon trill, the song of me rising
from bed and meeting the sun.

Have you reckon'd a thousand acres much? have you reckon'd
the earth much?
Have you practis'd so long to learn to read?
Have you felt so proud to get at the meaning of poems?

Stop this day and night with me and you shall possess the
origin of all poems,
You shall possess the good of the earth and sun, (there are
millions of suns left,)
You shall no longer take things at second or third hand, nor
look through the eyes of the dead, nor feed on the
spectres in books,
You shall not look through my eyes either, nor take things
from me,
You shall listen to all sides and filter them from your self.

3

I have heard what the talkers were talking, the talk of the be-
    ginning and the end,
But I do not talk of the beginning or the end.

There was never any more inception than there is now,
Nor any more youth or age than there is now,
And will never be any more perfection than there is now,
Nor any more heaven or hell than there is now.

Urge and urge and urge,
Always the procreant urge of the world.
Out of the dimness opposite equals advance, always substance
    and increase, always sex,
Always a knit of identity, always distinction, always a breed
    of life.

To elaborate is no avail, learn'd and unlearn'd feel that it is so.

Sure as the most certain sure, plumb in the uprights, well
    entretied, braced in the beams,
Stout as a horse, affectionate, haughty, electrical,
I and this mystery here we stand.

Clear and sweet is my soul, and clear and sweet is all that is
    not my soul.

Lack one lacks both, and the unseen is proved by the seen,
Till that becomes unseen and receives proof in its turn.

Showing the best and dividing it from the worst age vexes
    age,
Knowing the perfect fitness and equanimity of things, while
    they discuss I am silent, and go bathe and admire my-
    self.

Welcome is every organ and attribute of me, and of any man
    hearty and clean,
Not an inch nor a particle of an inch is vile, and none shall be
    less familiar than the rest.

I am satisfied—I see, dance, laugh, sing;
As the hugging and loving bed-fellow sleeps at my side
        through the night, and withdraws at the peep of the
        day with stealthy tread,
Leaving me baskets cover'd with white towels swelling the
    house with their plenty,
Shall I postpone my acceptation and realization and scream at
    my eyes,
That they turn from gazing after and down the road,
And forthwith cipher and show me to a cent,
Exactly the value of one and exactly the value of two, and
    which is ahead?

4

Trippers and askers surround me,
People I meet, the effect upon me of my early life or the
        ward and city I live in, or the nation,
The latest dates, discoveries, inventions, societies, authors old
    and new,
My dinner, dress, associates, looks, compliments, dues,
The real or fancied indifference of some man or woman I
    love,
The sickness of one of my folks or of myself, or ill-doing or loss
    or lack of money, or depressions or exaltations,
Battles, the horrors of fratricidal war, the fever of doubtful
    news, the fitful events;
These come to me days and nights and go from me again,
But they are not the Me myself.

Apart from the pulling and hauling stands what I am,
Stands amused, complacent, compassionate, idle, unitary,

Looks down, is erect, or bends an arm on an impalpable certain rest,
Looking with side-curved head curious what will come next,
Both in and out of the game and watching and wondering
at it.

Backward I see in my own days where I sweated through fog
with linguists and contenders,
I have no mockings or arguments, I witness and wait.

5

I believe in you my soul, the other I am must not abase itself
to you,
And you must not be abased to the other.

Loafe with me on the grass, loose the stop from your throat,
Not words, not music or rhyme I want, not custom or lecture,
not even the best,
Only the lull I like, the hum of your valvèd voice.

I mind how once we lay such a transparent summer morning,
How you settled your head athwart my hips and gently turn'd
over upon me,
And parted the shirt from my bosom-bone, and plunged your
tongue to my bare-stript heart,
And reach'd till you felt my beard, and reach'd till you held
my feet.

Swiftly arose and spread around me the peace and knowledge
that pass all the argument of the earth,
And I know that the hand of God is the promise of my own,
And I know that the spirit of God is the brother of my own,
And that all the men ever born are also my brothers, and the
women my sisters and lovers,
And that a kelson of the creation is love,
And limitless are leaves stiff or drooping in the fields,
And brown ants in the little wells beneath them,

And mossy scabs of the worm fence, heap'd stones, elder,
    mullein and poke-weed.

6

A child said *What is the grass?* fetching it to me with full
    hands;
How could I answer the child? I do not know what it is any
    more than he.

I guess it must be the flag of my disposition, out of hopeful
    green stuff woven.

Or I guess it is the handkerchief of the Lord,
A scented gift and remembrancer designedly dropt,
Bearing the owner's name someway in the corners, that we
    may see and remark, and say *Whose?*

Or I guess the grass is itself a child, the produced babe of the
    vegetation.

Or I guess it is a uniform hieroglyphic,
And it means, Sprouting alike in broad zones and narrow
    zones,
Growing among black folks as among white,
Kanuck, Tuckahoe, Congressman, Cuff, I give them the same,
    I receive them the same.

And now it seems to me the beautiful uncut hair of graves.
Tenderly will I use you curling grass,
It may be you transpire from the breasts of young men,
It may be if I had known them I would have loved them,
It may be you are from old people, or from offspring taken
    soon out of their mothers' laps,
And here you are the mothers' laps.

This grass is very dark to be from the white heads of old
    mothers,

Darker than the colorless beards of old men,
Dark to come from under the faint red roofs of mouths.

O I perceive after all so many uttering tongues,
And I perceive they do not come from the roofs of mouths
    for nothing.

I wish I could translate the hints about the dead young men
    and women,
And the hints about old men and mothers, and the offspring
    taken soon out of their laps.

What do you think has become of the young and old men?
And what do you think has become of the women and chil-
    dren?

They are alive and well somewhere,
The smallest sprout shows there is really no death,
And if ever there was it led forward life, and does not wait at
    the end to arrest it,
And ceas'd the moment life appear'd.

All goes onward and outward, nothing collapses,
And to die is different from what any one supposed, and
    luckier.

7

Has any one supposed it lucky to be born?
I hasten to inform him or her it is just as lucky to die, and I
    know it.

I pass death with the dying and birth with the new-wash'd
    babe, and am not contain'd between my hat and boots,
And peruse manifold objects, no two alike and every one good,
The earth good and the stars good, and their adjuncts all good.
I am not an earth nor an adjunct of an earth,

I am the mate and companion of people, all just as immortal
  and fathomless as myself,
(They do not know how immortal, but I know.)

Every kind for itself and its own, for me mine male and female,
For me those that have been boys and that love women,
For me the man that is proud and feels how it stings to be
  slighted,
For me the sweet-heart and the old maid, for me mothers and
  the mothers of mothers,
For me lips that have smiled, eyes that have shed tears,
For me children and the begetters of children.

Undrape! you are not guilty to me, or stale nor discarded,
I see through the broadcloth and gingham whether or no,
And am around, tenacious, acquisitive, tireless, and cannot be
  shaken away.

8

The little one sleeps in its cradle,
I lift the gauze and look a long time, and silently brush away
  flies with my hand.

The youngster and the red-faced girl turn aside up the bushy
  hill,
I peeringly view them from the top.

The suicide sprawls on the bloody floor of the bedroom,
I witness the corpse with its dabbled hair, I note where the
  pistol has fallen.

The blab of the pave, tires of carts, sluff of boot-soles, talk of
  the promenaders,
The heavy omnibus, the driver with his interrogating thumb,
  the clank of the shod horses on the granite floor,
The snow-sleighs, clinking, shouted jokes, pelts of snow-balls,
The hurrahs for popular favorites, the fury of rous'd mobs,

The flap of the curtain'd litter, a sick man inside borne to the
    hospital,
The meeting of enemies, the sudden oath, the blows and fall,
The excited crowd, the policeman with his star quickly work-
    ing his passage to the centre of the crowd,
The impassive stones that receive and return so many echoes,
What groans of over-fed or half-starv'd who fall sunstruck or
    in fits,
What exclamations of women taken suddenly who hurry home
    and give birth to babes,
What living and buried speech is always vibrating here, what
    howls restrain'd by decorum,
Arrests of criminals, slights, adulterous offers made, accept-
    ances, rejections with convex lips,
I mind them or the show or resonance of them—I come and I
    depart.

9

The big doors of the country barn stand open and ready,
The dried grass of the harvest-time loads the slow-drawn
    wagon,
The clear light plays on the brown gray and green inter-
    tinged,
The armfuls are pack'd to the sagging mow.

I am there, I help, I came stretch'd atop of the load,
I felt its soft jolts, one leg reclined on the other,
I jump from the cross-beams and seize the clover and timothy,
And roll head over heels and tangle my hair full of wisps.

10

Alone far in the wilds and mountains I hunt,
Wandering amazed at my own lightness and glee,
In the late afternoon choosing a safe spot to pass the night,
Kindling a fire and broiling the fresh-kill'd game,

Falling asleep on the gather'd leaves with my dog and gun by
    my side.

The Yankee clipper is under her sky-sails, she cuts the sparkle
    and scud,
My eyes settle the land, I bend at her prow or shout joyously
    from the deck.

The boatmen and clam-diggers arose early and stopt for me,
I tuck'd my trowser-ends in my boots and went and had a
    good time;
You should have been with us that day round the chowder-
    kettle.

I saw the marriage of the trapper in the open air in the far
    west, the bride was a red girl,
Her father and his friends sat near cross-legged and dumbly
    smoking, they had moccasins to their feet and large
    thick blankets hanging from their shoulders,
On a bank lounged the trapper, he was drest mostly in skins,
    his luxuriant beard and curls protected his neck, he
    held his bride by the hand,
She had long eyelashes, her head was bare, her coarse straight
    locks descended upon her voluptuous limbs and reach'd
    to her feet.

The runaway slave came to my house and stopt outside,
I heard his motions crackling the twigs of the woodpile,
Through the swung half-door of the kitchen I saw him limpsy
    and weak,
And went where he sat on a log and led him in and assured
    him,
And brought water and fill'd a tub for his sweated body and
    bruis'd feet,
And gave him a room that enter'd from my own, and gave
    him some coarse clean clothes,

And remember perfectly well his revolving eyes and his awk-
    wardness,
And remember putting plasters on the galls of his neck and
    ankles;
He staid with me a week before he was recuperated and
    pass'd north,
I had him sit next me at table, my fire-lock lean'd in the
    corner.

11

Twenty-eight young men bathe by the shore,
Twenty-eight young men and all so friendly;
Twenty-eight years of womanly life and all so lonesome.

She owns the fine house by the rise of the bank,
She hides handsome and richly drest aft the blinds of the
    window.

Which of the young men does she like the best?
Ah the homeliest of them is beautiful to her.

Where are you off to, lady? for I see you,
You splash in the water there, yet stay stock still in your
    room.

Dancing and laughing along the beach came the twenty-ninth
    bather,
The rest did not see her, but she saw them and loved them.

The beards of the young men glisten'd with wet, it ran from
    their long hair,
Little streams pass'd all over their bodies.

An unseen hand also pass'd over their bodies,
It descended tremblingly from their temples and ribs.

The young men float on their backs, their white bellies bulge
    to the sun, they do not ask who seizes fast to them,
They do not know who puffs and declines with pendant and
    bending arch,
They do not think whom they souse with spray.

12

The butcher-boy puts off his killing-clothes, or sharpens his
    knife at the stall in the market,
I loiter enjoying his repartee and his shuffle and break-down.

Blacksmiths with grimed and hairy chests environ the anvil,
Each has his main-sledge, they are all out, there is a great
    heat in the fire.

From the cinder-strew'd threshold I follow their movements,
The lithe sheer of their waists plays even with their massive
    arms,
Overhand the hammers swing, overhand so slow, overhand so
    sure,
They do not hasten, each man hits in his place.

13

The negro holds firmly the reins of his four horses, the block
    swags underneath on its tied-over chain,
The negro that drives the long dray of the stone-yard, steady
    and tall he stands pois'd on one leg on the string-piece,
His blue shirt exposes his ample neck and breast and loosens
    over his hip-band,
His glance is calm and commanding, he tosses the slouch of
    his hat away from his forehead,
The sun falls on his crispy hair and mustache, falls on the
    black of his polish'd and perfect limbs.

I behold the picturesque giant and love him, and I do not
    stop there,
I go with the team also.

In me the caresser of life wherever moving, backward as well
    as forward sluing,
To niches aside and junior bending, not a person or object
    missing,
Absorbing all to myself and for this song.

Oxen that rattle the yoke and chain or halt in the leafy shade,
    what is that you express in your eyes?
It seems to me more than all the print I have read in my life.

My tread scares the wood-drake and wood-duck on my dis-
    tant and day-long ramble,
They rise together, they slowly circle around.

I believe in those wing'd purposes,
And acknowledge red, yellow, white, playing within me,
And consider green and violet and the tufted crown inten-
    tional,
And do not call the tortoise unworthy because she is not
    something else,
And the jay in the woods never studied the gamut, yet trills
    pretty well to me,
And the look of the bay mare shames silliness out of me.

14

The wild gander leads his flock through the cool night,
Ya-honk he says, and sounds it down to me like an invitation,
The pert may suppose it meaningless, but I listening close,
Find its purpose and place up there toward the wintry sky.

The sharp-hoof'd moose of the north, the cat on the house-
    sill, the chickadee, the prairie-dog,
The litter of the grunting sow as they tug at her teats,
The brood of the turkey-hen and she with her half-spread
    wings,
I see in them and myself the same old law.

The press of my foot to the earth springs a hundred affections,
They scorn the best I can do to relate them.

I am enamour'd of growing out-doors,
Of men that live among cattle or taste of the ocean or woods,
Of the builders and steerers of ships and the wielders of axes
      and mauls, and the drivers of horses,
I can eat and sleep with them week in and week out.

What is commonest, cheapest, nearest, easiest, is Me,
Me going in for my chances, spending for vast returns,
Adorning myself to bestow myself on the first that will take
      me,
Not asking the sky to come down to my good will,
Scattering it freely forever.

15

The pure contralto sings in the organ loft,
The carpenter dresses his plank, the tongue of his foreplane
      whistles its wild ascending lisp,
The married and unmarried children ride home to their
      Thanksgiving dinner,
The pilot seizes the king-pin, he heaves down with a strong
      arm,
The mate stands braced in the whale-boat, lance and harpoon
      are ready,
The duck-shooter walks by silent and cautious stretches,
The deacons are ordain'd with cross'd hands at the altar,
The spinning-girl retreats and advances to the hum of the big
      wheel,
The farmer stops by the bars as he walks on a First-day loafe
      and looks at the oats and rye,
The lunatic is carried at last to the asylum a confirm'd case,
(He will never sleep any more as he did in the cot in his
      mother's bed-room;)
The jour printer with gray head and gaunt jaws works at his
      case,

He turns his quid of tobacco while his eyes blurr with the
    manuscript;
The malform'd limbs are tied to the surgeon's table,
What is removed drops horribly in a pail;
The quadroon girl is sold at the auction-stand, the drunkard
    nods by the bar-room stove,
The machinist rolls up his sleeves, the policeman travels his
    beat, the gate-keeper marks who pass,
The young fellow drives the express-wagon, (I love him,
    though I do not know him;)
The half-breed straps on his light boots to compete in the
    race,
The western turkey-shooting draws old and young, some lean
    on their rifles, some sit on logs,
Out from the crowd steps the marksman, takes his position,
    levels his piece;
The groups of newly-come immigrants cover the wharf or
    levee,
As the woolly-pates hoe in the sugar-field, the overseer views
    them from his saddle,
The bugle calls in the ball-room, the gentlemen run for their
    partners, the dancers bow to each other,
The youth lies awake in the cedar-roof'd garret and harks to
    the musical rain,
The Wolverine sets traps on the creek that helps fill the
    Huron,
The squaw wrapt in her yellow-hemm'd cloth is offering moc-
    casins and bead-bags for sale,
The connoisseur peers along the exhibition-gallery with half-
    shut eyes bent sideways,
As the deck-hands make fast the steamboat the plank is
    thrown for the shore-going passengers,
The young sister holds out the skein while the elder sister
    winds it off in a ball, and stops now and then for the
    knots,
The one-year wife is recovering and happy having a week
    ago borne her first child,

The clean-hair'd Yankee girl works with her sewing-machine
      or in the factory or mill,

The paving-man leans on his two-handed rammer, the re-
      porter's lead flies swiftly over the note-book, the sign-
      painter is lettering with blue and gold,

The canal boy trots on the tow-path, the book-keeper counts
      at his desk, the shoemaker waxes his thread,

The conductor beats time for the band and all the performers
      follow him,

The child is baptized, the convert is making his first profes-
      sions,

The regatta is spread on the bay, the race is begun, (how the
      white sails sparkle!)

The drover watching his drove sings out to them that would
      stray,

The pedler sweats with his pack on his back, (the purchaser
      higgling about the odd cent;)

The bride unrumples her white dress, the minute-hand of the
      clock moves slowly,

The opium-eater reclines with rigid head and just-open'd lips,

The prostitute draggles her shawl, her bonnet bobs on her
      tipsy and pimpled neck,

The crowd laugh at her blackguard oaths, the men jeer and
      wink to each other,

(Miserable! I do not laugh at your oaths nor jeer you;)

The President holding a cabinet council is surrounded by the
      great Secretaries,

On the piazza walk three matrons stately and friendly with
      twined arms,

The crew of the fish-smack pack repeated layers of halibut in
      the hold,

The Missourian crosses the plains toting his wares and his
      cattle,

As the fare-collector goes through the train he gives notice
      by the jingling of loose change,

The floor-men are laying the floor, the tinners are tinning the
      roof, the masons are calling for mortar,

In single file each shouldering his hod pass onward the
    laborers;
Seasons pursuing each other the indescribable crowd is
    gather'd, it is the fourth of Seventh-month, (what sa-
    lutes of cannon and small arms!)
Seasons pursuing each other the plougher ploughs, the mower
    mows, and the winter-grain falls in the ground;
Off on the lakes the pike-fisher watches and waits by the hole
    in the frozen surface,
The stumps stand thick round the clearing, the squatter strikes
    deep with his axe,
Flatboatmen make fast towards dusk near the cotton-wood or
    pecan-trees,
Coon-seekers go through the regions of the Red river or
    through those drain'd by the Tennessee, or through
    those of the Arkansas,
Torches shine in the dark that hangs on the Chattahoochee or
    Altamahaw,
Patriarchs sit at supper with sons and grandsons and great-
    grandsons around them,
In walls of adobie, in canvas tents, rest hunters and trappers
    after their day's sport,
The city sleeps and the country sleeps,
The living sleep for their time, the dead sleep for their time,
The old husband sleeps by his wife and the young husband
    sleeps by his wife;
And these tend inward to me, and I tend outward to them,
And such as it is to be of these more or less I am,
And of these one and all I weave the song of myself.

16

I am of old and young, of the foolish as much as the wise,
Regardless of others, ever regardful of others,
Maternal as well as paternal, a child as well as a man,
Stuff'd with the stuff that is coarse and stuff'd with the stuff
    that is fine,

One of the Nation of many nations, the smallest the same and
the largest the same,

A Southerner soon as a Northerner, a planter nonchalant and
hospitable down by the Oconee I live,

A Yankee bound my own way ready for trade, my joints the
limberest joints on earth and the sternest joints on
earth,

A Kentuckian walking the vale of the Elkhorn in my deer-
skin leggings, a Louisianian or Georgian,

A boatman over lakes or bays or along coasts, a Hoosier,
Badger, Buckeye;

At home on Kanadian snow-shoes or up in the bush, or with
fishermen off Newfoundland,

At home in the fleet of ice-boats, sailing with the rest and
tacking,

At home on the hills of Vermont or in the woods of Maine, or
the Texan ranch,

Comrade of Californians, comrade of free North-Westerners,
(loving their big proportions,)

Comrade of raftsmen and coalmen, comrade of all who shake
hands and welcome to drink and meat,

A learner with the simplest, a teacher of the thoughtfullest,

A novice beginning yet experient of myriads of seasons,

Of every hue and caste am I, of every rank and religion,

A farmer, mechanic, artist, gentleman, sailor, quaker,

Prisoner, fancy-man, rowdy, lawyer, physician, priest.

I resist any thing better than my own diversity,

Breathe the air but leave plenty after me,

And am not stuck up, and am in my place.

(The moth and the fish-eggs are in their place,

The bright suns I see and the dark suns I cannot see are in
their place,

The palpable is in its place and the impalpable is in its place.)

17

These are really the thoughts of all men in all ages and lands,
    they are not original with me,
If they are not yours as much as mine they are nothing, or
    next to nothing,
If they are not the riddle and the untying of the riddle they
    are nothing,
If they are not just as close as they are distant they are
    nothing.

This is the grass that grows wherever the land is and the
    water is,
This the common air that bathes the globe.

18

With music strong I come, with my cornets and my drums,
I play not marches for accepted victors only, I play marches
    for conquer'd and slain persons.

Have you heard that it was good to gain the day?
I also say it is good to fall, battles are lost in the same spirit
    in which they are won.

I beat and pound for the dead,
I blow through my embouchures my loudest and gayest for
    them.

Vivas to those who have fail'd!
And to those whose war-vessels sank in the sea!
And to those themselves who sank in the sea!
And to all generals that lost engagements, and all overcome
    heroes!
And the numberless unknown heroes equal to the greatest
    heroes known!

19

This is the meal equally set, this the meat for natural hunger,
It is for the wicked just the same as the righteous, I make appointments with all,
I will not have a single person slighted or left away,
The kept-woman, sponger, thief, are hereby invited,
The heavy-lipp'd slave is invited, the venerealee is invited;
There shall be no difference between them and the rest.

This is the press of a bashful hand, this the float and odor of hair,
This the touch of my lips to yours, this the murmur of yearning,
This the far-off depth and height reflecting my own face,
This the thoughtful merge of myself, and the outlet again.

Do you guess I have some intricate purpose?
Well I have, for the Fourth-month showers have, and the mica on the side of a rock has.

Do you take it I would astonish?
Does the daylight astonish? does the early redstart twittering through the woods?
Do I astonish more than they?

This hour I tell things in confidence,
I might not tell everybody, but I will tell you.

20

Who goes there? hankering, gross, mystical, nude;
How is it I extract strength from the beef I eat?

What is a man anyhow? what am I? what are you?

All I mark as my own you shall offset it with your own,
Else it were time lost listening to me.

I do not snivel that snivel the world over,
That months are vacuums and the ground but wallow and
    filth.

Whimpering and truckling fold with powders for invalids,
    conformity goes to the fourth-remov'd,
I wear my hat as I please indoors or out.

Why should I pray? why should I venerate and be ceremo-
    nious?

Having pried through the strata, analyzed to a hair, counsel'd
    with doctors and calculated close,
I find no sweeter fat than sticks to my own bones.

In all people I see myself, none more and not one a barley-
    corn less,
And the good or bad I say of myself I say of them.

I know I am solid and sound,
To me the converging objects of the universe perpetually flow,
All are written to me, and I must get what the writing means.

I know I am deathless,
I know this orbit of mine cannot be swept by a carpenter's
    compass,
I know I shall not pass like a child's carlacue cut with a
    burnt stick at night.

I know I am august,
I do not trouble my spirit to vindicate itself or be understood,
I see that the elementary laws never apologize,
(I reckon I behave no prouder than the level I plant my
    house by, after all.)

I exist as I am, that is enough,
If no other in the world be aware I sit content,
And if each and all be aware I sit content.

One world is aware and by far the largest to me, and that is
 myself,
And whether I come to my own to-day or in ten thousand or
 ten million years,
I can cheerfully take it now, or with equal cheerfulness I can
 wait.

My foothold is tenon'd and mortis'd in granite,
I laugh at what you call dissolution,
And I know the amplitude of time.

21

I am the poet of the Body and I am the poet of the Soul,
The pleasures of heaven are with me and the pains of hell are
 with me,
The first I graft and increase upon myself, the latter I translate into a new tongue.

I am the poet of the woman the same as the man,
And I say it is as great to be a woman as to be a man,
And I say there is nothing greater than the mother of men.

I chant the chant of dilation or pride,
We have had ducking and deprecating about enough,
I show that size is only development.

Have you outstript the rest? are you the President?
It is a trifle, they will more than arrive there every one, and
 still pass on.

I am he that walks with the tender and growing night,
I call to the earth and sea half-held by the night.
Press close bare-bosom'd night—press close magnetic nourish-
 ing night!
Night of south winds—night of the large few stars!
Still nodding night—mad naked summer night.

Smile O voluptuous cool-breath'd earth!
Earth of the slumbering and liquid trees!
Earth of departed sunset—earth of the mountains misty-topt!
Earth of the vitreous pour of the full moon just tinged with
      blue!
Earth of shine and dark mottling the tide of the river!
Earth of the limpid gray of clouds brighter and clearer for
      my sake!
Far-swooping elbow'd earth—rich apple-blossom'd earth!
Smile, for your lover comes.

Prodigal, you have given me love—therefore I to you give
      love!
O unspeakable passionate love.

22

You sea! I resign myself to you also—I guess what you mean,
I behold from the beach your crooked inviting fingers,
I believe you refuse to go back without feeling of me,
We must have a turn together, I undress, hurry me out of
      sight of the land,
Cushion me soft, rock me in billowy drowse,
Dash me with amorous wet, I can repay you.

Sea of stretch'd ground-swells,
Sea breathing broad and convulsive breaths,
Sea of the brine of life and of unshovell'd yet always-ready
      graves,
Howler and scooper of storms, capricious and dainty sea,
I am integral with you, I too am of one phase and of all
      phases.

Partaker of influx and efflux I, extoller of hate and concili-
      ation,
Extoller of amies and those that sleep in each others' arms.

I am he attesting sympathy,
(Shall I make my list of things in the house and skip the
house that supports them?)

I am not the poet of goodness only, I do not decline to be the
poet of wickedness also.

What blurt is this about virtue and about vice?
Evil propels me and reform of evil propels me, I stand indif-
ferent,
My gait is no fault-finder's or rejecter's gait,
I moisten the roots of all that has grown.

Did you fear some scrofula out of the unflagging pregnancy?
Did you guess the celestial laws are yet to be work'd over
and rectified?

I find one side a balance and the antipodal side a balance,
Soft doctrine as steady help as stable doctrine,
Thoughts and deeds of the present our rouse and early start.

This minute that comes to me over the past decillions,
There is no better than it and now.

What behaved well in the past or behaves well to-day is not
such a wonder,
The wonder is always and always how there can be a mean
man or an infidel.

23

Endless unfolding of words of ages!
And mine a word of the modern, the word En-Masse.

A word of the faith that never balks,
Here or henceforward it is all the same to me, I accept Time
absolutely.

It alone is without flaw, it alone rounds and completes all,
That mystic baffling wonder alone completes all.

I accept Reality and dare not question it,
Materialism first and last imbuing.

Hurrah for positive science! long live exact demonstration!
Fetch stonecrop mixt with cedar and branches of lilac,
This is the lexicographer, this the chemist, this made a gram-
      mar of the old cartouches,
These mariners put the ship through dangerous unknown seas,
This is the geologist, this works with the scalpel, and this is
      a mathematician.

Gentlemen, to you the first honors always!
Your facts are useful, and yet they are not my dwelling,
I but enter by them to an area of my dwelling.

Less the reminders of properties told my words,
And more the reminders they of life untold, and of freedom
      and extrication,
And make short account of neuters and geldings, and favor
      men and women fully equipt,
And beat the gong of revolt, and stop with fugitives and them
      that plot and conspire.

                              24

Walt Whitman, a kosmos, of Manhattan the son,
Turbulent, fleshy, sensual, eating, drinking and breeding,
No sentimentalist, no stander above men and women or apart
      from them,
No more modest than immodest.

Unscrew the locks from the doors!
Unscrew the doors themselves from their jambs!

Whoever degrades another degrades me,
And whatever is done or said returns at last to me.

Through me the afflatus surging and surging, through me the
      current and index.

I speak the pass-word primeval, I give the sign of democracy,
By God! I will accept nothing which all cannot have their
      counterpart of on the same terms.

Through me many long dumb voices,
Voices of the interminable generations of prisoners and slaves,
Voices of the diseas'd and despairing and of thieves and
      dwarfs,
Voices of cycles of preparation and accretion,
And of the threads that connect the stars, and of wombs and
      of the father-stuff,
And of the rights of them the others are down upon,
Of the deform'd, trivial, flat, foolish, despised,
Fog in the air, beetles rolling balls of dung.

Through me forbidden voices,
Voices of sexes and lusts, voices veil'd and I remove the veil,
Voices indecent by me clarified and transfigur'd.

I do not press my fingers across my mouth,
I keep as delicate around the bowels as around the head and
      heart,
Copulation is no more rank to me than death is.

I believe in the flesh and the appetites,
Seeing, hearing, feeling, are miracles, and each part and tag
      of me is a miracle.

Divine am I inside and out, and I make holy whatever I
      touch or am touch'd from,
The scent of these arm-pits aroma finer than prayer,
This head more than churches, bibles, and all the creeds.

If I worship one thing more than another it shall be the
      spread of my own body, or any part of it,
Translucent mould of me it shall be you!
Shaded ledges and rests it shall be you!
Firm masculine colter it shall be you!
Whatever goes to the tilth of me it shall be you!
You my rich blood! your milky stream pale strippings of my
      life!
Breast that presses against other breasts it shall be you!
My brain it shall be your occult convolutions!
Root of wash'd sweet-flag! timorous pond-snipe! nest of
      guarded duplicate eggs! it shall be you!
Mix'd tussled hay of head, beard, brawn, it shall be you!
Trickling sap of maple, fibre of manly wheat, it shall be you!
Sun so generous it shall be you!
Vapors lighting and shading my face it shall be you!
You sweaty brooks and dews it shall be you!
Winds whose soft-tickling genitals rub against me it shall be
      you!
Broad muscular fields, branches of live oak, loving lounger in
      my winding paths, it shall be you!
Hands I have taken, face I have kiss'd, mortal I have ever
      touch'd, it shall be you.

I dote on myself, there is that lot of me and all so luscious,
Each moment and whatever happens thrills me with joy,
I cannot tell how my ankles bend, nor whence the cause of
      my faintest wish,
Nor the cause of the friendship I emit, nor the cause of the
      friendship I take again.
That I walk up my stoop, I pause to consider if it really be,
A morning-glory at my window satisfies me more than the
      metaphysics of books.

To behold the day-break!
The little light fades the immense and diaphanous shadows,
The air tastes good to my palate.

Hefts of the moving world at innocent gambols silently ris-
    ing freshly exuding,
Scooting obliquely high and low.

Something I cannot see puts upward libidinous prongs,
Seas of bright juice suffuse heaven.

The earth by the sky staid with, the daily close of their junc-
    tion,
The heav'd challenge from the east that moment over my
    head,
The mocking taunt, See then whether you shall be master!

25

Dazzling and tremendous how quick the sun-rise would kill
    me,
If I could not now and always send sun-rise out of me.

We also ascend dazzling and tremendous as the sun,
We found our own O my soul in the calm and cool of the day-
    break.

My voice goes after what my eyes cannot reach,
With the twirl of my tongue I encompass worlds and volumes
    of worlds.

Speech is the twin of my vision, it is unequal to measure itself,
It provokes me forever, it says sarcastically,
Walt you contain enough, why don't you let it out then?

Come now I will not be tantalized, you conceive too much of
    articulation,
Do you not know O speech how the buds beneath you are
    folded?
Waiting in gloom, protected by frost,
The dirt receding before my prophetical screams,
I underlying causes to balance them at last,

My knowledge my live parts, it keeping tally with the mean-
     ing of all things,
Happiness, (which whoever hears me let him or her set out
     in search of this day.)

My final merit I refuse you, I refuse putting from me what I
     really am,
Encompass worlds, but never try to encompass me,
I crowd your sleekest and best by simple looking toward you.

Writing and talk do not prove me,
I carry the plenum of proof and every thing else in my face,
With the hush of my lips I wholly confound the skeptic.

26

Now I will do nothing but listen,
To accrue what I hear into this song, to let sounds contribute
     toward it.

I hear bravuras of birds, bustle of growing wheat, gossip of
     flames, clack of sticks cooking my meals,
I hear the sound I love, the sound of the human voice,
I hear all sounds running together, combined, fused or follow-
     ing,
Sounds of the city and sounds out of the city, sounds of the
     day and night.
Talkative young ones to those that like them, the loud laugh
     of work-people at their meals,
The angry base of disjointed friendship, the faint tones of the
     sick,
The judge with hands tight to the desk, his pallid lips pro-
     nouncing a death-sentence,
The heave'e'yo of stevedores unlading ships by the wharves,
     the refrain of the anchor-lifters,
The ring of alarm-bells, the cry of fire, the whirr of swift-
     streaking engines and hose-carts with premonitory
     tinkles and color'd lights,

The steam-whistle, the solid roll of the train of approaching
　　cars,
The slow march play'd at the head of the association march-
　　ing two and two,
(They go to guard some corpse, the flag-tops are draped with
　　black muslin.)

I hear the violoncello, ('tis the young man's heart's com-
　　plaint,)
I hear the key'd cornet, it glides quickly in through my ears,
It shakes mad-sweet pangs through my belly and breast.

I hear the chorus, it is a grand opera,
Ah this indeed is music—this suits me.

A tenor large and fresh as the creation fills me,
The orbic flex of his mouth is pouring and filling me full.

I hear the train'd soprano (what work with hers is this?)
The orchestra whirls me wider than Uranus flies,
It wrenches such ardors from me I did not know I possess'd
　　them,
It sails me, I dab with bare feet, they are lick'd by the in-
　　dolent waves,
I am cut by bitter and angry hail, I lose my breath,
Steep'd amid honey'd morphine, my windpipe throttled in
　　fakes of death,
At length let up again to feel the puzzle of puzzles,
And that we call Being.

27

To be in any form, what is that?
(Round and round we go, all of us, and ever come back
　　thither,)
If nothing lay more develop'd the quahaug in its callous shell
　　were enough.

Mine is no callous shell,
I have instant conductors all over me whether I pass or stop,
They seize every object and lead it harmlessly through me.

I merely stir, press, feel with my fingers, and am happy,
To touch my person to some one else's is about as much as I
    can stand.

28

Is this then a touch? quivering me to a new identity,
Flames and ether making a rush for my veins,
Treacherous tip of me reaching and crowding to help them,
My flesh and blood playing out lightning to strike what is
    hardly different from myself,
On all sides prurient provokers stiffening my limbs,
Straining the udder of my heart for its withheld drip,
Behaving licentious toward me, taking no denial,
Depriving me of my best as for a purpose,
Unbuttoning my clothes, holding me by the bare waist,
Deluding my confusion with the calm of the sunlight and
    pasture-fields,
Immodestly sliding the fellow-senses away,
They bribed to swap off with touch and go and graze at the
    edges of me,
No consideration, no regard for my draining strength or my
    anger,
Fetching the rest of the herd around to enjoy them a while,
Then all uniting to stand on a headland and worry me.

The sentries desert every other part of me,
They have left me helpless to a red marauder,
They all come to the headland to witness and assist against
    me.

I am given up by traitors,
I talk wildly, I have lost my wits, I and nobody else am the
    greatest traitor,

I went myself first to the headland, my own hands carried me
    there.

You villain touch! what are you doing? my breath is tight in
    its throat,
Unclench your floodgates, you are too much for me.

29

Blind loving wrestling touch, sheath'd hooded sharp-tooth'd
    touch!
Did it make you ache so, leaving me?

Parting track'd by arriving, perpetual payment of perpetual
    loan,
Rich showering rain, and recompense richer afterward.

Sprouts take and accumulate, stand by the curb prolific and
    vital,
Landscapes projected masculine, full-sized and golden.

30

All truths wait in all things,
They neither hasten their own delivery nor resist it,
They do not need the obstetric forceps of the surgeon,
The insignificant is as big to me as any,
(What is less or more than a touch?)

Logic and sermons never convince,
The damp of the night drives deeper into my soul.

(Only what proves itself to every man and woman is so,
Only what nobody denies is so.)

A minute and a drop of me settle my brain,
I believe the soggy clods shall become lovers and lamps,
And a compend of compends is the meat of a man or woman,

And a summit and flower there is the feeling they have for
    each other,
And they are to branch boundlessly out of that lesson until it
    becomes omnific,
And until one and all shall delight us, and we them.

31

I believe a leaf of grass is no less than the journey-work of the
    stars,
And the pismire is equally perfect, and a grain of sand, and
    the egg of the wren,
And the tree-toad is a chef-d'œuvre for the highest,
And the running blackberry would adorn the parlors of
    heaven,
And the narrowest hinge in my hand puts to scorn all ma-
    chinery,
And the cow crunching with depress'd head surpasses any
    statue,
And a mouse is miracle enough to stagger sextillions of in-
    fidels.

I find I incorporate gneiss, coal, long-threaded moss, fruits,
    grains, esculent roots,
And am stucco'd with quadrupeds and birds all over,
And have distanced what is behind me for good reasons,
But call any thing back again when I desire it.

In vain the speeding or shyness,
In vain the plutonic rocks send their old heat against my ap-
    proach,
In vain the mastodon retreats beneath its own powder'd bones,
In vain objects stand leagues off and assume manifold shapes,
In vain the ocean settling in hollows and the great monsters
    lying low,
In vain the buzzard houses herself with the sky,
In vain the snake slides through the creepers and logs,
In vain the elk takes to the inner passes of the woods,

In vain the razor-bill'd auk sails far north to Labrador,
I follow quickly, I ascend to the nest in the fissure of the cliff.

32

I think I could turn and live with animals, they are so placid
    and self-contain'd,
I stand and look at them long and long.

They do not sweat and whine about their condition,
They do not lie awake in the dark and weep for their sins,
They do not make me sick discussing their duty to God,
Not one is dissatisfied, not one is demented with the mania of
    owning things,
Not one kneels to another, nor to his kind that lived thousands
    of years ago,
Not one is respectable or unhappy over the whole earth.

So they show their relations to me and I accept them,
They bring me tokens of myself, they evince them plainly in
    their possession.

I wonder where they get those tokens,
Did I pass that way huge times ago and negligently drop
    them?
Myself moving forward then and now and forever,
Gathering and showing more always and with velocity,
Infinite and omnigenous, and the like of these among them,
Not too exclusive toward the reachers of my remembrancers,
Picking out here one that I love, and now go with him on
    brotherly terms.

A gigantic beauty of a stallion, fresh and responsive to my
    caresses,
Head high in the forehead, wide between the ears,
Limbs glossy and supple, tail dusting the ground,
Eyes full of sparkling wickedness, ears finely cut, flexibly
    moving.

His nostrils dilate as my heels embrace him,
His well-built limbs tremble with pleasure as we race around
    and return.

I but use you a minute, then I resign you, stallion,
Why do I need your paces when I myself out-gallop them?
Even as I stand or sit passing faster than you. . . .

         ✺   ✺   ✺

37

You laggards there on guard! look to your arms!
In at the conquer'd doors they crowd! I am possess'd!
Embody all presences outlaw'd or suffering,
See myself in prison shaped like another man,
And feel the dull unintermitted pain.

For me the keepers of convicts shoulder their carbines and
    keep watch,
It is I let out in the morning and barr'd at night.

Not a mutineer walks handcuff'd to jail but I am handcuff'd to
    him and walk by his side,
(I am less the jolly one there, and more the silent one with
    sweat on my twitching lips.)

Not a youngster is taken for larceny but I go up too, and am
    tried and sentenced.

Not a cholera patient lies at the last gasp but I also lie at the
    last gasp,
My face is ash-color'd, my sinews gnarl, away from me people
    retreat.

Askers embody themselves in me and I am embodied in them,
I project my hat, sit shame-faced, and beg.

38

Enough! enough! enough!
Somehow I have been stunn'd. Stand back!
Give me a little time beyond my cuff'd head, slumbers, dreams,
    gaping,
I discover myself on the verge of a usual mistake.

That I could forget the mockers and insults!
That I could forget the trickling tears and the blows of the
    bludgeons and hammers!
That I could look with a separate look on my own crucifixion
    and bloody crowning.

I remember now,
I resume the overstaid fraction,
The grave of rock multiplies what has been confided to it, or
    to any graves,
Corpses rise, gashes heal, fastenings roll from me.

I troop forth replenish'd with supreme power, one of an
    average unending procession,
Inland and sea-coast we go, and pass all boundary lines,
Our swift ordinances on their way over the whole earth,
The blossoms we wear in our hats the growth of thousands
    of years.

Eleves, I salute you! come forward!
Continue your annotations, continue your questionings.

39

The friendly and flowing savage, who is he?
Is he waiting for civilization, or past it and mastering it?
Is he some Southwesterner rais'd out-doors? is he Kanadian?
Is he from the Mississippi country? Iowa, Oregon, California?
The mountains? prairie-life, bush-life? or sailor from the sea?

Wherever he goes men and women accept and desire him,
They desire he should like them, touch them, speak to them,
     stay with them.

Behavior lawless as snow-flakes, words simple as grass, un-
     comb'd head, laughter, and naiveté,
Slow-stepping feet, common features, common modes and
     emanations,
They descend in new forms from the tips of his fingers,
They are wafted with the odor of his body or breath, they fly
     out of the glance of his eyes.

40

Flaunt of the sunshine I need not your bask—lie over!
You light surfaces only, I force surfaces and depths also.

Earth! you seem to look for something at my hands,
Say, old top-knot, what do you want?

Man or woman, I might tell how I like you, but cannot,
And might tell what it is in me and what it is in you, but can-
     not,
And might tell that pining I have, that pulse of my nights and
     days.

Behold, I do not give lectures or a little charity,
When I give I give myself.

You there, impotent, loose in the knees,
Open your scarf'd chops till I blow grit within you,
Spread your palms and lift the flaps of your pockets,
I am not to be denied, I compel, I have stores plenty and to
     spare,
And any thing I have I bestow.

I do not ask who you are, that is not important to me,
You can do nothing and be nothing but what I will infold you.

To cotton-field drudge or cleaner of privies I lean,
On his right cheek I put the family kiss,
And in my soul I swear I never will deny him.

On women fit for conception I start bigger and nimbler babes,
(This day I am jetting the stuff of far more arrogant re-
    publics.)

To any one dying, thither I speed and twist the knob of the
    door,
Turn the bed-clothes toward the foot of the bed,
Let the physician and the priest go home.

I seize the descending man and raise him with resistless will,
O despairer, here is my neck,
By God, you shall not go down! hang your whole weight upon
    me.

I dilate you with tremendous breath, I buoy you up,
Every room of the house do I fill with an arm'd force,
Lovers of me, bafflers of graves.

Sleep—I and they keep guard all night,
Not doubt, not decease shall dare to lay finger upon you,
I have embraced you, and henceforth possess you to myself,
And when you rise in the morning you will find what I tell
    you is so. . . .

* * *

48

I have said that the soul is not more than the body,
And I have said that the body is not more than the soul,
And nothing, not God, is greater to one than one's self is,
And whoever walks a furlong without sympathy walks to his
    own funeral drest in his shroud,

And I or you pocketless of a dime may purchase the pick of
　　the earth,
And to glance with an eye or show a bean in its pod con-
　　founds the learning of all times,
And there is no trade or employment but the young man fol-
　　lowing it may become a hero,
And there is no object so soft but it makes a hub for the
　　wheel'd universe,
And I say to any man or woman, Let your soul stand cool
　　and composed before a million universes.

And I say to mankind, Be not curious about God,
For I who am curious about each am not curious about God,
(No array of terms can say how much I am at peace about
　　God and about death.)

I hear and behold God in every object, yet understand God
　　not in the least,
Nor do I understand who there can be more wonderful than
　　myself.

Why should I wish to see God better than this day?
I see something of God each hour of the twenty-four, and each
　　moment then,
In the faces of men and women I see God, and in my own face
　　in the glass,
I find letters from God dropt in the street, and every one is
　　sign'd by God's name,
And I leave them where they are, for I know that wheresoe'er
　　I go,
Others will punctually come for ever and ever.

49

And as to you Death, and you bitter hug of mortality, it is
　　idle to try to alarm me.

To his work without flinching the accoucheur comes,
I see the elder-hand pressing receiving supporting,
I recline by the sills of the exquisite flexible doors,
And mark the outlet, and mark the relief and escape.

And as to you Corpse I think you are good manure, but that
    does not offend me,
I smell the white roses sweet-scented and growing,
I reach to the leafy lips, I reach to the polish'd breasts of
    melons.

And as to you Life I reckon you are the leavings of many
    deaths,
(No doubt I have died myself ten thousand times before.)

I hear you whispering there O stars of heaven,
O suns—O grass of graves—O perpetual transfers and promo-
    tions,
If you do not say any thing how can I say any thing?

Of the turbid pool that lies in the autumn forest,
Of the moon that descends the steeps of the soughing twilight,
Toss, sparkles of day and dusk—toss on the black stems that
    decay in the muck,
Toss to the moaning gibberish of the dry limbs.

I ascend from the moon, I ascend from the night,
I perceive that the ghastly glimmer is noonday sunbeams re-
    flected,
And debouch to the steady and central from the offspring
    great or small.

50

There is that in me—I do not know what it is—but I know it
    is in me.

Wrench'd and sweaty—calm and cool then my body becomes,
I sleep—I sleep long.

I do not know it—it is without name—it is a word unsaid,
It is not in any dictionary, utterance, symbol.

Something it swings on more than the earth I swing on,
To it the creation is the friend whose embracing awakes me.

Perhaps I might tell more. Outlines! I plead for my brothers
     and sisters.

Do you see O my brothers and sisters?
It is not chaos or death—it is form, union, plan—it is eternal
     life—it is Happiness.

51

The past and present wilt—I have fill'd them, emptied them,
And proceed to fill my next fold of the future.

Listener up there! what have you to confide to me?
Look in my face while I snuff the sidle of evening,
(Talk honestly, no one else hears you, and I stay only a
     minute longer.)

Do I contradict myself?
Very well then I contradict myself,
(I am large, I contain multitudes.)

I concentrate toward them that are nigh, I wait on the door-
     slab.

Who has done his day's work? who will soonest be through
     with his supper?
Who wishes to walk with me?

Will you speak before I am gone? will you prove already too
     late?

52

The spotted hawk swoops by and accuses me, he complains
    of my gab and my loitering.

I too am not a bit tamed, I too am untranslatable,
I sound my barbaric yawp over the roofs of the world.

The last scud of day holds back for me,
It flings my likeness after the rest and true as any on the
    shadow'd wilds,
It coaxes me to the vapor and the dusk.

I depart as air, I shake my white locks at the runaway sun,
I effuse my flesh in eddies, and drift it in lacy jags.

I bequeath myself to the dirt to grow from the grass I love,
If you want me again look for me under your boot-soles.

You will hardly know who I am or what I mean,
But I shall be good health to you nevertheless,
And filter and fibre your blood.

Failing to fetch me at first keep encouraged,
Missing me one place search another,
I stop somewhere waiting for you.

CHILDREN *of* ADAM

I SING THE BODY ELECTRIC

1

I sing the body electric,
The armies of those I love engirth me and I engirth them,
They will not let me off till I go with them, respond to them,
And discorrupt them, and charge them full with the charge
      of the soul.

Was it doubted that those who corrupt their own bodies con-
      ceal themselves?
And if those who defile the living are as bad as they who de-
      file the dead?
And if the body does not do fully as much as the soul?
And if the body were not the soul, what is the soul?

2

The love of the body of man or woman balks account, the
      body itself balks account,
That of the male is perfect, and that of the female is perfect.

The expression of the face balks account,
But the expression of a well-made man appears not only in
      his face,
It is in his limbs and joints also, it is curiously in the joints of
      his hips and wrists,

It is in his walk, the carriage of his neck, the flex of his waist
    and knees, dress does not hide him,
The strong sweet quality he has strikes through the cotton
    and broadcloth,
To see him pass conveys as much as the best poem, perhaps
    more,
You linger to see his back, and the back of his neck and
    shoulder-side.

The sprawl and fulness of babes, the bosoms and heads of
    women, the folds of their dress, their style as we pass in
    the street, the contour of their shape downwards,
The swimmer naked in the swimming-bath, seen as he swims
    through the transparent green-shine, or lies with his face
    up and rolls silently to and fro in the heave of the
    water,
The bending forward and backward of rowers in row-boats,
    the horseman in his saddle,
Girls, mothers, house-keepers, in all their performances,
The group of laborers seated at noon-time with their open
    dinner-kettles, and their wives waiting,
The female soothing a child, the farmer's daughter in the
    garden or cow-yard,
The young fellow hoeing corn, the sleigh-driver driving his
    six horses through the crowd,
The wrestle of wrestlers, two apprentice-boys, quite grown,
    lusty, good-natured, native-born, out on the vacant lot
    at sun-down after work,
The coats and caps thrown down, the embrace of love and
    resistance,
The upper-hold and under-hold, the hair rumpled over and
    blinding the eyes;
The march of firemen in their own costumes, the play of
    masculine muscle through clean-setting trowsers and
    waist-straps,
The slow return from the fire, the pause when the bell strikes
    suddenly again, and the listening on the alert,

The natural, perfect, varied attitudes, the bent head, the
    curv'd neck and the counting;
Such-like I love—I loosen myself, pass freely, am at the moth-
    er's breast with the little child,
Swim with the swimmers, wrestle with wrestlers, march in
    line with the firemen, and pause, listen, count.

3

I knew a man, a common farmer, the father of five sons,
And in them the fathers of sons, and in them the fathers of
    sons.
This man was of wonderful vigor, calmness, beauty of person,
The shape of his head, the pale yellow and white of his hair
    and beard, the immeasurable meaning of his black eyes,
    the richness and breadth of his manners,
These I used to go and visit him to see, he was wise also,
He was six feet tall, he was over eighty years old, his sons
    were massive, clean, bearded, tan-faced, handsome,
They and his daughters loved him, all who saw him loved
    him,
They did not love him by allowance, they loved him with per-
    sonal love,
He drank water only, the blood show'd like scarlet through
    the clear-brown skin of his face,
He was a frequent gunner and fisher, he sail'd his boat him-
    self, he had a fine one presented to him by a ship-
    joiner, he had fowling-pieces presented to him by men
    that loved him,
When he went with his five sons and many grand-sons to
    hunt or fish, you would pick him out as the most beauti-
    ful and vigorous of the gang,
You would wish long and long to be with him, you would
    wish to sit by him in the boat that you and he might
    touch each other.

4

I have perceiv'd that to be with those I like is enough,
To stop in company with the rest at evening is enough,
To be surrounded by beautiful, curious, breathing, laughing
    flesh is enough,
To pass among them or touch any one, or rest my arm ever
    so lightly round his or her neck for a moment, what
    is this then?
I do not ask any more delight, I swim in it as in a sea.

There is something in staying close to men and women and
    looking on them, and in the contact and odor of them,
    that pleases the soul well,
All things please the soul, but these please the soul well.

5

This is the female form,
A divine nimbus exhales from it from head to foot,
It attracts with fierce undeniable attraction,
I am drawn by its breath as if I were no more than a help-
    less vapor, all falls aside but myself and it,
Books, art, religion, time, the visible and solid earth, and what
    was expected of heaven or fear'd of hell, are now con-
    sumed,
Mad filaments, ungovernable shoots play out of it, the response
    likewise ungovernable,
Hair, bosom, hips, bend of legs, negligent falling hands all dif-
    fused, mine too diffused,
Ebb stung by the flow and flow stung by the ebb, love-flesh
    swelling and deliciously aching,
Limitless limpid jets of love hot and enormous, quivering jelly
    of love, white-blow and delirious juice,
Bridegroom night of love working surely and softly into the
    prostrate dawn,
Undulating into the willing and yielding day,

Lost in the cleave of the clasping and sweet-flesh'd day.

This the nucleus—after the child is born of woman, man is
 born of woman,
This the bath of birth, this the merge of small and large, and
 the outlet again.

Be not ashamed women, your privilege encloses the rest, and
 is the exit of the rest,
You are the gates of the body, and you are the gates of the
 soul.

The female contains all qualities and tempers them,
She is in her place and moves with perfect balance,
She is all things duly veil'd, she is both passive and active,
She is to conceive daughters as well as sons, and sons as well
 as daughters.

As I see my soul reflected in Nature,
As I see through a mist, One with inexpressible completeness,
 sanity, beauty,
See the bent head and arms folded over the breast, the Female I see.

6

The male is not less the soul nor more, he too is in his place,
He too is all qualities, he is action and power,
The flush of the known universe is in him,
Scorn becomes him well, and appetite and defiance become
 him well,
The wildest largest passions, bliss that is utmost, sorrow that
 is utmost become him well, pride is for him,
The full-spread pride of man is calming and excellent to the
 soul,
Knowledge becomes him, he likes it always, he brings every
 thing to the test of himself,

Whatever the survey, whatever the sea and the sail he strikes
      soundings at last only here,
(Where else does he strike soundings except here?)

The man's body is sacred and the woman's body is sacred,
No matter who it is, it is sacred—is it the meanest one in the
      laborers' gang?
Is it one of the dull-faced immigrants just landed on the
      wharf?
Each belongs here or anywhere just as much as the well-off,
      just as much as you,
Each has his or her place in the procession.

(All is a procession,
The universe is a procession with measured and perfect mo-
      tion.)

Do you know so much yourself that you call the meanest
      ignorant?
Do you suppose you have a right to a good sight, and he or
      she has no right to a sight?
Do you think matter has cohered together from its diffuse
      float, and the soil is on the surface, and water runs and
      vegetation sprouts,
For you only, and not for him and her?

7

A man's body at auction,
(For before the war I often go to the slave-mart and watch the
      sale,)
I help the auctioneer, the sloven does not half know his
      business.

Gentlemen look on this wonder,
Whatever the bids of the bidders they cannot be high enough
      for it,

For it the globe lay preparing quintillions of years without
  one animal or plant,
For it the revolving cycles truly and steadily roll'd.

In this head the all-baffling brain,
In it and below it the makings of heroes.

Examine these limbs, red, black, or white, they are cunning
  in tendon and nerve,
They shall be stript that you may see them.

Exquisite senses, life-lit eyes, pluck, volition,
Flakes of breast-muscle, pliant backbone and neck, flesh not
  flabby, good-sized arms and legs,
And wonders within there yet.

Within there runs blood,
The same old blood! the same red-running blood!
There swells and jets a heart, there all passions, desires, reach-
  ings, aspirations,
(Do you think they are not there because they are not ex-
  press'd in parlors and lecture-rooms?)

This is not only one man, this the father of those who shall be
  fathers in their turns,
In him the start of populous states and rich republics,
Of him countless immortal lives with countless embodiments
  and enjoyments.

How do you know who shall come from the offspring of his
  offspring through the centuries?
(Who might you find you have come from yourself, if you
  could trace back through the centuries?)

8

A woman's body at auction,
She too is not only herself, she is the teeming mother of
  mothers,

She is the bearer of them that shall grow and be mates to the
 mothers.

Have you ever loved the body of a woman?
Have you ever loved the body of a man?
Do you not see that these are exactly the same to all in all
 nations and times all over the earth?

If any thing is sacred the human body is sacred,
And the glory and sweet of a man is the token of manhood
 untainted,
And in man or woman a clean, strong, firm-fibred body, is
 more beautiful than the most beautiful face.

Have you seen the fool that corrupted his own live body?
 or the fool that corrupted her own live body?
For they do not conceal themselves, and cannot conceal themselves.

9

O my body! I dare not desert the likes of you in other men
 and women, nor the likes of the parts of you,
I believe the likes of you are to stand or fall with the likes of
 the soul, (and that they are the soul,)
I believe the likes of you shall stand or fall with my poems,
 and that they are my poems,
Man's, woman's, child's, youth's, wife's, husband's, mother's,
 father's, young man's, young woman's poems,
Head, neck, hair, ears, drop and tympan of the ears,
Eyes, eye-fringes, iris of the eye, eyebrows, and the waking or
 sleeping of the lids,
Mouth, tongue, lips, teeth, roof of the mouth, jaws, and the
 jaw-hinges,
Nose, nostrils of the nose, and the partition,
Cheeks, temples, forehead, chin, throat, back of the neck,
 neck-slue,
Strong shoulders, manly beard, scapula, hind-shoulders, and
 the ample side-round of the chest,

Upper-arm, armpit, elbow-socket, lower-arm, arm-sinews, arm-
bones,
Wrist and wrist-joints, hand, palm, knuckles, thumb, fore-
finger, finger-joints, finger-nails,
Broad breast-front, curling hair of the breast, breast-bone,
breast-side,
Ribs, belly, backbone, joints of the backbone,
Hips, hip-sockets, hip-strength, inward and outward round,
man-balls, man-root,
Strong set of thighs, well carrying the trunk above,
Leg-fibres, knee, knee-pan, upper-leg, under-leg,
Ankles, instep, foot-ball, toes, toe-joints, the heel;
All attitudes, all the shapeliness, all the belongings of my or
your body or of any one's body, male or female,
The lung-sponges, the stomach-sac, the bowels sweet and
clean,
The brain in its folds inside the skull-frame,
Sympathies, heart-valves, palate-valves, sexuality, maternity,
Womanhood, and all that is a woman, and the man that comes
from woman,
The womb, the teats, nipples, breast-milk, tears, laughter,
weeping, love-looks, love-perturbations and risings,
The voice, articulation, language, whispering, shouting aloud,
Food, drink, pulse, digestion, sweat, sleep, walking, swimming,
Poise on the hips, leaping, reclining, embracing, arm-curving
and tightening,
The continual changes of the flex of the mouth, and around
the eyes,
The skin, the sunburnt shade, freckles, hair,
The curious sympathy one feels when feeling with the hand
the naked meat of the body,
The circling rivers the breath, and breathing it in and out,
The beauty of the waist, and thence of the hips, and thence
downward toward the knees,
The thin red jellies within you or within me, the bones and the
marrow in the bones,
The exquisite realization of health;

O I say these are not the parts and poems of the body only,
    but of the soul,
O I say now these are the soul!

OUT OF THE ROLLING OCEAN THE CROWD

Out of the rolling ocean the crowd came a drop gently to me,
Whispering *I love you, before long I die,*
I have travel'd a long way merely to look on you to touch you,
For I could not die till I once look'd on you,
For I fear'd I might afterward lose you.

Now we have met, we have look'd, we are safe,
Return in peace to the ocean my love,
I too am part of that ocean my love, we are not so much
    separated,
Behold the great rondure, the cohesion of all, how perfect!
But as for me, for you, the irresistible sea is to separate us,
As for an hour carrying us diverse, yet cannot carry us diverse
    forever;
Be not impatient—a little space—know you I salute the air, the
    ocean and the land,
Every day at sundown for your dear sake my love.

I AM HE THAT ACHES WITH LOVE

I am he that aches with amorous love;
Does the earth gravitate? does not all matter, aching, attract
    all matter?
So the body of me to all I meet or know.

NATIVE MOMENTS

Native moments—when you come upon me—ah you are here
    now,
Give me now libidinous joys only,
Give me the drench of my passions, give me life coarse and
    rank,
To-day I go consort with Nature's darlings, to-night too,
I am for those who believe in loose delights,
    I share the midnight orgies of young men,
I dance with the dancers and drink with the drinkers,
The echoes ring with our indecent calls, I pick out some low
    person for my dearest friend,

He shall be lawless, rude, illiterate, he shall be one condemn'd
    by others for deeds done,
I will play a part no longer, why should I exile myself from
    my companions?
O you shunn'd persons, I at least do not shun you,
I come forthwith in your midst, I will be your poet,
I will be more to you than to any of the rest.

FACING WEST FROM CALIFORNIA'S
SHORES

Facing west from California's shores,
Inquiring, tireless, seeking what is yet unfound,
I, a child, very old, over waves, towards the house of ma-
    ternity, the land of migrations, look afar,
Look off the shores of my Western sea, the circle almost
    circled;
For starting westward from Hindustan, from the vales of
    Kashmere,
From Asia, from the north, from the God, the sage, and the
    hero,

From the south, from the flowery peninsulas and the spice
    islands,
Long having wander'd since, round the earth having wan-
    der'd,
Now I face home again, very pleas'd and joyous,
(But where is what I started for so long ago?
And why is it yet unfound?)

AS ADAM EARLY IN THE MORNING

As Adam early in the morning,
Walking forth from the bower refresh'd with sleep,
Behold me where I pass, hear my voice, approach,
Touch me, touch the palm of your hand to my body as I pass,
Be not afraid of my body.

CALAMUS

IN PATHS UNTRODDEN

In paths untrodden,
In the growth by margins of pond-waters,
Escaped from the life that exhibits itself,
From all the standards hitherto publish'd, from the pleasures,
    profits, conformities,
Which too long I was offering to feed my soul,
Clear to me now standards not yet publish'd, clear to me that
    my soul,
That the soul of the man I speak for rejoices in comrades,
Here by myself away from the clank of the world,
Tallying and talk'd to here by tongues aromatic,

No longer abash'd, (for in this secluded spot I can respond as
    I would not dare elsewhere,)
Strong upon me the life that does not exhibit itself, yet con-
    tains all the rest,
Resolv'd to sing no songs to-day but those of manly attach-
    ment,
Projecting them along that substantial life,
Bequeathing hence types of athletic love,
Afternoon this delicious Ninth-month in my forty-first year,
I proceed for all who are or have been young men,
To tell the secret of my nights and days,
To celebrate the needs of comrades.

SCENTED HERBAGE OF MY BREAST

Scented herbage of my breast,
Leaves from you I glean, I write, to be perused best after-
    wards,
Tomb-leaves, body-leaves growing up above me above death,
Perennial roots, tall leaves, O the winter shall not freeze you
    delicate leaves.
Every year shall you bloom again, out from where you re-
    tired you shall emerge again;
O I do not know whether many passing by will discover you
    or inhale your faint odor, but I believe a few will;
O slender leaves! O blossoms of my blood! I permit you to tell
    in your own way of the heart that is under you,
O I do not know what you mean there underneath yourselves,
    you are not happiness,
You are often more bitter than I can bear, you burn and sting
    me,
Yet you are beautiful to me you faint tinged roots, you make
    me think of death,
Death is beautiful from you, (what indeed is finally beautiful
    except death and love?)
O I think it is not for life I am chanting here my chant of
    lovers, I think it must be for death,

For how calm, how solemn it grows to ascend to the atmosphere of lovers,

Death or life I am then indifferent, my soul declines to prefer,

(I am not sure but the high soul of lovers welcomes death most,)

Indeed O death, I think now these leaves mean precisely the same as you mean,

Grow up taller sweet leaves that I may see! grow up out of my breast!

Spring away from the conceal'd heart there!

Do not fold yourself so in your pink-tinged roots timid leaves!

Do not remain down there so ashamed, herbage of my breast!

Come I am determin'd to unbare this broad breast of mine, I have long enough stifled and choked;

Emblematic and capricious blades I leave you, now you serve me not,

I will say what I have to say by itself,

I will sound myself and comrades only, I will never again utter a call only their call,

I will raise with it immortal reverberations through the States,

I will give an example to lovers to take permanent shape and will through the States,

Through me shall the words be said to make death exhilarating,

Give me your tone therefore O death, that I may accord with it,

Give me yourself, for I see that you belong to me now above all, and are folded inseparably together, you love and death are,

Nor will I allow you to balk me any more with what I was calling life,

For now it is convey'd to me that you are the purports essential,

That you hide in their shifting forms of life, for reasons, and that they are mainly for you,

That you beyond them come forth to remain, the real reality,

That behind the mask of materials you patiently wait, no matter how long,

That you will one day perhaps take control of all,
That you will perhaps dissipate this entire show of appearance,
That may-be you are what it is all for, but it does not last so
    very long,
But you will last very long.

WHOEVER YOU ARE HOLDING ME
NOW IN HAND

Whoever you are holding me now in hand,
Without one thing all will be useless,
I give you fair warning before you attempt me further,
I am not what you supposed, but far different.

Who is he that would become my follower?
Who would sign himself a candidate for my affections?

The way is suspicious, the result uncertain, perhaps destruc-
    tive,
You would have to give up all else, I alone would expect to be
    your sole and exclusive standard,
Your novitiate would even then be long and exhausting,
The whole past theory of your life and all conformity to the
    lives around you would have to be abandon'd,
Therefore release me now before troubling yourself any fur-
    ther, let go your hand from my shoulders,
Put me down and depart on your way.

Or else by stealth in some wood for trial,
Or back of a rock in the open air,
(For in any roof'd room of a house I emerge not, nor in
    company,
And in libraries I lie as one dumb, a gawk, or unborn, or
    dead,)

But just possibly with you on a high hill, first watching lest
      any person for miles around approach unawares,
Or possibly with you sailing at sea, or on the beach of the
      sea or some quiet island,
Here to put your lips upon mine I permit you,
With the comrade's long-dwelling kiss or the new husband's
      kiss,
For I am the new husband and I am the comrade.

Or if you will, thrusting me beneath your clothing,
Where I may feel the throbs of your heart or rest upon your
      hip,
Carry me when you go forth over land or sea;
For thus merely touching you is enough, is best,
And thus touching you would I silently sleep and be carried
      eternally.

But these leaves conning you con at peril,
For these leaves and me you will not understand,
They will elude you at first and still more afterward, I will
      certainly elude you,
Even while you should think you had unquestionably caught
      me, behold!
Already you see I have escaped from you.

For it is not for what I have put into it that I have written
      this book,
Nor is it by reading it you will acquire it,
Nor do those know best who admire me and vauntingly praise
      me,
Nor will the candidates for my love (unless at most a very
      few) prove victorious,
Nor will my poems do good only, they will do just as much
      evil, perhaps more,
For all is useless without that which you may guess at many
      times and not hit, that which I hinted at;
Therefore release me and depart on your way.

CITY OF ORGIES

City of orgies, walks and joys,
City whom that I have lived and sung in your midst will one
    day make you illustrious,
Not the pageants of you, nor your shifting tableaus, your
    spectacles, repay me,
Not the interminable rows of your houses, nor the ships at the
    wharves,
Nor the processions in the streets, nor the bright windows with
    goods in them,
Nor to converse with learn'd persons, or bear my share in the
    soiree or feast;
Not those, but as I pass O Manhattan, your frequent and swift
    flash of eyes offering me love,
Offering response to my own—these repay me,
Lovers, continual lovers, only repay me.

I SAW IN LOUISIANA A LIVE-OAK
GROWING

I saw in Louisiana a live-oak growing,
All alone stood it and the moss hung down from the branches,
Without any companion it grew there uttering joyous leaves
    of dark green,
And its look, rude, unbending, lusty, made me think of my-
    self,
But I wonder'd how it could utter joyous leaves standing
    alone there without its friend near, for I knew I could
    not,
And I broke off a twig with a certain number of leaves upon
    it, and twined around it a little moss,
And brought it away, and I have placed it in sight in my
    room,

It is not needed to remind me as of my own dear friends,
(For I believe lately I think of little else than of them,)
Yet it remains to me a curious token, it makes me think of
      manly love;
For all that, and though the live-oak glistens there in Lou-
      isiana solitary in a wide flat space,
Uttering joyous leaves all its life without a friend a lover near,
I know very well I could not.

TO A STRANGER

Passing stranger! you do not know how longingly I look upon
      you,
You must be he I was seeking, or she I was seeking, (it comes
      to me as of a dream,)
I have somewhere surely lived a life of joy with you,
All is recall'd as we flit by each other, fluid, affectionate,
      chaste, matured,
You grew up with me, were a boy with me or a girl with me,
I ate with you and slept with you, your body has become not
      yours only nor left my body mine only,
You give me the pleasure of your eyes, face, flesh, as we pass,
      you take of my beard, breast, hands, in return,
I am not to speak to you, I am to think of you when I sit alone
      or wake at night alone,
I am to wait, I do not doubt I am to meet you again,
I am to see to it that I do not lose you.

HERE THE FRAILEST LEAVES OF ME

Here the frailest leaves of me and yet my strongest lasting,
Here I shade and hide my thoughts, I myself do not expose
      them,
And yet they expose me more than all my other poems.

THIS MOMENT YEARNING AND THOUGHTFUL

This moment yearning and thoughtful sitting alone,
It seems to me there are other men in other lands yearning
    and thoughtful,
It seems to me I can look over and behold them in Germany,
    Italy, France, Spain,
Or far, far away, in China, or in Russia or Japan, talking
    other dialects,
And it seems to me if I could know those men I should be-
    come attached to them as I do to men in my own lands,
O I know we should be brethren and lovers,
I know I should be happy with them.

I HEAR IT WAS CHARGED AGAINST ME

I hear it was charged against me that I sought to destroy
    institutions,
But really I am neither for nor against institutions,
(What indeed have I in common with them? or what with the
    destruction of them?)
Only I will establish in the Mannahatta and in every city of
    these States inland and seaboard,
And in the fields and woods, and above every keel little or
    large that dents the water,
Without edifices or rules or trustees or any argument,
The institution of the dear love of comrades.

THE PRAIRIE-GRASS DIVIDING

The prairie-grass dividing, its special odor breathing,
I demand of it the spiritual corresponding,
Demand the most copious and close companionship of men,
Demand the blades to rise of words, acts, beings,
Those of the open atmosphere, coarse, sunlit, fresh, nutritious,
Those that go their own gait, erect, stepping with freedom
  and command, leading not following,
Those with a never-quell'd audacity, those with sweet and
  lusty flesh clear of taint,
Those that look carelessly in the faces of Presidents and gov-
  ernors, as to say *Who are you?*
Those of earth-born passion, simple, never constrain'd, never
  obedient,
Those of inland America.

WHEN I PERUSE THE CONQUER'D FAME

When I peruse the conquer'd fame of heroes and the victories
  of mighty generals, I do not envy the generals,
Nor the President in his Presidency, nor the rich in his great
  house,
But when I hear of the brotherhood of lovers, how it was with
  them,
How together through life, through dangers, odium, unchang-
  ing, long and long,
Through youth and through middle and old age, how unfaltering, how affectionate and faithful they were,
Then I am pensive—I hastily walk away fill'd with the bitter-
  est envy.

NO LABOR-SAVING MACHINE

No labor-saving machine,
Nor discovery have I made,
Nor will I be able to leave behind me any wealthy bequest to
found a hospital or library,
Nor reminiscence of any deed of courage for America,
Nor literary success nor intellect, nor book for the book-shelf,
But a few carols vibrating through the air I leave,
For comrades and lovers.

SONG of the OPEN ROAD

1

Afoot and light-hearted I take to the open road,
Healthy, free, the world before me,
The long brown path before me leading wherever I choose.

Henceforth I ask not good-fortune, I myself am good-fortune,
Henceforth I whimper no more, postpone no more, need noth-
ing,
Done with indoor complaints, libraries, querulous criticisms,
Strong and content I travel the open road.

The earth, that is sufficient,
I do not want the constellations any nearer,
I know they are very well where they are,
I know they suffice for those who belong to them.

(Still here I carry my old delicious burdens,
I carry them, men and women, I carry them with me wherever I go,

I swear it is impossible for me to get rid of them,
I am fill'd with them, and I will fill them in return.)

2

You road I enter upon and look around, I believe you are not
    all that is here,
I believe that much unseen is also here.

Here the profound lesson of reception, nor preference nor de-
    nial,
The black with his woolly head, the felon, the diseas'd, the
    illiterate person, are not denied;
The birth, the hasting after the physician, the beggar's tramp,
    the drunkard's stagger, the laughing party of mechanics,
The escaped youth, the rich person's carriage, the fop, the
    eloping couple,
The early market-man, the hearse, the moving of furniture
    into the town, the return back from the town,
They pass, I also pass, any thing passes, none can be inter-
    dicted,
None but are accepted, none but shall be dear to me.

3

You air that serves me with breath to speak!
You objects that call from diffusion my meanings and give
    them shape!
You light that wraps me and all things in delicate equable
    showers!
You paths worn in the irregular hollows by the roadsides!
I believe you are latent with unseen existences, you are so
    dear to me.

You flagg'd walks of the cities! you strong curbs at the edges!
You ferries! you planks and posts of wharves! you timber-
    lined sides! you distant ships!

You rows of houses! you window-pierc'd façades! you roofs!
You porches and entrances! you copings and iron guards!
You windows whose transparent shells might expose so much!
You doors and ascending steps! you arches!
You gray stones of interminable pavements! you trodden
  crossings!
From all that has touch'd you I believe you have imparted to
  yourselves, and now would impart the same secretly to
  me,
From the living and the dead you have peopled your impas-
  sive surfaces, and the spirits thereof would be evident
  and amicable with me.

4

The earth expanding right hand and left hand,
The picture alive, every part in its best light,
The music falling in where it is wanted, and stopping where
  it is not wanted,
The cheerful voice of the public road, the gay fresh sentiment
  of the road.

O highway I travel, do you say to me *Do not leave me?*
Do you say *Venture not—if you leave me you are lost?*
Do you say *I am already prepared, I am well-beaten and un-
  denied, adhere to me?*

O public road, I say back I am not afraid to leave you, yet I
  love you,
You express me better than I can express myself,
You shall be more to me than my poem.

I think heroic deeds were all conceiv'd in the open air, and
  all free poems also,
I think I could stop here myself and do miracles,
I think whatever I shall meet on the road I shall like, and
  whoever beholds me shall like me,
I think whoever I see must be happy.

5

From this hour I ordain myself loos'd of limits and imaginary
lines,
Going where I list, my own master total and absolute,
Listening to others, considering well what they say,
Pausing, searching, receiving, contemplating,
Gently, but with undeniable will, divesting myself of the holds
that would hold me.

I inhale great draughts of space,
The east and the west are mine, and the north and the south
are mine.

I am larger, better than I thought,
I did not know I held so much goodness.

All seems beautiful to me,
I can repeat over to men and women You have done such
good to me I would do the same to you,
I will recruit for myself and you as I go,
I will scatter myself among men and women as I go,
I will toss a new gladness and roughness among them,
Whoever denies me it shall not trouble me,
Whoever accepts me he or she shall be blessed and shall bless
me.

6

Now if a thousand perfect men were to appear it would not
amaze me,
Now if a thousand beautiful forms of women appear'd it
would not astonish me.

Now I see the secret of the making of the best persons,
It is to grow in the open air and to eat and sleep with the
earth.

Here a great personal deed has room,
(Such a deed seizes upon the hearts of the whole race of men,
Its effusion of strength and will overwhelms law and mocks
    all authority and all argument against it.)

Here is the test of wisdom,
Wisdom is not finally tested in schools,
Wisdom cannot be pass'd from one having it to another not
    having it,
Wisdom is of the soul, is not susceptible of proof, is its own
    proof,
Applies to all stages and objects and qualities and is content,
Is the certainty of the reality and immortality of things, and
    the excellence of things;
Something there is in the float of the sight of things that pro-
    vokes it out of the soul.

Now I re-examine philosophies and religions,
They may prove well in lecture-rooms, yet not prove at all
    under the spacious clouds and along the landscape and
    flowing currents.

Here is realization,
Here is a man tallied—he realizes here what he has in him,
The past, the future, majesty, love—if they are vacant of you,
    you are vacant of them.

Only the kernel of every object nourishes;
Where is he who tears off the husks for you and me?
Where is he that undoes stratagems and envelopes for you
    and me?

Here is adhesiveness, it is not previously fashion'd, it is
    apropos;
Do you know what it is as you pass to be loved by strangers?
Do you know the talk of those turning eye-balls?

7

Here is the efflux of the soul,
The efflux of the soul comes from within through embower'd
      gates, ever provoking questions,
These yearnings why are they? these thoughts in the darkness
      why are they?
Why are there men and women that while they are nigh me
      the sunlight expands my blood?
Why when they leave me do my pennants of joy sink flat and
      lank?
Why are there trees I never walk under but large and melo-
      dious thoughts descend upon me?
(I think they hang there winter and summer on those trees
      and always drop fruit as I pass;)
What is it I interchange so suddenly with strangers?
What with some driver as I ride on the seat by his side?
What with some fisherman drawing his seine by the shore as
      I walk by and pause?
What gives me to be free to a woman's and man's good-will?
      what gives them to be free to mine?

8

The efflux of the soul is happiness, here is happiness,
I think it pervades the open air, waiting at all times,
Now it flows unto us, we are rightly charged.

Here rises the fluid and attaching character,
The fluid and attaching character is the freshness and sweet-
      ness of man and woman,
(The herbs of the morning sprout no fresher and sweeter ev-
      ery day out of the roots of themselves, than it sprouts
      fresh and sweet continually out of itself.)
Toward the fluid and attaching character exudes the sweat of
      the love of young and old,

From it falls distill'd the charm that mocks beauty and attain-
   ments,
Toward it heaves the shuddering longing ache of contact.

9

Allons! whoever you are come travel with me!
Traveling with me you find what never tires.

The earth never tires,
The earth is rude, silent, incomprehensible at first, Nature is
   rude and incomprehensible at first,
Be not discouraged, keep on, there are divine things well
   envelop'd,
I swear to you there are divine things more beautiful than
   words can tell.

Allons! we must not stop here,
However sweet these laid-up stores, however convenient this
   dwelling we cannot remain here,
However shelter'd this port and however calm these waters
   we must not anchor here,
However welcome the hospitality that surrounds us we are
   permitted to receive it but a little while.

10

Allons! the inducements shall be greater,
We will sail pathless and wild seas,
We will go where winds blow, waves dash, and the Yankee
   clipper speeds by under full sail.

Allons! with power, liberty, the earth, the elements,
Health, defiance, gayety, self-esteem, curiosity;
Allons! from all formules!
From your formules, O bat-eyed and materialistic priests.

The stale cadaver blocks up the passage—the burial waits no
   longer.

Allons! yet take warning!
He traveling with me needs the best blood, thews, endurance,
None may come to the trial till he or she bring courage and
    health, -
Come not here if you have already spent the best of yourself,
Only those may come who come in sweet and determin'd
    bodies,
No diseas'd person, no rum-drinker or venereal taint is per-
    mitted here.

(I and mine do not convince by arguments, similes, rhymes,
We convince by our presence.)

11

Listen! I will be honest with you,
I do not offer the old smooth prizes, but offer rough new
    prizes,
These are the days that must happen to you:
You shall not heap up what is call'd riches,
You shall scatter with lavish hand all that you earn or achieve,
You but arrive at the city to which you were destin'd, you
    hardly settle yourself to satisfaction before you are
    call'd by an irresistible call to depart,
You shall be treated to the ironical smiles and mockings of
    those who remain behind you,
What beckonings of love you receive you shall only answer
    with passionate kisses of parting,
You shall not allow the hold of those who spread their reach'd
    hands toward you.

12

Allons! after the great Companions, and to belong to them!
They too are on the road—they are the swift and majestic
    men—they are the greatest women,
Enjoyers of calms of seas and storms of seas,
Sailors of many a ship, walkers of many a mile of land,

Habituès of many distant countries, habituès of far-distant
    dwellings,
Trusters of men and women, observers of cities, solitary
    toilers,
Pausers and contemplators of tufts, blossoms, shells of the
    shore,
Dancers at wedding-dances, kissers of brides, tender helpers
    of children, bearers of children,
Soldiers of revolts, standers by gaping graves, lowerers-down
    of coffins,
Journeyers over consecutive seasons, over the years, the curi-
    ous years each emerging from that which preceded it,
Journeyers as with companions, namely their own diverse
    phases,
Forth-steppers from the latent unrealized baby-days,
Journeyers gayly with their own youth, journeyers with their
    bearded and well-grain'd manhood,
Journeyers with their womanhood, ample, unsurpass'd, con-
    tent,
Journeyers with their own sublime old age of manhood or
    womanhood,
Old age, calm, expanded, broad with the haughty breadth of
    the universe,
Old age, flowing free with the delicious near-by freedom of
    death.

13

Allons! to that which is endless as it was beginningless,
To undergo much, tramps of days, rests of nights,
To merge all in the travel they tend to, and the days and
    nights they tend to,
Again to merge them in the start of superior journeys,
To see nothing anywhere but what you may reach it and pass
    it,
To conceive no time, however distant, but what you may
    reach it and pass it,
To look up or down no road but it stretches and waits for
    you, however long but it stretches and waits for you,

To see no being, not God's or any, but you also go thither,

To see no possession but you may possess it, enjoying all
without labor or purchase, abstracting the feast yet not
abstracting one particle of it,

To take the best of the farmer's farm and the rich man's elegant villa, and the chaste blessings of the well-married
couple, and the fruits of orchards and flowers of gardens,

To take to your use out of the compact cities as you pass
through,

To carry buildings and streets with you afterward wherever
you go,

To gather the minds of men out of their brains as you en-
counter them, to gather the love out of their hearts,

To take your lovers on the road with you, for all that you
leave them behind you,

To know the universe itself as a road, as many roads, as roads
for traveling souls.

All parts away for the progress of souls,

All religion, all solid things, arts, governments—all that was
or is apparent upon this globe or any globe, falls into
niches and corners before the procession of souls along
the grand roads of the universe.

Of the progress of the souls of men and women along the
grand roads of the universe, all other progress is the
needed emblem and sustenance.

Forever alive, forever forward,

Stately, solemn, sad, withdrawn, baffled, mad, turbulent, feeble, dissatisfied,

Desperate, proud, fond, sick, accepted by men, rejected by
men,

They go! they go! I know that they go, but I know not where
they go,

But I know that they go toward the best—toward something
great.

Whoever you are, come forth! or man or woman come forth!
You must not stay sleeping and dallying there in the house,
though you built it, or though it has been built for you.

Out of the dark confinement! out from behind the screen!
It is useless to protest, I know all and expose it.

Behold through you as bad as the rest,
Through the laughter, dancing, dining, supping, of people,
Inside of dresses and ornaments, inside of those wash'd and
trimm'd faces,
Behold a secret silent loathing and despair.

No husband, no wife, no friend, trusted to hear the confes-
sion,
Another self, a duplicate of every one, skulking and hiding it
goes,
Formless and wordless through the streets of the cities, polite
and bland in the parlors,
In the cars of railroads, in steamboats, in the public assembly,
Home to the houses of men and women, at the table, in the
bedroom, everywhere,
Smartly attired, countenance smiling, form upright, death un-
der the breast-bones, hell under the skull-bones,
Under the broadcloth and gloves, under the ribbons and arti-
ficial flowers,
Keeping fair with the customs, speaking not a syllable of it-
self,
Speaking of any thing else but never of itself.

14

Allons! through struggles and wars!
The goal that was named cannot be countermanded.

Have the past struggles succeeded?
What has succeeded? yourself? your nation? Nature?

Now understand me well—it is provided in the essence of
   things that from any fruition of success, no matter
   what, shall come forth something to make a greater
   struggle necessary.

My call is the call of battle, I nourish active rebellion,
He going with me must go well arm'd,
He going with me goes often with spare diet, poverty, angry
   enemies, desertions.

15

Allons! the road is before us!
It is safe—I have tried it—my own feet have tried it well—be
   not detain'd!
Let the paper remain on the desk unwritten, and the book on
   the shelf unopen'd!
Let the tools remain in the workshop! let the money remain
   unearn'd!
Let the school stand! mind not the cry of the teacher!
Let the preacher preach in his pulpit! let the lawyer plead in
   the court, and the judge expound the law.

Camerado, I give you my hand!
I give you my love more precious than money,
I give you myself before preaching or law;
Will you give me yourself? will you come travel with me?
Shall we stick by each other as long as we live?

CROSSING BROOKLYN FERRY

1

Flood-tide below me! I see you face to face!
Clouds of the west—sun there half an hour high—I see you
    also face to face.

Crowds of men and women attired in the usual costumes,
    how curious you are to me!
On the ferry-boats the hundreds and hundreds that cross, re-
    turning home, are more curious to me than you sup-
    pose,
And you that shall cross from shore to shore years hence are
    more to me, and more in my meditations, than you
    might suppose.

2

The impalpable sustenance of me from all things at all hours
    of the day,
The simple, compact, well-join'd scheme, myself disinte-
    grated, every one disintegrated yet part of the scheme,
The similitudes of the past and those of the future,
The glories strung like beads on my smallest sights and hear-
    ings, on the walk in the street and the passage over the
    river,
The current rushing so swiftly and swimming with me far
    away,
The others that are to follow me, the ties between me and
    them,
The certainty of others, the life, love, sight, hearing of others.

Others will enter the gates of the ferry and cross from shore
    to shore,
Others will watch the run of the flood-tide,
Others will see the shipping of Manhattan north and west,
    and the heights of Brooklyn to the south and east,
Others will see the islands large and small;
Fifty years hence, others will see them as they cross, the sun
    half an hour high,
A hundred years hence, or ever so many hundred years hence,
    others will see them,
Will enjoy the sunset, the pouring-in of the flood-tide, the
    falling-back to the sea of the ebb-tide.

3

It avails not, time nor place—distance avails not,
I am with you, you men and women of a generation, or ever
    so many generations hence,
Just as you feel when you look on the river and sky, so I felt,
Just as any of you is one of a living crowd, I was one of a
    crowd,
Just as you are refresh'd by the gladness of the river and the
    bright flow, I was refresh'd,
Just as you stand and lean on the rail, yet hurry with the
    swift current, I stood yet was hurried,
Just as you look on the numberless masts of ships and the
    thick-stemm'd pipes of steamboats, I look'd.

I too many and many a time cross'd the river of old,
Watched the Twelfth-month sea-gulls, saw them high in the
    air floating with motionless wings, oscillating their
    bodies,
Saw how the glistening yellow lit up parts of their bodies and
    left the rest in strong shadow,
Saw the slow-wheeling circles and the gradual edging toward
    the south,
Saw the reflection of the summer sky in the water,
Had my eyes dazzled by the shimmering track of beams,

Look'd at the fine centrifugal spokes of light round the shape
    of my head in the sunlit water,
Look'd on the haze on the hills southward and south-west-
    ward,
Look'd on the vapor as it flew in fleeces tinged with violet,
Look'd toward the lower bay to notice the vessels arriving,
Saw their approach, saw aboard those that were near me,
Saw the white sails of schooners and sloops, saw the ships at
    anchor,
The sailors at work in the rigging or out astride the spars,
The round masts, the swinging motion of the hulls, the slen-
    der serpentine pennants,
The large and small steamers in motion, the pilots in their
    pilot-houses,
The white wake left by the passage, the quick tremulous
    whirl of the wheels,
The flags of all nations, the falling of them at sunset,
The scallop-edged waves in the twilight, the ladled cups, the
    frolicsome crests and glistening,
The stretch afar growing dimmer and dimmer, the gray walls
    of the granite storehouses by the docks,
On the river the shadowy group, the big steam-tug closely
    flank'd on each side by the barges, the hay-boat, the
    belated lighter,
On the neighboring shore the fires from the foundry chim-
    neys burning high and glaringly into the night,
Casting their flicker of black contrasted with wild red and
    yellow light over the tops of houses, and down into the
    clefts of streets.

4

These and all else were to me the same as they are to you,
I loved well those cities, loved well the stately and rapid river,
The men and women I saw were all near to me,
Others the same—others who look back on me because I
    look'd forward to them,
(The time will come, though I stop here to-day and to-night.)

5

What is it then between us?
What is the count of the scores or hundreds of years between
us?

Whatever it is, it avails not—distance avails not, and place
avails not,
I too lived, Brooklyn of ample hills was mine,
I too walk'd the streets of Manhattan island, and bathed in
the waters around it,
I too felt the curious abrupt questionings stir within me,
In the day among crowds of people sometimes they came
upon me,
In my walks home late at night or as I lay in my bed they
came upon me,
I too had been struck from the float forever held in solution,
I too had receiv'd identity by my body,
That I was I knew was of my body, and what I should be I
knew I should be of my body.

6

It is not upon you alone the dark patches fall,
The dark threw its patches down upon me also,
The best I had done seem'd to me blank and suspicious,
My great thoughts as I supposed them, were they not in real-
ity meagre?
Nor is it you alone who know what it is to be evil,
I am he who knew what it was to be evil,
I too knitted the old knot of contrariety,
Blabb'd, blush'd, resented, lied, stole, grudg'd,
Had guile, anger, lust, hot wishes I dared not speak,
Was wayward, vain, greedy, shallow, sly, cowardly, malig-
nant,
The wolf, the snake, the hog, not wanting in me,
The cheating look, the frivolous word, the adulterous wish,
not wanting,

Refusals, hates, postponements, meanness, laziness, none of
    these wanting,
Was one with the rest, the days and haps of the rest,
Was call'd by my nighest name by clear loud voices of young
    men as they saw me approaching or passing,
Felt their arms on my neck as I stood, or the negligent lean-
    ing of their flesh against me as I sat,
Saw many I loved in the street or ferry-boat or public assem-
    bly, yet never told them a word,
Lived the same life with the rest, the same old laughing,
    gnawing, sleeping,
Play'd the part that still looks back on the actor or actress,
The same old role, the role that is what we make it, as great
    as we like,
Or as small as we like, or both great and small.

7

Closer yet I approach you,
What thought you have of me now, I had as much of you—I
    laid in my stores in advance,
I consider'd long and seriously of you before you were born.

Who was to know what should come home to me?
Who knows but I am enjoying this?
Who knows, for all the distance, but I am as good as looking
    at you now, for all you cannot see me?

8

Ah, what can ever be more stately and admirable to me than
    mast-hemm'd Manhattan?
River and sunset and scallop-edg'd waves of flood-tide?
The sea-gulls oscillating their bodies, the hay-boat in the twi-
    light, and the belated lighter?

What gods can exceed these that clasp me by the hand, and
    with voices I love call me promptly and loudly by my
    nighest name as I approach?

What is more subtle than this which ties me to the woman or
    man that looks in my face?
Which fuses me into you now, and pours my meaning into
    you?

We understand then do we not?
What I promis'd without mentioning it, have you not ac-
    cepted?
What the study could not teach—what the preaching could
    not accomplish is accomplish'd, is it not?

9

Flow on, river! flow with the flood-tide, and ebb with the
    ebb-tide!
Frolic on, crested and scallop-edg'd waves!
Gorgeous clouds of the sunset! drench with your splendor me,
    or the men and women generations after me!
Cross from shore to shore, countless crowds of passengers!
Stand up, tall masts of Mannahatta! stand up, beautiful hills
    of Brooklyn!
Throb, baffled and curious brain! throw out questions and
    answers!
Suspend here and everywhere, eternal float of solution!
Gaze, loving and thirsting eyes, in the house or street or pub-
    lic assembly!
Sound out, voices of young men! loudly and musically call me
    by my nighest name!
Live, old life! play the part that looks back on the actor or
    actress!
Play the old role, the role that is great or small according as
    one makes it!
Consider, you who peruse me, whether I may not in unknown
    ways be looking upon you;
Be firm, rail over the river, to support those who lean idly,
    yet haste with the hasting current;
Fly on, sea-birds! fly sideways, or wheel in large circles high
    in the air;

Receive the summer sky, you water, and faithfully hold it
    till all downcast eyes have time to take it from you!

Diverge, fine spokes of light, from the shape of my head, or
    any one's head, in the sunlit water!

Come on, ships from the lower bay! pass up or down, white-
    sail'd schooners, sloops, lighters!

Flaunt away, flags of all nations! be duly lower'd at sunset!

Burn high your fires, foundry chimneys! cast black shadows
    at nightfall! cast red and yellow light over the tops of
    the houses!

Appearances, now or henceforth, indicate what you are,

You necessary film, continue to envelop the soul,

About my body for me, and your body for you, be hung our
    divinest aromas,

Thrive, cities—bring your freight, bring your shows, ample
    and sufficient rivers,

Expand, being than which none else is perhaps more spiritual,

Keep your places, objects than which none else is more last-
    ing.

You have waited, you always wait, you dumb, beautiful min-
    isters,

We receive you with free sense at last, and are insatiate
    henceforward,

Not you any more shall be able to foil us, or withhold your-
    selves from us,

We use you, and do not cast you aside—we plant you perma-
    nently within us,

We fathom you not—we love you—there is perfection in you
    also,

You furnish your parts toward eternity,

Great or small, you furnish your parts toward the soul.

A SONG of the ROLLING EARTH

1

A song of the rolling earth, and of words according,
Were you thinking that those were the words, those upright
    lines? those curves, angles, dots?
No, those are not the words, the substantial words are in the
    ground and sea,
They are in the air, they are in you.

Were you thinking that those were the words, those delicious
    sounds out of your friends' mouths?
No, the real words are more delicious than they.

Human bodies are words, myriads of words,
(In the best poems re-appears the body, man's or woman's,
    well-shaped, natural, gay,
Every part able, active, receptive, without shame or the need
    of shame.)

Air, soil, water, fire—those are words,
I myself am a word with them—my qualities interpenetrate
    with theirs—my name is nothing to them,
Though it were told in the three thousand languages, what
    would air, soil, water, fire, know of my name?

A healthy presence, a friendly or commanding gesture, are
    words, sayings, meanings,
The charms that go with the mere looks of some men and
    women, are sayings and meanings also.

The workmanship of souls is by those inaudible words of the
  earth,
The masters know the earth's words and use them more than
    audible words.

Amelioration is one of the earth's words,
The earth neither lags nor hastens,
It has all attributes, growths, effects, latent in itself from the
    jump,
It is not half beautiful only, defects and excrescences show
    just as much as perfections show.

The earth does not withhold, it is generous enough,
The truths of the earth continually wait, they are not so con-
    ceal'd either,
They are calm, subtle, untransmissible by print,
They are imbued through all things conveying themselves
    willingly,
Conveying a sentiment and invitation, I utter and utter,
I speak not, yet if you hear me not of what avail am I to you?
To bear, to better, lacking these of what avail am I?

(Accouche! accouchez!
Will you rot your own fruit in yourself there?
Will you squat and stifle there?)

The earth does not argue,
Is not pathetic, has no arrangements,
Does not scream, haste, persuade, threaten, promise,
Makes no discriminations, has no conceivable failures,
Closes nothing, refuses nothing, shuts none out,
Of all the powers, objects, states, it notifies, shuts none out.

The earth does not exhibit itself nor refuse to exhibit itself,
    possesses still underneath,

Underneath the ostensible sounds, the august chorus of heroes, the wail of slaves,
Persuasions of lovers, curses, gasps of the dying, laughter of
  young people, accents of bargainers,
Underneath these possessing words that never fail.

To her children the words of the eloquent dumb great mother
  never fail,
The true words do not fail, for motion does not fail and reflection does not fail,
Also the day and night do not fail, and the voyage we pursue
  does not fail.

Of the interminable sisters,
Of the ceaseless cotillons of sisters,
Of the centripetal and centrifugal sisters, the elder and
  younger sisters,
The beautiful sister we know dances on with the rest.

With her ample back towards every beholder,
With the fascinations of youth and the equal fascinations of
  age,
Sits she whom I too love like the rest, sits undisturb'd,
Holding up in her hand what has the character of a mirror,
  while her eyes glance back from it,
Glance as she sits, inviting none, denying none,
Holding a mirror day and night tirelessly before her own face.

Seen at hand or seen at a distance,
Duly the twenty-four appear in public every day,
Duly approach and pass with their companions or a com-
  panion,
Looking from no countenances of their own, but from the
  countenances of those who are with them,
From the countenances of children or women or the manly
  countenance,

From the open countenances of animals or from inanimate
    things,
From the landscape or waters or from the exquisite apparition
    of the sky,
From our countenances, mine and yours, faithfully returning
    them,
Every day in public appearing without fail, but never twice
    with the same companions.

Embracing man, embracing all, proceed the three hundred
    and sixty-five resistlessly round the sun;
Embracing all, soothing, supporting, follow close three hun-
    dred and sixty-five offsets of the first, sure and neces-
    sary as they.

Tumbling on steadily, nothing dreading,
Sunshine, storm, cold, heat, forever withstanding, passing,
    carrying,
The soul's realization and determination still inheriting,
The fluid vacuum around and ahead still entering and divid-
    ing,
No balk retarding, no anchor anchoring, on no rock striking,
Swift, glad, content, unbereav'd, nothing losing,
Of all able and ready at any time to give strict account,
The divine ship sails the divine sea.

2

Whoever you are! motion and reflection are especially for you,
The divine ship sails the divine sea for you.

Whoever you are! you are he or she for whom the earth is
    solid and liquid,
You are he or she for whom the sun and moon hang in the
    sky,

For none more than you are the present and the past,
For none more than you is immortality.

Each man to himself and each woman to herself, is the word
      of the past and present, and the true word of immor-
      tality;
No one can acquire for another—not one,
Not one can grow for another—not one.

The song is to the singer, and comes back most to him,
The teaching is to the teacher, and comes back most to him,
The murder is to the murderer, and comes back most to him,
The theft is to the thief, and comes back most to him,
The love is to the lover, and comes back most to him,
The gift is to the giver, and comes back most to him—it can-
      not fail,
The oration is to the orator, the acting is to the actor and
      actress not to the audience,
And no man understands any greatness or goodness but his
      own, or the indication of his own.

3

I swear the earth shall surely be complete to him or her who
      shall be complete,
The earth remains jagged and broken only to him or her who
      remains jagged and broken.

I swear there is no greatness or power that does not emulate
      those of the earth,
There can be no theory of any account unless it corroborates
      the theory of the earth,
No politics, song, religion, behavior, or what not, is of ac-
      count, unless it compare with the amplitude of the
      earth,

Unless it face the exactness, vitality, impartiality, rectitude of
 the earth.

I swear I begin to see love with sweeter spasms than that
 which responds love,
It is that which contains itself, which never invites and never
 refuses.

I swear I begin to see little or nothing in audible words,
All merges toward the presentation of the unspoken meanings of the earth,
Toward him who sings the songs of the body and of the truths
 of the earth,
Toward him who makes the dictionaries of words that print
 cannot touch.

I swear I see what is better than to tell the best,
It is always to leave the best untold.

When I undertake to tell the best I find I cannot,
My tongue is ineffectual on its pivots,
My breath will not be obedient to its organs,
I become a dumb man.

The best of the earth cannot be told anyhow, all or any is
 best,
It is not what you anticipated, it is cheaper, easier, nearer,
Things are not dismiss'd from the places they held before,
The earth is just as positive and direct as it was before,
Facts, religions, improvements, politics, trades, are as real as
 before,
But the soul is also real, it too is positive and direct,
No reasoning, no proof has establish'd it,
Undeniable growth has establish'd it.

4

These to echo the tones of souls and the phrases of souls,
(If they did not echo the phrases of souls what were they
then?
If they had not reference to you in especial what were they
then?)

I swear I will never henceforth have to do with the faith that
tells the best,
I will have to do only with that faith that leaves the best untold.

Say on, sayers! sing on, singers!
Delve! mould! pile the words of the earth!
Work on, age after age, nothing is to be lost,
It may have to wait long, but it will certainly come in use,
When the materials are all prepared and ready, the architects
shall appear.

I swear to you the architects shall appear without fail,
I swear to you they will understand you and justify you,
The greatest among them shall be he who best knows you,
and encloses all and is faithful to all,
He and the rest shall not forget you, they shall perceive that
you are not an iota less than they,
You shall be fully glorified in them.

PIONEERS! O PIONEERS!

Come my tan-faced children,
Follow well in order, get your weapons ready,
Have you your pistols? have you your sharp-edged axes?
Pioneers! O pioneers!

For we cannot tarry here,
We must march my darlings, we must bear the brunt of danger,
We the youthful sinewy races, all the rest on us depend,
Pioneers! O pioneers!

O you youths, Western youths,
So impatient, full of action, full of manly pride and friendship,
Plain I see you Western youths, see you tramping with the foremost,
Pioneers! O pioneers!

Have the elder races halted?
Do they droop and end their lesson, wearied over there beyond the seas?
We take up the task eternal, and the burden and the lesson,
Pioneers! O pioneers!

All the past we leave behind,
We debouch upon a newer mightier world, varied world,
Fresh and strong the world we seize, world of labor and the march,
Pioneers! O pioneers!

We detachments steady throwing,
Down the edges, through the passes, up the mountains steep,
Conquering, holding, daring, venturing as we go the unknown
　　　　　ways,
　　　　Pioneers! O pioneers!

We primeval forests felling,
We the rivers stemming, vexing we and piercing deep the
　　　　　mines within,
We the surface broad surveying, we the virgin soil upheaving,
　　　　Pioneers! O pioneers!

Colorado men are we,
From the peaks gigantic, from the great sierras and the high
　　　　　plateaus,
From the mine and from the gully, from the hunting trail we
　　　　　come,
　　　　Pioneers! O pioneers!

From Nebraska, from Arkansas,
Central inland race are we, from Missouri, with the continen-
　　　　　tal blood intervein'd,
All the hands of comrades clasping, all the Southern, all the
　　　　　Northern,
　　　　Pioneers! O pioneers!

O resistless restless race!
O beloved race in all! O my breast aches with tender love for
　　　　　all!
O I mourn and yet exult, I am rapt with love for all,
　　　　Pioneers! O pioneers!

Raise the mighty mother mistress,
Waving high the delicate mistress, over all the starry mistress,
　　　　　(bend your heads all,)
Raise the fang'd and warlike mistress, stern, impassive, weap-
　　　　　on'd mistress,
　　　　Pioneers! O pioneers!

See my children, resolute children,
By those swarms upon our rear we must never yield or falter,
Ages back in ghostly millions frowning there behind us urg-
ing,
Pioneers! O pioneers!

On and on the compact ranks,
With accessions ever waiting, with the places of the dead
quickly fill'd,
Through the battle, through defeat, moving yet and never
stopping,
Pioneers! O pioneers!

O to die advancing on!
Are there some of us to droop and die? has the hour come?
Then upon the march we fittest die, soon and sure the gap is
fill'd,
Pioneers! O pioneers!

All the pulses of the world,
Falling in they beat for us, with the Western movement beat,
Holding single or together, steady moving to the front, all for
us,
Pioneers! O pioneers!

Life's involv'd and varied pageants,
All the forms and shows, all the workmen at their work,
All the seamen and the landsmen, all the masters with their
slaves,
Pioneers! O pioneers!

All the hapless silent lovers,
All the prisoners in the prisons, all the righteous and the
wicked,
All the joyous, all the sorrowing, all the living, all the dying,
Pioneers! O pioneers!

I too with my soul and body,
We, a curious trio, picking, wandering on our way,
Through these shores amid the shadows, with the apparitions
      pressing,
      Pioneers! O pioneers!

Lo, the darting bowling orb!
Lo, the brother orbs around, all the clustering suns and
      planets,
All the dazzling days, all the mystic nights with dreams,
      Pioneers! O pioneers!

These are of us, they are with us,
All for primal needed work, while the followers there in em-
      bryo wait behind,
We to-day's procession heading, we the route for travel clear-
      ing,
      Pioneers! O pioneers!

O you daughters of the West!
O you young and elder daughters! O you mothers and you
      wives!
Never must you be divided, in our ranks you move united,
      Pioneers! O pioneers!

Minstrels latent on the prairies!
(Shrouded bards of other lands, you may rest, you have done
      your work,)
Soon I hear you coming warbling, soon you rise and tramp
      amid us,
      Pioneers! O pioneers!

Not for delectations sweet,
Not the cushion and the slipper, not the peaceful and the
      studious,
Not the riches safe and palling, not for us the tame enjoy-
      ment,
      Pioneers! O pioneers!

Do the feasters gluttonous feast?
Do the corpulent sleepers sleep? have they lock'd and bolted
doors?
Still be ours the diet hard, and the blanket on the ground,
Pioneers! O pioneers!

Has the night descended?
Was the road of late so toilsome? did we stop discouraged
nodding on our way?
Yet a passing hour I yield you in your tracks to pause oblivi-
ous,
Pioneers! O pioneers!

Till with sound of trumpet,
Far, far off the daybreak call—hark! how loud and clear I
hear it wind,
Swift! to the head of the army!—swift! spring to your places,
Pioneers! O pioneers!

FRANCE

The 18th Year of These States

A great year and place,
A harsh discordant natal scream out-sounding, to touch the
mother's heart closer than any yet.

I walk'd the shores of my Eastern sea,
Heard over the waves the little voice,
Saw the divine infant where she woke mournfully wailing,
amid the roar of cannon, curses, shouts, crash of falling
buildings,
Was not so sick from the blood in the gutters running, nor
from the single corpses, nor those in heaps, nor those
borne away in the tumbrils,
Was not so desperate at the battues of death—was not so
shock'd at the repeated fusillades of the guns.

Pale, silent, stern, what could I say to that long-accrued retri-
    bution?
Could I wish humanity different?
Could I wish the people made of wood and stone?
Or that there be no justice in destiny or time?

O Liberty! O mate for me!
Here too the blaze, the grape-shot and the axe, in reserve, to
    fetch them out in case of need,
Here too, though long represt, can never be destroy'd,
Here too could rise at last murdering and ecstatic,
Here too demanding full arrears of vengeance.

Hence I sign this salute over the sea,
And I do not deny that terrible red birth and baptism,
But remember the little voice that I heard wailing, and wait
    with perfect trust, no matter how long,
And from to-day sad and cogent I maintain the bequeath'd
    cause, as for all lands,
And I send these words to Paris with my love,
And I guess some chansonniers there will understand them,
For I guess there is latent music yet in France, floods of it,
O I hear already the bustle of instruments, they will soon be
    drowning all that would interrupt them,
O I think the east wind brings a triumphal and free march,
It reaches hither, it swells me to joyful madness,
I will run transpose it in words, to justify it,
I will yet sing a song for you ma femme.

MYSELF AND MINE

Myself and mine gymnastic ever,
To stand the cold or heat, to take good aim with a gun, to sail
    a boat, to manage horses, to beget superb children,
To speak readily and clearly, to feel at home among common
    people,
And to hold our own in terrible positions on land and sea.

Not for an embroiderer,
(There will always be plenty of embroiderers, I welcome them
     also,)
But for the fibre of things and for inherent men and women.

Not to chisel ornaments,
But to chisel with free stroke the heads and limbs of plen-
     teous supreme Gods, that the States may realize them
     walking and talking.

Let me have my own way,
Let others promulge the laws, I will make no account of the
     laws,
Let others praise eminent men and hold up peace, I hold up
     agitation and conflict,
I praise no eminent man, I rebuke to his face the one that
     was thought most worthy.

(Who are you? and what are you secretly guilty of all your
     life?
Will you turn aside all your life? will you grub and chatter all
     your life?
And who are you, blabbing by rote, years, pages, languages,
     reminiscences,
Unwitting to-day that you do not know how to speak proper-
     ly a single word?)

Let others finish specimens, I never finish specimens,
I start them by exhaustless laws as Nature does, fresh and
     modern continually.

I give nothing as duties,
What others give as duties I give as living impulses,
(Shall I give the heart's action as a duty?)
Let others dispose of questions, I dispose of nothing, I arouse
     unanswerable questions,
Who are they I see and touch, and what about them?
What about these likes of myself that draw me so close by
     tender directions and indirections?

I call to the world to distrust the accounts of my friends, but
 listen to my enemies, as I myself do,
I charge you forever reject those who would expound me, for
 I cannot expound myself,
I charge that there be no theory or school founded out of me,
I charge you to leave all free, as I have left all free.

After me, vista!
O I see life is not short, but immeasurably long,
I henceforth tread the world chaste, temperate, an early riser,
 a steady grower,
Every hour the semen of centuries, and still of centuries.

I must follow up these continual lessons of the air, water,
 earth,
I perceive I have no time to lose.

YEAR OF METEORS

(1859–60)

Year of meteors! brooding year!
I would bind in words retrospective some of your deeds and
 signs,
I would sing your contest for the 19th Presidentiad,
I would sing how an old man, tall, with white hair, mounted
 the scaffold in Virginia,
(I was at hand, silent I stood with teeth shut close, I watch'd,
I stood very near you old man when cool and indifferent, but
 trembling with age and your unheal'd wounds you
 mounted the scaffold;)
I would sing in my copious song your census returns of the
 States,
The tables of population and products, I would sing of your
 ships and their cargoes,

The proud black ships of Manhattan arriving, some fill'd with
    immigrants, some from the isthmus with cargoes of
    gold,

Songs thereof would I sing, to all that hitherward comes
    would I welcome give,

And you would I sing, fair stripling! welcome to you from
    me, young prince of England!

(Remember you surging Manhattan's crowds as you pass'd
    with your cortege of nobles?

There in the crowds stood I, and singled you out with attach-
    ment;)

Nor forget I to sing of the wonder, the ship as she swam up
    my bay,

Well-shaped and stately the Great Eastern swam up my bay,
    she was 600 feet long,

Her moving swiftly surrounded by myriads of small craft I
    forget not to sing;

Nor the comet that came unannounced out of the north flar-
    ing in heaven,

Nor the strange huge meteor-procession dazzling and clear
    shooting over our heads,

(A moment, a moment long it sail'd its balls of unearthly light
    over our heads,

Then departed, dropt in the night, and was gone;)

Of such, and fitful as they, I sing—with gleams from them
    would I gleam and patch these chants,

Your chants, O year all mottled with evil and good—year of
    forebodings!

Year of comets and meteors transient and strange—lo! even
    here one equally transient and strange!

As I flit through you hastily, soon to fall and be gone, what is
    this chant,

What am I myself but one of your meteors?

SEA-DRIFT

OUT OF THE CRADLE ENDLESSLY ROCKING

Out of the cradle endlessly rocking,
Out of the mocking-bird's throat, the musical shuttle,
Out of the Ninth-month midnight,
Over the sterile sands and the fields beyond, where the child
     leaving his bed wander'd alone, bareheaded, barefoot,
Down from the shower'd halo,
Up from the mystic play of shadows twining and twisting as
     if they were alive,
Out from the patches of briers and blackberries,
From the memories of the bird that chanted to me,
From your memories sad brother, from the fitful risings and
     fallings I heard,
From under that yellow half-moon late-risen and swollen as if
     with tears,
From those beginning notes of yearning and love there in the
     mist,
From the thousand responses of my heart never to cease,
From the myriad thence-arous'd words,
From the word stronger and more delicious than any,
From such as now they start the scene revisiting,
As a flock, twittering, rising, or overhead passing,
Borne hither, ere all eludes me, hurriedly,
A man, yet by these tears a little boy again,

Throwing myself on the sand, confronting the waves,
I, chanter of pains and joys, uniter of here and hereafter,
Taking all hints to use them, but swiftly leaping beyond them,
A reminiscence sing.

Once Paumanok,
When the lilac-scent was in the air and Fifth-month grass
     was growing,
Up this seashore in some briers,
Two feather'd guests from Alabama, two together,
And their nest, and four light-green eggs spotted with brown,
And every day the he-bird to and fro near at hand,
And every day the she-bird crouch'd on her nest, silent, with
     bright eyes,
And every day I, a curious boy, never too close, never dis-
     turbing them,
Cautiously peering, absorbing, translating.

Shine! shine! shine!
Pour down your warmth, great sun!
While we bask, we two together.

Two together!
Winds blow south, or winds blow north,
Day come white, or night come black,
Home, or rivers and mountains from home,
Singing all time, minding no time,
While we two keep together.

Till of a sudden,
May-be kill'd, unknown to her mate,
One forenoon the she-bird crouch'd not on the nest,
Nor return'd that afternoon, nor the next,
Nor ever appear'd again.

And thenceforward all summer in the sound of the sea,
And at night under the full of the moon in calmer weather,

Over the hoarse surging of the sea,
Or flitting from brier to brier by day,
I saw, I heard at intervals the remaining one, the he-bird,
The solitary guest from Alabama.

Blow! blow! blow!
Blow up sea-winds along Paumanok's shore;
I wait and I wait till you blow my mate to me.

Yes, when the stars glisten'd,
All night long on the prong of a moss-scallop'd stake,
Down almost amid the slapping waves,
Sat the lone singer wonderful causing tears.

He call'd on his mate,
He pour'd forth the meanings which I of all men know.

Yes my brother I know,
The rest might not, but I have treasur'd every note,
For more than once dimly down to the beach gliding,
Silent, avoiding the moonbeams, blending myself with the
    shadows,
Recalling now the obscure shapes, the echoes, the sounds and
    sights after their sorts,
The white arms out in the breakers tirelessly tossing,
I, with bare feet, a child, the wind wafting my hair,
Listen'd long and long.

Listen'd to keep, to sing, now translating the notes,
Following you my brother.

Soothe! soothe! soothe!
Close on its wave soothes the wave behind,
And again another behind embracing and lapping, every one
    close,
But my love soothes not me, not me.

Low hangs the moon, it rose late,
It is lagging—O I think it is heavy with love, with love.

O madly the sea pushes upon the land,
With love, with love.

O night! do I not see my love fluttering out among the break-
*   ers?*
What is that little black thing I see there in the white?

Loud! loud! loud!
Loud I call to you, my love!
High and clear I shoot my voice over the waves,
Surely you must know who is here, is here,
You must know who I am, my love.

Low-hanging moon!
What is that dusky spot in your brown yellow?
O it is the shape, the shape of my mate!
O moon do not keep her from me any longer.

Land! land! O land!
Whichever way I turn, O I think you could give me my mate
*   back again if you only would,*
For I am almost sure I see her dimly whichever way I look.

O rising stars!
Perhaps the one I want so much will rise, will rise with some
*   of you.*

O throat! O trembling throat!
Sound clearer through the atmosphere!
Pierce the woods, the earth,
Somewhere listening to catch you must be the one I want.

Shake out carols!
Solitary here, the night's carols!

Carols of lonesome love! death's carols!
Carols under that lagging, yellow, waning moon!
O under that moon where she droops almost down into the
    sea!
O reckless despairing carols.

But soft! sink low!
Soft! let me just murmur,
And do you wait a moment you husky-nois'd sea,
For somewhere I believe I heard my mate responding to me,
So faint, I must be still, be still to listen,
But not altogether still, for then she might not come im-
    mediately to me.

Hither my love!
Here I am! here!
With this just-sustain'd note I announce myself to you,
This gentle call is for you my love, for you.

Do not be decoy'd elsewhere,
That is the whistle of the wind, it is not my voice,
That is the fluttering, the fluttering of the spray,
Those are the shadows of leaves.

O darkness! O in vain!
O I am very sick and sorrowful.

O brown halo in the sky near the moon, drooping upon the
    sea!
O troubled reflection in the sea!
O throat! O throbbing heart!
And I singing uselessly, uselessly all the night.

O past! O happy life! O songs of joy!
In the air, in the woods, over fields,
Loved! loved! loved! loved! loved!
But my mate no more, no more with me!
We two together no more.

The aria sinking,
All else continuing, the stars shining,
The winds blowing, the notes of the bird continuous echoing,
With angry moans the fierce old mother incessantly moaning,
On the sands of Paumanok's shore gray and rustling,
The yellow half-moon enlarged, sagging down, drooping, the
    face of the sea almost touching,
The boy ecstatic, with his bare feet the waves, with his hair
    the atmosphere dallying,
The love in the heart long pent, now loose, now at last tu-
    multuously bursting,
The aria's meaning, the ears, the soul, swiftly depositing,
The strange tears down the cheeks coursing,
The colloquy there, the trio, each uttering,
The undertone, the savage old mother incessantly crying,
To the boy's soul's questions sullenly timing, some drown'd
    secret hissing,
To the outsetting bard.

Demon or bird! (said the boy's soul,)
Is it indeed toward your mate you sing? or is it really to me?
For I, that was a child, my tongue's use sleeping, now I have
    heard you,
Now in a moment I know what I am for, I awake,
And already a thousand singers, a thousand songs, clearer,
    louder and more sorrowful than yours,
A thousand warbling echoes have started to life within me,
    never to die.

O you singer solitary, singing by yourself, projecting me,
O solitary me listening, never more shall I cease perpetuating
    you,
Never more shall I escape, never more the reverberations,
Never more the cries of unsatisfied love be absent from me,
Never again leave me to be the peaceful child I was before
    what there in the night,
By the sea under the yellow and sagging moon,

The messenger there arous'd, the fire, the sweet hell within,
The unknown want, the destiny of me.

O give me the clew! (it lurks in the night here somewhere,)
O if I am to have so much, let me have more!

A word then, (for I will conquer it,)
The word final, superior to all,
Subtle, sent up—what is it?—I listen;
Are you whispering it, and have been all the time, you sea-
    waves?
Is that it from your liquid rims and wet sands?

Whereto answering, the sea,
Delaying not, hurrying not,
Whisper'd me through the night, and very plainly before day-
    break,
Lisp'd to me the low and delicious word death,
And again death, death, death, death,
Hissing melodious, neither like the bird nor like my arous'd
    child's heart,
But edging near as privately for me rustling at my feet,
Creeping thence steadily up to my ears and laving me softly
    all over,
Death, death, death, death, death.

Which I do not forget,
But fuse the song of my dusky demon and brother,
That he sang to me in the moonlight on Paumanok's gray
    beach,
With the thousand responsive songs at random,
My own songs awaked from that hour,
And with them the key, the word up from the waves,
The word of the sweetest song and all songs,
That strong and delicious word which, creeping to my feet,
(Or like some old crone rocking the cradle, swathed in sweet
    garments, bending aside,)
The sea whisper'd me.

AS I EBB'D WITH THE OCEAN OF LIFE

1

As I ebb'd with the ocean of life,
As I wended the shores I know,
As I walk'd where the ripples continually wash you Paumanok,
Where they rustle up hoarse and sibilant,
Where the fierce old mother endlessly cries for her castaways,
I musing late in the autumn day, gazing off southward,
Held by this electric self out of the pride of which I utter
    poems,
Was seiz'd by the spirit that trails in the lines underfoot,
The rim, the sediment that stands for all the water and all the
    land of the globe.

Fascinated, my eyes reverting from the south, dropt, to follow
    those slender windrows,
Chaff, straw, splinters of wood, weeds, and the sea-gluten,
Scum, scales from shining rocks, leaves of salt-lettuce, left by
    the tide,
Miles walking, the sound of breaking waves the other side of
    me,
Paumanok there and then as I thought the old thought of like-
    nesses,
These you presented to me you fish-shaped island,
As I wended the shores I know,
As I walk'd with that electric self seeking types.

2

As I wend to the shores I know not,
As I list to the dirge, the voices of men and women wreck'd,
As I inhale the impalpable breezes that set in upon me,
As the ocean so mysterious rolls toward me closer and closer,

I too but signify at the utmost a little wash'd-up drift,
A few sands and dead leaves to gather,
Gather, and merge myself as part of the sands and drift.

O baffled, balk'd, bent to the very earth,
Oppress'd with myself that I have dared to open my mouth,
Aware now that amid all that blab whose echoes recoil upon
     me I have not once had the least idea who or what I am,
But that before all my arrogant poems the real Me stands yet
     untouch'd, untold, altogether unreach'd,
Withdrawn far, mocking me with mock-congratulatory signs
     and bows,
With peals of distant ironical laughter at every word I have
     written,
Pointing in silence to these songs, and then to the sand be-
     neath.

I perceive I have not really understood any thing, not a single
     object, and that no man ever can,
Nature here in sight of the sea taking advantage of me to dart
     upon me and sting me,
Because I have dared to open my mouth to sing at all.

3

You oceans both, I close with you,
We murmur alike reproachfully rolling sands and drift, know-
     ing not why,
These little shreds indeed standing for you and me and all.

You friable shore with trails of debris,
You fish-shaped island, I take what is underfoot,
What is yours is mine my father.

I too Paumanok,
I too have bubbled up, floated the measureless float, and been
     wash'd on your shores,

I too am but a trail of drift and debris,
I too leave little wrecks upon you, you fish-shaped island.

I throw myself upon your breast my father,
I cling to you so that you cannot unloose me,
I hold you so firm till you answer me something.

Kiss me my father,
Touch me with your lips as I touch those I love,
Breathe to me while I hold you close the secret of the mur-
	muring I envy.

4

Ebb, ocean of life, (the flow will return,)
Cease not your moaning you fierce old mother,
Endlessly cry for your castaways, but fear not, deny not me,
Rustle not up so hoarse and angry against my feet as I touch
	you or gather from you.

I mean tenderly by you and all,
I gather for myself and for this phantom looking down where
	we lead, and following me and mine.

Me and mine, loose windrows, little corpses,
Froth, snowy white, and bubbles,
(See, from my dead lips the ooze exuding at last,
See, the prismatic colors glistening and rolling,)
Tufts of straw, sands, fragments,
Buoy'd hither from many moods, one contradicting another,
From the storm, the long calm, the darkness, the swell,
Musing, pondering, a breath, a briny tear, a dab of liquid or
	soil,
Up just as much out of fathomless workings fermented and
	thrown,
A limp blossom or two, torn, just as much over waves float-
	ing, drifted at random,
Just as much for us that sobbing dirge of Nature,

Just as much whence we come that blare of the cloud-trum-
    pets,
We, capricious, brought hither we know not whence, spread
    out before you,
You up there walking or sitting,
Whoever you are, we too lie in drifts at your feet.

TO THE MAN-OF-WAR-BIRD

Thou who hast slept all night upon the storm,
Waking renew'd on thy prodigious pinions,
(Burst the wild storm? above it thou ascended'st,
And rested on the sky, thy slave that cradled thee,)
Now a blue point, far, far in heaven floating,
As to the light emerging here on deck I watch thee,
(Myself a speck, a point on the world's floating vast.)

Far, far at sea,
After the night's fierce drifts have strewn the shore with
    wrecks,
With re-appearing day as now so happy and serene,
The rosy and elastic dawn, the flashing sun,
The limpid spread of air cerulean,
Thou also re-appearest.

Thou born to match the gale, (thou art all wings,)
To cope with heaven and earth and sea and hurricane,
Thou ship of air that never furl'st thy sails,
Days, even weeks untired and onward, through spaces, realms
    gyrating,
At dusk that look'st on Senegal, at morn America,
That sport'st amid the lightning-flash and thunder-cloud,
In them, in thy experiences, had'st thou my soul,
What joys! what joys were thine!

TEARS

Tears! tears! tears!
In the night, in solitude, tears,
On the white shore dripping, dripping, suck'd in by the sand,
Tears, not a star shining, all dark and desolate,
Moist tears from the eyes of a muffled head;
O who is that ghost? that form in the dark, with tears?
What shapeless lump is that, bent, crouch'd there on the sand?
Streaming tears, sobbing tears, throes, choked with wild cries;
O storm, embodied, rising, careering with swift steps along
        the beach!
O wild and dismal night storm, with wind—O belching and
        desperate!
O shade so sedate and decorous by day, with calm counte-
        nance and regulated pace,
But away at night as you fly, none looking—O then the un-
        loosen'd ocean,
Of tears! tears! tears!

ABOARD AT A SHIP'S HELM

Aboard at a ship's helm,
A young steersman steering with care.

Through fog on a sea-coast dolefully ringing,
An ocean-bell—O a warning bell, rock'd by the waves.

O you give good notice indeed, you bell by the sea-reefs ring-
        ing,
Ringing, ringing, to warn the ship from its wreck-place.

For as on the alert O steersman, you mind the loud admonition,
The bows turn, the freighted ship tacking speeds away under
        her gray sails,

The beautiful and noble ship with all her precious wealth
    speeds away gayly and safe.

But O the ship, the immortal ship! O ship aboard the ship!
Ship of the body, ship of the soul, voyaging, voyaging, voy-
    aging.

ON THE BEACH AT NIGHT

On the beach at night,
Stands a child with her father,
Watching the east, the autumn sky.

Up through the darkness,
While ravening clouds, the burial clouds, in black masses
    spreading,
Lower sullen and fast athwart and down the sky,
Amid a transparent clear belt of ether yet left in the east,
Ascends large and calm the lord-star Jupiter,
And nigh at hand, only a very little above,
Swim the delicate sisters the Pleiades.

From the beach the child holding the hand of her father,
Those burial-clouds that lower victorious soon to devour all,
Watching, silently weeps.

Weep not, child,
Weep not, my darling,
With these kisses let me remove your tears,
The ravening clouds shall not long be victorious,
They shall not long possess the sky, they devour the stars only
    in apparition,
Jupiter shall emerge, be patient, watch again another night,
    the Pleiades shall emerge,
They are immortal, all those stars both silvery and golden
    shall shine out again,

The great stars and the little ones shall shine out again, they
      endure,
The vast immortal suns and the long-enduring pensive moons
      shall again shine.

Then dearest child mournest thou only for Jupiter?
Considerest thou alone the burial of the stars?

Something there is,
(With my lips soothing thee, adding I whisper,
I give thee the first suggestion, the problem and indirection,)
Something there is more immortal even than the stars,
(Many the burials, many the days and nights, passing away,)
Something that shall endure longer even than lustrous Jupiter,
Longer than sun or any revolving satellite,
Or the radiant sisters the Pleiades.

THE WORLD BELOW THE BRINE

The world below the brine,
Forests at the bottom of the sea, the branches and leaves,
Sea-lettuce, vast lichens, strange flowers and seeds, the thick
      tangle, openings, and pink turf,
Different colors, pale gray and green, purple, white, and gold,
      the play of light through the water,
Dumb swimmers there among the rocks, coral, gluten, grass,
      rushes, and the aliment of the swimmers,
Sluggish existences grazing there suspended, or slowly crawl-
      ing close to the bottom,
The sperm-whale at the surface blowing air and spray, or dis-
      porting with his flukes,
The leaden-eyed shark, the walrus, the turtle, the hairy sea-
      leopard, and the sting-ray,
Passions there, wars, pursuits, tribes, sight in those ocean-
      depths, breathing that thick-breathing air, as so many
      do,

The change thence to the sight here, and to the subtle air
　　breathed by beings like us who walk this sphere,
The change onward from ours to that of beings who walk
　　other spheres.

ON THE BEACH AT NIGHT ALONE

On the beach at night alone,
As the old mother sways her to and fro singing her husky song,
As I watch the bright stars shining, I think a thought of the
　　clef of the universes and of the future.

A vast similitude interlocks all,
All spheres, grown, ungrown, small, large, suns, moons,
　　planets,
All distances of place however wide,
All distances of time, all inanimate forms,
All souls, all living bodies though they be ever so different, or
　　in different worlds,
All gaseous, watery, vegetable, mineral processes, the fishes,
　　the brutes,
All nations, colors, barbarisms, civilizations, languages,
All identities that have existed or may exist on this globe, or
　　any globe,
All lives and deaths, all of the past, present, future,
This vast similitude spans them, and always has spann'd,
And shall forever span them and compactly hold and enclose
　　them.

SONG FOR ALL SEAS, ALL SHIPS

1

To-day a rude brief recitative,
Of ships sailing the seas, each with its special flag or ship-
　　signal,

Of unnamed heroes in the ships—of waves spreading and
    spreading far as the eye can reach,
Of dashing spray, and the winds piping and blowing,
And out of these a chant for the sailors of all nations,
Fitful, like a surge.

Of sea-captains young or old, and the mates, and of all intrepid
    sailors,
Of the few, very choice, taciturn, whom fate can never surprise
    nor death dismay,
Pick'd sparingly without noise by thee old ocean, chosen by
    thee,
Thou sea that pickest and cullest the race in time, and unitest
    nations,
Suckled by thee, old husky nurse, embodying thee,
Indomitable, untamed as thee.

(Ever the heroes on water or on land, by ones or twos appear-
    ing,
Ever the stock preserv'd and never lost, though rare, enough
    for seed preserv'd.)

2

Flaunt out O sea your separate flags of nations!
Flaunt out visible as ever the various ship-signals!
But do you reserve especially for yourself and for the soul of
    man one flag above all the rest,
A spiritual woven signal for all nations, emblem of man elate
    above death,
Token of all brave captains and all intrepid sailors and mates,
And all that went down doing their duty,
Reminiscent of them, twined from all intrepid captains young
    or old,
A pennant universal, subtly waving all time, o'er all brave
    sailors,
All seas, all ships.

PATROLING BARNEGAT

Wild, wild the storm, and the sea high running,
Steady the roar of the gale, with incessant undertone mutter-
　　ing,
Shouts of demoniac laughter fitfully piercing and pealing,
Waves, air, midnight, their savagest trinity lashing,
Out in the shadows their milk-white combs careering,
On beachy slush and sand spirts of snow fierce slanting,
Where through the murk the easterly death-wind breasting,
Through cutting swirl and spray watchful and firm advancing,
(That in the distance! is that a wreck? is the red signal
　　flaring?)
Slush and sand of the beach tireless till daylight wending,
Steadily, slowly, through hoarse roar never remitting,
Along the midnight edge by those milk-white combs career-
　　ing,
A group of dim, weird forms, struggling, the night confront-
　　ing,
That savage trinity warily watching.

AFTER THE SEA-SHIP

After the sea-ship, after the whistling winds,
After the white-gray sails taut to their spars and ropes,
Below, a myriad myriad waves hastening, lifting up their
　　necks,
Tending in ceaseless flow toward the track of the ship,
Waves of the ocean bubbling and gurgling, blithely prying,
Waves, undulating waves, liquid, uneven, emulous waves,
Toward that whirling current, laughing and buoyant, with
　　curves,
Where the great vessel sailing and tacking displaced the sur-
　　face,

Larger and smaller waves in the spread of the ocean yearn-
    fully flowing,
The wake of the sea-ship after she passes, flashing and frolic-
    some under the sun,
A motley procession with many a fleck of foam and many frag-
    ments,
Following the stately and rapid ship, in the wake following.

BY *the* ROADSIDE

A BOSTON BALLAD
(1854)

To get betimes in Boston town I rose this morning early,
Here's a good place at the corner, I must stand and see the
    show.

Clear the way there Jonathan!
Way for the President's marshal—way for the government can-
    non!
Way for the Federal foot and dragoons, (and the apparitions
    copiously tumbling.)

I love to look on the Stars and Stripes, I hope the fifes will play
    Yankee Doodle.

How bright shine the cutlasses of the foremost troops!
Every man holds his revolver, marching stiff through Boston
    town.

A fog follows, antiques of the same come limping,
Some appear wooden-legged, and some appear bandaged and
　　bloodless.

Why this is indeed a show—it has called the dead out of the
　　earth!
The old graveyards of the hills have hurried to see!
Phantoms! phantoms countless by flank and rear!
Cock'd hats of mothy mould—crutches made of mist!
Arms in slings—old men leaning on young men's shoulders.

What troubles you Yankee phantoms? what is all this chatter-
　　ing of bare gums?
Does the ague convulse your limbs? do you mistake your
　　crutches for firelocks and level them?

If you blind your eyes with tears you will not see the Presi-
　　dent's marshal,
If you groan such groans you might balk the government
　　cannon.

For shame old maniacs—bring down those toss'd arms, and let
　　your white hair be,
Here gape your great grandsons, their wives gaze at them from
　　the windows,
See how well dress'd, see how orderly they conduct them-
　　selves.

Worse and worse—can't you stand it? are you retreating?
Is this hour with the living too dead for you?

Retreat then—pell-mell!
To your graves—back—back to the hills old limpers!
I do not think you belong here anyhow.

But there is one thing that belongs here—shall I tell you what
　　it is, gentlemen of Boston?

will whisper it to the Mayor, he shall send a committee to
    England,
They shall get a grant from the Parliament, go with a cart to
    the royal vault,
Dig out King George's coffin, unwrap him quick from the
    grave-clothes, box up his bones for a journey,
Find a swift Yankee clipper—here is freight for you, black-
    bellied clipper,
Up with your anchor—shake out your sails—steer straight to-
    ward Boston bay.

Now call for the President's marshal again, bring out the gov-
    ernment cannon,
Fetch home the roarers from Congress, make another proces-
    sion, guard it with foot and dragoons.

This centre-piece for them;
Look, all orderly citizens—look from the windows, women!

The committee open the box, set up the regal ribs, glue those
    that will not stay,
Clap the skull on top of the ribs, and clap a crown on top of
    the skull.

You have got your revenge, old buster—the crown is come to
    its own, and more than its own.

Stick your hands in your pockets, Jonathan—you are a made
    man from this day,
You are mighty cute—and here is one of your bargains.

EUROPE

The 72d and 73d Years of These States

Suddenly out of its stale and drowsy lair, the lair of slaves,
Like lightning it le'pt forth half startled at itself,
Its feet upon the ashes and the rags, its hands tight to the
throats of kings.

O hope and faith!
O aching close of exiled patriots' lives!
O many a sicken'd heart!
Turn back unto this day and make yourselves afresh.

And you, paid to defile the People—you liars, mark!
Not for numberless agonies, murders, lusts,
For court thieving in its manifold mean forms, worming from
his simplicity the poor man's wages,
For many a promise sworn by royal lips and broken and
laugh'd at in the breaking,
Then in their power not for all these did the blows strike
revenge, or the heads of the nobles fall;
The People scorn'd the ferocity of kings.
But the sweetness of mercy brew'd bitter destruction, and the
frighten'd monarchs come back,
Each comes in state with his train, hangman, priest, tax
gatherer,
Soldier, lawyer, lord, jailer, and sycophant.

Yet behind all lowering stealing, lo, a shape,
Vague as the night, draped interminably, head, front and form
in scarlet folds,
Whose face and eyes none may see,
Out of its robes only this, the red robes lifted by the arm,
One finger crook'd pointed high over the top, like the head of
a snake appears.

Meanwhile corpses lie in new-made graves, bloody corpses of
     young men,
The rope of the gibbet hangs heavily, the bullets of princes
     are flying, the creatures of power laugh aloud,
And all these things bear fruits, and they are good.

Those corpses of young men,
Those martyrs that hang from the gibbets, those hearts pierc'd
     by the gray lead,
Cold and motionless as they seem live elsewhere with un-
     slaughter'd vitality.

They live in other young men O kings!
They live in brothers again ready to defy you,
They were purified by death, they were taught and exalted.

Not a grave of the murder'd for freedom but grows seed for
     freedom, in its turn to bear seed,
Which the winds carry afar and re-sow, and the rains and the
     snows nourish.

Not a disembodied spirit can the weapons of tyrants let loose,
But it stalks invisibly over the earth, whispering, counseling,
     cautioning.

Liberty, let others despair of you—I never despair of you.

Is the house shut? is the master away?
Nevertheless, be ready, be not weary of watching,
He will soon return, his messengers come anon.

TO A PRESIDENT

All you are doing and saying is to America dangled mirages,
You have not learn'd of Nature—of the politics of Nature you
      have not learn'd the great amplitude, rectitude, im-
      partiality,
You have not seen that only such as they are for these States,
And that what is less than they must sooner or later lift off
      from these States.

I SIT AND LOOK OUT

I sit and look out upon all the sorrows of the world, and upon
      all oppression and shame,
I hear secret convulsive sobs from young men at anguish with
      themselves, remorseful after deeds done,
I see in low life the mother misused by her children, dying,
      neglected, gaunt, desperate,
I see the wife misused by her husband, I see the treacherous
      seducer of young women,
I mark the ranklings of jealousy and unrequited love attempted
      to be hid, I see these sights on the earth,
I see the workings of battle, pestilence, tyranny, I see martyrs
      and prisoners,
I observe a famine at sea, I observe the sailors casting lots who
      shall be kill'd to preserve the lives of the rest,
I observe the slights and degradations cast by arrogant persons
      upon laborers, the poor, and upon negroes, and the like;
All these—all the meanness and agony without end I sitting
      look out upon,
See, hear, and am silent.

TO RICH GIVERS

What you give me I cheerfully accept,
A little sustenance, a hut and garden, a little money, as I
    rendezvous with my poems,
A traveler's lodging and breakfast as I journcy through the
    States,—why should I be ashamed to own such gifts?
    why to advertise for them?
For I myself am not one who bestows nothing upon man and
    woman,
For I bestow upon any man or woman the entrance to all the
    gifts of the universe.

THE DALLIANCE OF THE EAGLES

Skirting the river road, (my forenoon walk, my rest,)
Skyward in air a sudden muffled sound, the dalliance of the
    eagles,
The rushing amorous contact high in space together,
The clinching interlocking claws, a living, fierce, gyrating
    wheel,
Four beating wings, two beaks, a swirling mass tight grap-
    pling,
In tumbling turning clustering loops, straight downward fall-
    ing,
Till o'er the river pois'd, the twain yet one, a moment's lull,
A motionless still balance in the air, then parting, talons
    loosing,
Upward again on slow-firm pinions slanting, their separate
    diverse flight,
She hers, he his, pursuing.

ROAMING IN THOUGHT

(After reading HEGEL*)*

Roaming in thought over the Universe, I saw the little that
    is Good steadily hastening towards immortality,
And the vast all that is call'd Evil I saw hastening to merge
    itself and become lost and dead.

A FARM PICTURE

Through the ample open door of the peaceful country barn,
A sunlit pasture field with cattle and horses feeding,
And haze and vista, and the far horizon fading away.

A CHILD'S AMAZE

Silent and amazed even when a little boy,
I remember I heard the preacher every Sunday put God in
    his statements,
As contending against some being or influence.

THE RUNNER

On a flat road runs the well-train'd runner,
He is lean and sinewy with muscular legs,
He is thinly clothed, he leans forward as he runs,
With lightly closed fists and arms partially rais'd.

BEAUTIFUL WOMEN

Women sit or move to and fro, some old, some young,
The young are beautiful—but the old are more beautiful than
    the young.

MOTHER AND BABE

I see the sleeping babe nestling the breast of its mother,
The sleeping mother and babe—hush'd, I study them long
and long.

THOUGHT

Of obedience, faith, adhesiveness;
As I stand aloof and look there is to me something profoundly
affecting in large masses of men following the lead of
those who do not believe in men.

VISOR'D

A mask, a perpetual natural disguiser of herself,
Concealing her face, concealing her form,
Changes and transformations every hour, every moment,
Falling upon her even when she sleeps.

THOUGHT

Of Justice—as if Justice could be any thing but the same
ample law, expounded by natural judges and saviors,
As if it might be this thing or that thing, according to decisions.

GLIDING O'ER ALL

Gliding o'er all, through all,
Through Nature, Time, and Space,
As a ship on the waters advancing,
The voyage of the soul—not life alone,
Death, many deaths I'll sing.

HAST NEVER COME TO THEE AN HOUR

Hast never come to thee an hour,
A sudden gleam divine, precipitating, bursting all these bubbles, fashions, wealth?
These eager business aims—books, politics, art, amours,
To utter nothingness?

THOUGHT

Of Equality—as if it harm'd me, giving others the same chances and rights as myself—as if it were not indispensable to my own rights that others possess the same.

TO OLD AGE

I see in you the estuary that enlarges and spreads itself grandly as it pours in the great sea.

LOCATIONS AND TIMES

Locations and times—what is it in me that meets them all, whenever and wherever, and makes me at home?
Forms, colors, densities, odors—what is it in me that corresponds with them?

OFFERINGS

A thousand perfect men and women appear,
Around each gathers a cluster of friends, and gay children and youths, with offerings.

TO THE STATES

To Identify the 16th, 17th, or 18th Presidentiad

Why reclining, interrogating? why myself and all drowsing?
What deepening twilight—scum floating atop of the waters,
Who are they as bats and night-dogs askant in the capitol?
What a filthy Presidentiad! (O South, your torrid suns! O
    North, your arctic freezings!)
Are those really Congressmen? are those the great Judges? is
    that the President?
Then I will sleep awhile yet, for I see that these States sleep,
    for reasons;
(With gathering murk, with muttering thunder and lambent
    shoots we all duly awake,
South, North, East, West, inland and seaboard, we will sure-
    ly awake.)

DRUM-TAPS

EIGHTEEN SIXTY-ONE

Arm'd year—year of the struggle,
No dainty rhymes or sentimental love verses for you terrible
    year,
Not you as some pale poetling seated at a desk lisping
    cadenzas piano,
But as a strong man erect, clothed in blue clothes, advancing,
    carrying a rifle on your shoulder,
With well-gristled body and sunburnt face and hands, with a
    knife in the belt at your side,

As I heard you shouting loud, your sonorous voice ringing
    across the continent,
Your masculine voice O year, as rising amid the great cities,
Amid the men of Manhattan I saw you as one of the work-
    men, the dwellers in Manhattan,
Or with large steps crossing the prairies out of Illinois and
    Indiana,
Rapidly crossing the West with springy gait and descending
    the Alleghanies,
Or down from the great lakes or in Pennsylvania, or on deck
    along the Ohio river,
Or southward along the Tennessee or Cumberland rivers, or
    at Chattanooga on the mountain top,
Saw I your gait and saw I your sinewy limbs clothed in blue,
    bearing weapons, robust year,
Heard your determin'd voice launch'd forth again and again,
Year that suddenly sang by the mouths of the round-lipp'd
    cannon,
I repeat you, hurrying, crashing, sad, distracted year.

BEAT! BEAT! DRUMS!

Beat! beat! drums!—blow! bugles! blow!
Through the windows—through doors—burst like a ruthless
    force,
Into the solemn church, and scatter the congregation,
Into the school where the scholar is studying;
Leave not the bridegroom quiet—no happiness must he have
    now with his bride,
Nor the peaceful farmer any peace, ploughing his field or
    gathering his grain,
So fierce you whirr and pound you drums—so shrill you bugles
    blow.

Beat! beat! drums!—blow! bugles! blow!
Over the traffic of cities—over the rumble of wheels in the
    streets;

Are beds prepared for sleepers at night in the houses? no
   sleepers must sleep in those beds,
No bargainers' bargains by day—no brokers or speculators—
   would they continue?
Would the talkers be talking? would the singer attempt to
   sing?
Would the lawyer rise in the court to state his case before
   the judge?
Then rattle quicker, heavier drums—you bugles wilder blow.

Beat! beat! drums!—blow! bugles! blow!
Make no parley—stop for no expostulation,
Mind not the timid—mind not the weeper or prayer,
Mind not the old man beseeching the young man,
Let not the child's voice be heard, nor the mother's entreaties,
Make even the trestles to shake the dead where they lie
   awaiting the hearses,
So strong you thump O terrible drums—so loud you bugles
   blow.

CAVALRY CROSSING A FORD

A line in long array where they wind betwixt green islands,
They take a serpentine course, their arms flash in the sun—
   hark to the musical clank,
Behold the silvery river, in it the splashing horses loitering
   stop to drink,
Behold the brown-faced men, each group, each person a pic-
   ture, the negligent rest on the saddles,
Some emerge on the opposite bank, others are just entering
   the ford—while,
Scarlet and blue and snowy white,
The guidon flags flutter gayly in the wind.

FROM PAUMANOK STARTING I FLY
LIKE A BIRD

From Paumanok starting I fly like a bird,
Around and around to soar to sing the idea of all,
To the north betaking myself to sing there arctic songs,
To Kanada till I absorb Kanada in myself, to Michigan then,
To Wisconsin, Iowa, Minnesota, to sing their songs, (they are
      inimitable;)
Then to Ohio and Indiana to sing theirs, to Missouri and
      Kansas and Arkansas to sing theirs,
To Tennessee and Kentucky, to the Carolinas and Georgia
      to sing theirs,
To Texas and so along up toward California, to roam ac-
      cepted everywhere;
To sing first, (to the tap of the war-drum if need be,)
The idea of all, of the Western world one and inseparable,
And then the song of each member of these States.

BIVOUAC ON A MOUNTAIN SIDE

I see before me now a traveling army halting,
Below a fertile valley spread, with barns and the orchards of
      summer,
Behind, the terraced sides of a mountain, abrupt, in places
      rising high,
Broken, with rocks, with clinging cedars, with tall shapes
      dingily seen,
The numerous camp-fires scatter'd near and far, some away
      up on the mountain,
The shadowy forms of men and horses, looming, large-sized
      flickering,
And over all the sky—the sky! far, far out of reach, studded
      breaking out, the eternal stars.

AN ARMY CORPS ON THE MARCH

With its cloud of skirmishers in advance,
With now the sound of a single shot snapping like a whip,
        and now an irregular volley,
The swarming ranks press on and on, the dense brigades
        press on,
Glittering dimly, toiling under the sun—the dust-cover'd men,
In columns rise and fall to the undulations of the ground,
With artillery interspers'd—the wheels rumble, the horses
        sweat,
As the army corps advances.

BY THE BIVOUAC'S FITFUL FLAME

By the bivouac's fitful flame,
A procession winding around me, solemn and sweet and slow
        —but first I note,
The tents of the sleeping army, the fields' and woods' dim
        outline,
The darkness lit by spots of kindled fire, the silence,
Like a phantom far or near an occasional figure moving,
The shrubs and trees, (as I lift my eyes they seem to be
        stealthily watching me,)
While wind in procession thoughts, O tender and wondrous
        thoughts,
Of life and death, of home and the past and loved, and of
        those that are far away;
A solemn and slow procession there as I sit on the ground,
By the bivouac's fitful flame.

VIGIL STRANGE I KEPT ON THE FIELD ONE NIGHT

Vigil strange I kept on the field one night;

When you my son and my comrade dropt at my side that day,

One look I but gave which your dear eyes return'd with a look I shall never forget,

One touch of your hand to mine O boy, reach'd up as you lay on the ground,

Then onward I sped in the battle, the even-contested battle,

Till late in the night reliev'd to the place at last again I made my way,

Found you in death so cold dear comrade, found your body son of responding kisses, (never again on earth responding,)

Bared your face in the starlight, curious the scene, cool blew the moderate night-wind,

Long there and then in vigil I stood, dimly around me the battle-field spreading,

Vigil wondrous and vigil sweet there in the fragrant silent night,

But not a tear fell, not even a long-drawn sigh, long, long I gazed,

Then on the earth partially reclining sat by your side leaning my chin in my hands,

Passing sweet hours, immortal and mystic hours with you dearest comrade—not a tear, not a word,

Vigil of silence, love and death, vigil for you my son and my soldier,

As onward silently stars aloft, eastward new ones upward stole,

Vigil final for you brave boy, (I could not save you, swift was your death,

I faithfully loved you and cared for you living, I think we shall surely meet again,)

ill at latest lingering of the night, indeed just as the dawn
    appear'd,

Iy comrade I wrapt in his blanket, envelop'd well his form,

olded the blanket well, tucking it carefully over head and
    carefully under feet,

nd there and then and bathed by the rising sun, my son in
    his grave, in his rude-dug grave I deposited,

nding my vigil strange with that, vigil of night and battle-
    field dim,

igil for boy of responding kisses, (never again on earth re-
    sponding,)

igil for comrade swiftly slain, vigil I never forget, how as
    day brighten'd,

rose from the chill ground and folded my soldier well in his
    blanket,

nd buried him where he fell.

A MARCH IN THE RANKS
HARD-PREST, AND THE ROAD
UNKNOWN

march in the ranks hard-prest, and the road unknown,

route through a heavy wood with muffled steps in the dark-
    ness,

ur army foil'd with loss severe, and the sullen remnant re-
    treating,

ll after midnight glimmer upon us the lights of a dim-
    lighted building,

e come to an open space in the woods, and halt by the
    dim-lighted building,

is a large old church at the crossing roads, now an im-
    promptu hospital,

ntering but for a minute I see a sight beyond all the pic-
    tures and poems ever made,

adows of deepest, deepest black, just lit by moving can-
    dles and lamps,

And by one great pitchy torch stationary with wild red flame
    and clouds of smoke,
By these, crowds, groups of forms vaguely I see on the floor,
    some in the pews laid down,
At my feet more distinctly a soldier, a mere lad, in danger of
    bleeding to death, (he is shot in the abdomen,)
I stanch the blood temporarily, (the youngster's face is white
    as a lily,)
Then before I depart I sweep my eyes o'er the scene fain to
    absorb it all,
Faces, varieties, postures beyond description, most in obscu-
    rity, some of them dead,
Surgeons operating, attendants holding lights, the smell of
    ether, the odor of blood,
The crowd, O the crowd of the bloody forms, the yard out-
    side also fill'd,
Some on the bare ground, some on planks or stretchers, some
    in the death-spasm sweating,
An occasional scream or cry, the doctor's shouted orders or
    calls,
The glisten of the little steel instruments catching the glint
    of the torches,
These I resume as I chant, I see again the forms, I smell the
    odor,
Then hear outside the orders given, *Fall in, my men, fall in,*
But first I bend to the dying lad, his eyes open, a half-smile
    gives he me,
Then the eyes close, calmly close, and I speed forth to the
    darkness,
Resuming, marching, ever in darkness marching, on in the
    ranks,
The unknown road still marching.

SIGHT IN CAMP IN THE DAYBREAK GRAY AND DIM

sight in camp in the daybreak gray and dim,
s from my tent I emerge so early sleepless,
s slow I walk in the cool fresh air the path near by the hos-
    pital tent,
hree forms I see on stretchers lying, brought out there un-
    tended lying,
ver each the blanket spread, ample brownish woolen blan-
    ket,
ray and heavy blanket, folding, covering all.

urious I halt and silent stand,
en with light fingers I from the face of the nearest the first
    just lift the blanket;
ho are you elderly man so gaunt and grim, with well-gray'd
    hair, and flesh all sunken about the eyes?
ho are you my dear comrade?

en to the second I step—and who are you my child and
    darling?
ho are you sweet boy with cheeks yet blooming?

en to the third—a face nor child nor old, very calm, as of
    beautiful yellow-white ivory;
ung man I think I know you—I think this face is the face
    of the Christ himself,
ead and divine and brother of all, and here again he lies.

LONG, TOO LONG AMERICA

ng, too long America,
aveling roads all even and peaceful you learn'd from joys
    and prosperity only,

But now, ah now, to learn from crises of anguish, advancing
     grappling with direst fate and recoiling not,
And now to conceive and show to the world what your chi
     dren en-masse really are,
(For who except myself has yet conceiv'd what your childre
     en-masse really are?)

YEAR THAT TREMBLED AND
REEL'D BENEATH ME

Year that trembled and reel'd beneath me!
Your summer wind was warm enough, yet the air I breathe
     froze me,
A thick gloom fell through the sunshine and darken'd me,
Must I change my triumphant songs? said I to myself,
Must I indeed learn to chant the cold dirges of the baffled?
And sullen hymns of defeat?

ETHIOPIA SALUTING THE COLOR

Who are you dusky woman, so ancient hardly human,
With your woolly-white and turban'd head, and bare bo
     feet?
Why rising by the roadside here, do you the colors greet?

('Tis while our army lines Carolina's sands and pines,
Forth from thy hovel door thou Ethiopia com'st to me,
As under doughty Sherman I march toward the sea.)

Me master years a hundred since from my parents sunder
A little child, they caught me as the savage beast is caug
Then hither me across the sea the cruel slaver brought.

No further does she say, but lingering all the day,
Her high-borne turban'd head she wags, and rolls her da
     ling eye,

And courtesies to the regiments, the guidons moving by.

What is it fateful woman, so blear, hardly human?
Why wag your head with turban bound, yellow, red and
　　green?
Are the things so strange and marvelous you see or have seen?

NOT YOUTH PERTAINS TO ME

Not youth pertains to me,
Nor delicatesse, I cannot beguile the time with talk,
Awkward in the parlor, neither a dancer nor elegant,
In the learn'd coterie sitting constrain'd and still, for learning
　　inures not to me,
Beauty, knowledge, inure not to me—yet there are two or
　　three things inure to me,
I have nourish'd the wounded and sooth'd many a dying
　　soldier,
And at intervals waiting or in the midst of camp,
Composed these songs.

LO, VICTRESS ON THE PEAKS

Lo, Victress on the peaks,
Where thou with mighty brow regarding the world,
(The world O Libertad, that vainly conspired against thee,)
Out of its countless beleaguering toils, after thwarting them
　　all,
Dominant, with the dazzling sun around thee,
Flauntest now unharm'd in immortal soundness and bloom—
　　lo, in these hours supreme,
No poem proud, I chanting bring to thee, nor mastery's rap-
　　turous verse,
But a cluster containing night's darkness and blood-dripping
　　wounds,
And psalms of the dead.

RACE OF VETERANS

Race of veterans—race of victors!
Race of the soil, ready for conflict—race of the conquering
     march!
(No more credulity's race, abiding-temper'd race,)
Race henceforth owning no law but the law of itself,
Race of passion and the storm.

WORLD TAKE GOOD NOTICE

World take good notice, silver stars fading,
Milky hue ript, weft of white detaching,
Coals thirty-eight, baleful and burning,
Scarlet, significant, hands off warning,
Now and henceforth flaunt from these shores.

O TAN-FACED PRAIRIE-BOY

O tan-faced prairie-boy,
Before you came to camp came many a welcome gift,
Praises and presents came and nourishing food, till at last
     among the recruits,
You came, taciturn, with nothing to give—we but look'd on
     each other,
When lo! more than all the gifts of the world you gave me.

WHEN LILACS LAST IN THE DOORYARD BLOOM'D

1

When lilacs last in the dooryard bloom'd,
And the great star early droop'd in the western sky in the
    night,
I mourn'd, and yet shall mourn with ever-returning spring.

Ever-returning spring, trinity sure to me you bring,
Lilac blooming perennial and drooping star in the west,
And thought of him I love.

2

O powerful western fallen star!
O shades of night—O moody, tearful night!
O great star disappear'd—O the black murk that hides the
    star!
O cruel hands that hold me powerless—O helpless soul of me!
O harsh surrounding cloud that will not free my soul.

3

In the dooryard fronting an old farm-house near the white-
    wash'd palings,
Stands the lilac-bush tall-growing with heart-shaped leaves of
    rich green,
With many a pointed blossom rising delicate, with the per-
    fume strong I love,

With every leaf a miracle—and from this bush in the door-
    yard,
With delicate-color'd blossoms and heart-shaped leaves of
    rich green,
A sprig with its flower I break.

4

In the swamp in secluded recesses,
A shy and hidden bird is warbling a song.

Solitary the thrush,
The hermit withdrawn to himself, avoiding the settlements,
Sings by himself a song.

Song of the bleeding throat,
Death's outlet song of life, (for well dear brother I know,
If thou wast not granted to sing thou would'st surely die.)

5

Over the breast of the spring, the land, amid cities,
Amid lanes and through old woods, where lately the violets
    peep'd from the ground, spotting the gray debris,
Amid the grass in the fields each side of the lanes, passing the
    endless grass,
Passing the yellow-spear'd wheat, every grain from its shroud
    in the dark-brown fields uprisen,
Passing the apple-tree blows of white and pink in the or-
    chards,
Carrying a corpse to where it shall rest in the grave,
Night and day journeys a coffin.

6

Coffin that passes through lanes and streets,
Through day and night with the great cloud darkening the
    land,

With the pomp of the inloop'd flags with the cities draped
    in black,
With the show of the States themselves as of crape-veil'd
    women standing,
With processions long and winding and the flambeaus of the
    night,
With the countless torches lit, with the silent sea of faces and
    the unbared heads,
With the waiting depot, the arriving coffin, and the sombre
    faces,
With dirges through the night, with the thousand voices ris-
    ing strong and solemn,
With all the mournful voices of the dirges pour'd around the
    coffin,
The dim-lit churches and the shuddering organs—where amid
    these you journey,
With the tolling tolling bells' perpetual clang,
Here, coffin that slowly passes,
I give you my sprig of lilac.

7

(Nor for you, for one alone,
Blossoms and branches green to coffins all I bring,
For fresh as the morning, thus would I chant a song for you
    O sane and sacred death.

All over bouquets of roses,
O death, I cover you over with roses and early lilies,
But mostly and now the lilac that blooms the first,
Copious I break, I break the sprigs from the bushes,
With loaded arms I come, pouring for you,
For you and the coffins all of you O death.)

8

O western orb sailing the heaven,
Now I know what you must have meant as a month since I
    walk'd,

As I walk'd in silence the transparent shadowy night,
As I saw you had something to tell as you bent to me night
     after night,
As you droop'd from the sky low down as if to my side,
     (while the other stars all look'd on,)
As we wander'd together the solemn night, (for something I
     know not what kept me from sleep,)
As the night advanced, and I saw on the rim of the west how
     full you were of woe,
As I stood on the rising ground in the breeze in the cool trans-
     parent night,
As I watch'd where you pass'd and was lost in the netherward
     black of the night,
As my soul in its trouble dissatisfied sank, as where you sad
     orb,
Concluded, dropt in the night, and was gone.

9

Sing on there in the swamp,
O singer bashful and tender, I hear your notes, I hear your
     call,
I hear, I come presently, I understand you,
But a moment I linger, for the lustrous star has detain'd me,
The star my departing comrade holds and detains me.

10

O how shall I warble myself for the dead one there I loved?
And how shall I deck my song for the large sweet soul that
     has gone?
And what shall my perfume be for the grave of him I love?

Sea-winds blown from east and west,
Blown from the Eastern sea and blown from the Western
     sea, till there on the prairies meeting,
These and with these and the breath of my chant,
I'll perfume the grave of him I love.

11

O what shall I hang on the chamber walls?
And what shall the pictures be that I hang on the walls,
To adorn the burial-house of him I love?

Pictures of growing spring and farms and homes,
With the Fourth-month eve at sundown, and the gray smoke
    lucid and bright,
With floods of the yellow gold of the gorgeous, indolent, sink-
    ing sun, burning, expanding the air,
With the fresh sweet herbage under foot, and the pale green
    leaves of the trees prolific,
In the distance the flowing glaze, the breast of the river, with
    a wind-dapple here and there,
With ranging hills on the banks, with many a line against the
    sky, and shadows,
And the city at hand with dwellings so dense, and stacks of
    chimneys,
And all the scenes of life and the workshops, and the work-
    men homeward returning.

12

Lo, body and soul—this land,
My own Manhattan with spires, and the sparkling and hurry-
    ing tides, and the ships,
The varied and ample land, the South and the North in the
    light, Ohio's shores and flashing Missouri,
And ever the far-spreading prairies cover'd with grass
    and corn.

Lo, the most excellent sun so calm and haughty,
The violet and purple morn with just-felt breezes,
The gentle soft-born measureless light,
The miracle spreading bathing all, the fulfill'd noon,
The coming eve delicious, the welcome night and the stars,
Over my cities shining all, enveloping man and land.

13

Sing on, sing on you gray-brown bird,
Sing from the swamps, the recesses, pour your chant from
      the bushes,
Limitless out of the dusk, out of the cedars and pines.

Sing on dearest brother, warble your reedy song,
Loud human song, with voice of uttermost woe.

O liquid and free and tender!
O wild and loose to my soul—O wondrous singer!
You only I hear—yet the star holds me, (but will soon depart,)
Yet the lilac with mastering odor holds me.

14

Now while I sat in the day and look'd forth,
In the close of the day with its light and the fields of spring,
      and the farmers preparing their crops,
In the large unconscious scenery of my land with its lakes
      and forests,
In the heavenly aerial beauty, (after the perturb'd winds and
      the storms,)
Under the arching heavens of the afternoon swift passing, and
      the voices of children and women,
The many-moving sea-tides, and I saw the ships how they
      sail'd,
And the summer approaching with richness, and the fields all
      busy with labor,
And the infinite separate houses, how they all went on, each
      with its meals and minutia of daily usages,
And the streets how their throbbings throbb'd, and the cities
      pent—lo, then and there,
Falling upon them all and among them all, enveloping me
      with the rest,
Appear'd the cloud, appear'd the long black trail,
And I knew death, its thought, and the sacred knowledge
      of death.

Then with the knowledge of death as walking one side of
    me,
And the thought of death close-walking the other side of me,
And I in the middle as with companions, and as holding the
    hands of companions,
I fled forth to the hiding receiving night that talks not,
Down to the shores of the water, the path by the swamp in
    the dimness,
To the solemn shadowy cedars and ghostly pines so still.

And the singer so shy to the rest receiv'd me,
The gray-brown bird I know receiv'd us comrades three,
And he sang the carol of death, and a verse for him I love.

From deep secluded recesses,
From the fragrant cedars and the ghostly pines so still,
Came the carol of the bird.

And the charm of the carol rapt me,
As I held as if by their hands my comrades in the night,
And the voice of my spirit tallied the song of the bird.

Come lovely and soothing death,
Undulate round the world, serenely arriving, arriving,
In the day, in the night, to all, to each,
Sooner or later delicate death.

Prais'd be the fathomless universe,
For life and joy, and for objects and knowledge curious,
And for love, sweet love—but praise! praise! praise!
For the sure-enwinding arms of cool-enfolding death.

Dark mother always gliding near with soft feet,
Have none chanted for thee a chant of fullest welcome?
Then I chant it for thee, I glorify thee above all,
I bring thee a song that when thou must indeed come, come
    unfalteringly.

Approach strong deliveress,
When it is so, when thou hast taken them I joyously sing the
dead,
Lost in the loving floating ocean of thee,
Laved in the flood of thy bliss O death.

From me to thee glad serenades,
Dances for thee I propose saluting thee, adornments and
feastings for thee,
And the sights of the open landscape and the high-spread sky
are fitting,
And life and the fields, and the huge and thoughtful night.

The night in silence under many a star,
The ocean shore and the husky whispering wave whose voice
I know,
And the soul turning to thee O vast and well-veil'd death,
And the body gratefully nestling close to thee.

Over the tree-tops I float thee a song,
Over the rising and sinking waves, over the myriad fields and
the prairies wide,
Over the dense-pack'd cities all and the teeming wharves and
ways,
I float this carol with joy, with joy to thee O death.

15

To the tally of my soul,
Loud and strong kept up the gray-brown bird,
With pure deliberate notes spreading filling the night.

Loud in the pines and cedars dim,
Clear in the freshness moist and the swamp-perfume,
And I with my comrades there in the night.

While my sight that was bound in my eyes unclosed,
As to long panoramas of visions.

And I saw askant the armies,
I saw as in noiseless dreams hundreds of battle-flags,
Borne through the smoke of the battles and pierc'd with
    missiles I saw them,
And carried hither and yon through the smoke, and torn and
    bloody,
And at last but a few shreds left on the staffs, (and all in
    silence,)
And the staffs all splinter'd and broken.

I saw battle-corpses, myriads of them,
And the white skeletons of young men, I saw them,
I saw the debris and debris of all the slain soldiers of the war,
But I saw they were not as was thought,
They themselves were fully at rest, they suffer'd not,
The living remain'd and suffer'd, the mother suffer'd,
And the wife and the child and the musing comrade suffer'd,
And the armies that remain'd suffer'd.

16

Passing the visions, passing the night,
Passing, unloosing the hold of my comrades' hands,
Passing the song of the hermit bird and the tallying song of
    my soul,
Victorious song, death's outlet song, yet varying ever-altering
    song,
As low and wailing, yet clear the notes, rising and falling,
    flooding the night,
Sadly sinking and fainting, as warning and warning, and yet
    again bursting with joy,
Covering the earth and filling the spread of the heaven,
As that powerful psalm in the night I heard from recesses,
Passing, I leave thee lilac with heart-shaped leaves,
I leave thee there in the door-yard, blooming, returning with
    spring.

I cease from my song for thee,
From my gaze on thee in the west, fronting the west, communing with thee,
O comrade lustrous with silver face in the night.

Yet each to keep and all, retrievements out of the night,
The song, the wondrous chant of the gray-brown bird,
And the tallying chant, the echo arous'd in my soul,
With the lustrous and drooping star with the countenance full of woe,
With the holders holding my hand nearing the call of the bird,
Comrades mine and I in the midst, and their memory ever to keep, for the dead I loved so well,
For the sweetest, wisest soul of all my days and lands—and this for his dear sake,
Lilac and star and bird twined with the chant of my soul,
There in the fragrant pines and the cedars dusk and dim.

O CAPTAIN! MY CAPTAIN

O Captain! my Captain! our fearful trip is done,
The ship has weather'd every rack, the prize we sought is won,
The port is near, the bells I hear, the people all exulting,
While follow eyes the steady keel, the vessel grim and daring;
　　　　But O heart! heart! heart!
　　　　　O the bleeding drops of red,
　　　　　　Where on the deck my Captain lies,
　　　　　　　Fallen cold and dead.

O Captain! my Captain! rise up and hear the bells;
Rise up—for you the flag is flung—for you the bugle trills,
For you bouquets and ribbon'd wreaths—for you the shores a-crowding,

For you they call, the swaying mass, their eager faces turning;
> Here Captain! dear father!
>> This arm beneath your head!
>>> It is some dream that on the deck,
>>>> You've fallen cold and dead.

My Captain does not answer, his lips are pale and still,
My father does not feel my arm, he has no pulse nor will,
The ship is anchor'd safe and sound, its voyage closed and
> done,
From fearful trip the victor ship comes in with object won;
> Exult O shores, and ring O bells!
>> But I with mournful tread,
>>> Walk the deck my Captain lies,
>>>> Fallen cold and dead.

HUSH'D BE THE CAMPS TO-DAY

(May 4, 1865)

Hush'd be the camps to-day,
And soldiers let us drape our war-worn weapons,
And each with musing soul retire to celebrate,
Our dear commander's death.

No more for him life's stormy conflicts,
Nor victory, nor defeat—no more time's dark events,
Charging like ceaseless clouds across the sky.

But sing poet in our name,
Sing of the love we bore him—because you, dweller in camps,
> know it truly.

As they invault the coffin there,
Sing—as they close the doors of earth upon him—one verse,
For the heavy hearts of soldiers.

THIS DUST WAS ONCE THE MAN

This dust was once the man,
Gentle, plain, just and resolute, under whose cautious hand,
Against the foulest crime in history known in any land or age,
Was saved the Union of these States.

BY BLUE ONTARIO'S SHORE

1

By blue Ontario's shore,
As I mused of these warlike days and of peace return'd, and
    the dead that return no more,
A Phantom gigantic superb, with stern visage accosted me,
Chant me the poem, it said, *that comes from the soul of
    America, chant me the carol of victory,*
*And strike up the marches of Libertad, marches more power-
    ful yet,*
*And sing me before you go the song of the throes of Democ-
    racy.*

(Democracy, the destin'd conqueror, yet treacherous lip-
    smiles everywhere,
And death and infidelity at every step.)

2

A Nation announcing itself,
I myself make the only growth by which I can be appreci-
    ated,
I reject none, accept all, then reproduce all in my own forms.

A breed whose proof is in time and deeds,
What we are we are, nativity is answer enough to objections,
We wield ourselves as a weapon is wielded,
We are powerful and tremendous in ourselves,
We are executive in ourselves, we are sufficient in the variety
    of ourselves,
We are the most beautiful to ourselves and in ourselves,
We stand self-pois'd in the middle, branching thence over the
    world,
From Missouri, Nebraska, or Kansas, laughing attacks to
    scorn.

Nothing is sinful to us outside of ourselves,
Whatever appears, whatever does not appear, we are beau-
    tiful or sinful in ourselves only.

(O Mother—O Sisters dear!
If we are lost, no victor else has destroy'd us,
It is by ourselves we go down to eternal night.)

3

Have you thought there could be but a single supreme?
There can be any number of supremes—one does not counter-
    vail another any more than one eyesight countervails
    another, or one life countervails another.

All is eligible to all,
All is for individuals, all is for you,
No condition is prohibited, not God's or any.

All comes by the body, only health puts you in rapport with
    the universe.

Produce great Persons, the rest follows.

4

Piety and conformity to them that like,
Peace, obesity, allegiance, to them that like,
I am he who tauntingly compels men, women, nations,
Crying, Leap from your seats and contend for your lives!

I am he who walks the States with a barb'd tongue, ques-
　　tioning every one I meet,
Who are you that wanted only to be told what you knew be-
　　fore?
Who are you that wanted only a book to join you in your
　　nonsense?

(With pangs and cries as thine own O bearer of many chil-
　　dren,
These clamors wild to a race of pride I give.)
O lands, would you be freer than all that has ever been be-
　　fore?
If you would be freer than all that has been before, come
　　listen to me.

Fear grace, elegance, civilization, delicatesse,
Fear the mellow sweet, the sucking of honey-juice,
Beware the advancing mortal ripening of Nature,
Beware what precedes the decay of the ruggedness of states
　　and men.

5

Ages, precedents, have long been accumulating undirected
　　materials,
America brings builders, and brings its own styles.

The immortal poets of Asia and Europe have done their work
　　and pass'd to other spheres,
A work remains, the work of surpassing all they have done.

America, curious toward foreign characters, stands by its own
at all hazards,
Stands removed, spacious, composite, sound, initiates the true
use of precedents,
Does not repel them or the past or what they have produced
under their forms,
Takes the lesson with calmness, perceives the corpse slowly
borne from the house,
Perceives that it waits a little while in the door, that it was
fittest for its days,
That its life has descended to the stalwart and well-shaped
heir who approaches,
And that he shall be fittest for his days.

Any period one nation must lead,
One land must be the promise and reliance of the future.

These States are the amplest poem,
Here is not merely a nation but a teeming Nation of nations,
Here the doings of men correspond with the broadcast doings
of the day and night,
Here is what moves in magnificent masses careless of particu-
lars,
Here are the roughs, beards, friendliness, combativeness, the
soul loves,
Here the flowing trains, here the crowds, equality, diversity,
the soul loves.

6

Land of lands and bards to corroborate!
Of them standing among them, one lifts to the light a west-
bred face,
To him the hereditary countenance bequeath'd both mother's
and father's,
His first parts substances, earth, water, animals, trees,
Built of the common stock, having room for far and near,
Used to dispense with other lands, incarnating this land,

Attracting it body and soul to himself, hanging on its neck
  with incomparable love,
Plunging his seminal muscle into its merits and demerits,
Making its cities, beginnings, events, diversities, wars, vocal
  in him,
Making its rivers, lakes, bays, embouchure in him,
Mississippi with yearly freshets and changing chutes, Colum-
  bia, Niagara, Hudson, spending themselves lovingly in
  him,
If the Atlantic coast stretch or the Pacific coast stretch, he
  stretching with them North or South,
Spanning between them East and West, and touching what-
  ever is between them,
Growths growing from him to offset the growths of pine,
  cedar, hemlock, live-oak, locust, chestnut, hickory, cot-
  tonwood, orange, magnolia,
Tangles as tangled in him as any canebrake or swamp,
He likening sides and peaks of mountains, forests coated with
  northern transparent ice,
Off him pasturage sweet and natural as savanna, upland,
  prairie,
Through him flights, whirls, screams, answering those of the
  fish-hawk, mocking-bird, night-heron, and eagle,
His spirit surrounding his country's spirit, unclosed to good
  and evil,
Surrounding the essences of real things, old times and present
  times,
Surrounding just found shores, islands, tribes of red aborigines,
Weather-beaten vessels, landings, settlements, embryo stature
  and muscle,
The haughty defiance of the Year One, war, peace, the formation of the Constitution,
The separate States, the simple elastic scheme, the immigrants,
The Union always swarming with blatherers and always sure
  and impregnable,

The unsurvey'd interior, log-houses, clearings, wild animals, hunters, trappers,

Surrounding the multiform agriculture, mines, temperature, the gestation of new States,

Congress conveying every Twelfth-month, the members duly coming up from the uttermost parts,

Surrounding the noble character of mechanics and farmers, especially the young men,

Responding their manners, speech, dress, friendships, the gait they have of persons who never knew how it felt to stand in the presence of superiors,

The freshness and candor of their physiognomy, the copiousness and decision of their phrenology,

The picturesque looseness of their carriage, their fierceness when wrong'd,

The fluency of their speech, their delight in music, their curiosity, good temper and open-handedness, the whole composite make,

The prevailing ardor and enterprise, the large amativeness,

The perfect equality of the female with the male, the fluid movement of the population,

The superior marine, free commerce, fisheries, whaling, gold-digging,

Wharf-hemm'd cities, railroad and steamboat lines intersecting all points,

Factories, mercantile life, labor-saving machinery, the Northeast, Northwest, Southwest,

Manhattan firemen, the Yankee swap, southern plantation life,

Slavery—the murderous, treacherous conspiracy to raise it upon the ruins of all the rest,

On and on to the grapple with it—Assassin! then your life or ours be the stake, and respite no more.

7

(Lo, high toward heaven, this day,
Libertad, from the conqueress' field return'd,
I mark the new aureola around your head,

No more of soft astral, but dazzling and fierce,
With war's flames and the lambent lightnings playing,
And your port immovable where you stand,
With still the inextinguishable glance and the clinch'd and
    lifted fist,
And your foot on the neck of the menacing one, the scorner
    utterly crush'd beneath you,
The menacing arrogant one that strode and advanced with
    his senseless scorn, bearing the murderous knife,
The wide-swelling one, the braggart that would yesterday do
    so much,
To-day a carrion dead and damn'd, the despised of all the
    earth,
An offal rank, to the dunghill maggots spurn'd.)

8

Others take finish, but the Republic is ever constructive and
    ever keeps vista,
Others adorn the past, but you O days of the present, I adorn
    you,
O days of the future I believe in you—I isolate myself for
    your sake,
O America because you build for mankind I build for you,
O well-beloved stone-cutters, I lead them who plan with de-
    cision and science,
Lead the present with friendly hand toward the future.

(Bravas to all impulses sending sane children to the next age!
But damn that which spends itself with no thought of the
    stain, pains, dismay, feebleness, it is bequeathing.)

9

I listened to the Phantom by Ontario's shore,
I heard the voice arising demanding bards,
By them all native and grand, by them alone can these States
    be fused into the compact organism of a Nation.

To hold men together by paper and seal or by compulsion is
    no account,
That only holds men together which aggregates all in a living
    principle, as the hold of the limbs of the body or the
    fibres of plants.

Of all races and eras these States with veins full of poetical
    stuff most needs poets, and are to have the greatest, and
    use them the greatest,
Their Presidents shall not be their common referee so much
    as their poets shall.

(Soul of love and tongue of fire!
Eye to pierce the deepest deeps and sweep the world!
Ah Mother, prolific and full in all besides, yet how long bar-
    ren, barren?)

10

Of these States the poet is the equable man,
Not in him but off from him things are grotesque, eccentric,
    fail of their full returns,
Nothing out of its place is good, nothing in its place is bad,
He bestows on every object or quality its fit proportion,
    neither more nor less,
He is the arbiter of the diverse, he is the key,
He is the equalizer of his age and land,
He supplies what wants supplying, he checks what wants
    checking,
In peace out of him speaks the spirit of peace, large, rich,
    thrifty, building populous towns, encouraging agricul-
    ture, arts, commerce, lighting the study of man, the
    soul, health, immortality, government,
In war he is the best backer of the war, he fetches artillery as
    good as the engineer's, he can make every word he
    speaks draw blood,
The years straying toward infidelity he withholds by his
    steady faith,

He is no arguer, he is judgment, (Nature accepts him ab-
      solutely,)
He judges not as the judge judges but as the sun falling
      round a helpless thing,
As he sees the farthest he has the most faith,
His thoughts are the hymns of the praise of things,
In the dispute on God and eternity he is silent,
He sees eternity less like a play with a prologue and de-
      nouement,
He sees eternity in men and women, he does not see men
      and women as dreams or dots.

For the great Idea, the idea of perfect and free individuals,
For that, the bard walks in advance, leader of leaders,
The attitude of him cheers up slaves and horrifies foreign
      despots.

Without extinction is Liberty, without retrograde is Equality,
They live in the feelings of young men and the best women,
(Not for nothing have the indomitable heads of the earth
      been always ready to fall for Liberty.)

11

For the great Idea,
That, O my brethren, that is the mission of poets.

Songs of stern defiance ever ready,
Songs of the rapid arming and the march,
The flag of peace quick-folded, and instead the flag we know,
Warlike flag of the great Idea.

(Angry cloth I saw there leaping!
I stand again in leaden rain your flapping folds saluting,
I sing you over all, flying beckoning through the fight—O the
      hard-contested fight!
The cannons ope their rosy-flashing muzzles—the hurtled balls
      scream,

The battle-front forms amid the smoke—the volleys pour in-
        cessant from the line,
Hark, the ringing word *Charge!*—now the tussle and the furi-
        ous maddening yells,
Now the corpses tumble curl'd upon the ground,
Cold, cold in death, for precious life of you,
Angry cloth I saw there leaping.)

12

Are you he who would assume a place to teach or be a poet
        here in the States?
The place is august, the terms obdurate.

Who would assume to teach here may well prepare himself
        body and mind,
He may well survey, ponder, arm, fortify, harden, make lithe
        himself,
He shall surely be question'd beforehand by me with many
        and stern questions.

Who are you indeed who would talk or sing to America?
Have you studied out the land, its idioms and men?
Have you learn'd the physiology, phrenology, politics, ge-
        ography, pride, freedom, friendship of the land? its
        substratums and objects?
Have you consider'd the organic compact of the first day of
        the first year of Independence, sign'd by the Com-
        missioners, ratified by the States, and read by Wash-
        ington at the head of the army?
Have you possess'd yourself of the Federal Constitution?
Do you see who have left all feudal processes and poems be-
        hind them, and assumed the poems and processes of
        Democracy?
Are you faithful to things? do you teach what the land and
        sea, the bodies of men, womanhood, amativeness,
        heroic angers, teach?
Have you sped through fleeting customs, popularities?

Can you hold your hand against all seductions, follies, whirls,
fierce contentions? are you very strong? are you really
of the whole People?

Are you not of some coterie? some school or mere religion?

Are you done with reviews and criticisms of life? animating
now to life itself?

Have you vivified yourself from the maternity of these States?

Have you too the old ever-fresh forbearance and impartiality?

Do you hold the like love for those hardening to maturity?
for the last-born? little and big? and for the errant?

What is this you bring my America?

Is it uniform with my country?

Is it not something that has been better told or done before?

Have you not imported this or the spirit of it in some ship?

Is it not a mere tale? a rhyme? a prettiness?—is the good old
cause in it?

Has it not dangled long at the heels of the poets, politicians,
literats, of enemies' lands?

Does it not assume that what is notoriously gone is still here?

Does it answer universal needs? will it improve manners?

Does it sound with trumpet-voice the proud victory of the
Union in that secession war?

Can your performance face the open fields and the seaside?

Will it absorb into me as I absorb food, air, to appear again in
my strength, gait, face?

Have real employments contributed to it? original makers, not
mere amanuenses?

Does it meet modern discoveries, calibres, facts, face to face?

What does it mean to American persons, progresses, cities?
Chicago, Kanada, Arkansas?

Does it see behind the apparent custodians the real custodians
standing, menacing, silent, the mechanics, Manhattan-
ese, Western men, Southerners, significant alike in their
apathy, and in the promptness of their love?

Does it see what finally befalls, and has always finally be-
fallen, each temporizer, patcher, outsider, partialist,

alarmist, infidel, who has ever ask'd any thing of
America?
What mocking and scornful negligence?
The track strew'd with the dust of skeletons,
By the roadside others disdainfully toss'd.

13

Rhymes and rhymers pass away, poems distill'd from poems
pass away,
The swarms of reflectors and the polite pass, and leave ashes,
Admirers, importers, obedient persons, make but the soil of
literature,
America justifies itself, give it time, no disguise can deceive
it or conceal from it, it is impassive enough,
Only toward the likes of itself will it advance to meet them,
If its poets appear it will in due time advance to meet them,
there is no fear of mistake,
(The proof of a poet shall be sternly deferr'd till his country
absorbs him as affectionately as he has absorb'd it.)

He masters whose spirit masters, he tastes sweetest who results sweetest in the long run,
The blood of the brawn beloved of time is unconstraint;
In the need of songs, philosophy, an appropriate native grand-
opera, shipcraft, any craft,
He or she is greatest who contributes the greatest original
practical example.

Already a nonchalant breed, silently emerging, appears on the
streets,
People's lips salute only doers, lovers, satisfiers, positive know-
ers,
There will shortly be no more priests, I say their work is done,
Death is without emergencies here, but life is perpetual emergencies here,
Are your body, days, manners, superb? after death you shall
be superb,

Justice, health, self-esteem, clear the way with irresistible
     power;
How dare you place any thing before a man?

14

Fall behind me States!
A man before all—myself, typical, before all.

Give me the pay I have served for,
Give me to sing the songs of the great Idea, take all the rest,
I have loved the earth, sun, animals, I have despised riches,
I have given alms to every one that ask'd, stood up for the
     stupid and crazy, devoted my income and labor to
     others,
Hated tyrants, argued not concerning God, had patience and
     indulgence toward the people, taken off my hat to
     nothing known or unknown,
Gone freely with powerful uneducated persons and with the
     young, and with the mothers of families,
Read these leaves to myself in the open air, tried them by
     trees, stars, rivers,
Dismiss'd whatever insulted my own soul or defiled my body,
Claim'd nothing to myself which I have not carefully claim'd
     for others on the same terms,
Sped to the camps, and comrades found and accepted from
     every State,
(Upon this breast has many a dying soldier lean'd to breathe
     his last,
This arm, this hand, this voice, have nourish'd, rais'd, restored,
To life recalling many a prostrate form;)
I am willing to wait to be understood by the growth of the
     taste of myself,
Rejecting none, permitting all.

(Say O Mother, have I not to your thought been faithful?
Have I not through life kept you and yours before me?)

15

I swear I begin to see the meaning of these things,
It is not the earth, it is not America who is so great,
It is I who am great or to be great, it is You up there, or any
    one,
It is to walk rapidly through civilizations, governments,
    theories,
Through poems, pageants, shows, to form individuals.

Underneath all, individuals,
I swear nothing is good to me now that ignores individuals,
The American compact is altogether with individuals,
The only government is that which makes minute of indi-
    viduals,
The whole theory of the universe is directed unerringly to one
    single individual—namely to You.

(Mother! with subtle sense severe, with the naked sword in
    your hand,
I saw you at last refuse to treat but directly with individuals.)

16

Underneath all, Nativity,
I swear I will stand by my own nativity, pious or impious so
    be it;
I swear I am charm'd with nothing except nativity,
Men, women, cities, nations, are only beautiful from nativity.

Underneath all is the Expression of love for men and women,
(I swear I have seen enough of mean and impotent modes of
    expressing love for men and women,
After this day I take my own modes of expressing love for
    men and women.)

I swear I will have each quality of my race in myself,

(Talk as you like, he only suits these States whose manners
      favor the audacity and sublime turbulence of the
      States.)

Underneath the lessons of things, spirits, Nature, govern-
      ments, ownerships, I swear I perceive other lessons,
Underneath all to me is myself, to you yourself, (the same
      monotonous old song.)

17

O I see flashing that this America is only you and me,
Its power, weapons, testimony, are you and me,
Its crimes, lies, thefts, defections, are you and me,
Its Congress is you and me, the officers, capitols, armies, ships,
      are you and me,
Its endless gestations of new States are you and me,
The war, (that war so bloody and grim, the war I will hence-
      forth forget), was you and me,
Natural and artificial are you and me,
Freedom, language, poems, employments, are you and me,
Past, present, future, are you and me.

I dare not shirk any part of myself,
Not any part of America good or bad,
Not to build for that which builds for mankind,
Not to balance ranks, complexions, creeds, and the sexes,
Not to justify science nor the march of equality,
Nor to feed the arrogant blood of the brawn belov'd of time.

I am for those that have never been master'd,
For men and women whose tempers have never been master'd,
For those whom laws, theories, conventions, can never mas-
      ter.

I am for those who walk abreast with the whole earth,
Who inaugurate one to inaugurate all.

I will not be outfaced by irrational things,
I will penetrate what it is in them that is sarcastic upon me,
I will make cities and civilizations defer to me,
This is what I have learnt from America—it is the amount, and
      it I teach again.

(Democracy, while weapons were everywhere aim'd at your
      breast,
I saw you serenely give birth to immortal children, saw in
      dreams your dilating form,
Saw you with spreading mantle covering the world.)

18

I will confront these shows of the day and night,
I will know if I am to be less than they,
I will see if I am not as majestic as they,
I will see if I am not as subtle and real as they,
I will see if I am to be less generous than they,
I will see if I have no meaning, while the houses and ships
      have meaning,
I will see if the fishes and birds are to be enough for them-
      selves, and I am not to be enough for myself.

I match my spirit against yours you orbs, growths, mountains,
      brutes,
Copious as you are I absorb you all in myself, and become
      the master myself,
America isolated yet embodying all, what is it finally except
      myself?
These States, what are they except myself?
I know now why the earth is gross, tantalizing, wicked, it is
      for my sake,
I take you specially to be mine, you terrible, rude forms.

(Mother, bend down, bend close to me your face,
I know not what these plots and wars and deferments are for,
I know not fruition's success, but I know that through war
      and crime your work goes on, and must yet go on.)

19

Thus by blue Ontario's shore,
While the winds fann'd me and the waves came trooping to-
    ward me,
I thrill'd with the power's pulsations, and the charm of my
    theme was upon me,
Till the tissues that held me parted their ties upon me.

And I saw the free souls of poets,
The loftiest bards of past ages strode before me,
Strange large men, long unwaked, undisclosed, were disclosed
    to me.

20

O my rapt verse, my call, mock me not!
Not for the bards of the past, not to invoke them have I
    launch'd you forth,
Not to call even those lofty bards here by Ontario's shores,
Have I sung so capricious and loud my savage song.

Bards for my own land only I invoke,
(For the war the war is over, the field is clear'd,)
Till they strike up marches henceforth triumphant and on-
    ward,
To cheer O Mother your boundless expectant soul.

Bards of the great Idea! bards of the peaceful inventions! (for
    the war, the war is over!)
Yet bards of latent armies, a million soldiers waiting ever-
    ready,
Bards with songs as from burning coals or the lightning's
    fork'd stripes!
Ample Ohio's, Kanada's bards—bards of California! inland
    bards—bards of the war!
You by my charm I invoke.

REVERSALS

Let that which stood in front go behind,
Let that which was behind advance to the front,
Let bigots, fools, unclean persons, offer new propositions,
Let the old propositions be postponed,
Let a man seek pleasure everywhere except in himself,
Let a woman seek happiness everywhere except in herself.

PROUD MUSIC of the STORM

1

Proud music of the storm,
Blast that careers so free, whistling across the prairies,
Strong hum of forest tree-tops—wind of the mountains,
Personified dim shapes—you hidden orchestras,
You serenades of phantoms with instruments alert,
Blending with Nature's rhythmus all the tongues of nations;
You chords left as by vast composers—you choruses,
You formless, free, religious dances—you from the Orient,
You undertone of rivers, roar of pouring cataracts,
You sounds from distant guns with galloping cavalry,
Echoes of camps with all the different bugle-calls,

Trooping tumultuous, filling the midnight late, bending me
    powerless,
Entering my lonesome slumber-chamber, why have you seiz'd
    me?

2

Come forward O my soul, and let the rest retire,
Listen, lose not, it is toward thee they tend,
Parting the midnight, entering my slumber-chamber,
For thee they sing and dance O soul.

A festive song,
The duet of the bridegroom and the bride, a marriage-march,
With lips of love, and hearts of lovers fill'd to the brim with
    love,
The red-flush'd cheeks and perfumes, the cortege swarming
    full of friendly faces young and old,
To flutes' clear notes and sounding harps' cantabile.

Now loud approaching drums,
Victoria! see'st thou in powder-smoke the banners torn but
    flying? the rout of the baffled?
Hearest those shouts of a conquering army?
(Ah soul, the sobs of women, the wounded groaning in agony,
The hiss and crackle of flames, the blacken'd ruins, the em-
    bers of cities,
The dirge and desolation of mankind.)

Now airs antique and mediæval fill me,
I see and hear old harpers with their harps at Welsh festivals,
I hear the minnesingers singing their lays of love,
I hear the minstrels, gleemen, troubadours, of the middle
    ages.

Now the great organ sounds,
Tremulous, while underneath, (as the hid footholds of the
    earth,

On which arising rest, and leaping forth depend,
All shapes of beauty, grace and strength, all hues we know,
Green blades of grass and warbling birds, children that gam-
      bol and play, the clouds of heaven above,)
The strong base stands, and its pulsations intermits not,
Bathing, supporting, merging all the rest, maternity of all the
      rest,
And with it every instrument in multitudes,
The players playing, all the world's musicians,
The solemn hymns and masses rousing adoration,
All passionate heart-chants, sorrowful appeals,
The measureless sweet vocalists of ages,
And for their solvent setting earth's own diapason,
Of winds and woods and mighty ocean waves,
A new composite orchestra, binder of years and climes, ten-
      fold renewer,
As of the far-back days the poets tell, the Paradiso,
The straying thence, the separation long, but now the wander-
      ing done,
The journey done, the journeyman come home,
And man and art with Nature fused again.

Tutti! for earth and heaven;
(The Almighty leader now for once has signal'd with his
      wand.)

The manly strophe of the husbands of the world,
And all the wives responding.

The tongues of violins,
(I think O tongues ye tell this heart, that cannot tell itself,
This brooding yearning heart, that cannot tell itself.)

3

Ah from a little child,
Thou knowest soul how to me all sounds became music,
My mother's voice in lullaby or hymn,

(The voice, O tender voices, memory's loving voices,
Last miracle of all, O dearest mother's, sister's, voices;)
The rain, the growing corn, the breeze among the long-leav'd
    corn,
The measur'd sea-surf beating on the sand,
The twittering bird, the hawk's sharp scream,
The wild-fowl's notes at night as flying low migrating north
    or south,
The psalm in the country church or mid the clustering trees,
    the open air camp-meeting,
The fiddler in the tavern, the glee, the long-strung sailor-song,
The lowing cattle, bleating sheep, the crowing cock at dawn.

All songs of current lands come sounding round me,
The German airs of friendship, wine and love,
Irish ballads, merry jigs and dances, English warbles,
Chansons of France, Scotch tunes, and o'er the rest,
Italia's peerless compositions.

Across the stage with pallor on her face, yet lurid passion,
Stalks Norma brandishing the dagger in her hand.

I see poor crazed Lucia's eyes' unnatural gleam,
Her hair down her back falls loose and dishevel'd.

I see where Ernani walking the bridal garden,
Amid the scent of night-roses, radiant, holding his bride by
    the hand,
Hears the infernal call, the death-pledge of the horn.

To crossing swords and gray hairs bared to heaven,
The clear electric base and baritone of the world,
The trombone duo, Libertad forever!

From Spanish chestnut trees' dense shade,
By old and heavy convent walls a wailing song,

Song of lost love, the torch of youth and life quench'd in
    despair,
Song of the dying swan, Fernando's heart is breaking.

Awaking from her woes at last retriev'd Amina sings,
Copious as stars and glad as morning light the torrents of her
    joy.

(The teeming lady comes,
The lustrious orb, Venus contralto, the blooming mother,
Sister of loftiest gods, Alboni's self I hear.)

4

I hear those odes, symphonies, operas,
I hear in the *William Tell* the music of an arous'd and angry
    people,
I hear Meyerbeer's *Huguenots*, the *Prophet*, or *Robert*,
Gounod's *Faust*, or Mozart's *Don Juan*.

I hear the dance-music of all nations,
The waltz, some delicious measure, lapsing, bathing me in
    bliss,
The bolero to tinkling guitars and clattering castanets.

I see religious dances old and new,
I hear the sound of the Hebrew lyre,
I see the crusaders marching bearing the cross on high, to the
    martial clang of cymbals,
I hear dervishes monotonously chanting, interspers'd with
    frantic shouts, as they spin around turning always to-
    wards Mecca,
I see the rapt religious dances of the Persians and the Arabs,
Again, at Eleusis, home of Ceres, I see the modern Greeks
    dancing,
I hear them clapping their hands as they bend their bodies,
I hear the metrical shuffling of their feet.

I see again the wild old Corybantian dance, the performers
    wounding each other,
I see the Roman youth to the shrill sound of flageolets throw-
    ing and catching their weapons,
As they fall on their knees and rise again.

I hear from the Mussulman mosque the muezzin calling,
I see the worshippers within, nor form nor sermon, argument
    nor word,
But silent, strange, devout, rais'd, glowing heads, ecstatic
    faces.

I hear the Egyptian harp of many strings,
The primitive chants of the Nile boatmen,
The sacred imperial hymns of China,
To the delicate sounds of the king, (the stricken wood and
    stone,)
Or to Hindu flutes and the fretting twang of the vina,
A band of bayaderes.

5

Now Asia, Africa leave me, Europe seizing inflates me,
To organs huge and bands I hear as from vast concourses of
    voices,
Luther's strong hymn *Eine feste Burg ist unser Gott*,
Rossini's *Stabat Mater dolorosa*,
Or floating in some high cathedral dim with gorgeous color'd
    windows,
The passionate *Agnus Dei* or *Gloria in Excelsis*.

Composers! mighty maestros!
And you, sweet singers of old lands, soprani, tenori, bassi!
To you a new bard caroling in the West,
Obeisant sends his love.

(Such led to thee O soul,
All senses, shows and objects, lead to thee,
But now it seems to me sound leads o'er all the rest.)

I hear the annual singing of the children in St. Paul's cathedral,
Or, under the high roof of some colossal hall, the symphonies,
oratorios of Beethoven, Handel, or Haydn,
The *Creation* in billows of godhood laves me.

Give me to hold all sounds, (I madly struggling cry,)
Fill me with all the voices of the universe,
Endow me with their throbbings, Nature's also,
The tempests, waters, winds, operas and chants, marches and
dances,
Utter, pour in, for I would take them all!

6

Then I woke softly,
And pausing, questioning awhile the music of my dream,
And questioning all those reminiscences, the tempest in its
fury,
And all the songs of sopranos and tenors,
And those rapt oriental dances of religious fervor,
And the sweet varied instruments, and the diapason of organs,
And all the artless plaints of love and grief and death,
I said to my silent curious soul out of the bed of the slumber-
chamber,
Come, for I have found the clew I sought so long,
Let us go forth refresh'd amid the day,
Cheerfully tallying life, walking the world, the real,
Nourish'd henceforth by our celestial dream.

And I said, moreover,
Haply what thou hast heard O soul was not the sound of
winds,
Nor dream of raging storm, nor sea-hawk's flapping wings nor
harsh scream,
Nor vocalism of sun-bright Italy,
Nor German organ majestic, nor vast concourse of voices, nor
layers of harmonies,

Nor strophes of husbands and wives, nor sound of marching
　　soldiers,
Nor flutes, nor harps, nor the bugle-calls of camps,
But to a new rhythmus fitted for thee,
Poems bridging the way from Life to Death, vaguely wafted
　　in night air, uncaught, unwritten,
Which let us go forth in the bold day and write.

PASSAGE to INDIA

1

Singing my days,
Singing the great achievements of the present,
Singing the strong light works of engineers,
Our modern wonders, (the antique ponderous Seven outvied,)
In the Old World the east the Suez canal,
The New by its mighty railroad spann'd,
The seas inlaid with eloquent gentle wires;
Yet first to sound, and ever sound, the cry with thee O soul,
The Past! the Past! the Past!

The Past—the dark unfathom'd retrospect!
The teeming gulf—the sleepers and the shadows!
The past—the infinite greatness of the past!
For what is the present after all but a growth out of the past?
(As a projectile form'd, impell'd, passing a certain line, still
　　keeps on,
So the present, utterly form'd, impell'd by the past.)

2

Passage O soul to India!
Eclaircise the myths Asiatic, the primitive fables.

Not you alone proud truths of the world,
Nor you alone ye facts of modern science,
But myths and fables of eld, Asia's, Africa's fables,
The far-darting beams of the spirit, the unloos'd dreams,
The deep diving bibles and legends,
The daring plots of the poets, the elder religions;
O you temples fairer than lilies pour'd over by the rising sun!
O you fables spurning the known, eluding the hold of the
         known, mounting to heaven!
You lofty and dazzling towers, pinnacled, red as roses, bur-
         nish'd with gold!
Towers of fables immortal fashion'd from mortal dreams!
You too I welcome and fully the same as the rest!
You too with joy I sing.

Passage to India!
Lo, soul, seest thou not God's purpose from the first?
The earth to be spann'd, connected by network,
The races, neighbors, to marry and be given in marriage,
The oceans to be cross'd, the distant brought near,
The lands to be welded together.

A worship new I sing,
You captains, voyagers, explorers, yours,
You engineers, you architects, machinists, yours,
You, not for trade or transportation only,
But in God's name, and for thy sake O soul.

3

Passage to India!
Lo soul for thee of tableaus twain,
I see in one the Suez canal initiated, open'd,
I see the procession of steamships, the Empress Eugenie's
         leading the van,
I mark from on deck the strange landscape, the pure sky, the
         level sand in the distance,
I pass swiftly the picturesque groups, the workmen gather'd,
The gigantic dredging machines.

In one again, different, (yet thine, all thine, O soul, the same,)
I see over my own continent the Pacific railroad surmounting
    every barrier,
I see continual trains of cars winding along the Platte carry-
    ing freight and passengers,
I hear the locomotives rushing and roaring, and the shrill
    steam-whistle,
I hear the echoes reverberate through the grandest scenery
    in the world,
I cross the Laramie plains, I note the rocks in grotesque
    shapes, the buttes,
I see the plentiful larkspur and wild onions, the barren, color-
    less, sage-deserts,
I see in glimpses afar or towering immediately above me the
    great mountains, I see the Wind river and the Wahsatch
    mountains,
I see the Monument mountain and the Eagle's Nest, I pass
    the Promontory, I ascend the Nevadas,
I scan the noble Elk mountain and wind around its base,
I see the Humboldt range, I thread the valley and cross the
    river,
I see the clear waters of lake Tahoe, I see forests of majestic
    pines,
Or crossing the great desert, the alkaline plains, I behold en-
    chanting mirages of waters and meadows,
Marking through these and after all, in duplicate slender
    lines,
Bridging the three or four thousand miles of land travel,
Tying the Eastern to the Western sea,
The road between Europe and Asia.

(Ah Genoese thy dream! thy dream!
Centuries after thou art laid in thy grave,
The shore thou foundest verifies thy dream.)

4

Passage to India!
Struggles of many a captain, tales of many a sailor dead,

Over my mood stealing and spreading they come,
Like clouds and cloudlets in the unreach'd sky.

Along all history, down the slopes,
As a rivulet running, sinking now, and now again to the sur-
　　face rising,
A ceaseless thought, a varied train—lo, soul, to thee, thy sight,
　　they rise,
The plans, the voyages again, the expeditions;
Again Vasco de Gama sails forth,
Again the knowledge gain'd, the mariner's compass,
Lands found and nations born, thou born America,
For purpose vast, man's long probation fill'd,
Thou rondure of the world at last accomplish'd.

5

O vast Rondure, swimming in space,
Cover'd all over with visible power and beauty,
Alternate light and day and the teeming spiritual darkness,
Unspeakable high processions of sun and moon and count-
　　less stars above,
Below, the manifold grass and waters, animals, mountains,
　　trees,
With inscrutable purpose, some hidden prophetic intention,
Now first it seems my thought begins to span thee.

Down from the gardens of Asia descending radiating,
Adam and Eve appear, then their myriad progeny after them,
Wandering, yearning, curious, with restless explorations,
With questionings, baffled, formless, feverish, with never-
　　happy hearts,
With that sad incessant refrain, *Wherefore unsatisfied soul?*
　　and *Whither O mocking life?*

Ah who shall soothe these feverish children?
Who justify these restless explorations?
Who speak the secret of impassive earth?

Who bind it to us? what is this separate Nature so unnatural
What is this earth to our affections? (unloving earth, without
    a throb to answer ours,
Cold earth, the place of graves.)

Yet soul be sure the first intent remains, and shall be carried
    out,
Perhaps even now the time has arrived.

After the seas are all cross'd, (as they seem already cross'd,)
After the great captains and engineers have accomplish'd
    their work,
After the noble inventors, after the scientists, the chemist, the
    geologist, ethnologist,
Finally shall come the poet worthy that name,
The true son of God shall come singing his songs.
Then not your deeds only O voyagers, O scientists and inven-
    tors, shall be justified,
All these hearts as of fretted children shall be sooth'd,
All affection shall be fully responded to, the secret shall be
    told,
All these separations and gaps shall be taken up and hook'd
    and link'd together,
The whole earth, this cold, impassive, voiceless earth, shall
    be completely justified,
Trinitas divine shall be gloriously accomplish'd and com-
    pacted by the true son of God, the poet,
(He shall indeed pass the straits and conquer the mountains,
He shall double the cape of Good Hope to some purpose,)
Nature and Man shall be disjoin'd and diffused no more,
The true son of God shall absolutely fuse them.

6

Year at whose wide-flung door I sing!
Year of the purpose accomplish'd!
Year of the marriage of continents, climates and oceans!
(No mere doge of Venice now wedding the Adriatic,)

I see O year in you the vast terraqueous globe given and giv-
ing all,
Europe to Asia, Africa join'd, and they to the New World,
The lands, geographies, dancing before you, holding a fes-
tival garland,
As brides and bridegrooms hand in hand.

Passage to India!
Cooling airs from Caucasus far, soothing cradle of man,
The river Euphrates flowing, the past lit up again.

Lo soul, the retrospect brought forward,
The old, most populous, wealthiest of earth's lands,
The streams of the Indus and the Ganges and their many
affluents,
(I my shores of America walking to-day behold, resuming all,)
The tale of Alexander on his warlike marches suddenly dying,
On one side China and on the other side Persia and Arabia,
To the south the great seas and the bay of Bengal,
The flowing literatures, tremendous epics, religions, castes,
Old occult Brahma interminably far back, the tender and
junior Buddha,
Central and southern empires and all their belongings, pos-
sessors,
The wars of Tamerlane, the reign of Aurungzebe,
The traders, rulers, explorers, Moslems, Venetians, Byzan-
tium, the Arabs, Portuguese,
The first travelers famous yet, Marco Polo, Batouta the Moor,
Doubts to be solv'd, the map incognita, blanks to be fill'd,
The foot of man unstay'd, the hands never at rest,
Thyself O soul that will not brook a challenge.

The mediæval navigators rise before me,
The world of 1492, with its awaken'd enterprise,
Something swelling in humanity now like the sap of the earth
in spring,
The sunset splendor of chivalry declining.

And who art thou sad shade?
Gigantic, visionary, thyself a visionary,
With majestic limbs and pious beaming eyes,
Spreading around with every look of thine a golden world,
Enhuing it with gorgeous hues.

As the chief histrion,
Down to the footlights walks in some great scena,
Dominating the rest I see the Admiral himself,
(History's type of courage, action, faith,)
Behold him sail from Palos leading his little fleet,
His voyage behold, his return, his great fame,
His misfortunes, calumniators, behold him a prisoner, chain'd,
Behold his dejection, poverty, death.
(Curious in time I stand, noting the efforts of heroes,
Is the deferment long? bitter the slander, poverty, death?
Lies the seed unreck'd for centuries in the ground? lo, to God's
        due occasion,
Uprising in the night, it sprouts, blooms,
And fills the earth with use and beauty.)

7

Passage indeed O soul to primal thought,
Not lands and seas alone, thy own clear freshness,
The young maturity of brood and bloom,
To realms of budding bibles.

O soul, repressless, I with thee and thou with me,
Thy circumnavigation of the world begin,
Of man, the voyage of his mind's return,
To reason's early paradise,
Back, back to wisdom's birth, to innocent intuitions,
Again with fair creation.

8

O we can wait no longer,
We too take ship O soul,

Joyous we too launch out on trackless seas,
Fearless for unknown shores on waves of ecstasy to sail,
Amid the wafting winds, (thou pressing me to thee, I thee to
    me, O soul,)
Caroling free, singing our song of God,
Chanting our chant of pleasant exploration.

With laugh and many a kiss,
(Let others deprecate, let others weep for sin, remorse, hu-
    miliation,)
O soul thou pleasest me, I thee.

Ah more than any priest O soul we too believe in God,
But with the mystery of God we dare not dally.

O soul thou pleasest me, I thee,
Sailing these seas or on the hills, or waking in the night,
Thoughts, silent thoughts, of Time and Space and Death, like
    waters flowing,
Bear me indeed as through the regions infinite,
Whose air I breathe, whose ripples hear, lave me all over,
Bathe me O God in thee, mounting to thee,
I and my soul to range in range of thee.

O Thou transcendent,
Nameless, the fibre and the breath,
Light of the light, shedding forth universes, thou centre of
    them,
Thou mightier centre of the true, the good, the loving,
Thou moral, spiritual fountain—affection's source—thou reser-
    voir,
(O pensive soul of me—O thirst unsatisfied—waitest not there?
Waitest not haply for us somewhere there the Comrade per-
    fect?)
Thou pulse—thou motive of the stars, suns, systems,
That, circling, move in order, safe, harmonious,
Athwart the shapeless vastnesses of space,

How should I think, how breathe a single breath, how speak,
　　　if, out of myself,
I could not launch, to those, superior universes?

Swiftly I shrivel at the thought of God,
At Nature and its wonders, Time and Space and Death,
But that I, turning, call to thee O soul, thou actual Me,
And lo, thou gently masterest the orbs,
Thou matest Time, smilest content at Death,
And fillest, swellest full the vastnesses of Space.

Greater than stars or suns,
Bounding O soul thou journeyest forth;
What love than thine and ours could wider amplify?
What aspirations, wishes, outvie thine and ours O soul?
What dreams of the ideal? what plans of purity, perfection,
　　　strength?
What cheerful willingness for others' sake to give up all?
For others' sake to suffer all?

Reckoning ahead O soul, when thou, the time achiev'd,
The seas all cross'd, weather'd the capes, the voyage done,
Surrounded, copest, frontest God, yieldest, the aim attain'd,
As fill'd with friendship, love complete, the Elder Brother
　　　found,
The Younger melts in fondness in his arms.

9

Passage to more than India!
Are thy wings plumed indeed for such far flights?
O soul, voyagest thou indeed on voyages like those?
Disportest thou on waters such as those?
Soundest below the Sanscrit and the Vedas?
Then have thy bent unleash'd.

Passage to you, your shores, ye aged fierce enigmas!
Passage to you, to mastership of you, ye strangling problems!

You, strew'd with the wrecks of skeletons, that, living, never
    reach'd you.

Passage to more than India!
O secret of the earth and sky!
Of you O waters of the sea! O winding creeks and rivers!
Of you O woods and fields! of you strong mountains of my
    land!
Of you O prairies! of you gray rocks!
O morning red! O clouds! O rain and snows!
O day and night, passage to you!

O sun and moon and all you stars! Sirius and Jupiter!
Passage to you!

Passage, immediate passage! the blood burns in my veins!
Away O soul! hoist instantly the anchor!
Cut the hawsers—haul out—shake out every sail!
Have we not stood here like trees in the ground long enough?
Have we not grovel'd here long enough, eating and drinking
    like mere brutes?
Have we not darken'd and dazed ourselves with books long
    enough?

Sail forth—steer for the deep waters only,
Reckless O soul, exploring, I with thee, and thou with me,
For we are bound where mariner has not yet dared to go,
And we will risk the ship, ourselves and all.

O my brave soul!
O farther farther sail!
O daring joy, but safe! are they not all the seas of God?
O farther, farther, farther sail!

THE SLEEPERS

1

I wander all night in my vision,
Stepping with light feet, swiftly and noiselessly stepping and
     stopping,
Bending with open eyes over the shut eyes of sleepers,
Wandering and confused, lost to myself, ill-assorted, contra-
     dictory,
Pausing, gazing, bending, and stopping.

How solemn they look there, stretch'd and still,
How quiet they breathe, the little children in their cradles.

The wretched features of ennuyés, the white features of
     corpses, the livid faces of drunkards, the sick-gray faces
     of onanists,
The gash'd bodies on battle-fields, the insane in their strong-
     door'd rooms, the sacred idiots, the new-born emerging
     from gates, and the dying emerging from gates,
The night pervades them and infolds them.

The married couple sleep calmly in their bed, he with his
     palm on the hip of the wife, and she with her palm on
     the hip of the husband,
The sisters sleep lovingly side by side in their bed,
The men sleep lovingly side by side in theirs,
And the mother sleeps with her little child carefully wrapt.

The blind sleep, and the deaf and dumb sleep,
The prisoner sleeps well in the prison, the runaway son sleeps,

The murderer that is to be hung next day, how does he sleep?
And the murder'd person, how does he sleep?

The female that loves unrequited sleeps,
And the male that loves unrequited sleeps,
The head of the money maker that plotted all day sleeps,
And the enraged and treacherous dispositions, all, all sleep.

I stand in the dark with drooping eyes by the worst-suffering
        and the most restless,
I pass my hands soothingly to and fro a few inches from
        them,
The restless sink in their beds, they fitfully sleep.

Now I pierce the darkness, new beings appear,
The earth recedes from me into the night,
I saw that it was beautiful, and I see that what is not the
        earth is beautiful.

I go from bedside to bedside, I sleep close with the other
        sleepers each in turn,
I dream in my dream all the dreams of the other dreamers,
And I become the other dreamers.

I am a dance—play up there! the fit is whirling me fast!
I am the ever-laughing—it is new moon and twilight,
I see the hiding of douceurs, I see nimble ghosts whichever
        way I look,
Cache and cache again deep in the ground and sea, and
        where it is neither ground nor sea.

Well do they do their jobs those journeymen divine,
Only from me can they hide nothing, and would not if they
        could,
I reckon I am their boss and they make me a pet besides,
And surround me and lead me and run ahead when I walk,
To lift their cunning covers to signify me with stretch'd arms,
        and resume the way;

Onward we move, a gay gang of blackguards! with mirth-
shouting music and wild-flapping pennants of joy!

I am the actor, the actress, the voter, the politician,
The emigrant and the exile, the criminal that stood in the box,
He who has been famous and he who shall be famous after
to-day,
The stammerer, the well-form'd person, the wasted or feeble
person.

I am she who adorn'd herself and folded her hair expectantly,
My truant lover has come, and it is dark.

Double yourself and receive me darkness,
Receive me and my lover too, he will not let me go without
him.
I roll myself upon you as upon a bed, I resign myself to the
dusk.

He whom I call answers me and takes the place of my lover,
He rises with me silently from the bed.

Darkness, you are gentler than my lover, his flesh was sweaty
and panting,
I feel the hot moisture yet that he left me.

My hands are spread forth, I pass them in all directions,
I would sound up the shadowy shore to which you are journeying.

Be careful darkness! already what was it touch'd me?
I thought my lover had gone, else darkness and he are one,
I hear the heart-beat, I follow, I fade away.

2

I descend my western course, my sinews are flaccid,
Perfume and youth course through me and I am their wake.

It is my face yellow and wrinkled instead of the old woman's,
I sit low in a straw-bottom chair and carefully darn my grand-
     son's stockings.

It is I too, the sleepless widow looking out on the winter mid-
     night,
I see the sparkles of starshine on the icy and pallid earth.

A shroud I see and I am the shroud, I wrap a body and lie in
     the coffin,
It is dark here under ground, it is not evil or pain here, it is
     blank here, for reasons.

(It seems to me that every thing in the light and air ought to
     be happy,
Whoever is not in his coffin and the dark grave let him know
     he has enough.)

3

I see a beautiful gigantic swimmer swimming naked through
     the eddies of the sea,
His brown hair lies close and even to his head, he strikes out
     with courageous arms, he urges himself with his legs,
I see his white body, I see his undaunted eyes,
I hate the swift-running eddies that would dash him
     head-foremost on the rocks.

What are you doing you ruffianly red-trickled waves?
Will you kill the courageous giant? will you kill him in the
     prime of his middle age?

Steady and long he struggles,
He is baffled, bang'd, bruis'd, he holds out while his strength
     holds out,
The slapping eddies are spotted with his blood, they bear him
     away, they roll him, swing him, turn him,

His beautiful body is borne in the circling eddies, it is con-
　　tinually bruis'd on rocks,
Swiftly and out of sight is borne the brave corpse.

4

I turn but do not extricate myself,
Confused, a past-reading, another, but with darkness yet.

The beach is cut by the razory ice-wind, the wreck-guns
　　sound,
The tempest lulls, the moon comes floundering through the
　　drifts.

I look where the ship helplessly heads end on, I hear the
　　burst as she strikes, I hear the howls of dismay, they
　　grow fainter and fainter.

I cannot aid with my wringing fingers,
I can but rush to the surf and let it drench me and freeze
　　upon me.

I search with the crowd, not one of the company is wash'd to
　　us alive,
In the morning I help pick up the dead and lay them in rows
　　in a barn.

5

Now of the older war-days, the defeat at Brooklyn,
Washington stands inside the lines, he stands on the in-
　　trench'd hills amid a crowd of officers,
His face is cold and damp, he cannot repress the weeping
　　drops,
He lifts the glass perpetually to his eyes, the color is blanch'd
　　from his cheeks,
He sees the slaughter of the southern braves confided to him
　　by their parents.

The same at last and at last when peace is declared,

He stands in the room of the old tavern, the well-belov'd soldiers all pass through,

The officers speechless and slow draw near in their turns,

The chief encircles their necks with his arm and kisses them on the cheek,

He kisses lightly the wet cheeks one after another, he shakes hands and bids good-by to the army.

6

Now what my mother told me one day as we sat at dinner together,

Of when she was a nearly grown girl living home with her parents on the old homestead.

A red squaw came one breakfast-time to the old homestead,

On her back she carried a bundle of rushes for rush-bottoming chairs,

Her hair, straight, shiny, coarse, black, profuse, half-envelop'd her face,

Her step was free and elastic, and her voice sounded exquisitely as she spoke.

My mother look'd in delight and amazement at the stranger,

She look'd at the freshness of her tall-borne face and full and pliant limbs,

The more she look'd upon her she loved her,

Never before had she seen such wonderful beauty and purity,

She made her sit on a bench by the jamb of the fireplace, she cook'd food for her,

She had no work to give her, but she gave her remembrance and fondness.

The red squaw staid all the forenoon, and toward the middle of the afternoon she went away,

O my mother was loth to have her go away,

All the week she thought of her, she watch'd for her many a
    month,
She remember'd her many a winter and many a summer,
But the red squaw never came nor was heard of there again.

7

A show of the summer softness—a contact of something un-
    seen—an amour of the light and air,
I am jealous and overwhelm'd with friendliness,
And will go gallivant with the light and air myself.

O love and summer, you are in the dreams and in me,
Autumn and winter are in the dreams, the farmer goes with
    his thrift,
The droves and crops increase, the barns are well-fill'd.

Elements merge in the night, ships make tacks in the dreams,
The sailor sails, the exile returns home,
The fugitive returns unharm'd, the immigrant is back beyond
    months and years,
The poor Irishman lives in the simple house of his childhood
    with the well-known neighbors and faces,
They warmly welcome him, he is barefoot again, he forgets
    he is well off,
The Dutchman voyages home, and the Scotchman and Welsh-
    man voyage home, and the native of the Mediterranean
    voyages home,
To every port of England, France, Spain, enter well-fill'd
    ships,
The Swiss foots it toward his hills, the Prussian goes his way,
    the Hungarian his way, and the Pole his way,
The Swede returns, and the Dane and Norwegian return.

The homeward bound and the outward bound,
The beautiful lost swimmer, the ennuyé, the onanist, the fe-
    male that loves unrequited, the money-maker,

The actor and actress, those through with their parts and
    those waiting to commence,
The affectionate boy, the husband and wife, the voter, the
    nominee that is chosen and the nominee that has fail'd,
The great already known and the great any time after to-day,
The stammerer, the sick, the perfect-form'd, the homely,
The criminal that stood in the box, the judge that sat and sen-
    tenced him, the fluent lawyers, the jury, the audience,
The laugher and weeper, the dancer, the midnight widow,
    the red squaw,
The consumptive, the erysipalite, the idiot, he that is wrong'd,
The antipodes, and every one between this and them in the
    dark,
I swear they are averaged now—one is no better than the
    other,
The night and sleep have liken'd them and restored them.

I swear they are all beautiful,
Every one that sleeps is beautiful, every thing in the dim
    light is beautiful,
The wildest and bloodiest is over, and all is peace.

Peace is always beautiful,
The myth of heaven indicates peace and night.

The myth of heaven indicates the soul,
The soul is always beautiful, it appears more or it appears
    less, it comes or it lags behind,
It comes from its embower'd garden and looks pleasantly on
    itself and encloses the world,
Perfect and clean the genitals previously jetting, and perfect
    and clean the womb cohering,
The head well-grown proportion'd and plumb, and the bowels
    and joints proportion'd and plumb.

The soul is always beautiful,
The universe is duly in order, every thing is in its place,

What has arrived is in its place and what waits shall be in its
　　　place,
The twisted skull waits, the watery or rotten blood waits,
The child of the glutton or venerealee waits long, and the
　　　child of the drunkard waits long, and the drunkard
　　　himself waits long,
The sleepers that lived and died wait, the far advanced are
　　　to go on in their turns, and the far behind are to come
　　　on in their turns,
The diverse shall be no less diverse, but they shall flow and
　　　unite—they unite now.

8

The sleepers are very beautiful as they lie unclothed,
They flow hand in hand over the whole earth from east to
　　　west as they lie unclothed,
The Asiatic and African are hand in hand, the European and
　　　American are hand in hand,
Learn'd and unlearn'd are hand in hand, and male and fe-
　　　male are hand in hand,
The bare arm of the girl crosses the bare breast of her lover,
　　　they press close without lust, his lips press her neck,
The father holds his grown or ungrown son in his arms with
　　　measureless love, and the son holds the father in his
　　　arms with measureless love,
The white hair of the mother shines on the white wrist of the
　　　daughter,
The breath of the boy goes with the breath of the man, friend
　　　is inarm'd by friend,
The scholar kisses the teacher and the teacher kisses the
　　　scholar, the wrong'd is made right,
The call of the slave is one with the master's call, and the
　　　master salutes the slave,
The felon steps forth from the prison, the insane becomes
　　　sane, the suffering of sick persons is reliev'd,
The sweatings and fevers stop, the throat that was unsound is

sound, the lungs of the consumptive are resumed, the
  poor distress'd head is free,
The joints of the rheumatic move as smoothly as ever, and
  smoother than ever,
Stiflings and passages open, the paralyzed become supple,
The swell'd and convuls'd and congested awake to themselves
  in condition,
They pass the invigoration of the night and the chemistry of
  the night, and awake.

I too pass from the night,
I stay a while away O night, but I return to you again and
  love you.

Why should I be afraid to trust myself to you?
I am not afraid, I have been well brought forward by you,
I love the rich running day, but I do not desert her in whom
  I lay so long,
I know not how I came of you and I know not where I go
  with you, but I know I came well and shall go well.

I will stop only a time with the night, and rise betimes,
I will duly pass the day O my mother, and duly return to you.

TRANSPOSITIONS

Let the reformers descend from the stands where they are
  forever bawling—let an idiot or insane person appear
  on each of the stands;

Let judges and criminals be transposed—let the prison-keep-
    ers be put in prison—let those that were prisoners take
    the keys;
Let them that distrust birth and death lead the rest.

TO THINK of TIME

1

To think of time—of all that retrospection,
To think of to-day, and the ages continued henceforward.

Have you guess'd you yourself would not continue?
Have you dreaded these earth-beetles?
Have you fear'd the future would be nothing to you?

Is to-day nothing? is the beginningless past nothing?
If the future is nothing they are just as surely nothing.

To think that the sun rose in the east—that men and women
    were flexible, real, alive—that every thing was alive,
To think that you and I did not see, feel, think, nor bear our
    part,
To think that we are now here and bear our part.

2

Not a day passes, not a minute or second without an ac-
    couchement,
Not a day passes, not a minute or second without a corpse.

The dull nights go over and the dull days also,
The soreness of lying so much in bed goes over,

The physician after long putting off gives the silent and ter-
  rible look for an answer,
The children come hurried and weeping, and the brothers and
  sisters are sent for,
Medicines stand unused on the shelf, (the camphor-smell has
  long pervaded the rooms,)
The faithful hand of the living does not desert the hand of
  the dying,
The twitching lips press lightly on the forehead of the dying,
The breath ceases and the pulse of the heart ceases,
The corpse stretches on the bed and the living look upon it,
It is palpable as the living are palpable.

The living look upon the corpse with their eyesight,
But without eyesight lingers a different living and looks
  curiously on the corpse.

3

To think the thought of death merged in the thought of materials,
To think of all these wonders of city and country, and others
  taking great interest in them, and we taking no interest in them.

To think how eager we are in building our houses,
To think others shall be just as eager, and we quite indifferent.

(I see one building the house that serves him a few years,
  or seventy or eighty years at most,
I see one building the house that serves him longer than that.)

Slow-moving and black lines creep over the whole earth—
  they never cease—they are the burial lines,
He that was President was buried, and he that is now President shall surely be buried.

4

A reminiscence of the vulgar fate,
A frequent sample of the life and death of workmen,
Each after his kind.

Cold dash of waves at the ferry-wharf, posh and ice in the
     river, half-frozen mud in the streets,
A gray discouraged sky overhead, the short last daylight of
     December,
A hearse and stages, the funeral of an old Broadway stage-
     driver, the cortege mostly drivers.

Steady the trot to the cemetery, duly rattles the death-bell,
The gate is pass'd, the new-dug grave is halted at, the living
     alight, the hearse uncloses,
The coffin is pass'd out, lower'd and settled, the whip is laid
     on the coffin, the earth is swiftly shovel'd in,
The mound above is flatted with the spades—silence,
A minute—no one moves or speaks—it is done,
He is decently put away—is there any thing more?

He was a good fellow, free-mouth'd, quick-temper'd, not bad-
     looking,
Ready with life or death for a friend, fond of women, gam-
     bled, ate hearty, drank hearty,
Had known what it was to be flush, grew low-spirited toward
     the last, sicken'd, was help'd by a contribution,
Died, aged forty-one years—and that was his funeral.

Thumb extended, finger uplifted, apron, cape, gloves, strap,
     wet-weather clothes, whip carefully chosen,
Boss, spotter, starter, hostler, somebody loafing on you, you
     loafing on somebody, headway, man before and man
     behind,
Good day's work, bad day's work, pet stock, mean stock, first
     out, last out, turning-in at night,
To think that these are so much and so nigh to other drivers,
     and he there takes no interest in them.

5

The market, the government, the working-man's wages, to
    think what account they are through our nights and
    days,
To think that other working-men will make just as great ac
    count of them, yet we make little or no account.

The vulgar and the refined, what you call sin and what you
    call goodness, to think how wide a difference,
To think the difference will still continue to others, yet we
    lie beyond the difference.

To think how much pleasure there is,
Do you enjoy yourself in the city? or engaged in business? or
    planning a nomination and election? or with your wife
    and family?
Or with your mother and sisters? or in womanly housework?
    or the beautiful maternal cares?
These also flow onward to others, you and I flow onward,
But in due time you and I shall take less interest in them.

Your farm, profits, crops—to think how engross'd you are,
To think there will still be farms, profits, crops, yet for you
    of what avail?

6

What will be will be well, for what is is well,
To take interest is well, and not to take interest shall be well.

The domestic joys, the daily housework or business, the build-
    ing of houses, are not phantasms, they have weight,
    form, location,
Farms, profits, crops, markets, wages, government, are none
    of them phantasms,
The difference between sin and goodness is no delusion,

The earth is not an echo, man and his life and all the things
of his life are well-consider'd.

You are not thrown to the winds, you gather certainly and
safely around yourself,
Yourself! yourself! yourself, for ever and ever!

7

It is not to diffuse you that you were born of your mother
and father, it is to identify you,
It is not that you should be undecided, but that you should
be decided,
Something long preparing and formless is arrived and form'd
in you,
You are henceforth secure, whatever comes or goes.

The threads that were spun are gather'd, the weft crosses the
warp, the pattern is systematic.
The preparations have every one been justified,
The orchestra have sufficiently tuned their instruments, the
baton has given the signal.

The guest that was coming, he waited long, he is now housed,
He is one of those who are beautiful and happy, he is one
of those that to look upon and be with is enough.

The law of the past cannot be eluded,
The law of the present and future cannot be eluded,
The law of the living cannot be eluded, it is eternal,
The law of promotion and transformation cannot be eluded,
The law of heroes and good-doers cannot be eluded,
The law of drunkards, informers, mean persons, not one iota
thereof can be eluded.

8

Slow moving and black lines go ceaselessly over the earth,

Northerner goes carried and Southerner goes carried, and they
 on the Atlantic side and they on the Pacific,
And they between, and all through the Mississippi country,
 and all over the earth.

The great masters and kosmos are well as they go, the heroes
 and good-doers are well,
The known leaders and inventors and the rich owners and
 pious and distinguish'd may be well,
But there is more account than that, there is strict account
 of all.

The interminable hordes of the ignorant and wicked are not
 nothing,
The barbarians of Africa and Asia are not nothing,
The perpetual successions of shallow people are not nothing
 as they go.

Of and in all these things,
I have dream'd that we are not to be changed so much, nor
 the law of us changed,
I have dream'd that heroes and good-doers shall be under
 the present and past law,
And that murderers, drunkards, liars, shall be under the present and past law,
For I have dream'd that the law they are under now is
 enough.

And I have dream'd that the purpose and essence of the
 known life, the transient,
Is to form and decide identity for the unknown life, the permanent.

If all came but to ashes of dung,
If maggots and rats ended us, then Alarum! for we are be-
 tray'd,
Then indeed suspicion of death.

Do you suspect death? if I were to suspect death I should
    die now,
Do you think I could walk pleasantly and well-suited toward
    annihilation?

Pleasantly and well-suited I walk,
Whither I walk I cannot define, but I know it is good,
The whole universe indicates that it is good,
The past and the present indicate that it is good.

How beautiful and perfect are the animals!
How perfect the earth, and the minutest thing upon it!
What is called good is perfect, and what is called bad is just
    as perfect,
The vegetables and minerals are all perfect, and the impon-
    derable fluids perfect;
Slowly and surely they have pass'd on to this, and slowly and
    surely they yet pass on.

9

I swear I think now that every thing without exception has
    an eternal soul!
The trees have, rooted in the ground! the weeds of the sea
    have! the animals!

I swear I think there is nothing but immortality!
That the exquisite scheme is for it, and the nebulous float is
    for it, and the cohering is for it!
And all preparation is for it—and identity is for it—and life
    and materials are altogether for it!

THOU MOTHER with THY EQUAL BROOD

1

Thou Mother with thy equal brood,
Thou varied chain of different States, yet one identity only,
A special song before I go I'd sing o'er all the rest,
For thee, the future.

I'd sow a seed for thee of endless Nationality,
I'd fashion thy ensemble including body and soul,
I'd show away ahead thy real Union, and how it may be ac-
    complish'd.

The paths to the house I seek to make,
But leave to those to come the house itself.

Belief I sing, and preparation;
As Life and Nature are not great with reference to the pres-
    ent only,
But greater still from what is yet to come,
Out of that formula for thee I sing.

2

As a strong bird on pinions free,
Joyous, the amplest spaces heavenward cleaving,
Such be the thought I'd think of thee America,
Such be the recitative I'd bring for thee.

The conceits of the poets of other lands I'd bring thee not,
Nor the compliments that have served their turn so long,

Nor rhyme, nor the classics, nor perfume of foreign court or
    indoor library;
But an odor I'd bring as from forests of pine in Maine, or
    breath of an Illinois prairie,
With open airs of Virginia or Georgia or Tennessee, or from
    Texas uplands, or Florida's glades,
Or the Saguenay's black stream, or the wide blue spread of
    Huron,
With presentment of Yellowstone's scene, or Yosemite,
And murmuring under, pervading all, I'd bring the rustling
    sea-sound,
That endlessly sounds from the two Great Seas of the world.

And for thy subtler sense subtler refrains dread Mother,
Preludes of intellect tallying these and thee, mind-formulas
    fitted for thee, real and sane and large as these and
    thee,
Thou! mounting higher, diving deeper than we knew, thou
    transcendental Union!
By thee fact to be justified, blended with thought,
Thought of man justified, blended with God,
Through thy idea, lo, the immortal reality!
Through thy reality, lo, the immortal idea!

3

Brain of the New World, what a task is thine,
To formulate the Modern—out of the peerless grandeur of
    the modern,
Out of thyself, comprising science, to recast poems, churches,
    art,
(Recast, may-be discard them, end them—may-be their work
    is done, who knows?)
By vision, hand, conception, on the background of the mighty
    past, the dead,·
To limn with absolute faith the mighty living present.

And yet thou living present brain heir of the dead, the Old
    World brain,
Thou that lay folded like an unborn babe within its folds so
    long,
Thou carefully prepared by it so long—haply thou but unfold-
    est it, only maturest it,
It to eventuate in thee—the essence of the by-gone time con-
    tain'd in thee,
Its poems, churches, arts, unwitting to themselves, destined
    with reference to thee;
Thou but the apples, long, long, long a-growing,
The fruit of all the Old ripening to-day in thee.

4

Sail, sail thy best, ship of Democracy,
Of value is thy freight, 'tis not the Present only,
The Past is also stored in thee,
Thou holdest not the venture of thyself alone, not of the
    Western continent alone,
Earth's *résumé* entire floats on thy keel O ship, is steadied by
    thy spars,
With thee Time voyages in trust, the antecedent nations sink
    or swim with thee,
With all their ancient struggles, martyrs, heroes, epics, wars,
    thou bear'st the other continents,
Theirs, theirs as much as thine, the destination-port trium-
    phant;
Steer then with good strong hand and wary eye O helmsman,
    thou carriest great companions,
Venerable priestly Asia sails this day with thee,
And royal feudal Europe sails with thee.

5

Beautiful world of new superber birth that rises to my eyes,
Like a limitless golden cloud filling the western sky,
Emblem of general maternity lifted above all,

Sacred shape of the bearer of daughters and sons,
Out of thy teeming womb thy giant babes in ceaseless procession issuing,
Acceding from such gestation, taking and giving continual strength and life,
World of the real—world of the twain in one,
World of the soul, born by the world of the real alone, led to identity, body, by it alone,
Yet in beginning only, incalculable masses of composite precious materials,
By history's cycles forwarded, by every nation, language, hither sent,
Ready, collected here, a freer, vast, electric world, to be constructed here,
(The true New World, the world of orbic science, morals, literatures to come,)
Thou wonder world yet undefined, unform'd, neither do I define thee,
How can I pierce the impenetrable blank of the future?
I feel thy ominous greatness evil as well as good,
I watch thee advancing, absorbing the present, transcending the past,
I see thy light lighting, and thy shadow shadowing, as if the entire globe,
But I do not undertake to define thee, hardly to comprehend thee,
I but thee name, thee prophesy, as now,
I merely thee ejaculate!

Thee in thy future,
Thee in thy only permanent life, career, thy own unloosen'd mind, thy soaring spirit,
Thee as another equally needed sun, radiant, ablaze, swift-moving, fructifying all,
Thee risen in potent, cheerfulness and joy, in endless great hilarity,
Scattering for good the cloud that hung so long, that weigh'd so long upon the mind of man,

The doubt, suspicion, dread, of gradual, certain decadence
    of man;
Thee in thy larger, saner brood of female, male—thee in thy
    athletes, moral, spiritual, South, North, West, East,
(To thy immortal breasts, Mother of All, thy every daughter,
    son, endear'd alike, forever equal,)
Thee in thy own musicians, singers, artists, unborn yet, but
    certain,
Thee in thy moral wealth and civilization, (until which thy
    proudest material civilization must remain in vain,)
Thee in thy all-supplying, all-enclosing worship—thee in no
    single bible, saviour, merely,
Thy saviours countless, latent within thyself, thy bibles in-
    cessant within thyself, equal to any, divine as any,
(Thy soaring course thee formulating, not in thy two great
    wars, nor in thy century's visible growth,
But far more in these leaves and chants, thy chants, great
    Mother!)
Thee in an education grown of thee, in teachers, studies, stu-
    dents, born of thee,
Thee in thy democratic fêtes en-masse, thy high original fes-
    tivals, operas, lecturers, preachers,
Thee in thy ultimata, (the preparations only now completed,
    the edifice on sure foundations tied,)
Thee in thy pinnacles, intellect, thought, thy topmost rational
    joys, thy love and godlike aspiration,
In thy resplendent coming literati, thy full-lung'd orators, thy
    sacerdotal bards, kosmic savans,
These! these in thee, (certain to come,) to-day I prophesy.

6

Land tolerating all, accepting all, not for the good alone, all
    good for thee,
Land in the realms of God to be a realm unto thyself,
Under the rule of God to be a rule unto thyself.

(Lo, where arise three peerless stars,
To be thy natal stars my country, Ensemble, Evolution, Free-
     dom,
Set in the sky of Law.)

Land of unprecedented faith, God's faith,
Thy soil, thy very subsoil, all upheav'd,
The general inner earth so long so sedulously draped over,
     now hence for what it is boldly laid bare,
Open'd by thee to heaven's light for benefit or bale.

Not for success alone,
Not to fair-sail unintermitted always,
The storm shall dash thy face, the murk of war and worse
     than war shall cover thee all over,
(Wert capable of war, its tug and trials? be capable of peace,
     its trials,
For the tug and mortal strain of nations come at last in pros-
     perous peace, not war;)
In many a smiling mask death shall approach beguiling thee,
     thou in disease shalt swelter,
The livid cancer spread its hideous claws, clinging upon thy
     breasts, seeking to strike thee deep within,
Consumption of the worst, moral consumption, shall rouge
     thy face with hectic,
But thou shalt face thy fortunes, thy diseases, and surmount
     them all,
Whatever they are to-day and whatever through time they
     may be,
They each and all shall lift and pass away and cease from
     thee,
While thou, Time's spirals rounding, out of thyself, thyself
     still extricating, fusing,
Equable, natural, mystical Union thou, (the mortal with im-
     mortal blent,)
Shalt soar toward the fulfilment of the future, the spirit of
     the body and the mind,
The soul, its destinies.

The soul, its destinies, the real real,
(Purport of all these apparitions of the real;)
In thee America, the soul, its destinies,
Thou globe of globes! thou wonder nebulous!
By many a throe of heat and cold convuls'd, (by these thy-
      self solidifying,)
Thou mental, moral orb—thou New, indeed new, Spiritual
      World!
The Present holds thee not—for such vast growth as thine,
For such unparallel'd flight as thine, such brood as thine,
The FUTURE only holds thee and can hold thee.

FROM NOON *to* STARRY NIGHT

THOU ORB ALOFT FULL-DAZZLING

Thou orb aloft full-dazzling! thou hot October noon!
Flooding with sheeny light the gray beach sand,
The sibilant near sea with vistas far and foam,
And tawny streaks and shades and spreading blue;
O sun of noon refulgent! my special word to thee.

Hear me illustrious!
Thy lover me, for always I have loved thee,
Even as basking babe, then happy boy alone by some wood
      edge, thy touching-distant beams enough,
Or man matured, or young or old, as now to thee I launch my
      invocation.

(Thou canst not with thy dumbness me deceive,
I know before the fitting man all Nature yields,

Though answering not in words, the skies, trees, hear his
      voice—and thou O sun,
As for thy throes, thy perturbations, sudden breaks and shafts
      of flame gigantic,
I understand them, I know those flames, those perturbations
      well.)

Thou that with fructifying heat and light,
O'er myriad farms, o'er lands and waters North and South,
O'er Mississippi's endless course, o'er Texas' grassy plains,
      Kanada's woods,
O'er all the globe that turns its face to thee shining in space,
Thou that impartially infoldest all, not only continents, seas,
Thou that to grapes and weeds and little wild flowers givest
      so liberally,
Shed, shed thyself on mine and me, with but a fleeting ray
      out of thy million millions,
Strike through these chants.

Nor only launch thy subtle dazzle and thy strength for these,
Prepare the later afternoon of me myself—prepare my length-
      ening shadows,
Prepare my starry nights.

WEAVE IN, MY HARDY LIFE

Weave in, weave in, my hardy life,
Weave yet a soldier strong and full for great campaigns to
      come,
Weave in red blood, weave sinews in like ropes, the senses,
      sight weave in,
Weave lasting sure, weave day and night the weft, the warp,
      incessant weave, tire not,
(We know not what the use O life, nor know the aim, the
      end, nor really aught we know,

But know the work, the need goes on and shall go on, the
    death-envelop'd march of peace as well as war goes on,)
For great campaigns of peace the same the wiry threads to
    weave,
We know not why or what, yet weave, forever weave.

SPAIN, 1873–74

Out of the murk of heaviest clouds,
Out of the feudal wrecks and heap'd-up skeletons of kings,
Out of that old entire European debris, the shatter'd mum-
    meries,
Ruin'd cathedrals, crumble of palaces, tombs of priests,
Lo, Freedom's features fresh undimm'd look forth—the same
    immortal face looks forth;
(A glimpse as of thy Mother's face Columbia,
A flash significant as of a sword,
Beaming towards thee.)

Nor think we forget thee maternal;
Lag'd'st thou so long? shall the clouds close again upon thee?
Ah, but thou hast thyself now appear'd to us—we know thee,
Thou hast given us a sure proof, the glimpse of thyself,
Thou waitest there as everywhere thy time.

BY BROAD POTOMAC'S SHORE

By broad Potomac's shore, again old tongue,
(Still uttering, still ejaculating, canst never cease this bab-
    ble?)
Again old heart so gay, again to you, your sense, the full flush
    spring returning,
Again the freshness and the odors, again Virginia's summer
    sky, pellucid blue and silver,
Again the forenoon purple of the hills,

Again the deathless grass, so noiseless soft and green,
Again the blood-red roses blooming.

Perfume this book of mine O blood-red roses!
Lave subtly with your waters every line Potomac!
Give me of you O spring, before I close, to put between its
      pages!
O forenoon purple of the hills, before I close, of you!
O deathless grass, of you!

OLD WAR-DREAMS

In midnight sleep of many a face of anguish,
Of the look at first of the mortally wounded, (of that inde-
      scribable look,)
Of the dead on their backs with arms extended wide,
         I dream, I dream, I dream.

Of scenes of Nature, fields and mountains,
Of skies so beauteous after a storm, and at night the moon so
      unearthly bright,
Shining sweetly, shining down, where we dig the trenches
      and gather the heaps,
         I dream, I dream, I dream.

Long have they pass'd, faces and trenches and fields,
Where through the carnage I moved with a callous com-
      posure, or away from the fallen,
Onward I sped at the time—but now of their forms at night,
         I dream, I dream, I dream.

THICK-SPRINKLED BUNTING

Thick-sprinkled bunting! flag of stars!
Long yet your road, fateful flag—long yet your road, and
      lined with bloody death,

For the prize I see at issue at last is the world,
All it ships and shores I see interwoven with your threads
     greedy banner;
Dream'd again the flags of kings, highest borne, to flaunt un-
     rival'd?
O hasten flag of man—O with sure and steady step, passing
     highest flags of kings,
Walk supreme to the heavens mighty symbol—run up above
     them all,
Flag of stars! thick-sprinkled bunting!

WHAT BEST I SEE IN THEE

To U. S. G. return'd from his World's Tour

What best I see in thee,
Is not that where thou mov'st down history's great highways,
Ever undimm'd by time shoots warlike victory's dazzle,
Or that thou sat'st where Washington sat, ruling the land in
     peace,
Or thou the man whom feudal Europe feted, venerable Asia
     swarm'd upon,
Who walk'd with kings with even pace the round world's
     promenade;
But that in foreign lands, in all thy walks with kings,
Those prairie sovereigns of the West, Kansas, Missouri, Illi-
     nois,
Ohio's, Indiana's millions, comrades, farmers, soldiers, all to
     the front,
Invisibly with thee walking with kings with even pace the
     round world's promenade,
Were all so justified.

AS I WALK THESE BROAD MAJESTIC
DAYS

As I walk these broad majestic days of peace,
(For the war, the struggle of blood finish'd, wherein, O ter-
    rific Ideal,
Against vast odds erewhile having gloriously won,
Now thou stridest on, yet perhaps in time toward denser wars,
Perhaps to engage in time in still more dreadful contests,
    dangers,
Longer campaigns and crises, labors beyond all others,)
Around me I hear that eclat of the world, politics, produce,
The announcements of recognized things, science,
The approved growth of cities and the spread of inventions.

I see the ships, (they will last a few years,)
The vast factories with their foremen and workmen,
And hear the indorsement of all, and do not object to it.

But I too announce solid things,
Science, ships, politics, cities, factories, are not nothing,
Like a grand procession to music of distant bugles pouring,
    triumphantly moving, and grander heaving in sight,
They stand for realities—all is as it should be.

Then my realities;
What else is so real as mine?
Libertad and the divine average, freedom to every slave on
    the face of the earth,
The rapt promises and luminè of seers, the spiritual world,
    these centuries-lasting songs,
And our visions, the visions of poets, the most solid announce-
    ments of any.

SPIRIT THAT FORM'D THIS SCENE

Written in Platte Cañon, Colorado

Spirit that form'd this scene,
These tumbled rock-piles grim and red,
These reckless heaven-ambition peaks,
These gorges, turbulent-clear streams, this naked freshness,
These formless wild arrays, for reasons of their own,
I know thee, savage spirit—we have communed together,
Mine too such wild arrays, for reasons of their own;
Was't charged against my chants they had forgotten art?
To fuse within themselves its rules precise and delicatesse?
The lyrist's measur'd beat, the wrought-out temple's grace—
      column and polish'd arch forgot?
But thou that revelest here—spirit that form'd this scene,
They have remember'd thee.

A CLEAR MIDNIGHT

This is thy hour O soul, thy free flight into the wordless,
Away from books, away from art, the day erased, the lesson
      done,
Thee fully forth emerging, silent, gazing, pondering the
      themes thou lovest best,
Night, sleep, death and the stars.

SONGS of PARTING

AS THE TIME DRAWS NIGH

As the time draws nigh glooming a cloud,
A dread beyond of I know not what darkens me.

I shall go forth,
I shall traverse the States awhile, but I cannot tell whither or
    how long,
Perhaps soon some day or night while I am singing my voice
    will suddenly cease.

O book, O chants! must all then amount to but this?
Must we barely arrive at this beginning of us?—and yet it is
    enough, O soul;
O soul, we have positively appear'd—that is enough.

YEARS OF THE MODERN

Years of the modern! years of the unperform'd!
Your horizon rises, I see it parting away for more august
    dramas,
I see not America only, not only Liberty's nation but other
    nations preparing,
I see tremendous entrances and exits, new combinations, the
    solidarity of races,
I see that force advancing with irresistible power on the
    world's stage,

(Have the old forces, the old wars, played their parts? are
    the acts suitable to them closed?)

I see Freedom, completely arm'd and victorious and very
    haughty, with Law on one side and Peace on the
    other,

A stupendous trio all issuing forth against the idea of caste;

What historic denouements are these we so rapidly approach?

I see men marching and countermarching by swift millions,

I see the frontiers and boundaries of the old aristocracies
    broken,

I see the landmarks of European kings removed,

I see this day the People beginning their landmarks, (all
    others give way;)

Never were such sharp questions ask'd as this day,

Never was average man, his soul, more energetic, more like a
    God,

Lo, how he urges and urges, leaving the masses no rest!

His daring foot is on land and sea everywhere, he colonizes
    the Pacific, the archipelagoes,

With the steamship, the electric telegraph, the newspaper, the
    wholesale engines of war,

With these and the world-spreading factories he interlinks all
    geography, all lands;

What whispers are these O lands, running ahead of you, pass-
    ing under the seas?

Are all nations communing? is there going to be but one heart
    to the globe?

Is humanity forming en-masse? for lo, tyrants tremble, crowns
    grow dim,

The earth, restive, confronts a new era, perhaps a general
    divine war,

No one knows what will happen next, such portents fill the
    days and nights;

Years prophetical! the space ahead as I walk, as I vainly try
    to pierce it, is full of phantoms,

Unborn deeds, thing soon to be, project their shapes around
    me,

This incredible rush and heat, this strange ecstatic fever of
    dreams O years!
Your dreams O years, how they penetrate through me! (I
    know not whether I sleep or wake;)
The perform'd America and Europe grow dim, retiring in
    shadow behind me,
The unperform'd, more gigantic than ever, advance, advance
    upon me.

SONG AT SUNSET

Splendor of ended day floating and filling me,
Hour prophetic, hour resuming the past,
Inflating my throat, you divine average,
You earth and life till the last ray gleams I sing.

Open mouth of my soul uttering gladness,
Eyes of my soul seeing perfection,
Natural life of me faithfully praising things,
Corroborating forever the triumph of things.

Illustrious every one!
Illustrious what we name space, sphere of unnumber'd spirits,
Illustrious the mystery of motion in all beings, even the
    tiniest insect,
Illustrious the attribute of speech, the senses, the body,
Illustrious the passing light—illustrious the pale reflection on
    the new moon in the western sky,
Illustrious whatever I see or hear or touch, to the last.

Good in all,
In the satisfaction and aplomb of animals,
In the annual return of the seasons,
In the hilarity of youth,
In the strength and flush of manhood,
In the grandeur and exquisiteness of old age,
In the superb vistas of death.

Wonderful to depart!
Wonderful to be here!
The heart, to jet the all-alike and innocent blood!
To breathe the air, how delicious!
To speak—to walk—to seize something by the hand!
To prepare for sleep, for bed, to look on my rose-color'd flesh!
To be conscious of my body, so satisfied, so large!
To be this incredible God I am!
To have gone forth among other Gods, these men and wom-
      en I love.

Wonderful how I celebrate you and myself!
How my thoughts play subtly at the spectacles around!
How the clouds pass silently overhead!
How the earth darts on and on! and how the sun, moon, stars,
      dart on and on!
How the water sports and sings! (surely it is alive!)
How the trees rise and stand up, with strong trunks, with
      branches and leaves!
(Surely there is something more in each of the trees, some
      living soul.)

O amazement of things—even the least particle!
O spirituality of things!
O strain musical flowing through ages and continents, now
      reaching me and America!
I take your strong chords, intersperse them, and cheerfully
      pass them forward.

I too carol the sun, usher'd or at noon, or as now, setting,
I too throb to the brain and beauty of the earth and of all the
      growths of the earth,
I too have felt the resistless call of myself.

As I steam'd down the Mississippi,
As I wander'd over the prairies,
As I have lived, as I have look'd through my windows my
      eyes,

As I went forth in the morning, as I beheld the light break-
　　ing in the east,
As I bathed on the beach of the Eastern Sea, and again on
　　the beach of the Western Sea,
As I roam'd the streets of inland Chicago, whatever streets I
　　have roam'd,
Or cities or silent woods, or even amid the sights of war,
Wherever I have been I have charged myself with content-
　　ment and triumph.

I sing to the last the equalities modern or old,
I sing the endless finalès of things,
I say Nature continues, glory continues,
I praise with electric voice,
For I do not see one imperfection in the universe,
And I do not see one cause or result lamentable at last in the
　　universe.

O setting sun! though the time has come,
I still warble under you, if none else does, unmitigated adora-
　　tion.

THE SOBBING OF THE BELLS

(Midnight, Sept. 19-20, 1881)

The sobbing of the bells, the sudden death-news everywhere,
The slumberers rouse, the rapport of the People,
(Full well they know that message in the darkness,
Full well return, respond within their breasts, their brains, the
　　sad reverberations,)
The passionate toll and clang—city to city, joining, sounding,
　　passing,
Those heart-beats of a Nation in the night.

MY LEGACY

The business man the acquirer vast,
After assiduous years surveying results, preparing for departure,
Devises houses and lands to his children, bequeaths stocks, goods, funds for a school or hospital,
Leaves money to certain companions to buy tokens, souvenirs of gems and gold.

But I, my life surveying, closing,
With nothing to show to devise from its idle years,
Nor houses nor lands, nor tokens of gems or gold for my friends,
Yet certain remembrances of the war for you, and after you,
And little souvenirs of camps and soldiers, with my love,
I bind together and bequeath in this bundle of songs.

JOY, SHIPMATE, JOY!

Joy, shipmate, joy!
(Pleas'd to my soul at death I cry,)
Our life is closed, our life begins,
The long, long anchorage we leave,
The ship is clear at last, she leaps!
She swiftly courses from the shore,
Joy, shipmate, joy.

THE UNTOLD WANT

The untold want by life and land ne'er granted,
Now voyager sail thou forth to seek and find.

PORTALS

What are those of the known but to ascend and enter the
  Unknown?
And what are those of life but for Death?

THESE CAROLS

These carols sung to cheer my passage through the world I
  see,
For completion I dedicate to the Invisible World.

NOW FINALÈ TO THE SHORE

Now finalè to the shore,
Now land and life finalè and farewell,
Now Voyager depart, (much, much for thee is yet in store,)
Often enough hast thou adventur'd o'er the seas,
Cautiously cruising, studying the charts,
Duly again to port and hawser's tie returning;
But now obey thy cherish'd secret wish,
Embrace thy friends, leave all in order,
To port and hawser's tie no more returning,
Depart upon thy endless cruise old Sailor.

SO LONG

To conclude, I announce what comes after me.

I remember I said before my leaves sprang at all,
I would raise my voice jocund and strong with reference to
  consummations.
When America does what was promis'd,

When through these States walk a hundred millions of su-
    perb persons,
When the rest part away for superb persons and contribute
    to them,
When breeds of the most perfect mothers denote America,
Then to me and mine our due fruition.

I have press'd through in my own right,
I have sung the body and the soul, war and peace have I
    sung, and the songs of life and death,
And the songs of birth, and shown that there are many births.

I have offer'd my style to every one, I have journey'd with
    confident step;
While my pleasure is yet at the full I whisper *So long!*
And take the young woman's hand and the young man's hand
    for the last time.

I announce natural persons to arise,
I announce justice triumphant,
I announce uncompromising liberty and equality,
I announce the justification of candor and the justification of
    pride.

I announce that the identity of these States is a single identity
    only,
I announce the Union more and more compact, indissoluble,
I announce splendors and majesties to make all the previous
    politics of the earth insignificant.

I announce adhesiveness, I say it shall be limitless, un-
    loosen'd,
I say you shall yet find the friend you were looking for.

I announce a man or woman coming, perhaps you are the
    one, *(So long!)*
I announce the great individual, fluid as Nature, chaste, affec-
    tionate, compassionate, fully arm'd.

I announce a life that shall be copious, vehement, spiritual,
  bold,
I announce an end that shall lightly and joyfully meet its
  translation.

I announce myriads of youths, beautiful, gigantic, sweet-
  blooded,
I announce a race of splendid and savage old men.

O thicker and faster—(*So long!*)
O crowding too close upon me,
I foresee too much, it means more than I thought,
It appears to me I am dying.

Hasten throat and sound your last,
Salute me—salute the days once more. Peal the old cry once
  more.

Screaming electric, the atmosphere using,
At random glancing, each as I notice absorbing,
Swiftly on, but a little while alighting,
Curious envelop'd messages delivering,
Sparkles hot, seed ethereal down in the dirt dropping,
Myself unknowing, my commission obeying, to question it
  never daring,
To ages and ages yet the growth of the seed leaving,
To troops out of the war arising, they the tasks I have set
  promulging,
To women certain whispers of myself bequeathing, their af-
  fection me more clearly explaining,
To young men my problems offering—no dallier I—I the
  muscle of their brains trying,
So I pass, a little time vocal, visible, contrary,
Afterward a melodious echo, passionately bent for, (death
  making me really undying,)
The best of me then when no longer visible, for toward that I
  have been incessantly preparing.

What is there more, that I lag and pause and crouch extended
    with unshut mouth?
Is there a single final farewell?

My songs cease, I abandon them,
From behind the screen where I hid I advance personally
    solely to you.

Camerado, this is no book,
Who touches this touches a man,
(Is it night? are we here together alone?)
It is I you hold and who holds you,
I spring from the pages into your arms—decease calls me
    forth.

O how your fingers drowse me,
Your breath falls around me like dew, your pulse lulls the
    tympans of my ears,
I feel immerged from head to foot,
Delicious, enough.

Enough O deed impromptu and secret,
Enough O gliding present—enough O summ'd-up past.

Dear friend whoever you are take this kiss,
I give it especially to you, do not forget me,
I feel like one who has done work for the day to retire
    awhile,
I receive now again of my many translations, from my ava-
    taras ascending, while others doubtless await me,
An unknown sphere more real than I dream'd, more direct,
    darts awakening rays about me, *So long!*
Remember my words, I may again return,
I love you, I depart from materials,
I am as one disembodied, triumphant, dead.

GOOD-BYE MY FANCY

PREFACE NOTE TO 2d ANNEX,

CONCLUDING L. OF G.—1891.

Had I not better withhold (in this old age and paralysis of me) such little tags and fringe-dots (maybe specks, stains,) as follow a long dusty journey, and witness it afterward? I have probably not been enough afraid of careless touches, from the first—and am not now—nor of parrot-like repetitions—nor platitudes and the commonplace. Perhaps I am too democratic for such avoidances. Besides, is not the verse-field, as originally plann'd by my theory, now sufficiently illustrated—and full time for me to silently retire?—(indeed amid no loud call or market for my sort of poetic utterance.)

In answer, or rather defiance, to that kind of well-put interrogation, here comes this little cluster, and conclusion of my preceding clusters. Though not at all clear that, as here collated, it is worth printing (certainly I have nothing fresh to write)—I while away the hours of my 72d year—hours of forced confinement in my den—by putting in shape this small old age collation:

> Last droplets of and after spontaneous rain,
> From many limpid distillations and past showers;
> (Will they germinate anything? mere exhalations as they
>   all are—the land's and sea's—America's;
> Will they filter to any deep emotion? any heart and brain?)

However that may be, I feel like improving to-day's opportunity and wind up. During the last two years I have sent out, in the lulls of illness and exhaustion, certain chirps—lingering-dying ones probably (undoubtedly)—which now I may as well gather and put in fair type while able to see correctly —(for my eyes plainly warn me they are dimming, and my brain more and more palpably neglects or refuses, month after month, even slight tasks or revisions.)

In fact, here I am these current years 1890 and '91, (each successive fortnight getting stiffer and stuck deeper) much like some hard-cased dilapidated grim ancient shell-fish or time-bang'd conch (no legs, utterly non-locomotive) cast up high and dry on the shore-sands, helpless to move anywhere— nothing left but behave myself quiet, and while away the days yet assign'd, and discover if there is anything for the said grim and time-bang'd conch to be got at last out of inherited good spirits and primal buoyant centre-pulses down there deep somewhere within his gray-blurr'd old shell....... (Reader, you must allow a little fun here—for one reason there are too many of the following poemets about death, &c., and for another the passing hours (July 5, 1890) are so sunny-fine. And old as I am I feel to-day almost a part of some frolicsome wave, or for sporting yet like a kid or kitten —probably a streak of physical adjustment and perfection here and now. I believe I have it in me perennially anyhow.)

Then behind all, the deep-down consolation (it is a glum one, but I dare not be sorry for the fact of it in the past, nor refrain from dwelling, even vaunting here at the end) that this late-years palsied old shorn and shell-fish condition of me is the indubitable outcome and growth, now near for 20 years along, of too over-zealous, over-continued bodily and emotional excitement and action through the times of 1862, '3, '4, and '5, visiting and waiting on wounded and sick army volunteers, both sides, in campaigns or contests, or after them, or in hospitals or fields south of Washington City, or in that place and elsewhere—those hot, sad, wrenching times —the army volunteers, all States,—or North or South—the wounded, suffering, dying—the exhausting, sweating summers, marches, battles, carnage—those trenches hurriedly heap'd by

the corpse-thousands, mainly unknown—Will the America of
the future—will this vast rich Union ever realize what itself
cost, back there after all?—those hecatombs of battle-deaths—
Those times of which, O far-off reader, this whole book is
indeed finally but a reminiscent memorial from thence by me
to you?

GOOD-BYE MY FANCY

Good-bye my fancy—(I had a word to say,
But 'tis not quite the time—The best of any man's word or say,
Is when its proper place arrives—and for its meaning,
I keep mine till the last.)

ON, ON THE SAME, YE JOCUND TWAIN!

On, on the same, ye jocund twain!
My life and recitative, containing birth, youth, mid-age years,
Fitful as motley-tongues of flame, inseparably twined and
     merged in one—combining all,
My single soul—aims, confirmations, failures, joys—Nor single
     soul alone,
I chant my nation's crucial stage, (America's, haply hu-
     manity's)—the trial great, the victory great,
A strange *eclaircissement* of all the masses past, the eastern
     world, the ancient, medieval,
Here, here from wanderings, strayings, lessons, wars, defeats—
     here at the west a voice triumphant—justifying all,

A gladsome pealing cry—a song for once of utmost pride and
    satisfaction;
I chant from it the common bulk, the general average horde,
    (the best no sooner than the worst)—And now I chant
    old age,
(My verses, written first for forenoon life, and for the sum-
    mer's, autumn's spread,
I pass to snow-white hairs the same, and give to pulses winter-
    cool'd the same;)
As here in careless trill, I and my recitatives, with faith and
    love,
Wafting to other work, to unknown songs, conditions,
On, on, ye jocund twain! continue on the same!

APPARITIONS

A vague mist hanging 'round half the pages:
(Sometimes how strange and clear to the soul,
That all these solid things are indeed but apparitions, con-
    cepts, non-realities.)

BRAVO, PARIS EXPOSITION

Add to your show, before you close it, France,
With all the rest, visible, concrete, temples, towers, goods,
    machines and ores,
Our sentiment wafted from many million heart-throbs, ethere-
    al but solid,
(We grand-sons and great-grand-sons do not forget your
    grand-sires,)
From fifty Nations and nebulous Nations, compacted, sent
    oversea to-day,
America's applause, love, memories and good-will.

L. OF G.'S PURPORT

Not to exclude or demarcate, or pick out evils from their
    formidable masses (even to expose them,)
But add, fuse, complete, extend—and celebrate the immortal
    and the good.

Haughty this song, its words and scope,
To span vast realms of space and time,
Evolution—the cumulative—growths and generations.

Begun in ripen'd youth and steadily pursued,
Wandering, peering, dallying with all—war, peace, day and
    night absorbing,
Never even for one brief hour abandoning my task,
I end it here in sickness, poverty, and old age.

I sing of life, yet mind me well of death:
To-day shadowy Death dogs my steps, my seated shape, and
    has for years—
Draws sometimes close to me, as face to face.

UNSEEN BUDS

Unseen buds, infinite, hidden well,
Under the snow and ice, under the darkness, in every square
    or cubic inch,
Germinal, exquisite, in delicate lace, microscopic, unborn,
Like babes in wombs, latent, folded, compact, sleeping;
Billions of billions, and trillions of trillions of them waiting,
(On earth and in the sea—the universe—the stars there in the
    heavens,)
Urging slowly, surely forward, forming endless,
And waiting ever more, forever more behind.

GOOD-BYE MY FANCY!

Good-bye my Fancy!
Farewell dear mate, dear love!
I'm going away, I know not where,
Or to what fortune, or whether I may ever see you again,
So Good-bye my Fancy.

Now for my last—let me look back a moment;
The slower fainter ticking of the clock is in me,
Exit, nightfall, and soon the heart-thud stopping.

Long have we lived, joy'd, caress'd together;
Delightful!—now separation—Good-bye my Fancy.

Yet let me not be too hasty,
Long indeed have we lived, slept, filter'd, become really
    blended into one;
Then if we die we die together, (yes, we'll remain one,)
If we go anywhere we'll go together to meet what happens,
May-be we'll be better off and blither, and learn something,
May-be it is yourself now really ushering me to the true
    songs, (who knows?)
May-be it is you the mortal knob really undoing, turning—so
    now finally,
Good-bye—and hail! my Fancy.

Specimen Days

[*Selections*]

A HAPPY HOUR'S COMMAND

Down in the Woods, July 2d, 1882.—If I do it at all I must delay no longer. Incongruous and full of skips and jumps as is that huddle of diary-jottings, war-memoranda of 1862–'65, Nature-notes of 1877–'81, with Western and Canadian observations afterwards, all bundled up and tied by a big string, the resolution and indeed mandate comes to me this day, this hour,—(and what a day! what an hour just passing! the luxury of riant grass and blowing breeze, with all the shows of sun and sky and perfect temperature, never before so filling me body and soul)—to go home, untie the bundle, reel out diary-scraps and memoranda, just as they are, large or small, one after another, into print-pages, and let the melange's lackings and wants of connection take care of themselves. It will illustrate one phase of humanity anyhow; how few of life's days and hours (and they not by relative value or proportion, but by chance) are ever noted. Probably another point too, how we give long preparations for some object, planning and delving and fashioning, and then, when the actual hour for doing arrives, find ourselves still quite unprepared, and tumble the thing together, letting hurry and crudeness tell the story better than fine work. At any rate I obey my happy hour's command, which seems curiously imperative. May-be, if I don't do anything else, I shall send out the most wayward, spontaneous, fragmentary book ever printed.

ANSWER TO AN INSISTING FRIEND

You ask for items, details of my early life—of genealogy and parentage, particularly of the women of my ancestry, and of its far back Netherlands stock on the maternal side—of the region where I was born and raised, and my father and mother before me, and theirs before them—with a word about Brooklyn and New York cities, the times I lived there as lad and young man. You say you want to get at these details mainly as the go-befores and embryons of "Leaves of Grass." Very good; you shall have at least some specimens of them all. I have often thought of the meaning of such things—that one can only encompass and complete matters of that kind by exploring behind, perhaps very far behind, themselves directly, and so into their genesis, antecedents, and cumulative stages. Then as luck would have it, I lately whiled away the tedium of a week's half-sickness and confinement, by collating these very items for another (yet unfulfill'd, probably abandon'd,) purpose; and if you will be satisfied with them, authentic in date-occurrence and fact simply, and told my own way, garrulous-like, here they are. I shall not hesitate to make extracts, for I catch at any thing to save labor; but those will be the best versions of what I want to convey.

GENEALOGY—VAN VELSOR
AND WHITMAN

The later years of the last century found the Van Velsor family, my mother's side, living on their own farm at Cold Spring, Long Island, New York State, near the eastern edge of Queens county, about a mile from the harbor. My father's side—probably the fifth generation from the first English arrivals in New England—were at the same time farmers on their own land—(and a fine domain it was, 500 acres, all good soil, gently sloping east and south, about one-tenth woods, plenty of grand old trees,) two or three miles off, at West Hills, Suffolk county. The Whitman name in the Eastern States, and so branching West and South, starts undoubtedly from one John Whitman, born 1602, in Old England, where he grew up, married, and his eldest son was born in 1629. He came over in the "True Love" in 1640 to America; and lived in Weymouth, Mass., which place became the mother-hive of the New-Englanders of the name: he died in 1692. His brother, Rev. Zechariah Whitman, also came over in the "True Love," either at that time or soon after, and lived at Milford, Conn. A son of this Zechariah, named Joseph, migrated to Huntington, Long Island, and permanently settled there. Savage's "Genealogical Dictionary" (vol iv, p 524) gets the Whitman family establish'd at Huntington, per this Joseph, before 1664. It is quite certain that from that beginning, and from Joseph, the West Hill Whitmans, and all others in Suffolk county, have since radiated, myself among the number. John and Zechariah both went to England and back again divers times; they had large families, and several of their children were born in the old country. We hear of the father of John and Zechariah, Abijah Whitman, who goes over into the 1500's, but we know little about him, except that he also was for some time in America.

These old pedigree-reminiscences come up to me vividly from a visit I made not long since (in my 63d year) to West Hills, and to the burial grounds of my ancestry, both sides. I extract from notes of that visit, written there and then:

THE OLD WHITMAN AND VAN VELSOR CEMETERIES

July 29, 1881.—After more than forty years' absence, (except a brief visit, to take my father there once more, two years before he died,) went down Long Island on a week's jaunt to the place where I was born, thirty miles from New York city. Rode around the old familiar spots, viewing and pondering and dwelling long upon them, everything coming back to me. Went to the old Whitman homestead on the upland and took a view eastward, inclining south, over the broad and beautiful farm lands of my grandfather (1780,) and my father. There was the new house (1810,) the big oak a hundred and fifty or two hundred years old; there the well, the sloping kitchen garden, and a little way off even the well-kept remains of the dwelling of my great-grandfather (1750–'60) still standing, with its mighty timbers and low ceilings. Near by, a stately grove of tall, vigorous black-walnuts, beautiful, Apollo-like, the sons or grandsons, no doubt, of black-walnuts during or before 1776. On the other side of the road spread the famous apple orchard, over twenty acres, the trees planted by hands long mouldering in the grave (my uncle Jesse's,) but quite many of them evidently capable of throwing out their annual blossoms and fruit yet.

I now write these lines seated on an old grave (doubtless of a century since at least) on the burial hill of the Whitmans, of many generations. Fifty and more graves are quite plainly traceable, and as many more decay'd out of all form—depress'd mounds, crumbled and broken stones, cover'd with moss—the gray and sterile hill, the clumps of chestnuts, outside, the silence, just varied by the soughing wind. There is always the deepest eloquence of sermon or poem in any of these ancient graveyards of which Long Island has so many; so what must this one have been to me? My whole family history, with its succession of links, from the first settlement down to date, told here—three centuries concentrate on this sterile acre.

The next day, July 30, I devoted to the maternal locality, and if possible was still more penetrated and impress'd. I write this paragraph on the burial hill of the Van Velsors, near Cold Spring, the most significant depository of the dead that could be imagin'd, without the slightest help from art, but far ahead of it, soil sterile, a mostly bare plateau-flat of half an acre, the top of a hill, brush and well grown trees and dense woods bordering all around, very primitive, secluded, no visitors, no road (you cannot drive here, you have to bring the dead on foot, and follow on foot.) Two or three-score graves quite plain; as many more almost rubb'd out. My grandfather Cornelius and my grandmother Amy (Naomi) and numerous relatives nearer or remoter, on my mother's side, lie buried here. The scene as I stood or sat, the delicate and wild odor of the woods, a slightly drizzling rain, the emotional atmosphere of the place, and the inferr'd reminiscences, were fitting accompaniments.

THE MATERNAL HOMESTEAD

I WENT down from this ancient grave place eighty or ninety rods to the site of the Van Velsor homestead, where my mother was born (1795,) and where every spot had been familiar to me as a child and youth (1825–'40.) Then stood there a long rambling, dark-gray, shingle-sided house, with sheds, pens, a great barn, and much open road-space. Now of all those not a vestige left; all had been pull'd down, erased, and the plough and harrow pass'd over foundations, road-spaces and everything, for many summers; fenced in at present, and grain and clover growing like any other fine fields. Only a big hole from the cellar, with some little heaps of broken stone, green with grass and weeds, identified the place. Even the copious old brook and spring seem'd to have mostly dwindled away. The whole scene, with what it arous'd, memories of my young days there half a century ago, the vast kitchen and ample fireplace and the sitting-room adjoining, the plain furniture, the meals, the house full of merry people, my grandmother Amy's sweet old face in its Quaker cap, my grandfather "the Major," jovial, red, stout, with sonorous voice and characteristic physiognomy, with the actual sights themselves, made the most pronounc'd half-day's experience of my whole jaunt.

For there with all those wooded, hilly, healthy surroundings, my dearest mother, Louisa Van Velsor, grew up—(her mother, Amy Williams, of the Friends' or Quakers' denomination—the Williams family, seven sisters and one brother—the father and brother sailors, both of whom met their deaths at sea.) The Van Velsor people were noted for fine horses, which the men bred and train'd from blooded stock. My mother, as a young woman, was a daily and daring rider. As to the head of the family himself, the old race of the Netherlands, so deeply grafted on Manhattan island and in Kings and Queens counties, never yielded a more mark'd and full Americanized specimen than Major Cornelius Van Velsor.

TWO OLD FAMILY INTERIORS

OF THE domestic and inside life of the middle of Long Island, at and just before that time, here are two samples:

"The Whitmans, at the beginning of the present century, lived in a long story-and-a-half farm-house, hugely timber'd, which is still standing. A great smoke-canopied kitchen, with vast hearth and chimney, form'd one end of the house. The existence of slavery in New York at that time, and the possession by the family of some twelve or fifteen slaves, house and field servants, gave things quite a patriarchal look. The very young darkies could be seen, a swarm of them, toward sundown, in this kitchen, squatted in a circle on the floor, eating their supper of Indian pudding and milk. In the house, and in food and furniture, all was rude, but substantial. No carpets or stoves were known, and no coffee, and tea or sugar only for the women. Rousing wood fires gave both warmth and light on winter nights. Pork, poultry, beef, and all the ordinary vegetables and grains were plentiful. Cider was the men's common drink, and used at meals. The clothes were mainly homespun. Journeys were made by both men and women on horseback. Both sexes labor'd with their own hands—the men on the farm—the women in the house and around it. Books were scarce. The annual copy of the almanac was a treat, and was pored over through the long winter evenings. I must not forget to mention that both these families were near enough to the sea to behold it from the high places, and to hear in still hours the roar of the surf; the latter, after a storm,

giving a peculiar sound at night. *Then all hands, male and female, went down frequently on beach and bathing parties, and the men on practical expeditions for cutting salt hay, and for clamming and fishing."*—John Burroughs's NOTES.

"*The ancestors of Walt Whitman, on both the paternal and maternal sides, kept a good table, sustain'd the hospitalities, decorums, and an excellent social reputation in the county, and they were often of mark'd individuality. If space permitted, I should consider some of the men worthy special description; and still more some of the women. His great-grandmother on the paternal side, for instance, was a large swarthy woman, who lived to a very old age. She smoked tobacco, rode on horseback like a man, managed the most vicious horse, and, becoming a widow in later life, went forth every day over her farm-lands, frequently in the saddle, directing the labor of her slaves, with language in which, on exciting occasions, oaths were not spared. The two immediate grandmothers were, in the best sense, superior women. The maternal one (Amy Williams before marriage) was a Friend, or Quakeress, of sweet, sensible character, housewifely proclivities, and deeply intuitive and spiritual. The other, (Hannah Brush,) was an equally noble, perhaps stronger character, lived to be very old, had quite a family of sons, was a natural lady, was in early life a school-mistress, and had great solidity of mind. W. W. himself makes much of the women of his ancestry.*"—The same.

Out from these arrieres of persons and scenes, I was born May 31, 1819. And now to dwell awhile on the locality itself— as the successive growth stages of my infancy, childhood, youth and manhood were all pass'd on Long Island, which I sometimes feel as if I had incorporated. I roam'd, as boy and man, and have lived in nearly all parts, from Brooklyn to Montauk point.

PAUMANOK, AND MY LIFE ON IT
AS CHILD AND YOUNG MAN

WORTH fully and particularly investigating indeed this Paumanok, (to give the spot its aboriginal name,) stretching east through Kings, Queens and Suffolk counties, 120 miles altogether—on the north Long Island sound, a beautiful, varied and picturesque series of inlets, "necks" and sea-like expansions, for a hundred miles to Orient point. On the ocean side the great south bay dotted with countless hummocks, mostly small, some quite large, occasionally long bars of sand out two hundred rods to a mile-and-a-half from the shore. While now and then, as at Rockaway and far east along the Hamptons, the beach makes right on the island, the sea dashing up without intervention. Several light-houses on the shores east; a long history of wrecks tragedies, some even of late years. As a youngster, I was in the atmosphere and traditions of many of these wrecks—of one or two almost an observer. Off Hempstead beach for example, was the loss of the ship "Mexico" in 1840, (alluded to in "the Sleepers" in L. of G.) And at Hampton, some years later, the destruction of the brig "Elizabeth," a fearful affair, in one of the worst winter gales, where Margaret Fuller went down, with her husband and child.

Inside the outer bars or beach this south bay is everywhere comparatively shallow; of cold winters all thick ice on the surface. As a boy I often went forth with a chum or two, on those frozen fields, with hand-sled, axe and eel-spear, after messes of eels. We would cut holes in the ice, sometimes striking quite an eel-bonanza, and filling our baskets with great, fat, sweet, white-meated fellows. The scenes, the ice, drawing the hand-sled, cutting holes, spearing the eels, &c., were of course just such fun as is dearest to boyhood. The shores of this bay, winter and summer, and my doings there in early life, are woven all through L. of G. One sport I was very fond of was to go on a bay-party in summer to gather sea-gull's eggs. (The gulls lay two or three eggs, more than half the size of hen's eggs, right on the sand, and leave the sun's heat to hatch them.)

The eastern end of Long Island, the Peconic bay region, I knew quite well too—sail'd more than once around Shelter island, and down to Montauk—spent many an hour on Turtle hill by the old light-house, on the extreme point, looking out over the ceaseless roll of the Atlantic. I used to like to go down there and fraternize with the blue-fishers, or the annual squads of sea-bass takers. Sometimes, along Montauk peninsula, (it is some 15 miles long, and good grazing,) met the strange, unkempt, half-barbarous herdsmen, at that time living there entirely aloof from society or civilization, in charge, on those rich pasturages, of vast droves of horses, kine or sheep, own'd by farmers of the eastern towns. Sometimes, too, the few remaining Indians, or half-breeds, at that period left on Montauk peninsula, but now I believe altogether extinct.

More in the middle of the island were the spreading Hempstead plains, then (1830–'40) quite prairie-like, open, uninhabited, rather sterile, cover'd with kill-calf and huckleberry bushes, yet plenty of fair pasture for the cattle, mostly milchcows, who fed there by hundreds, even thousands, and at evening, (the plains too were own'd by the towns, and this was the use of them in common,) might be seen taking their way home, branching off regularly in the right places. I have often been out on the edges of these plains toward sundown, and can yet recall in fancy the interminable cow processions, and hear the music of the tin or copper bells clanking far or near, and breathe the cool of the sweet and slightly aromatic evening air, and note the sunset.

Through the same region of the island, but further east, extended wide central tracts of pine and scrub-oak, (charcoal was largely made here,) monotonous and sterile. But many a good day or half-day did I have, wandering through those solitary cross-roads, inhaling the peculiar and wild aroma. Here, and all along the island and its shores, I spent intervals many years, all seasons, sometimes riding, sometimes boating, but generally afoot, (I was always then a good walker,) absorbing fields, shores, marine incidents, characters, the bay-men, farmers, pilots—always had a plentiful acquaintance with the latter, and with fishermen—went every summer on sailing trips—always liked the bare sea-beach, south side, and have some of my happiest hours on it to this day.

As I write, the whole experience comes back to me after the lapse of forty and more years—the soothing rustle of the waves, and the saline smell—boyhood's times, the clam-digging, barefoot, and with trowsers roll'd up—hauling down the creek—the perfume of the sedge-meadows—the hay-boat, and the chowder and fishing excursions;—or, of later years, little voyages down and out New York bay, in the pilot boats. Those same later years, also, while living in Brooklyn, (1836–'50) I went regularly every week in the mild seasons down to Coney island, at that time a long, bare unfrequented shore, which I had all to myself, and where I loved, after bathing, to race up and down the hard sand, and declaim Homer or Shakspere to the surf and sea-gulls by the hour. But I am getting ahead too rapidly, and must keep more in my traces.

MY FIRST READING—LAFAYETTE

From 1824 to '28 our family lived in Brooklyn in Front, Cranberry and Johnson streets. In the latter my father built a nice house for a home, and afterwards another in Tillary street. We occupied them, one after the other, but they were mortgaged, and we lost them. I yet remember Lafayette's visit. Most of these years I went to the public schools. It must have been about 1829 or '30 that I went with my father and mother to hear Elias Hicks preach in a ball-room on Brooklyn heights. At about the same time employ'd as a boy in an office, lawyers', father and two sons, Clarke's, Fulton street, near Orange. I had a nice desk and window-nook to myself; Edward C. kindly help'd me at my handwriting and composition, and, (the signal event of my life up to that time,) subscribed for me to a big circulating library. For a time I now revel'd in romance-reading of all kinds; first, the "Arabian

Nights," all the volumes, an amazing treat. Then, with sorties
in very many other directions, took in Walter Scott's novels,
one after another, and his poetry, (and continue to enjoy
novels and poetry to this day.)

PRINTING OFFICE—OLD BROOKLYN

AFTER about two years went to work in a weekly newspaper
and printing office, to learn the trade. The paper was the
"Long Island Patriot," owned by S. E. Clements, who was
also postmaster. An old printer in the office, William Hart-
shorne, a revolutionary character, who had seen Washington,
was a special friend of mine, and I had many a talk with him
about long past times. The apprentices, including myself,
boarded with his grand-daughter. I used occasionally to go
out riding with the boss, who was very kind to us boys; Sun-
days he took us all to a great old rough, fortress-looking stone
church, on Joralemon street, near where the Brooklyn city
hall now is—(at that time broad fields and country roads
everywhere around.) Afterward I work'd on the "Long Island
Star," Alden Spooner's paper. My father all these years pursuing his trade as carpenter and builder, with varying fortune.
There was a growing family of children—eight of us—my
brother Jesse the oldest, myself the second, my dear sisters
Mary and Hannah Louisa, my brothers Andrew, George,
Thomas Jefferson, and then my youngest brother, Edward,
born 1835, and always badly crippled, as I am myself of late
years.

GROWTH—HEALTH—WORK

I DEVELOPED (1833–4–5) into a healthy, strong youth (grew
too fast, though, was nearly as big as a man at 15 or 16.) Our
family at this period moved back to the country, my dear
mother very ill for a long time, but recover'd. All these years
I was down Long Island more or less every summer, now east,

now west, sometimes months at a stretch. At 16, 17, and so on, was fond of debating societies, and had an active membership with them, off and on, in Brooklyn and one or two country towns on the island. A most omnivorous novel-reader, these and later years, devour'd everything I could get. Fond of the theatre, also, in New York, went whenever I could—sometimes witnessing fine performances.

1836-7, work'd as compositor in printing offices in New York city. Then, when little more than eighteen, and for a while afterwards, went to teaching country schools down in Queens and Suffolk counties, Long Island, and "boarded round." (This latter I consider one of my best experiences and deepest lessons in human nature behind the scenes, and in the masses.) In '39, '40, I started and publish'd a weekly paper in my native town, Huntington. Then returning to New York city and Brooklyn, work'd on as printer and writer, mostly prose, but an occasional shy at "poetry."

MY PASSION FOR FERRIES

LIVING in Brooklyn or New York city from this time forward, my life, then, and still more the following years, was curiously identified with Fulton ferry, already becoming the greatest of its sort in the world for general importance, volume, variety, rapidity, and picturesqueness. Almost daily, later, ('50 to '60,) I cross'd on the boats, often up in the pilot-houses where I could get a full sweep, absorbing shows, accompaniments, surroundings. What oceanic currents, eddies, underneath—the great tides of humanity also, with ever-shifting movements. Indeed, I have always had a passion for ferries; to me they afford inimitable, streaming, never-failing, living poems. The river and bay scenery, all about New York island, any time of a fine day—the hurrying, splashing sea-tides—the changing panorama of steamers, all sizes, often a string of big ones outward bound to distant ports—the myriads of white-sail'd schooners, sloops, skiffs, and the marvellously beautiful yachts—the majestic sound boats as they rounded the Battery and came along towards 5, afternoon, eastward bound—the prospect off towards Staten island, or down the Narrows, or the other way up the Hudson—what refreshment of spirit such sights and experiences gave me years ago (and many a time since.) My old pilot friends, the Balsirs, Johnny Cole, Ira Smith, William White, and my young ferry friend, Tom Gere —how well I remember them all.

BROADWAY SIGHTS

BESIDES Fulton ferry, off and on for years, I knew and frequented Broadway—that noted avenue of New York's crowded and mixed humanity, and of so many notables. Here I saw, during those times, Andrew Jackson, Webster, Clay, Seward, Martin Van Buren, filibuster Walker, Kossuth, Fitz Greene Halleck, Bryant, the Prince of Wales, Charles Dickens, the first Japanese ambassadors, and lots of other celebrities of the time. Always something novel or inspiriting; yet mostly to me the hurrying and vast amplitude of those never-ending human currents. I remember seeing James Fenimore Cooper in a court-room in Chambers street, back of the city hall, where he was carrying on a law case—(I think it was a charge of libel he had brought against some one.) I also remember seeing Edgar A. Poe, and having a short interview with him, (it must have been in 1845 or '6,) in his office, second story of a corner building, (Duane or Pearl street.) He was editor and owner or part owner of "the Broadway Journal." The visit was about a piece of mine he had publish'd. Poe was very cordial, in a quiet way, appear'd well in person, dress, &c. I have a distinct and pleasing remembrance of his looks, voice, manner and matter; very kindly and human, but subdued, perhaps a little jaded. For another of my reminiscences, here on the west side, just below Houston street, I once saw (it must have been about 1832, of a sharp, bright January day) a bent, feeble but stout-built very old man, bearded, swathed in rich furs, with a great ermine cap on his head, led and assisted, almost carried, down the steps of his high front stoop (a dozen friends and

servants, emulous, carefully holding, guiding him) and then
lifted and tuck'd in a gorgeous sleigh, envelop'd in other furs,
for a ride. The sleigh was drawn by as fine a team of horses as
I ever saw. (You needn't think all the best animals are brought
up nowadays; never was such horseflesh as fifty years ago on
Long Island, or south, or in New York city; folks look'd for
spirit and mettle in a nag, not tame speed merely.) Well, I,
a boy of perhaps thirteen or fourteen, stopp'd and gazed long
at the spectacle of that fur-swathed old man, surrounded by
friends and servants, and the careful seating of him in the
sleigh. I remember the spirited, champing horses, the driver
with his whip, and a fellow-driver by his side, for extra
prudence. The old man, the subject of so much attention, I
can almost see now. It was John Jacob Astor.

The years 1846, '47, and there along, see me still in New
York city, working as writer and printer, having my usual
good health, and a good time generally.

OMNIBUS JAUNTS AND DRIVERS

ONE phase of those days must by no means go unrecorded—
namely, the Broadway omnibuses, with their drivers. The
vehicles still (I write this paragraph in 1881) give a portion
of the character of Broadway—the Fifth avenue, Madison avenue, and Twenty-third street lines yet running. But the flush
days of the old Broadway stages, characteristic and copious,
are over. The Yellow-birds, the Red-birds, the original Broadway, the Fourth avenue, the Knickerbocker, and a dozen
others of twenty or thirty years ago, are all gone. And the
men specially identified with them, and giving vitality and
meaning to them—the drivers—a strange, natural, quick-eyed
and wondrous race—(not only Rabelais and Cervantes would
have gloated upon them, but Homer and Shakspere would)—
how well I remember them, and must here give a word about
them. How many hours, forenoons and afternoons—how many
exhilarating night-times I have had—perhaps June or July, in
cooler air—riding the whole length of Broadway, listening

to some yarn, (and the most vivid yarns ever spun, and the rarest mimicry)—or perhaps I declaiming some stormy passage from Julius Cæsar or Richard, (you could roar as loudly as you chose in that heavy, dense, uninterrupted street-bass.) Yes, I knew all the drivers then, Broadway Jack, Dressmaker, Balky Bill, George Storms, Old Elephant, his brother Young Elephant (who came afterward,) Tippy, Pop Rice, Big Frank, Yellow Joe, Pete Callahan, Patsy Dee, and dozens more; for there were hundreds. They had immense qualities, largely animal—eating, drinking, women—great personal pride, in their way—perhaps a few slouches here and there, but I should have trusted the general run of them, in their simple good-will and honor, under all circumstances. Not only for comradeship, and sometimes affection—great studies I found them also. (I suppose the critics will laugh heartily, but the influence of those Broadway omnibus jaunts and drivers and declamations and escapades undoubtedly enter'd into the gestation of "Leaves of Grass.")

PLAYS AND OPERAS TOO

AND certain actors and singers, had a good deal to do with the business. All through these years, off and on, I frequented the old Park, the Bowery, Broadway and Chatham-square theatres, and the Italian operas at Chambers-street, Astorplace or the Battery—many seasons was on the free list, writing for papers even as quite a youth. The old Park theatre—what names, reminiscences, the words bring back! Placide, Clarke, Mrs. Vernon, Fisher, Clara F., Mrs. Wood, Mrs. Seguin, Ellen Tree, Hackett, the younger Kean, Macready, Mrs. Richardson, Rice—singers, tragedians, comedians. What perfect acting! Henry Placide in "Napoleon's Old Guard" or "Grandfather Whitehead,"—or "the Provoked Husband" of Cibber, with Fanny Kemble as Lady Townley—or Sheridan Knowles in his own "Virginius"—or inimitable Power in "Born to Good Luck." These, and many more, the years of youth and onward. Fanny Kemble—name to conjure up great mimic scenes withal—perhaps the greatest. I remember well her rendering of Bianca in "Fazio," and Marianna in "the Wife." Nothing finer did ever stage exhibit—the veterans of all nations said so, and my boyish heart and head felt it in every minute cell. The lady was just matured, strong, better than merely beautiful, born from the footlights, had had three years' practice in London and through the British towns, and then she came to give America that young maturity and roseate power in all their noon, or rather forenoon, flush. It was my good luck to see her nearly every night she play'd at the old Park— certainly in all her principal characters.

I heard, these years, well render'd, all the Italian and other operas in vogue, "Sonnambula," "the Puritans," "Der Freischutz," "Huguenots," "Fille d'Regiment," "Faust," "Etoile du Nord," "Poliuto," and others. Verdi's "Ernani," "Rigoletto," and "Trovatore," with Donnizetti's "Lucia" or "Favorita" or "Lucrezia," and Auber's "Massaniello," or Rossini's "William Tell" and "Gazza Ladra," were among my special enjoyments. I heard Alboni every time she sang in New York and vicinity—also Grisi, the tenor Mario, and the baritone Badiali, the finest in the world.

This musical passion follow'd my theatrical one. As boy or young man I had seen, (reading them carefully the day beforehand,) quite all Shakspere's acting dramas, play'd wonderfully well. Even yet I cannot conceive anything finer than old Booth in "Richard Third," or "Lear," (I don't know which was best,) or Iago, (or Pescara, or Sir Giles Overreach, to go outside of Shakspere)—or Tom Hamblin in "Macbeth"—or old Clarke, either as the ghost in "Hamlet," or as Prospero in "the Tempest," with Mrs. Austin as Ariel, and Peter Richings as Caliban. Then other dramas, and fine players in them, Forrest as Metamora or Damon or Brutus—John R. Scott as Tom Cringle or Rolla—or Charlotte Cushman's Lady Gay Spanker in "London Assurance." Then of some years later, at Castle Garden, Battery, I yet recall the splendid seasons of the Havana musical troupe under Maretzek—the fine band, the cool sea-breezes, the unsurpass'd vocalism—Steffanone, Bosio,

Truffi, Marini in "Marino Faliero," "Don Pasquale," or "Favorita." No better playing or singing ever in New York. It was here too I afterward heard Jenny Lind. (The Battery—its past associations—what tales those old trees and walks and seawalls could tell!)

THROUGH EIGHT YEARS

In 1848, '49, I was occupied as editor of the "daily Eagle" newspaper, in Brooklyn. The latter year went off on a leisurely journey and working expedition (my brother Jeff with me) through all the middle States, and down the Ohio and Mississippi rivers. Lived awhile in New Orleans, and work'd there on the editorial staff of "daily Crescent," newspaper. After a time plodded back northward, up the Mississippi, and around to, and by way of the great lakes, Michigan, Huron, and Erie, to Niagara falls and lower Canada, finally returning through central New York and down the Hudson; traveling altogether probably 8000 miles this trip, to and fro. '51, '53, occupied in housebuilding in Brooklyn. (For a little of the first part of that time in printing a daily and weekly paper, "the Freeman.") '55, lost my dear father this year by death. Commenced putting "Leaves of Grass" to press for good, at the job printing office of my friends, the brothers Rome, in Brooklyn, after many MS. doings and undoings—(I had great trouble in leaving out the stock "poetical" touches, but succeeded at last.) I am now (1856–'7) passing through my 37th year.

SOURCES OF CHARACTER—RESULTS
—1860

To sum up the foregoing from the outset (and, of course, far. far more unrecorded,) I estimate three leading sources and formative stamps to my own character, now solidified for good or bad, and its subsequent literary and other outgrowth—the maternal nativity-stock brought hither from far-away Nether-lands, for one, (doubtless the best)—the subterranean tenacity and central bony structure (obstinacy, wilfulness) which I get from my paternal English elements, for another—and the combination of my Long Island birth-spot, seashores, child-hood's scenes, absorptions, with teeming Brooklyn and New York—with, I suppose, my experiences afterward in the secession outbreak, for the third.

For, in 1862, startled by news that my brother George, an officer in the 51st New York volunteers, had been seriously wounded (first Fredericksburg battle, December 13th,) I hurriedly went down to the field of war in Virginia. But I must go back a little.

OPENING OF THE SECESSION WAR

NEWS of the attack on fort Sumter and *the flag* at Charleston harbor, S. C., was receiv'd in New York city late at night (13th April, 1861,) and was immediately sent out in extras of the newspapers. I had been to the opera in Fourteenth street that night, and after the performance was walking down Broadway toward twelve o'clock, on my way to Brooklyn, when I heard in the distance the loud cries of the newsboys, who came presently tearing and yelling up the street, rushing from side to side even more furiously than usual. I bought an extra and cross'd to the Metropolitan hotel (Niblo's) where the great lamps were still brightly blazing, and, with a crowd of others, who gather'd impromptu, read the news, which was evidently authentic. For the benefit of some who had no papers, one of us read the telegram aloud, while all listen'd silently and attentively. No remark was made by any of the crowd, which had increas'd to thirty or forty, but all stood a minute or two, I remember, before they dispers'd. I can almost see them there now, under the lamps at midnight again.

NATIONAL UPRISING AND VOLUNTEERING

I HAVE said somewhere that the three Presidentiads preceding 1861 show'd how the weakness and wickedness of rulers are just as eligible here in America under republican, as in Europe under dynastic influences. But what can I say of that prompt and splendid wrestling with secession slavery, the arch-enemy personified, the instant he unmistakably show'd his face? The volcanic upheaval of the nation, after that firing on the flag at Charleston, proved for certain something which had been previously in great doubt, and at once substantially settled the question of disunion. In my judgment it will remain as the grandest and most encouraging spectacle yet vouchsafed in any age, old or new, to political progress and democracy. It was not for what came to the surface merely—though that was important—but what it indicated below, which was of eternal importance. Down in the abysms of New World humanity there had form'd and harden'd a primal hard-pan of national Union will, determin'd and in the majority, refusing to be tamper'd with or argued against, confronting all emergencies, and capable at any time of bursting all surface bonds, and breaking out like an earthquake. It is, indeed, the best lesson of the century, or of America, and it is a mighty privilege to have been part of it. (Two great spectacles, immortal proofs of democracy, unequall'd in all the history of the past, are furnish'd by the secession war—one at the beginning, the other at its close. Those are, the general, voluntary, arm'd upheaval, and the peaceful and harmonious disbanding of the armies in the summer of 1865.)

CONTEMPTUOUS FEELING

EVEN after the bombardment of Sumter, however, the gravity of the revolt, and the power and will of the slave States for a strong and continued military resistance to national authority, were not at all realized at the North, except by a few. Nine-tenths of the people of the free States look'd upon the rebellion, as started in South Carolina, from a feeling one-half of contempt, and the other half composed of anger and incredulity. It was not thought it would be join'd in by Virginia, North Carolina, or Georgia. A great and cautious national official predicted that it would blow over "in sixty days," and folks generally believ'd the prediction. I remember talking about it on a Fulton ferry-boat with the Brooklyn mayor, who said he only "hoped the Southern fire-eaters would commit some overt act of resistance, as they would then be at once so effectually squelch'd, we would never hear of secession again—but he was afraid they never would have the pluck to really do anything." I remember, too, that a couple of companies of the Thirteenth Brooklyn, who rendezvou'd at the city armory, and started thence as thirty days' men, were all provided with pieces of rope, conspicuously tied to their musket-barrels, with which to bring back each man a prisoner from the audacious South, to be led in a noose, on our men's early and triumphant return!

BATTLE OF BULL RUN, JULY, 1861

ALL THIS sort of feeling was destin'd to be arrested and revers'd by a terrible shock—the battle of first Bull Run—certainly, as we now know it, one of the most singular fights on record. (All battles, and their results, are far more matters of accident than is generally thought; but this was throughout a casualty, a chance. Each side supposed it had won, till the last moment. One had, in point of fact, just the same right to be routed as the other. By a fiction, or series of fictions, the national forces at the last moment exploded in a panic and fled from the field.) The defeated troops commenced pouring into Washington over the Long Bridge at daylight on Monday, 22d—day drizzling all through with rain. The Saturday and Sunday of the battle (20th, 21st,) had been parch'd and hot to an extreme—the dust, the grime and smoke, in layers, sweated in, follow'd by other layers again sweated in, absorb'd by those excited souls—their clothes all saturated with the clay-powder filling the air—stirr'd up everywhere on the dry roads and trodden fields by the regiments, swarming wagons, artillery, &c.—all the men with this coating of murk and sweat and rain, now recoiling back, pouring over the Long Bridge—a horrible march of twenty miles, returning to Washington baffled, humiliated, panic-struck. Where are the vaunts, and the proud boasts with which you went forth? Where are your banners, and your bands of music, and your ropes to bring back your prisoners? Well, there isn't a band playing—and there isn't a flag but clings ashamed and lank to its staff.

The sun rises, but shines not. The men appear, at first sparsely and shame-faced enough, then thicker, in the streets of Washington—appear in Pennsylvania avenue, and on the steps and basement entrances. They come along in disorderly mobs, some in squads, stragglers, companies. Occasionally, a rare regiment, in perfect order, with its officers (some gaps, dead, the true braves,) marching in silence, with lowering faces, stern, weary to sinking, all black and dirty, but every man with his musket, and stepping alive; but these are the exceptions. Sidewalks of Pennsylvania avenue, Fourteenth street, &c., crowded, jamm'd with citizens, darkies, clerks, everybody, lookers-on; women in the windows, curious expressions from faces, as those swarms of dirt-cover'd return'd soldiers there (will they never end?) move by; but nothing said, no comments; (half our lookers-on secesh of the most venomous kind—they say nothing; but the devil snickers in their faces.) During the forenoon Washington gets all over motley with these defeated soldiers—queer-looking objects, strange eyes and faces, drench'd (the steady rain drizzles on all day) and fearfully worn, hungry, haggard, blister'd in the feet. Good people (but not over-many of them either,) hurry up something for their grub. They put wash-kettles on the fire, for soup, for coffee. They set tables on the side-walks—wagon-loads of bread are purchas'd, swiftly cut in stout chunks. Here are two aged ladies, beautiful, the first in the

city for culture and charm, they stand with store of eating and
drink at an improvis'd table of rough plank, and give food,
and have the store replenish'd from their house every half-
hour all that day; and there in the rain they stand, active,
silent, white-hair'd, and give food, though the tears stream
down their cheeks, almost without intermission, the whole
time. Amid the deep excitement, crowds and motion, and
desperate eagerness, it seems strange to see many, very many,
of the soldiers sleeping—in the midst of all, sleeping sound.
They drop down anywhere, on the steps of houses, up close
by the basements or fences, on the sidewalk, aside on some
vacant lot, and deeply sleep. A poor seventeen or eighteen
year old boy lies there, on the stoop of a grand house; he
sleeps so calmly, so profoundly. Some clutch their muskets
firmly even in sleep. Some in squads; comrades, brothers, close
together—and on them, as they lay, sulkily drips the rain.

As afternoon pass'd, and evening came, the streets, the bar-
rooms, knots everywhere, listeners, questioners, terrible yarns,
bugaboo, mask'd batteries, our regiment all cut up, &c.—
stories and story-tellers, windy, bragging, vain centres of
street-crowds. Resolution, manliness, seem to have abandon'd
Washington. The principal hotel, Willard's, is full of shoulder-
straps—thick, crush'd, creeping with shoulder-straps. (I see
them, and must have a word with them. There you are, shoulder-straps!—but where are your companies? where are your
men? Incompetents! never tell me of chances of battle, of
getting stray'd, and the like. I think this is your work, this
retreat, after all. Sneak, blow, put on airs there in Willard's
sumptuous parlors and bar-rooms, or anywhere—no explanation shall save you. Bull Run is your work; had you been half
or one-tenth worthy your men, this would never have happen'd.)

Meantime, in Washington, among the great persons and
their entourage, a mixture of awful consternation, uncertainty,
rage, shame, helplessness, and stupefying disappointment.
The worst is not only imminent, but already here. In a few
hours—perhaps before the next meal—the secesh generals,
with their victorious hordes, will be upon us. The dream of

humanity, the vaunted Union we thought so strong, so impregnable—lo! it seems already smash'd like a china plate. One bitter, bitter hour—perhaps proud America will never again know such an hour. She must pack and fly—no time to spare. Those white palaces—the dome-crown'd capitol there on the hill, so stately over the trees—shall they be left—or destroy'd first? For it is certain that the talk among certain of the magnates and officers and clerks and officials everywhere, for twenty-four hours in and around Washington after Bull Run, was loud and undisguised for yielding out and out, and substituting the southern rule, and Lincoln promptly abdicating and departing. If the secesh officers and forces had immediately follow'd, and by a bold Napoleonic movement had enter'd Washington the first day, (or even the second,) they could have had things their own way, and a powerful faction north to back them. One of our returning colonels express'd in public that night, amid a swarm of officers and gentlemen in a crowded room, the opinion that it was useless to fight, that the southerners had made their title clear, and that the best course for the national government to pursue was to desist from any further attempt at stopping them, and admit them again to the lead, on the best terms they were willing to grant. Not a voice was rais'd against this judgment, amid that large crowd of officers and gentlemen. (The fact is, the hour was one of the three or four of those crises we had then and afterward, during the fluctuations of four years, when human eyes appear'd at least just as likely to see the last breath of the Union as to see it continue.)

THE STUPOR PASSES— SOMETHING ELSE BEGINS

But the hour, the day, the night pass'd, and whatever returns, an hour, a day, a night like that can never again return. The President, recovering himself, begins that very night—sternly, rapidly sets about the task of reorganizing his forces, and placing himself in positions for future and surer work. If there were nothing else of Abraham Lincoln for history to stamp him with, it is enough to send him with his wreath to the memory of all future time, that he endured that hour, that day, bitterer than gall—indeed a crucifixion day—that it did not conquer him—that he unflinchingly stemm'd it, and resolv'd to lift himself and the Union out of it.

Then the great New York papers at once appear'd, (commencing that evening, and following it up the next morning, and incessantly through many days afterwards,) with leaders that rang out over the land with the loudest, most reverberating ring of clearest bugles, full of encouragement, hope, inspiration, unfaltering defiance. Those magnificent editorials! they never flagg'd for a fortnight. The "Herald" commenced them—I remember the articles well. The "Tribune" was equally cogent and inspiriting—and the "Times," "Evening Post," and other principal papers, were not a whit behind. They came in good time, for they were needed. For in the humiliation of Bull Run, the popular feeling north, from its extreme of superciliousness, recoil'd to the depth of gloom and apprehension.

(Of all the days of the war, there are two especially I can never forget. Those were the day following the news, in New York and Brooklyn, of that first Bull Run defeat, and the day of Abraham Lincoln's death. I was home in Brooklyn on both occasions. The day of the murder we heard the news very early in the morning. Mother prepared breakfast—and other meals afterward—as usual; but not a mouthful was eaten all day by either of us. We each drank half a cup of coffee; that was all. Little was said. We got every newspaper morning and evening, and the frequent extras of that period, and pass'd them silently to each other.)

DOWN AT THE FRONT

FALMOUTH, VA., *opposite Fredericksburg, December 21, 1862.*—Begin my visits among the camp hospitals in the army of the Potomac. Spend a good part of the day in a large brick mansion on the banks of the Rappahannock, used as a hospital since the battle—seems to have receiv'd only the worst cases. Out doors, at the foot of a tree, within ten yards of the front of the house, I notice a heap of amputated feet, legs, arms, hands, &c., a full load for a one-horse cart. Several dead bodies lie near, each cover'd with its brown woolen blanket. In the door-yard, towards the river, are fresh graves, mostly of officers, their names on pieces of barrel-staves or broken boards, stuck in the dirt. (Most of these bodies were subsequently taken up and transported north to their friends.) The large mansion is quite crowded upstairs and down, everything impromptu, no system, all bad enough, but I have no doubt the best that can be done; all the wounds pretty bad, some frightful, the men in their old clothes, unclean and bloody. Some of the wounded are rebel soldiers and officers, prisoners. One, a Mississippian, a captain, hit badly in leg, I talk'd with some time; he ask'd me for papers, which I gave him. (I saw him three months afterward in Washington, with his leg amputated, doing well.) I went through the rooms, downstairs and up. Some of the men were dying. I had nothing to give at that visit, but wrote a few letters to folks home, mothers, &c. Also talk'd to three or four, who seem'd most susceptible to it, and needing it.

AFTER FIRST FREDERICKSBURG

December 23 to 31.—The results of the late battle are exhibited everywhere about here in thousands of cases, (hundreds die every day,) in the camp, brigade, and division hospitals. These are merely tents, and sometimes very poor ones, the wounded lying on the ground, lucky if their blankets are spread on layers of pine or hemlock twigs, or small leaves. No cots; seldom even a mattress. It is pretty cold. The ground is frozen hard, and there is occasional snow. I go around from one case to another. I do not see that I do much good to these wounded and dying; but I cannot leave them. Once in a while some youngster holds on to me convulsively, and I do what I can for him; at any rate, stop with him and sit near him for hours, if he wishes it.

Besides the hospitals, I also go occasionally on long tours through the camps, talking with the men, &c. Sometimes at night among the groups around the fires, in their shebang enclosures of bushes. These are curious shows, full of characters and groups. I soon get acquainted anywhere in camp, with officers or men, and am always well used. Sometimes I go down on picket with the regiment I know best. As to rations, the army here at present seems to be tolerably well supplied, and the men have enough, such as it is, mainly salt pork and hard tack. Most of the regiments lodge in the flimsy little shelter-tents. A few have built themselves huts of logs and mud, with fire-places.

BACK TO WASHINGTON

January, '63.—Left camp at Falmouth, with some wounded, a few days since, and came here by Aquia creek railroad, and so on government steamer up the Potomac. Many wounded were with us on the cars and boat. The cars were just common platform ones. The railroad journey of ten or twelve miles was made mostly before sunrise. The soldiers guarding the road came out from their tents or shebangs of bushes with rumpled hair and half-awake look. Those on duty were walking their posts, some on banks over us, others down far below the level of the track. I saw large cavalry camps off the road. At Aquia creek landing were numbers of wounded going north. While I waited some three hours, I went around among them. Several wanted word sent home to parents, brothers, wives, &c., which I did for them, (by mail the next day from Washington.) On the boat I had my hands full. One poor fellow died going up.

I am now remaining in and around Washington, daily visiting the hospitals. Am much in Patent-office, Eighth street, H street, Armory-square, and others. Am now able to do a little good, having money, (as almoner of others home,) and getting experience. To-day, Sunday afternoon and till nine in the evening, visited Campbell hospital; attended specially to one case in ward 1, very sick with pleurisy and typhoid fever, young man, farmer's son, D. F. Russell, company E, 60th New York, downhearted and feeble; a long time before he would take any interest; wrote a letter home to his mother, in Malone, Franklin county, N. Y., at his request; gave him some fruit and one or two other gifts; envelop'd and directed his letter, &c. Then went thoroughly through ward 6, observ'd every case in the ward, without, I think, missing one; gave perhaps from twenty to thirty persons, each one some little gift, such as oranges, apples, sweet crackers, figs, &c.

Thursday, Jan. 21.—Devoted the main part of the day to Armory-square hospital; went pretty thoroughly through wards F, G, H, and I; some fifty cases in each ward. In ward F supplied the men throughout with writing paper and stamp'd envelope each; distributed in small portions, to proper subjects, a large jar of first-rate preserv'd berries, which had been donated to me by a lady—her own cooking. Found several cases I thought good subjects for small sums of money, which I furnish'd. (The wounded men often come up broke, and it helps their spirits to have even the small sum I give them.) My paper and envelopes all gone, but distributed a good lot of amusing reading matter; also, as I thought judicious, tobacco, oranges, apples, &c. Interesting cases in ward I; Charles Miller, bed 19, company D, 53d Pennsylvania, is only sixteen years of age, very bright, courageous boy, left leg amputated below the knee; next bed to him, another young lad very sick; gave each appropriate gifts. In the bed above, also, amputation of the left leg; gave him a little jar of raspberries; bed 1, this ward, gave a small sum; also to a soldier on crutches, sitting on his bed near. . . . (I am more and more surprised at the very great proportion of youngsters from fifteen to twenty-one in the army. I afterwards found a still greater proportion among the southerners.)

Evening, same day, went to see D. F. R., before alluded to; found him remarkably changed for the better; up and dress'd

—quite a triumph; he afterwards got well, and went back to his regiment. Distributed in the wards a quantity of note-paper, and forty or fifty stamp'd envelopes, of which I had recruited by stock, and the men were much in need.

FIFTY HOURS LEFT WOUNDED
ON THE FIELD

HERE is a case of a soldier I found among the crowded cots in the Patent-office. He likes to have some one to talk to, and we will listen to him. He got badly hit in his leg and side at Fredericksburg that eventful Saturday, 13th of December. He lay the succeeding two days and nights helpless on the field, between the city and those grim terraces of batteries; his company and regiment had been compell'd to leave him to his fate. To make matters worse, it happen'd he lay with his head slightly down hill, and could not help himself. At the end of some fifty hours he was brought off, with other wounded, under a flag of truce. I ask him how the rebels treated him as he lay during those two days and nights within reach of them—whether they came to him—whether they abused him? He answers that several of the rebels, soldiers and others, came to him at one time and another. A couple of them, who were together, spoke roughly and sarcastically, but nothing worse. One middle-aged man, however, who seem'd to be moving around the field, among the dead and wounded, for benevolent purposes, came to him in a way he will never forget; treated our soldier kindly, bound up his wounds, cheer'd him, gave him a couple of biscuits and a drink of whiskey and water; asked him if he could eat some beef. This good secesh, however, did not change our soldier's position, for it might have caused the blood to burst from the wounds, clotted and stagnated. Our soldier is from Pennsylvania; has had a pretty severe time; the wounds proved to be bad ones. But he retains a good heart, and is at present on the gain. (It is not uncommon for the men to remain on the field this way, one, two, or even four or five days.)

HOSPITAL SCENES AND PERSONS

Letter Writing.—When eligible, I encourage the men to write, and myself, when called upon, write all sorts of letters for them, (including love letters, very tender ones.) Almost as I reel off these memoranda, I write for a new patient to his wife. M. de F., of the 17th Connecticut, company H, has just come up (February 17th) from Windmill point, and is received in ward H, Armory-square. He is an intelligent looking man, has a foreign accent, black-eyed and hair'd, a Hebraic appearance. Wants a telegraphic message sent to his wife, New Canaan, Conn. I agree to send the message—but to make things sure I also sit down and write the wife a letter, and despatch it to the post-office immediately, as he fears she will come on, and he does not wish her to, as he will surely get well.

Saturday, January 30th.—Afternoon, visited Campbell hospital. Scene of cleaning up the ward, and giving the men all clean clothes—through the ward (6) the patients dressing or being dress'd—the naked upper half of the bodies—the good-humor and fun—the shirts, drawers, sheets of beds, &c., and the general fixing up for Sunday. Gave J. L. 50 cents.

Wednesday, February 4th.—Visited Armory-square hospital, went pretty thoroughly through wards E and D. Supplied paper and envelopes to all who wish'd—as usual, found plenty of men who needed those articles. Wrote letters. Saw and talk'd with two or three members of the Brooklyn 14th regt. A poor fellow in ward D, with a fearful wound in a fearful condition, was having some loose splinters of bone taken from the neighborhood of the wound. The operation was long, and one of great pain—yet, after it was well commenced, the soldier bore it in silence. He sat up, propp'd—was much wasted—had lain a long time quiet in one position (not for days only but weeks,) a bloodless, brown-skinn'd face, with eyes full of determination—belong'd to a New York regiment. There was an unusual cluster of surgeons, medical cadets, nurses, &c., around his bed—I thought the whole thing was done with tenderness, and done well. In one case, the wife sat by the side of her husband, his sickness typhoid fever, pretty bad. In another, by the side of her son, a mother—she told me she had seven children, and this was the youngest. (A fine, kind, healthy, gentle mother, good-looking, not very old, with a cap on her head, and dress'd like home—what a charm it gave to the whole ward.) I liked the woman nurse in ward E—I noticed how she sat a long time by a poor fellow who just had, that morning, in addition to his other sickness, bad hemorrhage—she gently assisted him, reliev'd him of the blood, holding a cloth to his mouth, as he coughed it up—he was so weak he could only just turn his head over on the pillow.

One young New York man, with a bright, handsome face, had been lying several months from a most disagreeable wound, receiv'd at Bull Run. A bullet had shot him right through the bladder, hitting him front, low in the belly, and coming out back. He had suffer'd much—the water came out of the wound, by slow but steady quantities, for many weeks—so that he lay almost constantly in a sort of puddle—and there were other disagreeable circumstances. He was of good heart, however. At present comparatively comfortable, had a bad throat, was delighted with a stick of horehound candy I gave him, with one or two other trifles.

PATENT-OFFICE HOSPITAL

February 23.—I must not let the great hospital at the Patent-office pass away without some mention. A few weeks ago the vast area of the second story of that noblest of Washington buildings was crowded close with rows of sick, badly wounded and dying soldiers. They were placed in three very large apartments. I went there many times. It was a strange, solemn, and, with all its features of suffering and death, a sort of fascinating sight. I go sometimes at night to soothe and relieve particular cases. Two of the immense apartments are fill'd with high and ponderous glass cases, crowded with models in miniature of every kind of utensil, machine or invention, it

ever enter'd into the mind of man to conceive; and with curi-
osities and foreign presents. Between these cases are lateral
openings, perhaps eight feet wide and quite deep, and in
these were placed the sick, besides a great long double row
of them up and down through the middle of the hall. Many of
them were very bad cases, wounds and amputations. Then
there was a gallery running above the hall in which there were
beds also. It was, indeed, a curious scene, especially at night
when lit up. The glass cases, the beds, the forms lying there,
the gallery above, and the marble pavement under foot—the
suffering, and the fortitude to bear it in various degrees—
occasionally, from some, the groan that could not be repress'd
—sometimes a poor fellow dying, with emaciated face and
glassy eye, the nurse by his side, the doctor also there, but no
friend, no relative—such were the sights but lately in the
Patent-office. (The wounded have since been removed from
there, and it is now vacant again.)

THE WHITE HOUSE BY MOONLIGHT

February 24th.—A spell of fine soft weather. I wander about a
good deal, sometimes at night under the moon. To-night took
a long look at the President's house. The white portico—the
palace-like, tall, round columns, spotless as snow—the walls
also—the tender and soft moonlight, flooding the pale marble,
and making peculiar faint languishing shades, not shadows—
everywhere a soft transparent hazy, thin, blue moon-lace,
hanging in the air—the brilliant and extra-plentiful clusters of
gas, on and around the façade, columns, portico, &c.—everything so white, so marbly pure and dazzling, yet soft—the
White House of future poems, and of dreams and dramas,
there in the soft and copious moon—the gorgeous front, in the
trees, under the lustrous flooding moon, full of reality, full of
illusion—the forms of the trees, leafless, silent, in trunk and
myriad-angles of branches, under the stars and sky—the White
House of the land, and of beauty and night—sentries at the

gates, and by the portico, silent, pacing there in blue overcoats —stopping you not at all, but eyeing you with sharp eyes, whichever way you move.

AN ARMY HOSPITAL WARD

LET me specialize a visit I made to the collection of barrack-like one-story edifices, Campbell hospital, out on the flats, at the end of the then horse railway route, on Seventh street. There is a long building appropriated to each ward. Let us go into ward 6. It contains to-day, I should judge, eighty or a hundred patients, half sick, half wounded. The edifice is nothing but boards, well whitewash'd inside, and the usual slender-framed iron bedsteads, narrow and plain. You walk down the central passage, with a row on either side, their feet towards you, and their heads to the wall. There are fires in large stoves, and the prevailing white of the walls is reliev'd by some ornaments, stars, circles, &c., made of evergreens. The view of the whole edifice and occupants can be taken at once, for there is no partition. You may hear groans or other sounds of unendurable suffering from two or three of the cots, but in the main there is quiet—almost a painful absence of demonstration; but the pallid face, the dull'd eye, and the moisture on the lip, are demonstration enough. Most of these sick or hurt are evidently young fellows from the country, farmers' sons, and such like. Look at the fine large frames, the bright and broad countenances, and the many yet lingering proofs of strong constitution and physique. Look at the patient and mute manner of our American wounded as they lie in such a sad collection; representatives from all New England, and from New York, and New Jersey, and Pennsylvania—indeed from all the States and all the cities—largely from the west. Most of them are entirely without friends or acquaintances here—no familiar face, and hardly a word of judicious sympathy or cheer, through their sometimes long and tedious sickness, or the pangs of aggravated wounds.

A CONNECTICUT CASE

THIS young man in bed 25 is H. D. B., of the 27th Connecticut, company B. His folks live at Northford, near New Haven. Though not more than twenty-one, or thereabouts, he has knock'd much around the world, on sea and land, and has seen some fighting on both. When I first saw him he was very sick, with no appetite. He declined offers of money—said he did not need anything. As I was quite anxious to do something, he confess'd that he had a hankering for a good home-made rice pudding—thought he could relish it better than anything. At this time his stomach was very weak. (The doctor, whom I consulted, said nourishment would do him more good than anything; but things in the hospital, though better than usual, revolted him.) I soon procured B. his rice-pudding. A Washington lady, (Mrs. O'C.), hearing his wish, made the pudding herself, and I took it up to him the next day. He subsequently told me he lived upon it for three or four days. This B. is a good sample of the American eastern young man—the typical Yankee. I took a fancy to him, and gave him a nice pipe, for a keepsake. He receiv'd afterwards a box of things from home, and nothing would do but I must take dinner with him, which I did, and a very good one it was.

TWO BROOKLYN BOYS

HERE in this same ward are two young men from Brooklyn, members of the 51st New York. I had known both the two as young lads at home, so they seem near to me. One of them, J. L., lies there with an amputated arm, the stump healing pretty well. (I saw him lying on the ground at Fredericksburg last December, all bloody, just after the arm was taken off. He was very phlegmatic about it, munching away at a cracker in the remaining hand—made no fuss.) He will recover, and thinks and talks yet of meeting the Johnny Rebs.

A SECESH BRAVE

THE grand soldiers are not comprised in those of one side, any more than the other. Here is a sample of an unknown southerner, a lad of seventeen. At the War department, a few days ago, I witness'd a presentation of captured flags to the Secretary. Among others a soldier named Gant, of the 104th Ohio volunteers, presented a rebel battle-flag, which one of the officers stated to me was borne to the mouth of our cannon and planted there by a boy but seventeen years of age, who actually endeavor'd to stop the muzzle of the gun with fence-rails. He was kill'd in the effort, and the flag-staff was sever'd by a shot from one of our men.

THE WOUNDED FROM CHANCELLORSVILLE

May, '63.—As I write this, the wounded have begun to arrive from Hooker's command from bloody Chancellorsville. I was down among the first arrivals. The men in charge told me the bad cases were yet to come. If that is so I pity them, for these are bad enough. You ought to see the scene of the wounded arriving at the landing here at the foot of Sixth street, at night. Two boat loads came about half-past seven last night. A little after eight it rain'd a long and violent shower. The pale, helpless soldiers had been debark'd, and lay around on the wharf and neighborhood anywhere. The rain was, probably, grateful to them; at any rate they were exposed to it. The few torches light up the spectacle. All around—on the wharf, on the ground, out on side places—the men are lying on blankets, old quilts, &c., with bloody rags bound round heads, arms, and legs. The attendants are few, and at night few outsiders also —only a few hard-work'd transportation men and drivers. (The wounded are getting to be common, and people grow callous.) The men, whatever their condition, lie there, and patiently wait till their turn comes to be taken up. Near by, the ambulances are now arriving in clusters, and one after another is call'd to back up and take its load. Extreme cases are sent off on stretchers. The men generally make little or no ado, whatever their sufferings. A few groans that cannot be suppress'd, and occasionally a scream of pain as they lift a man into the ambulance. To-day, as I write, hundreds more are expected, and to-morrow and the next day more, and so on for many days. Quite often they arrive at the rate of 1000 a day.

A NIGHT BATTLE, OVER A WEEK SINCE

May 12.—There was part of the late battle at Chancellorsville, (second Fredericksburg,) a little over a week ago, Saturday, Saturday night and Sunday, under Gen. Joe Hooker, I would like to give just a glimpse of—(a moment's look in a terrible storm at sea—of which a few suggestions are enough, and full details impossible.) The fighting had been very hot during the day, and after an intermission the latter part, was resumed at night, and kept up with furious energy till 3 o'clock in the morning. That afternoon (Saturday) an attack sudden and strong by Stonewall Jackson had gain'd a great advantage to the southern army, and broken our lines, entering us like a wedge, and leaving things in that position at dark. But Hooker at 11 at night made a desperate push, drove the secesh forces back, restored his original lines, and resumed his plans. This night scrimmage was very exciting, and afforded countless strange and fearful pictures. The fighting had been general both at Chancellorsville and northeast at Fredericksburg. (We hear of some poor fighting, episodes, skedaddling on our part. I think not of it. I think of the fierce bravery, the general rule.) One corps, the 6th, Sedgewick's, fights four dashing and bloody battles in thirty-six hours, retreating in great jeopardy, losing largely but maintaining itself, fighting with the sternest desperation under all circumstances, getting over the Rappahannock only by the skin of its teeth, yet getting over. It lost many, many brave men, yet it took vengeance, ample vengeance.

But it was the tug of Saturday evening, and through the night and Sunday morning, I wanted to make a special note of. It was largely in the woods, and quite a general engagement. The night was very pleasant, at times the moon shining out full and clear, all Nature so calm in itself, the early summer grass so rich, and foliage of the trees—yet there the battle raging, and many good fellows lying helpless, with new accessions to them, and every minute amid the rattle of muskets and crash of cannon, (for there was an artillery contest too,) the red life-blood oozing out from heads or trunks or limbs upon that green and dew-cool grass. Patches of the woods take fire, and several of the wounded, unable to move, are consumed—quite large spaces are swept over, burning the dead also—some of the men have their hair and beards singed —some, burns on their faces and hands—others holes burnt in their clothing. The flashes of fire from the cannon, the quick flaring flames and smoke, and the immense roar—the musketry so general, the light nearly bright enough for each side to see the other—the crashing, tramping of men—the yelling—close quarters—we hear the secesh yells—our men cheer loudly back, especially if Hooker is in sight—hand to hand conflicts, each side stands up to it, brave, determin'd as demons, they often charge upon us—a thousand deeds are done worth to write newer greater poems on—and still the woods on fire—still many are not only scorch'd—too many, unable to move, are burn'd to death.

Then the camps of the wounded—O heavens, what scene is this?—is this indeed *humanity*—these butchers' shambles? There are several of them. There they lie, in the largest, in an open space in the woods, from 200 to 300 poor fellows— the groans and screams—the odor of blood, mixed with the fresh scent of the night, the grass, the trees—that slaughter-house! O well is it their mothers, their sisters cannot see them —cannot conceive, and never conceiv'd, these things. One man is shot by a shell, both in the arm and leg—both are amputated

—there lie the rejected members. Some have their legs blown off—some bullets through the breast—some indescribably horrid wounds in the face or head, all mutilated, sickening, torn, gouged out—some in the abdomen—some mere boys—many rebels, badly hurt—they take their regular turns with the rest, just the same as any—the surgeons use them just the same. Such is the camp of the wounded—such a fragment, a reflection afar off of the bloody scene—while over all the clear, large moon comes out at times softly, quietly shining. Amid the woods, that scene of flitting souls—amid the crack and crash and yelling sounds—the impalpable perfume of the woods—and yet the pungent, stifling smoke—the radiance of the moon, looking from heaven at intervals so placid—the sky so heavenly—the clear-obscure up there, those buoyant upper oceans—a few large placid stars beyond, coming silently and languidly out, and then disappearing—the melancholy, draperied night above, around. And there, upon the roads, the fields, and in those woods, that contest, never one more desperate in any age or land—both parties now in force— masses—no fancy battle, no semi-play, but fierce and savage demons fighting there—courage and scorn of death the rule, exceptions almost none.

What history, I say, can ever give—for who can know—the mad, determin'd tussle of the armies, in all their separate large and little squads—as this—each steep'd from crown to toe in desperate, mortal purports? Who know the conflict, hand-to-hand—the many conflicts in the dark, those shadowy-tangled, flashing-moonbeam'd woods—the writhing groups and squads —the cries, the din, the cracking guns and pistols—the distant cannon—the cheers and calls and threats and awful music of the oaths—the indescribable mix—the officers' orders, persuasions, encouragements—the devils fully rous'd in human hearts —the strong shout, *Charge, men, charge*—the flash of the naked sword, and rolling flame and smoke? And still the broken, clear and clouded heaven—and still again the moonlight pouring silvery soft its radiant patches over all. Who paint the scene, the sudden partial panic of the afternoon, at dusk? Who paint the irrepressible advance of the second division of the Third corps, under Hooker himself, suddenly order'd up—those rapid-filing phantoms through the woods? Who show what moves there in the shadows, fluid and firm— to save, (and it did save,) the army's name, perhaps the nation? as there the veterans hold the field. (Brave Berry falls not yet—but death has mark'd him—soon he falls.)

UNNAMED REMAINS THE BRAVEST SOLDIER

OF SCENES like these, I say, who writes—whoe'er can write the story? Of many a score—aye, thousands, north and south, of unwrit heroes, unknown heroisms, incredible, impromptu, first-class desperations—who tells? No history ever—no poem sings, no music sounds, those bravest men of all—those deeds. No formal general's report, nor book in the library, nor column in the paper, embalms the bravest, north or south, east or west. Unnamed, unknown, remain, and still remain, the bravest soldiers. Our manliest—our boys—our hardy darlings; no picture gives them. Likely, the typic one of them (standing, no doubt, for hundreds, thousands,) crawls aside to some bush-clump, or ferny tuft, on receiving his death-shot—there sheltering a little while, soaking roots, grass and soil, with red blood—the battle advances, retreats, flits from the scene, sweeps by—and there, haply with pain and suffering, (yet less, far less, than is supposed,) the last lethargy winds like a serpent round him—the eyes glaze in death—none recks—perhaps the burial-squads, in truce, a week afterwards, search not the secluded spot—and there, at last, the Bravest Soldier crumbles in mother earth, unburied and unknown.

AMBULANCE PROCESSIONS

June 25, Sundown.—As I sit writing this paragraph I see a train of about thirty huge four-horse wagons, used as ambulances, fill'd with wounded, passing up Fourteenth street, on their way, probably, to Columbian, Carver, and mount Pleasant hospitals. This is the way the men come in now, seldom in small numbers, but almost always in these long, sad processions. Through the past winter, while our army lay opposite Fredericksburg, the like strings of ambulances were of frequent occurrence along Seventh street, passing slowly up from the steamboat wharf, with loads from Aquia creek.

BAD WOUNDS—THE YOUNG

THE soldiers are nearly all young men, and far more American than is generally supposed—I should say nine-tenths are native-born. Among the arrivals from Chancellorsville I find a large proportion of Ohio, Indiana, and Illinois men. As usual, there are all sorts of wounds. Some of the men fearfully burnt from the explosions of artillery caissons. One ward has a long row of officers, some with ugly hurts. Yesterday was perhaps worse than usual. Amputations are going on—the attendants are dressing wounds. As you pass by, you must be on your guard where you look. I saw the other day a gentleman, a visitor apparently from curiosity, in one of the wards, stop and turn a moment to look at an awful wound they were probing. He turn'd pale, and in a moment more he had fainted away and fallen on the floor.

THE MOST INSPIRITING OF ALL
WAR'S SHOWS

June 29.—Just before sundown this evening a very large cavalry force went by—a fine sight. The men evidently had seen service. First came a mounted band of sixteen bugles, drums and cymbals, playing wild martial tunes—made my heart jump. Then the principal officers, then company after company, with their officers at their heads, making of course the main part of the cavalcade; then a long train of men with led horses, lots of mounted negroes with special horses—and a long string of baggage-wagons, each drawn by four horses—and then a motley rear guard. It was a pronouncedly warlike and gay show; the sabres clank'd, the men look'd young and healthy and strong; the electric tramping of so many horses on the hard road, and the gallant bearing, fine seat, and bright faced appearance of a thousand and more handsome young American men, were so good to see. An hour later another troop went by, smaller in numbers, perhaps three hundred men. They too look'd like serviceable men, campaigners used to field and fight.

July 3.—This forenoon, for more than an hour, again long strings of cavalry, several regiments, very fine men and horses, four or five abreast. I saw them in Fourteenth street, coming in town from north. Several hundred extra horses, some of the mares with colts, trotting along. (Appear'd to be a number of prisoners too.) How inspiriting always the cavalry regiments. Our men are generally well mounted, feel good, are young, gay on the saddle, their blankets in a roll behind them, their sabres clanking at their sides. This noise and movement and the tramp of many horses' hoofs has a curious effect upon one. The bugles play—presently you hear them afar off, deaden'd, mix'd with other noises. Then just as they had all pass'd, a string of ambulances commenc'd from the other way, moving up Fourteenth street north, slowly wending along, bearing a large lot of wounded to the hospitals.

BATTLE OF GETTYSBURG

July 4th.—The weather to-day, upon the whole, is very fine, warm, but from a smart rain last night, fresh enough, and no dust, which is a great relief for this city. I saw the parade about noon, Pennsylvania avenue, from Fifteenth street down toward the capitol. There were three regiments of infantry, (I suppose the ones doing patrol duty here,) two or three societies of Odd Fellows, a lot of children in barouches, and a squad of policemen. (A useless imposition upon the soldiers —they have work enough on their backs without piling the like of this.) As I went down the Avenue, saw a big flaring placard on the bulletin board of a newspaper office, announcing "Glorious Victory for the Union Army!" Meade had fought Lee at Gettysburg, Pennsylvania, yesterday and day before, and repuls'd him most signally, taken 3,000 prisoners, &c. (I afterwards saw Meade's despatch, very modest, and a sort of order of the day from the President himself, quite religious, giving thanks to the Supreme, and calling on the people to do the same.) I walk'd on to Armory hospital—took along with me several bottles of blackberry and cherry syrup, good and strong, but innocent. Went through several of the wards, announc'd to the soldiers the news from Meade, and gave them all a good drink of the syrups with ice water, quite refreshing —prepar'd it all myself, and serv'd it around. Meanwhile the Washington bells are ringing their sundown peals for Fourth of July, and the usual fusilades of boys' pistols, crackers, and guns.

A CAVALRY CAMP

I am writing this, nearly sundown, watching a cavalry company (acting Signal service,) just come in through a shower, making their night's camp ready on some broad, vacant ground, a sort of hill, in full view opposite my window. There are the men in their yellow-striped jackets. All are dismounted; the freed horses stand with drooping heads and wet sides; they are to be led off presently in groups, to water. The little wall-tents and shelter tents spring up quickly. I see the fires already blazing, and pots and kettles over them. Some among the men are driving in tent-poles, wielding their axes with strong, slow blows. I see great huddles of horses, bundles of hay, groups of men (some with unbuckled sabres yet on their sides,) a few officers, piles of wood, the flames of the fires, saddles, harness, &c. The smoke streams upward, additional men arrive and dismount—some drive in stakes, and tie their horses to them; some go with buckets for water, some are chopping wood, and so on.

July 6th.—A steady rain, dark and thick and warm. A train of six-mule wagons has just pass'd bearing pontoons, great square-end flat-boats, and the heavy planking for overlaying them. We hear that the Potomac above here is flooded, and are wondering whether Lee will be able to get back across again, or whether Meade will indeed break him to pieces. The cavalry camp on the hill is a ceaseless field of observation for me. This forenoon there stand the horses, tether'd together, dripping, steaming, chewing their hay. The men emerge from their tents, dripping also. The fires are half quench'd.

July 10th.—Still the camp opposite—perhaps fifty or sixty tents. Some of the men are cleaning their sabres (pleasant to-day,) some brushing boots, some laying off, reading, writing—some cooking, some sleeping. On long temporary cross-sticks back of the tents are cavalry accoutrements—blankets and overcoats are hung out to air—there are the squads of horses tether'd, feeding, continually stamping and whisking their tails to keep off flies. I sit long in my third story window and look at the scene—a hundred little things going on—peculiar objects connected with the camp that could not be described, any one of them justly, without much minute drawing and coloring in words.

A NEW YORK SOLDIER

This afternoon, July 22d, I have spent a long time with Oscar F. Wilber, company G, 154th New York, low with chronic diarrhœa, and a bad wound also. He asked me to read him a chapter in the New Testament. I complied, and ask'd him what I should read. He said, "Make your own choice." I open'd at the close of one of the first books of the evangelists, and read the chapters describing the latter hours of Christ, and the scenes at the crucifixion. The poor, wasted young man ask'd me to read the following chapter also, how Christ rose again. I read very slowly, for Oscar was feeble. It pleased him very much, yet the tears were in his eyes. He ask'd me if I enjoy'd religion. I said, "Perhaps not, my dear, in the way you mean, and yet, may-be, it is the same thing." He said, "It is my chief reliance." He talk'd of death, and said he did not fear it. I said, "Why, Oscar, don't you think you will get well?" He said, "I may, but it is not probable." He spoke calmly of his condition. The wound was very bad, it discharg'd much. Then the diarrhœa had prostrated him, and I felt that he was even then the same as dying. He behaved very manly and affectionate. The kiss I gave him as I was about leaving he return'd fourfold. He gave me his mother's address, Mrs. Sally D. Wilber, Alleghany post-office, Cattaraugus county, N. Y. I had several such interviews with him. He died a few days after the one just described.

HOME-MADE MUSIC

August 8th.—To-night, as I was trying to keep cool, sitting by a wounded soldier in Armory-square, I was attracted by some pleasant singing in an adjoining ward. As my soldier was asleep, I left him, and entering the ward where the music was, I walk'd half-way down and took a seat by the cot of a young Brooklyn friend, S. R., badly wounded in the hand at Chancellorsville, and who has suffer'd much, but at that moment in the evening was wide awake and comparatively easy. He had turn'd over on his left side to get a better view of the singers, but the mosquito-curtains of the adjoining cots obstructed the sight. I stept round and loop'd them all up, so that he had a clear show, and then sat down again by him, and look'd and listen'd. The principal singer was a young lady-nurse of one of the wards, accompanying on a melodeon, and join'd by the lady-nurses of other wards. They sat there, making a charming group, with their handsome, healthy faces, and standing up a little behind them were some ten or fifteen of the convalescent soldiers, young men, nurses, &c., with books in their hands, singing. Of course it was not such a performance as the great soloists at the New York opera house take a hand in, yet I am not sure but I receiv'd as much pleasure under the circumstances, sitting there, as I have had from the best Italian compositions, express'd by world-famous performers. The men lying up and down the hospital, in their cots, (some badly wounded—some never to rise thence,) the cots themselves, with their drapery of white curtains, and the shadows down the lower and upper parts of the ward; then the silence of the men, and the attitudes they took—the whole was a sight to look around upon again and again. And there sweetly rose those voices up to the high, whitewash'd wooden roof, and pleasantly the roof sent it all back again. They sang very well, mostly quaint old songs and declamatory hymns, to fitting tunes. Here, for instance:

My days are swiftly gliding by, and I a pilgrim stranger,
Would not detain them as they fly, those hours of toil and danger;
For O we stand on Jordan's strand, our friends are passing over,
And just before, the shining shore we may almost discover.

We'll gird our loins my brethren dear, our distant home discerning,
Our absent Lord has left us word, let every lamp be burning,
For O we stand on Jordan's strand, our friends are passing over,
And just before, the shining shore we may almost discover.

ABRAHAM LINCOLN

August 12th.—I see the President almost every day, as I happen to live where he passes to or from his lodgings out of town. He never sleeps at the White House during the hot season, but has quarters at a healthy location some three miles north of the city, the Soldiers' home, a United States military establishment. I saw him this morning about 8½ coming in to business, riding on Vermont avenue, near L street. He always has a company of twenty-five or thirty cavalry, with sabres drawn and held upright over their shoulders. They say this guard was against his personal wish, but he let his counselors have their way. The party makes no great show in uniform or horses. Mr. Lincoln on the saddle generally rides a good-sized, easygoing gray horse, is dress'd in plain black, somewhat rusty and dusty, wears a black stiff hat, and looks about as ordinary in attire, &c., as the commonest man. A lieutenant, with yellow straps, rides at his left, and following behind, two by two, come the cavalry men, in their yellow-striped jackets. They are generally going at a slow trot, as that is the pace set them by the one they wait upon. The sabres and accoutrements clank, and the entirely unornamental *cortège* as it trots toward Lafayette square arouses no sensation, only some curious stranger stops and gazes. I see very plainly ABRAHAM LINCOLN's dark brown face, with the deep-cut lines, the eyes, always to me with a deep latent sadness in the expression. We have got so that we exchange bows, and very cordial ones. Sometimes the President goes and comes in an open barouche. The cavalry always accompany him, with drawn sabres. Often I notice as he goes out evenings—and sometimes in the morning, when he returns early—he turns off and halts at the large and handsome residence of the Secretary of War, on K street, and holds conference there. If in his barouche, I can see from my window he does not alight, but sits in his vehicle, and Mr. Stanton comes out to attend him. Sometimes one of his sons, a boy of ten or twelve, accompanies him, riding at his right on a pony. Earlier in the summer I occasionally saw the President and his wife, toward the latter part of the afternoon, out in a barouche, on a pleasure ride through the city. Mrs. Lincoln was dress'd in complete black, with a long crape veil. The equipage is of the plainest kind, only two horses, and they nothing extra. They pass'd me once very close, and I saw the President in the face fully, as they were moving slowly, and his look, though abstracted, happen'd to be directed steadily in my eye. He bow'd and smiled, but far beneath his smile I noticed well the expression I have alluded to. None of the artists or pictures has caught the deep, though

subtle and indirect expression of this man's face. There is
something else there. One of the great portrait painters of
two or three centuries ago is needed.

HEATED TERM

THERE has lately been much suffering here from heat; we
have had it upon us now eleven days. I go around with an
umbrella and a fan. I saw two cases of sun-stroke yesterday,
one in Pennsylvania avenue, and another in Seventh street.
The City railroad company loses some horses every day. Yet
Washington is having a livelier August, and is probably putting in a more energetic and satisfactory summer, than ever
before during its existence. There is probably more human
electricity, more population to make it, more business, more
light-heartedness, than ever before. The armies that swiftly
circumambiated from Fredericksburg—march'd, struggled,
fought, had out their mighty clinch and hurl at Gettysburg—
wheel'd, circumambiated again, return'd to their ways, touching us not, either at their going or coming. And Washington
feels that she has pass'd the worst; perhaps feels that she is
henceforth mistress. So here she sits with her surrounding hills
spotted with guns, and is conscious of a character and identity
different from what it was five or six short weeks ago, and
very considerably pleasanter and prouder.

SOLDIERS AND TALKS

SOLDIERS, soldiers, soldiers, you meet everywhere about the
city, often superb-looking men, though invalids dress'd in
worn uniforms, and carrying canes or crutches. I often have
talks with them, occasionally quite long and interesting. One,
for instance, will have been all through the peninsula under
McClellan—narrates to me the fights, the marches, the strange,
quick changes of that eventful campaign, and gives glimpses
of many things untold in any official reports or books or jour-

nals. These, indeed, are the things that are genuine and precious. The man was there, has been out two years, has been through a dozen fights, the superfluous flesh of talking is long work'd off him, and he gives me little but the hard meat and sinew. I find it refreshing, these hardy, bright, intuitive, American young men, (experienc'd soldiers with all their youth.) The vocal play and significance moves one more than books. Then there hangs something majestic about a man who has borne his part in battles, especially if he is very quiet regarding it when you desire him to unbosom. I am continually lost at the absence of blowing and blowers among these old-young American militaires. I have found some man or other who has been in every battle since the war began, and have talk'd with them about each one in every part of the United States, and many of the engagements on the rivers and harbors too. I find men here from every State in the Union, without exception. (There are more Southerners, especially border State men, in the Union army than is generally supposed.) I now doubt whether one can get a fair idea of what this war practically is, or what genuine America is, and her character, without some such experience as this I am having.

DEATH OF A WISCONSIN OFFICER

ANOTHER characteristic scene of that dark and bloody 1863, from notes of my visit to Armory-square hospital, one hot but pleasant summer day. In ward H we approach the cot of a young lieutenant of one of the Wisconsin regiments. Tread the bare board floor lightly here, for the pain and panting of death are in this cot. I saw the lieutenant when he was first brought here from Chancellorsville, and have been with him occasionally from day to day and night to night. He had been getting along pretty well till night before last, when a sudden hemorrhage that could not be stopt came upon him, and to-day it still continues at intervals. Notice that water-pail by the side of the bed, with a quantity of blood and bloody pieces of muslin, nearly full; that tells the story. The poor young man is struggling painfully for breath, his great dark eyes with a glaze already upon them, and the choking faint but audible in his throat. An attendant sits by him, and will not leave him till the last; yet little or nothing can be done. He will die here in an hour or two, without the presence of kith or kin. Meantime the ordinary chat and business of the ward a little way off goes on indifferently. Some of the inmates are laughing and joking, others are playing checkers or cards, others are reading, &c.

I have noticed through most of the hospitals that as long as there is any chance for a man, no matter how bad he may be, the surgeon and nurses work hard, sometimes with curious tenacity, for his life, doing everything, and keeping somebody by him to execute the doctor's orders, and minister to him every minute night and day. See that screen there. As you advance through the dusk of early candle-light, a nurse will step forth on tip-toe, and silently but imperiously forbid you to make any noise, or perhaps to come near at all. Some soldier's life is flickering there, suspended between recovery and death. Perhaps at this moment the exhausted frame has just fallen into a light sleep that a step might shake. You must retire. The neighboring patients must move in their stocking feet. I have been several times struck with such mark'd efforts—everything bent to save a life from the very grip of the destroyer. But when that grip is once firmly fix'd, leaving no hope or chance at all, the surgeon abandons the patient. If it is a case where stimulus is any relief, the nurse gives milk-punch or brandy, or whatever is wanted, *ad libitum*. There is no fuss made. Not a bit of sentimentalism or whining have I seen about a single death-bed in hospital or on the field, but generally impassive indifference. All is over, as far as any efforts can avail; it is useless to expend emotions or labors. While there is a prospect they strive hard—at least most surgeons do; but death certain and evident, they yield the field.

A SILENT NIGHT RAMBLE

October 20th.—To-night, after leaving the hospital at 10 o'clock, (I had been on self-imposed duty some five hours, pretty closely confined,) I wander'd a long time around Washington. The night was sweet, very clear, sufficiently cool, a voluptuous half-moon, slightly golden, the space near it of a transparent blue-gray tinge. I walk'd up Pennsylvania avenue, and then to Seventh street, and a long while around the Patent-office. Somehow it look'd rebukefully strong, majestic, there in the delicate moonlight. The sky, the planets, the constellations all so bright, so calm, so expressively silent, so soothing, after those hospital scenes. I wander'd to and fro till the moist moon set, long after midnight.

SPIRITUAL CHARACTERS AMONG THE SOLDIERS

EVERY now and then, in hospital or camp, there are beings I meet—specimens of unworldliness, disinterestedness, and animal purity and heroism—perhaps some unconscious Indianian, or from Ohio or Tennessee—on whose birth the calmness of heaven seems to have descended, and whose gradual growing up, whatever the circumstances of work-life or change, or hardship, or small or no education that attended it, the power of a strange spiritual sweetness, fibre and inward health, have also attended. Something veil'd and abstracted is often a part of the manners of these beings. I have met them, I say, not seldom in the army, in camp, and in the hospitals. The Western regiments contain many of them. They are often young men, obeying the events and occasions about them, marching, soldiering, fighting, foraging, cooking, working on farms or at some trade before the war—unaware of their own nature, (as to that, who is aware of his own nature?) their companions only understanding that they are different from the rest, more silent, "something odd about them," and apt to go off and meditate and muse in solitude.

CATTLE DROVES ABOUT
WASHINGTON

AMONG other sights are immense droves of cattle with their drivers, passing through the streets of the city. Some of the men have a way of leading the cattle by a peculiar call, a wild, pensive hoot, quite musical, prolong'd, indescribable, sounding something between the cooing of a pigeon and the hoot of an owl. I like to stand and look at the sight of one of these immense droves—a little way off—(as the dust is great.) There are always men on horseback, cracking their whips and shouting—the cattle low—some obstinate ox or steer attempts to escape—then a lively scene—the mounted men, always excellent riders and on good horses, dash after the recusant, and wheel and turn—a dozen mounted drovers, their great slouch'd, broad-brimm'd hats, very picturesque—another dozen on foot—everybody cover'd with dust—long goads in their hands—an immense drove of perhaps 1000 cattle—the shouting, hooting, movement, &c.

HOSPITAL PERPLEXITY

To ADD to other troubles, amid the confusion of this great army of sick, it is almost impossible for a stranger to find any friend or relative, unless he has the patient's specific address to start upon. Besides the directory printed in the newspapers here, there are one or two general directories of the hospitals kept at provost's headquarters, but they are nothing like complete; they are never up to date, and, as things are, with the daily streams of coming and going and changing, cannot be. I have known cases, for instance such as a farmer coming here from northern New York to find a wounded brother, faithfully hunting round for a week, and then compell'd to leave and go home without getting any trace of him. When he got home he found a letter from the brother giving the right address.

DOWN AT THE FRONT

CULPEPPER, VA., *Feb. '64.*—Here I am pretty well down toward the extreme front. Three or four days ago General S., who is now in chief command, (I believe Meade is absent, sick,) moved a strong force southward from camp as if intending business. They went to the Rapidan; there has since been some manœuvring and a little fighting, but nothing of consequence. The telegraphic accounts given Monday morning last, make entirely too much of it, I should say. What General S. intended we here know not, but we trust in that competent commander. We were somewhat excited, (but not so very much either,) on Sunday, during the day and night, as orders were sent out to pack up and harness, and be ready to evacuate, to fall back towards Washington. But I was very sleepy and went to bed. Some tremendous shouts arousing me during the night, I went forth and found it was from the men above mention'd, who were returning. I talk'd with some of the men; as usual I found them full of gayety, endurance, and many fine little outshows, the signs of the most excellent good manliness of the world. It was a curious sight to see those shadowy columns moving through the night. I stood unobserv'd in the darkness and watch'd them long. The mud was very deep. The men had their usual burdens, overcoats, knapsacks, guns and blankets. Along and along they filed by me, with often a laugh, a song, a cheerful word, but never once a murmur. It may have been odd, but I never before so realized the majesty and reality of the American people *en masse*. It fell upon me like a great awe. The strong ranks moved neither fast nor slow. They had march'd seven or eight miles already through the slipping unctuous mud. The brave First corps stopt here. The equally brave Third corps moved on to Brandy station. The famous Brooklyn 14th are here, guarding the town. You see their red legs actively moving everywhere. Then they have a theatre of their own here. They give musical performances, nearly everything done capitally. Of course the audience is a jam. It is good sport to attend one of these entertainments of the 14th. I like to look around at the soldiers, and the general collection in front of the curtain, more than the scene on the stage.

PAYING THE BOUNTIES

ONE of the things to note here now is the arrival of the paymaster with his strong box, and the payment of bounties to veterans re-enlisting. Major H. is here to-day, with a small mountain of greenbacks, rejoicing the hearts of the 2d division of the First corps. In the midst of a rickety shanty, behind a little table, sit the major and clerk Eldridge, with the rolls before them, and much moneys. A re-enlisted man gets in cash about $200 down, (and heavy instalments following, as the pay-days arrive, one after another.) The show of the men crowding around is quite exhilarating; I like to stand and look. They feel elated, their pockets full, and the ensuing furlough, the visit home. It is a scene of sparkling eyes and flush'd cheeks. The soldier has many gloomy and harsh experiences, and this makes up for some of them. Major H. is order'd to pay first all the re-enlisted men of the First corps their bounties and back pay, and then the rest. You hear the peculiar sound of the rustling of the new and crisp greenbacks by the hour, through the nimble fingers of the major and my friend clerk E.

RUMORS, CHANGES, &c.

ABOUT the excitement of Sunday, and the orders to be ready to start, I have heard since that the said orders came from some cautious minor commander, and that the high principalities knew not and thought not of any such move; which is likely. The rumor and fear here intimated a long circuit by Lee, and flank attack on our right. But I cast my eyes at the mud, which was then at its deepest and palmiest condition, and retired composedly to rest. Still it is about time for Culpepper to have a change. Authorities have chased each other here like clouds in a stormy sky. Before the first Bull Run this was the rendezvous and camp of instruction of the secession troops. I am stopping at the house of a lady who has witness'd all the eventful changes of the war, along this route of contending armies. She is a widow, with a family of young children, and lives here with her sister in a large handsome house. A number of army officers board with them.

VIRGINIA

DILAPIDATED, fenceless, and trodden with war as Virginia is, wherever I move across her surface, I find myself rous'd to surprise and admiration. What capacity for products, improvements, human life, nourishment and expansion. Everywhere that I have been in the Old Dominion, (the subtle mockery of that title now!) such thoughts have fill'd me. The soil is yet far above the average of any of the northern States. And how full of breadth the scenery, everywhere distant mountains, everywhere convenient rivers. Even yet prodigal in forest woods, and surely eligible for all the fruits, orchards, and flowers. The skies and atmosphere most luscious, as I feel certain, from more than a year's residence in the State, and movements hither and yon. I should say very healthy, as a general thing. Then a rich and elastic quality, by night and by day. The sun rejoices in his strength, dazzling and burning, and yet, to me, never unpleasantly weakening. It is not the panting tropical heat, but invigorates. The north tempers it. The nights are often unsurpassable. Last evening (Feb. 8,) I saw the first of the new moon, the outlined old moon clear along with it; the sky and air so clear, such transparent hues of color, it seem'd to me I had never really seen the new moon before. It was the thinnest cut crescent possible. It hung delicate just above the sulky shadow of the Blue mountains. Ah, if it might prove an omen and good prophecy for this unhappy State.

SUMMER OF 1864

I AM back again in Washington, on my regular daily and nightly rounds. Of course there are many specialties. Dotting a ward here and there are always cases of poor fellows, long-suffering under obstinate wounds, or weak and dishearten'd from typhoid fever, or the like; mark'd cases, needing special and sympathetic nourishment. These I sit down and either talk to, or silently cheer them up. They always like it hugely, (and so do I.) Each case has its peculiarities, and needs some new adaptation. I have learnt to thus conform—learnt a good deal of hospital wisdom. Some of the poor young chaps, away from home for the first time in their lives, hunger and thirst for affection; this is sometimes the only thing that will reach their condition. The men like to have a pencil, and something to write in. I have given them cheap pocket-diaries, and almanacs for 1864, interleav'd with blank paper. For reading I generally have some old pictorial magazines or story papers—they are always acceptable. Also the morning or evening papers of the day. The best books I do not give, but lend to read through the wards, and then take them to others, and so on; they are very punctual about returning the books. In these wards, or on the field, as I thus continue to go round, I have come to adapt myself to each emegency, after its kind or call, however trivial, however solemn, every one justified and made real under its circumstances—not only visits and cheering talk and little gifts—not only washing and dressing wounds, (I have some cases where the patient is unwilling any one should do this but me)—but passages from the Bible, expounding them, prayer at the bedside, explanations of doctrine, &c. (I think I see my friends smiling at this confession, but I was never more in earnest in my life.) In camp and everywhere, I was in the habit of reading or giving recitations to the men. They were very fond of it, and liked declamatory poetical pieces. We would gather in a large group by ourselves, after supper, and spend the time in such readings, or in talking, and occasionally by an amusing game called the game of twenty questions.

A NEW ARMY ORGANIZATION FIT
FOR AMERICA

IT IS plain to me out of the events of the war, north and south, and out of all considerations, that the current military theory, practice, rules and organization, (adopted from Europe from the feudal institutes, with, of course, the "modern improvements," largely from the French,) though tacitly follow'd, and believ'd in by the officers generally, are not at all consonant with the United States, nor our people, nor our days. What it will be I know not—but I know that as entire an abnegation of the present military system, and the naval too, and a building up from radically different root-bases and centres appropriate to us, must eventually result, as that our political system has resulted and become establish'd, different from feudal Europe, and built up on itself from original, perennial, democratic premises. We have undoubtedly in the United States the greatest military power—an exhaustless, intelligent, brave and reliable rank and file—in the world, any land, perhaps all lands. The problem is to organize this in the manner fully appropriate to it, to the principles of the republic, and to get the best service out of it. In the present struggle, as already seen and review'd, probably three-fourths of the losses, men, lives, &c., have been sheer superfluity, extravagance, waste.

DEATH OF A HERO

I WONDER if I could ever convey to another—to you, for instance, reader dear—the tender and terrible realities of such cases, (many, many happen'd,) as the one I am now going to mention. Stewart C. Glover, company E, 5th Wisconsin—was wounded May 5, in one of those fierce tussles of the Wilderness—died May 21—aged about 20. He was a small and beardless young man—a splendid soldier—in fact almost an ideal American, of his age. He had serv'd nearly three years, and would have been entitled to his discharge in a few days. He was in Hancock's corps. The fighting had about ceas'd for the day, and the general commanding the brigade rode by and call'd for volunteers to bring in the wounded. Glover responded among the first—went out gayly—but while in the act of bearing in a wounded sergeant to our lines, was shot in the knee by a rebel sharpshooter; consequence, amputation and death. He had resided with his father, John Glover, an aged and feeble man, in Batavia, Genesee county, N. Y., but was at school in Wisconsin, after the war broke out, and there enlisted—soon took to soldier-life, liked it, was very manly, was belov'd by officers and comrades. He kept a little diary, like so many of the soldiers. On the day of his death he wrote the following in it, *to-day the doctor says I must die —all is over with me—ah, so young to die.* On another blank leaf he pencill'd to his brother, *dear brother Thomas, I have been brave but wicked—pray for me.*

HOSPITAL SCENES—INCIDENTS

It is Sunday afternoon, middle of summer hot and oppressive, and very silent through the ward. I am taking care of a critical case, now lying in a half lethargy. Near where I sit is a suffering rebel, from the 8th Louisiana; his name is Irving. He has been here a long time, badly wounded, and lately had his leg amputated; it is not doing very well. Right opposite me is a sick soldier-boy, laid down with his clothes on, sleeping, looking much wasted, his pallid face on his arm. I see by the yellow trimming on his jacket that he is a cavalry boy. I step softly over and find by his card that he is named William Cone, of the 1st Maine cavalry, and his folks live in Skowhegan.

Ice Cream Treat.—One hot day toward the middle of June, I gave the inmates of Carver hospital a general ice cream treat, purchasing a large quantity, and, under convoy of the doctor or head nurse, going around personally through the wards to see to its distribution.

An Incident.—In one of the fights before Atlanta, a rebel soldier, of large size, evidently a young man, was mortally wounded top of the head, so that the brains partially exuded. He lived three days, lying on his back on the spot where he first dropt. He dug with his heel in the ground during that time a hole big enough to put in a couple of ordinary knapsacks. He just lay there in the open air, and with little intermission kept his heel going night and day. Some of our soldiers then moved him to a house, but he died in a few minutes.

Another.—After the battles at Columbia, Tennessee, where we repuls'd about a score of vehement rebel charges, they left a great many wounded on the ground, mostly within our range. Whenever any of these wounded attempted to move away by any means, generally by crawling off, our men without exception brought them down by a bullet. They let none crawl away, no matter what his condition.

A YANKEE SOLDIER

As I turn'd off the Avenue one cool October evening into Thirteenth street, a soldier with knapsack and overcoat stood at the corner inquiring his way. I found he wanted to go part of the road in my direction, so we walk'd on together. We soon fell into conversation. He was small and not very young, and a tough little fellow, as I judged in the evening light, catching glimpses by the lamps we pass'd. His answers were short, but clear. His name was Charles Carroll; he belong'd to one of the Massachusetts regiments, and was born in or near Lynn. His parents were living, but were very old. There were four sons, and all had enlisted. Two had died of starvation and misery in the prison at Andersonville, and one had been kill'd in the west. He only was left. He was now going home, and by the way he talk'd I inferr'd that his time was nearly out. He made great calculations on being with his parents to comfort them the rest of their days.

UNION PRISONERS SOUTH

Michael Stansbury, 48 years of age, a sea-faring man, a southerner by birth and raising, formerly captain of U. S. light ship Long Shoal, station'd at Long Shoal point, Pamlico sound —though a southerner, a firm Union man—was captur'd Feb. 17, 1863, and has been nearly two years in the Confederate prisons; was at one time order'd releas'd by Governor Vance, but a rebel officer re-arrested him; then sent on to Richmond for exchange—but instead of being exchanged was sent down (as a southern citizen, not a soldier,) to Salisbury, N. C., where he remain'd until lately, when he escap'd among the exchang'd by assuming the name of a dead soldier, and coming up via Wilmington with the rest. Was about sixteen months in Salisbury. Subsequent to October, '64, there were about 11,000 Union prisoners in the stockade; about 100 of them southern unionists, 200 U. S. deserters. During the past winter 1500 of the prisoners, to save their lives, join'd the confederacy, on condition of being assign'd merely to guard duty. Out of the 11,000 not more than 2500 came out; 500 of these were pitiable, helpless wretches—the rest were in a condition to travel. There were often 60 dead bodies to be buried in the morning; the daily average would be about 40. The regular food was a meal of corn, the cob and husk ground together, and sometimes once a week a ration of sorghum molasses. A diminutive ration of meat might possibly come once a month, not oftener. In the stockade, containing the 11,000 men, there was a partial show of tents, not enough for 2000. A large proportion of the men lived in holes in the ground, in the utmost wretchedness. Some froze to death, others had their hands and feet frozen. The rebel guards would occasionally, and on the least pretence, fire into the prison from mere demonism and wantonness. All the horrors that can be named, starvation, lassitude, filth, vermin, despair, swift loss of self-respect, idiocy, insanity, and frequent murder, were there. Stansbury has a wife and child living in Newbern—has written to them from here—is in the U. S. light-house employ still—

(had been home to Newbern to see his family, and on his return to the ship was captured in his boat.) Has seen men
brought there to Salisbury as hearty as you ever see in your
life—in a few weeks completely dead gone, much of it from
thinking on their condition—hope all gone. Has himself a hard,
sad, strangely deaden'd kind of look, as of one chill'd for
years in the cold and dark, where his good manly nature had
no room to exercise itself.

DESERTERS

Oct. 24.—Saw a large squad of our own deserters, (over 300)
surrounded with a cordon of arm'd guards, marching along
Pennsylvania avenue. The most motley collection I ever saw,
all sorts of rig, all sorts of hats and caps, many fine-looking
young fellows, some of them shame-faced, some sickly, most
of them dirty, shirts very dirty and long worn, &c. They
tramp'd along without order, a huge huddling mass, not in
ranks. I saw some of the spectators laughing, but I felt like
anything else but laughing. These deserters are far more
numerous than would be thought. Almost every day I see
squads of them, sometimes two or three at a time, with a small
guard; sometimes ten or twelve, under a larger one. (I hear
that desertions from the army now in the field have often
averaged 10,000 a month. One of the commonest sights in
Washington is a squad of deserters.)

A GLIMPSE OF WAR'S
HELL-SCENES

In one of the late movements of our troops in the valley, (near
Upperville, I think,) a strong force of Moseby's mounted
guerillas attack'd a train of wounded, and the guard of cavalry
convoying them. The ambulances contain'd about 60
wounded, quite a number of them officers of rank. The rebels

were in strength, and the capture of the train and its partial guard after a short snap was effectually accomplish'd. No sooner had our men surrender'd, the rebels instantly commenced robbing the train and murdering their prisoners, even the wounded. Here is the scene or a sample of it, ten minutes after. Among the wounded officers in the ambulances were one, a lieutenant of regulars, and another of higher rank. These two were dragg'd out on the ground on their backs, and were now surrounded by the guerillas, a demoniac crowd, each member of which was stabbing them in different parts of their bodies. One of the officers had his feet pinn'd firmly to the ground by bayonets stuck through them and thrust into the ground. These two officers, as afterwards found on examination, had receiv'd about twenty such thrusts, some of them through the mouth, face, &c. The wounded had all been dragg'd (to give a better chance also for plunder,) out of their wagons; some had been effectually dispatch'd, and their bodies were lying there lifeless and bloody. Others, not yet dead, but horribly mutilated, were moaning or groaning. Of our men who surrender'd, most had been thus maim'd or slaughter'd.

At this instant a force of our cavalry, who had been following the train at some interval, charged suddenly upon the secesh captors, who proceeded at once to make the best escape they could. Most of them got away, but we gobbled two officers and seventeen men, in the very acts just described. The sight was one which admitted of little discussion, as may be imagined. The seventeen captur'd men and two officers were put under guard for the night, but it was decided there and then that they should die. The next morning the two officers were taken in the town, separate places, put in the centre of the street, and shot. The seventeen men were taken to an open ground, a little one side. They were placed in a hollow square, half-encompass'd by two of our cavalry regiments, one of which regiments had three days before found the bloody corpses of three of their men hamstrung and hung up by the heels to limbs of trees by Moseby's guerillas, and the other had not long before had twelve men, after surrendering, shot and then hung by the neck to limbs of trees, and jeering inscriptions pinn'd to the breast of one of the corpses, who had been a sergeant. Those three, and those twelve, had been found, I say, by these environing regiments. Now, with revolvers, they form'd the grim cordon of the seventeen prisoners. The latter were placed in the midst of the hollow square, unfasten'd, and the ironical remark made to them that they were now to be given "a chance for themselves." A few ran for it. But what use? From every side the deadly pills came. In a few minutes the seventeen corpses strew'd the hollow square. I was curious to know whether some of the Union soldiers, some few, (some one or two at least of the youngsters,) did not abstain from shooting on the helpless men. Not one. There was no exultation, very little said, almost nothing, yet every man there contributed his shot.

Multiply the above by scores, aye hundreds—verify it in all the forms that different circumstances, individuals, places, could afford—light it with every lurid passion, the wolf's, the lion's lapping thirst for blood—the passionate, boiling volcanoes of human revenge for comrades, brothers slain—with the light of burning farms, and heaps of smutting, smouldering black embers—and in the human heart everywhere black, worse embers—and you have an inkling of this war.

GIFTS—MONEY—DISCRIMINATION

As a very large proportion of the wounded came up from the front without a cent of money in their pockets, I soon discover'd that it was about the best thing I could do to raise their spirits, and show them that somebody cared for them, and practically felt a fatherly or brotherly interest in them, to give them small sums in such cases, using tact and discretion about it. I am regularly supplied with funds for this purpose by good women and men in Boston, Salem, Providence, Brooklyn, and New York. I provide myself with a quantity of bright new ten-cent and five-cent bills, and, when I think it incumbent, I give 25 or 30 cents, or perhaps 50 cents, and occasionally a still larger sum to some particular case. As I have started this subject, I take opportunity to ventilate the financial question. My supplies, altogether voluntary, mostly confidential, often seeming quite Providential, were numerous and varied. For instance, there were two distant and wealthy ladies, sisters, who sent regularly, for two years, quite heavy sums, enjoining that their names should be kept secret. The same delicacy was indeed a frequent condition. From several had *carte blanche*. Many were entire strangers. From these sources, during from two to three years, in the manner described, in the hospitals, I bestowed, as almoner for others, many, many thousands of dollars. I learn'd one thing conclusively—that beneath all the ostensible greed and heartlessness of our times there is no end to the generous benevolence of men and women in the United States, when once sure of their object. Another thing became clear to me—while *cash* is not amiss to bring up the rear, tact and magnetic sympathy and unction are, and ever will be, sovereign still.

ARMY SURGEONS—AID
DEFICIENCIES

I MUST bear my most emphatic testimony to the zeal, manliness, and professional spirit and capacity, generally prevailing among the surgeons, many of them young men, in the hospitals and the army. I will not say much about the exceptions, for they are few; (but I have met some of those few, and very incompetent and airish they were.) I never ceas'd to find the best men, and the hardest and most disinterested workers, among the surgeons in the hospitals. They are full of genius, too. I have seen many hundreds of them and this is my testimony. There are, however, serious deficiencies, wastes, sad want of system, in the commissions, contributions, and in all the voluntary, and a great part of the governmental nursing, edibles, medicines, stores, &c. (I do not say surgical attendance, because the surgeons cannot do more than human endurance permits.) Whatever puffing accounts there may be in the papers of the North, this is the actual fact. No thorough previous preparation, no system, no foresight, no genius. Always plenty of stores, no doubt, but never where they are needed, and never the proper application. Of all harrowing experiences, none is greater than that of the days following a heavy battle. Scores, hundreds of the noblest men on earth, uncomplaining, lie helpless, mangled, faint, alone, and so bleed to death, or die from exhaustion, either actually untouch'd at all, or merely the laying of them down and leaving them, when there ought to be means provided to save them.

THE BLUE EVERYWHERE

THIS city, its suburbs the capitol, the front of the White House, the places of amusement, the Avenue, and all the main streets, swarm with soldiers this winter, more than ever before. Some are out from the hospitals, some from the neighboring camps, &c. One source or another, they pour plenteously, and make, I should say, the mark'd feature in the human movement and costume-appearance of our national city. Their blue pants and overcoats are everywhere. The clump of crutches is heard up the stairs of the paymasters' offices, and there are characteristic groups around the doors of the same, often waiting long and wearily in the cold. Toward the latter part of the afternoon, you see the furlough'd men, sometimes singly, sometimes in small squads, making their way to the Baltimore depot. At all times, except early in the morning, the patrol detachments are moving around, especially during the earlier hours of evening, examining passes, and arresting all soldiers without them. They do not question the one-legged, or men badly disabled or maim'd, but all others are stopt. They also go around evenings through the auditoriums of the theatres, and make officers and all show their passes, or other authority, for being there.

A MODEL HOSPITAL

Sunday, January 29th, 1865.—Have been in Armory-square this afternoon. The wards are very comfortable, new floors and plaster walls, and models of neatness. I am not sure but this is a model hospital after all, in important respects. I found several sad cases of old lingering wounds. One Delaware soldier, William H. Millis, from Bridgeville, whom I had been with after the battles of the Wilderness, last May, where he receiv'd a very bad wound in the chest, with another in the left arm, and whose case was serious (pneumonia had set in) all last June and July, I now find well enough to do light duty. For three weeks at the time mention'd he just hovered between life and death.

BOYS IN THE ARMY

As I walk'd home about sunset, I saw in Fourteenth street a very young soldier, thinly clad, standing near the house I was about to enter. I stopt a moment in front of the door and call'd him to me. I knew that an old Tennessee regiment, and also an Indiana regiment, were temporarily stopping in new barracks, near Fourteenth street. This boy I found belonged to the Tennessee regiment. But I could hardly believe he carried a musket. He was but 15 years old, yet had been twelve months a soldier, and had borne his part in several battles, even historic ones. I ask'd him if he did not suffer from the cold, and if he had no overcoat. No, he did not suffer from cold, and had no overcoat, but could draw one whenever he wish'd. His father was dead, and his mother living in some part of East Tennessee; all the men were from that part of the country. The next forenoon I saw the Tennessee and Indiana regiments marching down the Avenue. My boy was with the former, stepping along with the rest. There were many other boys no older. I stood and watch'd them as they tramp'd along with slow, strong, heavy, regular steps. There

did not appear to be a man over 30 years of age, and a large
proportion were from 15 to perhaps 22 or 23. They had all the
look of veterans, worn, stain'd, impassive, and a certain un
bent, lounging gait, carrying in addition to their regular arm
and knapsacks, frequently a frying-pan, broom, &c. They were
all of pleasant physiognomy; no refinement, nor blanch'd with
intellect, but as my eye pick'd them, moving along, rank by
rank, there did not seem to be a single repulsive, brutal or
markedly stupid face among them.

BURIAL OF A LADY NURSE

HERE is an incident just occurr'd in one of the hospitals. A
lady named Miss or Mrs. Billings, who has long been a prac
tical friend of soldiers, and nurse in the army, and had become
attached to it in a way that no one can realize but him or
her who has had experience, was taken sick, early this winter
linger'd some time, and finally died in the hospital. It was her
request that she should be buried among the soldiers, and
after the military method. This request was fully carried out.
Her coffin was carried to the grave by soldiers, with the usual
escort, buried, and a salute fired over the grave. This was at
Annapolis a few days since.

FEMALE NURSES FOR SOLDIERS

THERE are many women in one position or another, among the
hospitals, mostly as nurses here in Washington, and among
the military stations; quite a number of them young ladies
acting as volunteers. They are a help in certain ways, and de
serve to be mention'd with respect. Then it remains to be
distinctly said that few or no young ladies, under the irresisti
ble conventions of society, answer the practical requirement
of nurses for soldiers. Middle-aged or healthy and good con
dition'd elderly women, mothers of children, are always best
Many of the wounded must be handled. A hundred things

which cannot be gainsay'd, must occur and must be done. The presence of a good middle-aged or elderly woman, the magnetic touch of hands, the expressive features of the mother, the silent soothing of her presence, her words, her knowledge and privileges arrived at only through having had children, are precious and final qualification. It is a natural faculty that is required; it is not merely having a genteel young woman at a table in a ward. One of the finest nurses I met was a red-faced illiterate old Irish woman; I have seen her take the poor wasted naked boys so tenderly up in her arms. There are plenty of excellent clean old black women that would make tip-top nurses.

THE CAPITOL BY GAS-LIGHT

To-night I have been wandering awhile in the capitol, which is all lit up. The illuminated rotunda looks fine. I like to stand aside and look a long, long while, up at the dome; it comforts me somehow. The House and Senate were both in session till very late. I look'd in upon them, but only a few moments; they were hard at work on tax and appropriation bills. I wander'd through the long and rich corridors and apartments under the Senate; an old habit of mine, former winters, and now more satisfaction than ever. Not many persons down there, occasionally a flitting figure in the distance.

THE INAUGURATION

March 4.—The President very quietly rode down to the capitol in his own carriage, by himself, on a sharp trot, about noon, either because he wish'd to be on hand to sign bills, or to get rid of marching in line with the absurd procession, the muslin temple of liberty, and pasteboard monitor. I saw him on his return, at three o'clock, after the performance was over. He was in his plain two-horse barouche, and look'd very much worn and tired; the lines, indeed, of vast responsibilities, intricate questions, and demands of life and death, cut deeper than ever upon his dark brown face; yet all the old goodness, tenderness, sadness, and canny shrewdness, underneath the furrows. (I never see that man without feeling that he is one to become personally attach'd to, for his combination of purest, heartiest tenderness, and native western form of manliness.) By his side sat his little boy, of ten years. There were no soldiers, only a lot of civilians on horseback, with huge yellow scarfs over their shoulders, riding around the carriage. (At the inauguration four years ago, he rode down and back again surrounded by a dense mass of arm'd cavalrymen eight deep, with drawn sabres; and there were sharp-shooters station'd at every corner on the route.) I ought to make mention of the closing levee of Saturday night last. Never before was such a compact jam in front of the White House—all the grounds fill'd, and away out to the spacious sidewalks. I was there, as I took a notion to go—was in the rush inside with the crowd—surged along the passage-ways, the blue and other rooms, and through the great east room. Crowds of country people, some very funny. Fine music from the Marine band, off in a side place. I saw Mr. Lincoln, drest all in black, with white kid gloves and a claw-hammer coat, receiving, as in duty bound, shaking hands, looking very disconsolate, and as if he would give anything to be somewhere else.

ATTITUDE OF FOREIGN GOVERN-
MENTS DURING THE WAR

LOOKING over my scraps, I find I wrote the following during 1864. The happening to our America, abroad as well as at home, these years, is indeed most strange. The democratic republic has paid her to-day the terrible and resplendent compliment of the united wish of all the nations of the world that her union should be broken, her future cut off, and that she should be compell'd to descend to the level of kingdoms and empires ordinarily great. There is certainly not one govern ment in Europe but is now watching the war in this country, with the ardent prayer that the United States may be effectually split, crippled, and dismember'd by it. There is not one but would help toward that dismemberment, if it dared. I say such is the ardent wish to-day of England and of France, as governments, and of all the nations of Europe, as governments. I think indeed it is to-day the real, heartfelt wish of all the nations of the world, with the single exception of Mexico— Mexico, the only one to whom we have ever really done wrong, and now the only one who prays for us and for our triumph, with genuine prayer. Is it not indeed strange? America, made up of all, cheerfully from the beginning opening her arms to all, the result and justifier of all, of Britain, Germany, France and Spain—all here—the accepter, the friend, hope, last resource and general house of all—she who has harm'd none, but been bounteous to so many, to millions, the mother of strangers and exiles, all nations—should now I say be paid this dread compliment of general governmental fear and hatred. Are we indignant? alarm'd? Do we feel jeopardized? No; help'd, braced, concentrated, rather. We are all too prone to wander from ourselves, to affect Europe, and watch her frowns and smiles. We need this hot lesson of general hatred, and henceforth must never forget it. Never again will we trust the moral sense nor abstract friendliness of a single *government* of the old world.

THE WEATHER—DOES IT SYMPATHIZE WITH THESE TIMES?

WHETHER the rains, the heat and cold, and what underlies them all, are affected with what affects man in masses, and follow his play of passionate action, strain'd stronger than usual, and on a larger scale than usual—whether this, or no, it is certain that there is now, and has been for twenty months or more, on this American continent north, many a remarkable, many an unprecedented expression of the subtile world of air above us and around us. There, since this war, and the wide and deep national agitation, strange analogies, different combinations, a different sunlight, or absence of it; different products even out of the ground. After every great battle, a great storm. Even civic events the same. On Saturday last, a forenoon like whirling demons, dark, with slanting rain, full of rage; and then the afternoon, so calm, so bathed with flooding splendor from heaven's most excellent sun, with atmosphere of sweetness; so clear, it show'd the stars, long, long before they were due. As the President came out on the capitol portico, a curious little white cloud, the only one in that part of the sky, appear'd like a hovering bird, right over him.

Indeed, the heavens, the elements, all the meteorological influences, have run riot for weeks past. Such caprices, abruptest alternation of frowns and beauty, I never knew. It is a common remark that (as last summer was different in its spells of intense heat from any preceding it,) the winter just completed has been without parallel. It has remain'd so down to the hour I am writing. Much of the daytime of the past month was sulky, with leaden heaviness, fog, interstices of bitter cold, and some insane storms. But there have been samples of another description. Nor earth nor sky ever knew spectacles of superber beauty than some of the nights lately here. The western star, Venus, in the earlier hours of evening, has never been so large, so clear; it seems as if it told something, as if it held rapport indulgent with humanity, with us Americans. Five or six nights since, it hung close by the moon, then a little past its first quarter. The star was wonderful, the moon like young mother. The sky, dark blue, the transparent night, the planets, the moderate west wind, the elastic temperature, the miracle of that great star, and the young and swelling moon swimming in the west, suffused the soul. Then I heard, slow and clear, the deliberate notes of a bugle come up out of the silence, sounding so good through the night's mystery, no hurry, but firm and faithful, floating along, rising, falling leisurely, with here and there a long-drawn note; the bugle, well play'd, sounding tattoo, in one of the army hospitals near here, where the wounded (some of them personally so

dear to me,) are lying in their cots, and many a sick boy
come down to the war from Illinois, Michigan, Wisconsin,
Iowa, and the rest.

INAUGURATION BALL

March 6.—I have been up to look at the dance and supper-
rooms, for the inauguration ball at the Patent office; and I
could not help thinking, what a different scene they presented
to my view a while since, fill'd with a crowded mass of the
worst wounded of the war, brought in from second Bull Run,
Antietam, and Fredericksburg. To-night, beautiful women,
perfumes, the violins' sweetness, the polka and the waltz; then
the amputation, the blue face, the groan, the glassy eye of the
dying, the clotted rag, the odor of wounds and blood, and
many a mother's son amid strangers, passing away untended
there, (for the crowd of the badly hurt was great, and much
for nurse to do, and much for surgeon.)

SCENE AT THE CAPITOL

I MUST mention a strange scene at the capitol, the hall of
Representatives, the morning of Saturday last, (March 4th.)
The day just dawn'd, but in half-darkness, everything dim,
leaden, and soaking. In that dim light, the members nervous
from long drawn duty, exhausted, some asleep, and many half
asleep. The gas-light, mix'd with the dingy day-break, produced an unearthly effect. The poor little sleepy, stumbling
pages, the smell of the hall, the members with heads leaning
on their desks, the sounds of the voices speaking, with unusual intonations—the general moral atmosphere also of the
close of this important session—the strong hope that the war
is approaching its close—the tantalizing dread lest the hope
may be a false one—the grandeur of the hall itself, with its
effect of vast shadows up toward the panels and spaces over
the galleries—all made a mark'd combination.

In the midst of this, with the suddenness of a thunderbolt, burst one of the most angry and crashing storms of rain and hail ever heard. It beat like a deluge on the heavy glass roof of the hall, and the wind literally howl'd and roar'd. For a moment, (and no wonder,) the nervous and sleeping Representatives were thrown into confusion. The slumberers awaked with fear, some started for the doors, some look'd up with blanch'd cheeks and lips to the roof, and the little pages began to cry; it was a scene. But it was over almost as soon as the drowsied men were actually awake. They recover'd themselves; the storm raged on, beating, dashing, and with loud noises at times. But the House went ahead with its business then, I think, as calmly and with as much deliberation as at any time in its career. Perhaps the shock did it good. (One is not without impression, after all, amid these members of Congress, of both the Houses, that if the flat routine of their duties should ever be broken in upon by some great emergency involving real danger, and calling for first-class personal qualities, those qualities would be found generally forthcoming, and from men not now credited with them.)

A YANKEE ANTIQUE

March 27, 1865.—Sergeant Calvin F. Harlowe, company C, 29th Massachusetts, 3d brigade, 1st division, Ninth corps—a mark'd sample of heroism and death, (some may say bravado, but I say *heroism*, of grandest, oldest order)—in the late attack by the rebel troops, and temporary capture by them, of fort Steadman, at night. The fort was surprised at dead of night. Suddenly awaken'd from their sleep, and rushing from their tents, Harlowe, with others, found himself in the hands of the secesh—they demanded his surrender—he answer'd, *Never while I live.* (Of course it was useless. The others surrender'd; the odds were too great.) Again he was ask'd to yield, this time by a rebel captain. Though surrounded, and quite calm, he again refused, call'd sternly to his comrades to fight on, and himself attempted to do so. The rebel captain then shot him—

but at the same instant he shot the captain. Both fell together mortally wounded. Harlowe died almost instantly. The rebels were driven out in a very short time. The body was buried next day, but soon taken up and sent home, (Plymouth county, Mass.) Harlowe was only 22 years of age—was a tall, slim, dark-hair'd, blue-eyed young man—had come out originally with the 29th; and that is the way he met his death, after four years' campaign. He was in the Seven Days fight before Richmond, in second Bull Run, Antietam, first Fredericksburg, Vicksburg, Jackson, Wilderness, and the campaigns following—was as good a soldier as ever wore the blue, and every old officer in the regiment will bear that testimony. Though so young, and in a common rank, he had a spirit as resolute and brave as any hero in the books, ancient or modern—It was too great to say the words "I surrender"— and so he died. (When I think of such things, knowing them well, all the vast and complicated events of the war, on which history dwells and makes its volumes, fall aside, and for the moment at any rate I see nothing but young Calvin Harlowe's figure in the night, disdaining to surrender.)

WOUNDS AND DISEASES

The war is over, but the hospitals are fuller than ever, from former and current cases. A large majority of the wounds are in the arms and legs. But there is every kind of wound, in every part of the body. I should say of the sick, from my observation, that the prevailing maladies are typhoid fever and the camp fevers generally, diarrhœa, catarrhal affections and bronchitis, rheumatism and pneumonia. These forms of sickness lead; all the rest follow. There are twice as many sick as there are wounded. The deaths range from seven to ten per cent. of those under treatment.

DEATH OF PRESIDENT LINCOLN

April 16, '65.—I find in my notes of the time, this passage on the death of Abraham Lincoln: He leaves for America's history and biography, so far, not only its most dramatic reminiscence —he leaves, in my opinion, the greatest, best, most characteristic, artistic, moral personality. Not but that he had faults, and show'd them in the Presidency; but honesty, goodness, shrewdness, conscience, and (a new virtue, unknown to other lands, and hardly yet really known here, but the foundation and tie of all, as the future will grandly develop,) UNIONISM, in its truest and amplest sense, form'd the hard-pan of his character. These he seal'd with his life. The tragic splendor of his death, purging, illuminating all, throws round his form, his head, an aureole that will remain and will grow brighter through time, while history lives, and love of country lasts. By many has this Union been help'd; but if one name, one man, must be pick'd out, he, most of all, is the conservator of it, to the future. He was assassinated—but the Union is not assassinated—*ça ira!* One falls, and another falls. The soldier drops, sinks like a wave—but the ranks of the ocean eternally press on. Death does its work, obliterates a hundred, a thousand—President, general, captain, private—but the Nation is immortal.

SHERMAN'S ARMY'S JUBILATION— ITS SUDDEN STOPPAGE

WHEN Sherman's armies, (long after they left Atlanta,) were marching through South and North Carolina—after leaving Savannah, the news of Lee's capitulation having been receiv'd —the men never mov'd a mile without from some part of the line sending up continued, inspiriting shouts. At intervals all day long sounded out the wild music of those peculiar army cries. They would be commenc'd by one regiment or brigade, immediately taken up by others, and at length whole corps and armies would join in these wild triumphant choruses. It was one of the characteristic expressions of the western troops, and became a habit, serving as a relief and outlet to the men—a vent for their feelings of victory, returning peace, &c. Morning, noon, and afternoon, spontaneous, for occasion or without occasion, these huge, strange cries, differing from any other, echoing through the open air for many a mile, expressing youth, joy, wildness, irrepressible strength, and the ideas of advance and conquest, sounded along the swamps and uplands of the South, floating to the skies. ('There never were men that kept in better spirits in danger or defeat—what then could they do in victory?'—said one of the 15th corps to me, afterwards.) This exuberance continued till the armies arrived at Raleigh. There the news of the President's murder was receiv'd. Then no more shouts or yells, for a week. All the marching was comparatively muffled. It was very significant—hardly a loud word or laugh in many of the regiments. A hush and silence pervaded all.

NO GOOD PORTRAIT OF LINCOLN

PROBABLY the reader has seen physiognomies (often old farmers, sea-captains, and such) that, behind their homeliness, or even ugliness, held superior points so subtle, yet so palpable, making the real life of their faces almost as impossible to depict as a wild perfume or fruit-taste, or a passionate tone of the living voice—and such was Lincoln's face, the peculiar color, the lines of it, the eyes, mouth, expression. Of technical beauty it had nothing—but to the eye of a great artist it furnished a rare study, a feast and fascination. The current portraits are all failures—most of them caricatures.

RELEAS'D UNION PRISONERS
FROM SOUTH

THE releas'd prisoners of war are now coming up from the southern prisons. I have seen a number of them. The sight is worse than any sight of battle-fields, or any collection of wounded, even the bloodiest. There was, (as a sample,) one large boat load, of several hundreds, brought about the 25th, to Annapolis; and out of the whole number only three individuals were able to walk from the boat. The rest were carried ashore and laid down in one place or another. Can those be *men*—those little livid brown, ash-streak'd, monkey-looking dwarfs?—are they really not mummied, dwindled corpses? They lay there, most of them, quite still, but with a horrible look in their eyes and skinny lips (often with not enough flesh on the lips to cover their teeth.) Probably no more appalling sight was ever seen on this earth. (There are deeds, crimes, that may be forgiven; but this is not among them. It steeps its perpetrators in blackest, escapeless, endless damnation. Over 50,000 have been compell'd to die the death of starvation—reader, did you ever try to realize what *starvation* actually is?—in those prisons—and in a land of plenty.) An indescribable meanness, tyranny, aggravating course of insults, almost incredible—was evidently the rule of treatment through all the southern military prisons. The dead there are not to be pitied as much as some of the living that come from there—if they can be call'd living—many of them are mentally imbecile, and will never recuperate.

THE GRAND REVIEW

FOR two days now the broad spaces of Pennsylvania avenue along to Treasury hill, and so by detour around to the President's house, and so up to Georgetown, and across the aqueduct bridge, have been alive with a magnificent sight, the returning armies. In their wide ranks stretching clear across the Avenue, I watch them march or ride along, at a brisk pace, through two whole days—infantry, cavalry, artillery—some 200,000 men. Some days afterwards one or two other corps; and then, still afterwards, a good part of Sherman's immense army, brought up from Charleston, Savannah, &c.

WESTERN SOLDIERS

May 26–7.—The streets, the public buildings and grounds of Washington, still swarm with soldiers from Illinois, Indiana, Ohio, Missouri, Iowa, and all the Western States. I am continually meeting and talking with them. They often speak to me first, and always show great sociability, and glad to have a good interchange of chat. These Western soldiers are more slow in their movements, and in their intellectual quality also; have no extreme alertness. They are larger in size, have a more serious physiognomy, are continually looking at you as they pass in the street. They are largely animal, and handsomely so. During the war I have been at times with the Fourteenth, Fifteenth, Seventeenth, and Twentieth Corps. I always feel drawn toward the men, and like their personal contact when we are crowded close together, as frequently these days in the street-cars. They all think the world of General Sherman; call him "old Bill," or sometimes "uncle Billy."

A SOLDIER ON LINCOLN

May 28.—As I sat by the bedside of a sick Michigan soldier in hospital to-day, a convalescent from the adjoining bed rose and came to me, and presently we began talking. He was a middle-aged man, belonged to the 2d Virginia regiment, but lived in Racine, Ohio, and had a family there. He spoke of President Lincoln, and said: "The war is over, and many are lost. And now we have lost the best, the fairest, the truest man in America. Take him altogether, he was the best man this country ever produced. It was quite a while I thought very different; but some time before the murder, that's the way I have seen it." There was deep earnestness in the soldier. (I found upon further talk he had known Mr. Lincoln personally, and quite closely, years before.) He was a veteran; was now in the fifth year of his service; was a cavalry man, and had been in a good deal of hard fighting.

TWO BROTHERS, ONE SOUTH, ONE NORTH

May 28–9.—I staid to-night a long time by the bedside of a new patient, a young Baltimorean, aged about 19 years, W. S. P., (2d Maryland, southern,) very feeble, right leg amputated, can't sleep hardly at all—has taken a great deal of morphine, which, as usual, is costing more than it comes to. Evidently very intelligent and well bred—very affectionate—held on to my hand, and put it by his face, not willing to let me leave. As I was lingering, soothing him in his pain, he says to me suddenly, "I hardly think you know who I am—I don't wish to impose upon you—I am a rebel soldier." I said I did not know that, but it made no difference. Visiting him daily for about two weeks after that, while he lived, (death had mark'd him, and he was quite alone,) I loved him much, always kiss'd him, and he did me. In an adjoining ward I found his brother, an officer of rank, a Union soldier, a brave and religious man, (Col. Clifton K. Prentiss, sixth Maryland infantry, Sixth corps, wounded in one of the engagements at Petersburg, April 2—linger'd, suffer'd much, died in Brooklyn, Aug. 20, '65.) It was in the same battle both were hit. One was a strong Unionist, the other Secesh; both fought on their respective sides, both badly wounded, and both brought together here after a separation of four years. Each died for his cause.

SOME SAD CASES YET

May 31.—James H. Williams, aged 21, 3d Virginia cavalry.—About as mark'd a case of a strong man brought low by a complication of diseases, (laryngitis, fever, debility and diarrhœa,) as I have ever seen—has superb physique, remains swarthy yet, and flushed and red with fever—is altogether flighty—flesh of his great breast and arms tremulous, and pulse pounding away with treble quickness—lies a good deal of the time in a partial sleep, but with low muttering and groans—a sleep in which there is no rest. Powerful as he is, and so young, he will not be able to stand many more days of the strain and sapping heat of yesterday and to-day. His throat is in a bad way, tongue and lips parch'd. When I ask him how he feels, he is able just to articulate, "I feel pretty bad yet, old man," and looks at me with his great bright eyes. Father, John Williams, Millensport, Ohio.

June 9–10.—I have been sitting late to-night by the bedside of a wounded captain, a special friend of mine, lying with a painful fracture of left leg in one of the hospitals, in a large ward partially vacant. The lights were put out, all but a little candle, far from where I sat. The full moon shone in through the windows, making long, slanting silvery patches on the floor. All was still, my friend too was silent, but could not sleep; so I sat there by him, slowly wafting the fan, and occupied with the musings that arose out of the scene, the long shadowy ward, the beautiful ghostly moonlight on the floor, the white beds, here and there an occupant with huddled form, the bed-clothes thrown off. The hospitals have a number of cases of sun-stroke and exhaustion by heat, from the late reviews. There are many such from the Sixth corps, from the hot parade of day before yesterday. (Some of these shows cost the lives of scores of men.)

Sunday, Sep. 10.—Visited Douglas and Stanton hospitals. They are quite full. Many of the cases are bad ones, lingering wounds, and old sickness. There is a more than usual look of despair on the countenances of many of the men; hope has left them. I went through the wards, talking as usual. There are several here from the confederate army whom I had seen in other hospitals, and they recognized me. Two were in a dying condition.

CALHOUN'S REAL MONUMENT

IN ONE of the hospital tents for special cases, as I sat to-day tending a new amputation, I heard a couple of neighboring soldiers talking to each other from their cots. One down with fever, but improving, had come up belated from Charleston not long before. The other was what we now call an "old veteran," (*i.e.*, he was a Connecticut youth, probably of less than the age of twenty-five years, the four last of which he had spent in active service in the war in all parts of the country.) The two were chatting of one thing and another. The fever soldier spoke of John C. Calhoun's monument, which he had seen, and was describing it. The veteran said: "I have seen Calhoun's monument. That you saw is not the real monument. But I have seen it. It is the desolated, ruined south; nearly the whole generation of young men between seventeen and thirty destroyed or maim'd; all the old families used up— the rich impoverish'd, the plantations cover'd with weeds, the slaves unloos'd and become the masters, and the name of southerner blacken'd with every shame—all that is Calhoun's real monument."

"CONVULSIVENESS"

As I have look'd over the proof-sheets of the preceding pages, I have once or twice fear'd that my diary would prove, at best, but a batch of convulsively written reminiscences. Well, be it so. They are but parts of the actual distraction, heat, smoke and excitement of those times. The war itself, with the temper of society preceding it, can indeed be best described by that very word *convulsiveness*.

THREE YEARS SUMM'D UP

DURING those three years in hospital, camp or field, I made over six hundred visits or tours, and went, as I estimate, counting all, among from eighty thousand to a hundred thousand of the wounded and sick, as sustainer of spirit and body in some degree, in time of need. These visits varied from an hour or two, to all day or night; for with dear or critical cases I generally watch'd all night. Sometimes I took up my quarters in the hospital, and slept or watch'd there several nights in succession. Those three years I consider the greatest privilege and satisfaction, (with all their feverish excitements and physical deprivations and lamentable sights,) and, of course, the most profound lesson of my life. I can say that in my ministerings I comprehended all, whoever came in my way, northern or southern, and slighted none. It arous'd and brought out and decided undream'd-of depths of emotion. It has given me my most fervent views of the true *ensemble* and extent of the States. While I was with wounded and sick in thousands of cases from the New England States, and from New York, New Jersey, and Pennsylvania, and from Michigan, Wisconsin, Ohio, Indiana, Illinois, and all the Western States, I was with more or less from all the States, North and South, without exception. I was with many from the border States, especially from Maryland and Virginia, and found, during those lurid years 1862–63, far more Union southerners, especially Tennesseans, than is supposed. I was with many rebel officers and men among our wounded, and gave them always what I had, and tried to cheer them the same as any. I was among the army teamsters considerably, and, indeed, always found myself drawn to them. Among the black soldiers, wounded or sick, and in the contraband camps, I also took my way whenever in their neighborhood, and did what I could for them.

THE MILLION DEAD, TOO,
SUMM'D UP

THE dead in this war—there they lie, strewing the fields and
woods and valleys and battle-fields of the south—Virginia, the
Peninsula—Malvern hill and Fair Oaks—the banks of the
Chickahominy—the terraces of Fredericksburg—Antietam
bridge—the grisly ravines of Manassas—the bloody promenade
of the Wilderness—the varieties of the *strayed* dead, (the
estimate of the War department is 25,000 national soldiers
kill'd in battle and never buried at all, 5,000 drown'd—15,000
inhumed by strangers, or on the march in haste, in hitherto
unfound localities—2,000 graves cover'd by sand and mud
by Mississippi freshets, 3,000 carried away by caving-in of
banks, &c.,)—Gettysburg, the West, Southwest—Vicksburg—
Chattanooga—the trenches of Petersburg—the numberless
battles, camps, hospitals everywhere—the crop reap'd by the
mighty reapers, typhoid, dysentery, inflammations—and blackest and loathesomest of all, the dead and living burial-pits, the
prison-pens of Andersonville, Salisbury, Belle-Isle, &c., (not
Dante's pictured hell and all its woes, its degradations, filthy
torments, excell'd those prisons)—the dead, the dead, the dead
—*our* dead—or South or North, ours all, (all, all, all, finally
dear to me)—or East or West—Atlantic coast or Mississippi
valley—somewhere they crawl'd to die, alone, in bushes, low
gullies, or on the sides of hills—(there, in secluded spots, their
skeletons, bleach'd bones, tufts of hair, buttons, fragments of
clothing, are occasionally found yet)—our young men once so
handsome and so joyous, taken from us—the son from the
mother, the husband from the wife, the dear friend from
the dear friend—the clusters of camp graves, in Georgia, the
Carolinas, and in Tennessee—the single graves left in the
woods or by the road-side, (hundreds, thousands, obliterated)
—the corpses floated down the rivers, and caught and lodged,
(dozens, scores, floated down the upper Potomac, after the
cavalry engagements, the pursuit of Lee, following Gettys-

burg)—some lie at the bottom of the sea—the general million, and the special cemeteries in almost all the States—the infinite dead—(the land entire saturated, perfumed with their impalpable ashes' exhalation in Nature's chemistry distill'd, and shall be so forever, in every future grain of wheat and ear of corn, and every flower that grows, and every breath we draw) —not only Northern dead leavening Southern soil—thousands, aye tens of thousands, of Southerners, crumble to-day in Northern earth.

And everywhere among these countless graves—everywhere in the many soldiers' Cemeteries of the Nation, (there are now, I believe, over seventy of them)—as at the time in the vast trenches, the depositories of slain, Northern and Southern, after the great battles—not only where the scathing trail passed those years, but radiating since in all the peaceful quarters of the land—we see, and ages yet may see, on monuments and gravestones, singly or in masses, to thousands or tens of thousands, the significant word UNKNOWN.

(In some of the cemeteries nearly *all* the dead are unknown. At Salisbury, N. C., for instance, the known are only 85, while the unknown are 12,027, and 11,700 of these are buried in trenches. A national monument has been put up here, by order of Congress, to mark the spot—but what visible, material monument can ever fittingly commemorate that spot?)

THE REAL WAR WILL NEVER GET IN THE BOOKS

AND so good-bye to the war. I know not how it may have been, or may be, to others—to me the main interest I found, (and still, on recollection, find,) in the rank and file of the armies, both sides, and in those specimens amid the hospitals, and even the dead on the field. To me the points illustrating the latent personal character and eligibilities of these States, in the two or three millions of American young and middle-aged men, North and South, embodied in those armies—and especially the one-third or one-fourth of their number, stricken by wounds or disease at some time in the course of the contest—were of more significance even than the political interests involved. (As so much of a race depends on how it faces death, and how it stands personal anguish and sickness. As, in the glints of emotions under emergencies, and the indirect traits and asides in Plutarch, we get far profounder clues to the antique world than all its more formal history.)

Future years will never know the seething hell and the black infernal background of countless minor scenes and interiors, (not the official surface-courteousness of the Generals, not the few great battles) of the Secession war; and it is best they should not—the real war will never get in the books. In the mushy influences of current times, too, the fervid atmosphere and typical events of those years are in danger of being totally forgotten. I have at night watch'd by the side of a sick man in the hospital, one who could not live many hours. I have seen his eyes flash and burn as he raised himself and recurr'd to the cruelties on his surrender'd brother, and mutilations of the corpse afterward. (See, in the preceding pages, the incident at Upperville—the seventeen kill'd as in the description, were left there on the ground. After they dropt dead, no one touch'd them—all were made sure of, however. The carcasses were left for the citizens to bury or not, as they chose.)

Such was the war. It was not a quadrille in a ball-room. Its interior history will not only never be written—its practicality, minutiæ of deeds and passions, will never be even suggested. The actual soldier of 1862–'65, North and South, with all his ways, his incredible dauntlessness, habits, practices, tastes, language, his fierce friendship, his appetite, rankness, his superb strength and animality, lawless gait, and a hundred unnamed lights and shades of camp, I say, will never be written—perhaps must not and should not be.

The preceding notes may furnish a few stray glimpses into that life, and into those lurid interiors, never to be fully convey'd to the future. The hospital part of the drama from '61 to '65, deserves indeed to be recorded. Of that many-threaded

drama, with its sudden and strange surprises, its confounding
of prophecies, its moments of despair, the dread of foreign
interference, the interminable campaigns, the bloody battles,
the mighty and cumbrous and green armies, the drafts and
bounties—the immense money expenditure, like a heavy-pour-
ing constant rain—with, over the whole land, the last three
years of the struggle, an unending, universal mourning-wail
of women, parents, orphans—the marrow of the tragedy concentrated in those Army Hospitals—(it seem'd sometimes as
if the whole interest of the land, North and South, was one
vast central hospital, and all the rest of the affair but flanges)
—those forming the untold and unwritten history of the war—
infinitely greater (like life's) than the few scraps and distor-
tions that are ever told or written. Think how much, and of
importance, will be—how much, civic and military, has already been—buried in the grave, in eternal darkness.

AN INTERREGNUM PARAGRAPH

SEVERAL years now elapse before I resume my diary. I continued at Washington working in the Attorney-General's department through '66 and '67, and some time afterward. In
February '73 I was stricken down by paralysis, gave up my
desk, and migrated to Camden, New Jersey, where I lived
during '74 and '75, quite unwell—but after that began to grow
better; commenc'd going for weeks at a time, even for months,
down in the country, to a charmingly recluse and rural spot
along Timber creek, twelve or thirteen miles from where it
enters the Delaware river. Domicil'd at the farm-house of my
friends, the Staffords, near by, I lived half the time along
this creek and its adjacent fields and lanes. And it is to my life
here that I, perhaps, owe partial recovery (a sort of second
wind, or semi-renewal of the lease of life) from the prostration
of 1874–'75. If the notes of that outdoor life could only prove
as glowing to you, reader dear, as the experience itself was
to me. Doubtless in the course of the following, the fact of
invalidism will crop out, (I call myself *a half-Paralytic* these

days, and reverently bless the Lord it is no worse,) between some of the lines—but I get my share of fun and healthy hours, and shall try to indicate them. (The trick is, I find, to tone your wants and tastes low down enough, and make much of negatives, and of mere daylight and the skies.)

NEW THEMES ENTERED UPON

1876, '77.—I find the woods in mid-May and early June my best places for composition. Seated on logs or stumps there, or resting on rails, nearly all the following memoranda have been jotted down. Wherever I go, indeed, winter or summer, city or country, alone at home or traveling, I must take notes— (the ruling passion strong in age and disablement, and even the approach of—but I must not say it yet.) Then underneath the following excerpta—crossing the *t*'s and dotting the *i*'s of certain moderate movements of late years—I am fain to fancy the foundations of quite a lesson learn'd. After you have exhausted what there is in business, politics, conviviality, love, and so on—have found that none of these finally satisfy, or permanently wear—what remains? Nature remains; to bring out from their torpid recesses, the affinities of a man or woman with the open air, the trees, fields, the changes of seasons—the sun by day and the stars of heaven by night. We will begin from these convictions. Literature flies so high and is so hotly spiced, that our notes may seem hardly more than breaths of common air, or draughts of water to drink. But that is part of our lesson.

Dear, soothing, healthy, restoration-hours—after three confining years of paralysis—after the long strain of the war, and its wounds and death.

ENTERING A LONG FARM-LANE

As every man has his hobby-liking, mine is for a real farm-lane fenced by old chestnut-rails gray-green with dabs of moss and lichen, copious weeds and briers growing in spots athwart the heaps of stray-pick'd stones at the fence bases—irregular paths worn between, and horse and cow tracks—all characteristic accompaniments marking and scenting the neighborhood in their seasons—apple-tree blossoms in forward April—pigs, poultry, a field of August buckwheat, and in another the long flapping tassels of maize—and so to the pond, the expansion of the creek, the secluded-beautiful, with young and old trees and such recesses and vistas.

TO THE SPRING AND BROOK

So, STILL sauntering on, to the spring under the willows—musical as soft clinking glasses—pouring a sizeable stream, thick as my neck, pure and clear, out from its vent where the bank arches over like a great brown shaggy eyebrow or mouth-roof—gurgling, gurgling ceaselessly—meaning, saying something, of course (if one could only translate it)—always gurgling there, the whole year through—never giving out—oceans of mint, blackberries in summer—choice of light and shade—just the place for my July sun-baths and water-baths too—but mainly the inimitable soft sound-gurgles of it, as I sit there hot afternoon. How they and all grow into me, day after day—everything in keeping—the wild, just-palpable perfume, and the dapple of leaf-shadows, and all the natural-medicinal, elemental-moral influences of the spot.

Babble on, O brook, with that utterance of thine! I too will express what I have gather'd in my days and progress, native, subterranean, past—and now thee. Spin and wind thy way—I with thee, a little while, at any rate. As I haunt thee so often, season by season, thou knowest, reckest not me, (yet why be so certain? who can tell?)—but I will learn from thee, and dwell on thee—receive, copy, print from thee.

AN EARLY SUMMER REVEILLE

AWAY then to loosen, to unstring the divine bow, so tense, so long. Away, from curtain, carpet, sofa, book—from "society" —from city house, street, and modern improvements and luxuries—away to the primitive winding, aforementioned wooded creek, with its untrimm'd bushes and turfy banks— away from ligatures, tight boots, buttons, and the whole cast-iron civilizee life—from entourage of artificial store, machine, studio, office, parlor—from tailordom and fashion's clothes— from any clothes, perhaps, for the nonce, the summer heats advancing, there in those watery, shaded solitudes. Away, thou soul, (let me pick thee out singly, reader dear, and talk in perfect freedom, negligently, confidentially,) for one day and night at least, returning to the naked source-life of us all— to the breast of the great silent savage all-acceptive Mother. Alas! how many of us are so sodden—how many have wander'd so far away, that return is almost impossible.

But to my jottings, taking them as they come, from the heap, without particular selection. There is little consecutive-ness in dates. They run any time within nearly five or six years. Each was carelessly pencilled in the open air, at the time and place. The printers will learn this to some vexation perhaps, as much of their copy is from those hastily-written first notes.

BIRDS MIGRATING AT MIDNIGHT

DID you ever chance to hear the midnight flight of birds passing through the air and darkness overhead, in countless armies, changing their early or late summer habitat? It is something not to be forgotten. A friend called me up just after 12 last night to mark the peculiar noise of unusually immense flocks migrating north (rather late this year.) In the silence, shadow and delicious odor of the hour, (the natural perfume belonging to the night alone,) I thought it rare music. You could *hear* the characteristic motion—once or twice "the rush of mighty wings," but oftener a velvety rustle, long drawn out—sometimes quite near—with continual calls and chirps, and some song-notes. It all lasted from 12 till after 3. Once in a while the species was plainly distinguishable; I could make out the bobolink, tanager, Wilson's thrush, white-crown'd sparrow, and occasionally from high in the air came the notes of the plover.

CEDAR-APPLES

As I journey'd to-day in a light wagon ten or twelve miles through the country, nothing pleas'd me more, in their homely beauty and novelty (I had either never seen the little things to such advantage, or had never noticed them before) than that peculiar fruit, with its profuse clear-yellow dangles of inch-long silk or yarn, in boundless profusion spotting the dark-green cedar bushes—contrasting well with their bronze tufts—the flossy shreds covering the knobs all over, like a shock of wild hair on elfin pates. On my ramble afterward down by the creek I pluck'd one from its bush, and shall keep it. These cedar-apples last only a little while however, and soon crumble and fade.

SUMMER SIGHTS AND
INDOLENCES

June 10th.—As I write, 5½ P.M., here by the creek, nothing can exceed the quiet splendor and freshness around me. We had a heavy shower, with brief thunder and lightning, in the middle of the day; and since, overhead, one of those not uncommon yet indescribable skies (in quality, not details or forms) of limpid blue, with rolling silver-fringed clouds, and a pure-dazzling sun. For underlay, trees in fulness of tender foliage—liquid, reedy, long-drawn notes of birds—based by the fretful mewing of a querulous cat-bird, and the pleasant chippering-shriek of two kingfishers. I have been watching the

latter the last half hour, on their regular evening frolic over
and in the stream; evidently a spree of the liveliest kind. They
pursue each other, whirling and wheeling around, with many
a jocund downward dip, splashing the spray in jets of diamonds—and then off they swoop, with slanting wings and
graceful flight, sometimes so near me I can plainly see their
dark-gray feather-bodies and milk-white necks.

SUNDOWN PERFUME—QUAIL-NOTES
—THE HERMIT-THRUSH

June 19, 4 to 6½, P.M.—Sitting alone by the creek—solitude
here, but the scene bright and vivid enough—the sun shining,
and quite a fresh wind blowing (some heavy showers last
night), the grass and trees looking their best—the clare-obscure
of different greens, shadows, half-shadows, and the dappling
glimpses of the water, through recesses—the wild flageolet-
note of a quail near by—the just-heard fretting of some hylas
down there in the pond—crows cawing in the distance—a
drove of young hogs rooting in soft ground near the oak under
which I sit—some come sniffing near me, and then scamper
away, with grunts. And still the clear notes of the quail—the
quiver of leaf-shadows over the paper as I write—the sky aloft,
with white clouds, and the sun well declining to the west—the
swift darting of many sand-swallows coming and going, their
holes in a neighboring marl-bank—the odor of the cedar and
oak, so palpable, as evening approaches—perfume, color, the
bronze-and-gold of nearly ripen'd wheat—clover-fields, with
honey-scent—the well-up maize, with long and rustling leaves
—the great patches of thriving potatoes, dusky green, fleck'd
all over with white blossoms—the old, warty, venerable oak
above me—and ever, mix'd with the dual notes of the quail,
the soughing of the wind through some near-by pines.

As I rise for return, I linger long to a delicious song-epilogue
(is it the hermit-thrush?) from some bushy recess off there in
the swamp, repeated leisurely and pensively over and over
again. This, to the circle-gambols of the swallows flying by

dozens in concentric rings in the last rays of sunset, like
flashes of some airy wheel.

A JULY AFTERNOON BY THE POND

THE fervent heat, but so much more endurable in this pure
air—the white and pink pond-blossoms, with great heart-
shaped leaves; the glassy waters of the creek, the banks, with
dense bushery, and the picturesque beeches and shade and
turf; the tremulous, reedy call of some bird from recesses,
breaking the warm, indolent, half voluptuous silence; an occasional wasp, hornet, honey-bee or bumble (they hover near
my hands or face, yet annoy me not, nor I them, as they appear to examine, find nothing, and away they go)—the vast
space of the sky overhead so clear, and the buzzard up there
sailing his slow whirl in majestic spirals and discs; just over
the surface of the pond, two large slate-color'd dragon-flies,
with wings of lace, circling and darting and occasionally
balancing themselves quite still, their wings quivering all the
time, (are they not showing off for my amusement?)—the
pond itself, with the sword-shaped calamus; the water snakes
—occasionally a flitting blackbird, with red dabs on his shoulders, as he darts slantingly by—the sounds that bring out
the solitude, warmth, light and shade—the quawk of some
pond duck—(the crickets and grasshoppers are mute in the
noon heat, but I hear the song of the first cicadas;)—then at
some distance the rattle and whirr of a reaping machine as the
horses draw it on a rapid walk through a rye field on the opposite side of the creek—(what was the yellow or light-brown
bird, large as a young hen, with short neck and long-stretch'd
legs I just saw, in flapping and awkward flight over there
through the trees?) the prevailing delicate, yet palpable,
spicy, grassy, clovery perfume to my nostrils; and over all,
encircling all, to my sight and soul, the free space of the sky,
transparent and blue—and hovering there in the west, a mass
of white-gray fleecy clouds the sailors call "shoals of mackerel"
—the sky, with silver swirls like locks of toss'd hair, spreading,

expanding—a vast voiceless, formless simulacrum—yet may-be the most real reality and formulator of everything—who knows?

LOCUSTS AND KATYDIDS

Aug. 22.—Reedy monotones of locust, or sounds of katydid— I hear the latter at night, and the other both day and night. I thought the morning and evening warble of birds delightful; but I find I can listen to these strange insects with just as much pleasure. A single locust is now heard near noon from a tree two hundred feet off, as I write—a long whirring, continued, quite loud noise graded in distinct whirls, or swinging circles, increasing in strength and rapidity up to a certain point, and then a fluttering, quietly tapering fall. Each strain is continued from one to two minutes. The locust-song is very appropriate to the scene—gushes, has meaning, is masculine, is like some fine old wine, not sweet, but far better than sweet.

But the katydid—how shall I describe its piquant utterances? One sings from a willow-tree just outside my open bedroom window, twenty yards distant; every clear night for a fortnight past has sooth'd me to sleep. I rode through a piece of woods for a hundred rods the other evening, and heard the katydids by myriads—very curious for once; but I like better my single neighbor on the tree.

Let me say more about the song of the locust, even to repetition; a long, chromatic, tremulous crescendo, like a brass disk whirling round and round, emitting wave after wave of notes, beginning with a certain moderate beat or measure, rapidly increasing in speed and emphasis, reaching a point of great energy and significance, and then quickly and gracefully dropping down and out. Not the melody of the singing-bird—far from it; the common musician might think without melody, but surely having to the finer ear a harmony of its own; monotonous—but what a swing there is in that brassy drone, round and round, cymbal-line—or like the whirling of brass quoits.

THE LESSON OF A TREE

Sept. 1.—I should not take either the biggest or the most picturesque tree to illustrate it. Here is one of my favorites now
before me, a fine yellow poplar, quite straight perhaps 90 feet
high, and four thick at the butt. How strong, vital, enduring!
how dumbly eloquent! What suggestions of imperturbability
and *being*, as against the human trait of mere *seeming*. Then
the qualities, almost emotional, palpably artistic, heroic, of a
tree; so innocent and harmless, yet so savage. It *is*, yet says
nothing. How it rebukes by its tough and equable serenity all
weathers, this gusty-temper'd little whiffet, man, that runs
indoors at a mite of rain or snow. Science (or rather half-way
science) scoffs at reminiscence of dryad, and hamadryad, and
of trees speaking. But, if they don't, they do as well as most
speaking, writing, poetry, sermons—or rather they do a great
deal better. I should say indeed that those old dryad-reminis-
cences are quite as true as any, and profounder than most
reminiscences we get. ("Cut this out," as the quack
mediciners say, and keep by you.) Go and sit in a grove or
woods, with one or more of those voiceless companions, and
read the foregoing, and think.

One lesson from affiliating a tree—perhaps the greatest
moral lesson anyhow from earth, rocks, animals, is that same
lesson of inherency, of *what is*, without the least regard to
what the looker on (the critic) supposes or says, or whether
he likes or dislikes. What worse—what more general malady
pervades each and all of us, our literature, education, attitude
toward each other, (even toward ourselves,) then a morbid
trouble about *seems*, (generally temporarily seems too,) and
no trouble at all, or hardly any, about the sane, slow-growing,
perennial, real parts of character, books, friendship, marriage
—humanity's invisible foundations and hold-together? (As
the all-basis, the nerve, the great-sympathetic, the plenum
within humanity, giving stamp to everything, is necessarily invisible.)

Aug. 4, 6 P.M.—Lights and shades and rare effects on tree-foliage and grass—transparent greens, grays, &c., all in sunset pomp and dazzle. The clear beams are now thrown in many new places, on the quilted, seam'd, bronze-drab, lower tree-trunks, shadow'd except at this hour—now flooding their young and old columnar ruggedness with strong light, unfolding to my sense new amazing features of silent, shaggy charm, the solid bark, the expression of harmless impassiveness, with many a bulge and gnarl unreck'd before. In the revealings of such light, such exceptional hour, such mood, one does not wonder at the old story fables, (indeed, why fables?) of people falling into love-sickness with trees, seiz'd extatic with the mystic realism of the resistless silent strength in them—*strength*, which after all is perhaps the last, completest, highest beauty.

Trees I am familiar with here

Willows.

Catalpas.

Persimmons.

Mountain-ash.

Hickories.

Maples, many kinds.

Locusts.

Birches.

Dogwood.

Pine.

the Elm.

Chestnut.

Linden.

Aspen.

Spruce.

Hornbeam.

Laurel.

Holly.

Oaks, (many kinds—one sturdy old fellow, vital, green, bushy, five feet thick at the butt, I sit under every day.)

Cedars, plenty.

Tulip trees, (*Liriodendron*, is of the magnolia family—I have seen it in Michigan and southern Illinois, 140 feet high and 8 feet thick at the butt; does not transplant well; best rais'd from seeds—the lumbermen call it yellow poplar.)

Sycamores.

Gum-trees, both sweet and sour.

Beeches.

Black-walnuts.

Sassafras.

THE SKY—DAYS AND NIGHTS— HAPPINESS

Oct. 20.—A clear, crispy day—dry and breezy air, full of oxygen. Out of the sane, silent, beauteous miracles that envelope and fuse me—trees, water, grass, sunlight, and early frost—the one I am looking at most to-day is the sky. It has that delicate, transparent blue, peculiar to autumn, and the only clouds are little or larger white ones, giving their still and spiritual motion to the great concave. All through the earlier day (say from 7 to 11) it keeps a pure, yet vivid blue. But as noon approaches the color gets lighter, quite gray for two or three hours—then still paler for a spell, till sun-down—which last I watch dazzling through the interstices of a knoll of big trees—darts of fire and a gorgeous show of light-yellow, liver-color and red, with a vast silver glaze askant on the water—the transparent shadows, shafts, sparkle, and vivid colors beyond all the paintings ever made.

I don't know what or how, but it seems to me mostly owing to these skies, (every now and then I think, while I have of course seen them every day of my life, I never really saw the skies before,) I have had this autumn some wondrously contented hours—may I not say perfectly happy ones? As I've read, Byron just before his death told a friend that he had known but three happy hours during his whole existence. Then there is the old German legend of the king's bell, to the same point. While I was out there by the wood, that beautiful sunset through the trees, I thought of Byron's and the bell story, and the notion started in me that I was having a happy hour. (Though perhaps my best moments I never jot down; when they come I cannot afford to break the charm by inditing memoranda. I just abandon myself to the mood, and let it float on, carrying me in its placid extasy.)

What is happiness, anyhow? Is this one of its hours, or the like of it?—so impalpable—a mere breath, an evanescent tinge? I am not sure—so let me give myself the benefit of the doubt.

Hast Thou, pellucid, in Thy azure depths, medicine for case like mine? (Ah, the physical shatter and troubled spirit of me the last three years.) And dost Thou subtly mystically now drip it through the air invisibly upon me?

Night of Oct. 28.—The heavens unusually transparent—the stars out by myriads—the great path of the Milky Way, with its branch, only seen of very clear nights—Jupiter, setting in the west, looks like a huge hap-hazard splash, and has a little star for companion.

> *Clothed in his white garments,*
> *Into the round and clear arena slowly entered the*
> *brahmin,*
> *Holding a little child by the hand,*
> *Like the moon with the planet Jupiter in a cloudless*
> *night-sky.*
>
> Old Hindu Poem.

Early in November.—At its farther end the lane already described opens into a broad grassy upland field of over twenty acres, slightly sloping to the south. Here I am accustom'd to walk for sky views and effects, either morning or sundown. To-day from this field my soul is calm'd and expanded beyond description, the whole forenoon by the clear blue arching over all, cloudless, nothing particular, only sky and daylight. Their soothing accompaniments, autumn leaves, the cool dry air, the faint aroma—crows cawing in the distance—two great buzzards wheeling gracefully and slowly far up there—the occasional murmur of the wind, sometimes quite gently, then threatening through the trees—a gang of farm-laborers loading corn-stalks in a field in sight, and the patient horses waiting.

BIRDS AND BIRDS AND BIRDS

A little later—bright weather.—An unusual melodiousness, these days, (last of April and first of May) from the blackbirds; indeed all sorts of birds, darting, whistling, hopping or perch'd on trees. Never before have I seen, heard, or been in the midst of, and got so flooded and saturated with them and their performances, as this current month. Such oceans, such successions of them. Let me make a list of those I find here:

Black birds (plenty,)	Meadow-larks (plenty,)
Ring doves,	Cat-birds (plenty,)
Owls,	Cuckoos,
Woodpeckers,	Pond snipes (plenty,)
King-birds,	Cheewinks,
Crows (plenty,)	Quawks,
Wrens,	Ground robins,
Kingfishers,	Ravens,
Quails,	Gray snipes,
Turkey-buzzards,	Eagles,
Hen-hawks,	High-holes,
Yellow birds,	Herons,
Thrushes,	Tits,
Reed birds,	Woodpigeons.

Early came the

Blue birds,	Meadow lark,
Killdeer,	White-bellied swallow,
Plover,	Sandpiper,
Robin,	Wilson's thrush,
Woodcock,	Flicker.

FULL-STARR'D NIGHTS

May 21.—Back in Camden. Again commencing one of those unusually transparent, full-starr'd, blue-black nights, as if to show that however lush and pompous the day may be, there is something left in the not-day that can outvie it. The rarest, finest sample of long-drawn-out clear-obscure, from sundown to 9 o'clock. I went down to the Delaware, and cross'd and cross'd. Venus like blazing silver well up in the west. The large pale thin crescent of the new moon, half an hour high, sinking languidly under a bar-sinister of cloud, and then emerging. Arcturus right overhead. A faint fragrant sea-odor wafted up from the south. The gloaming, the temper'd coolness, with every feature of the scene, indescribably soothing and tonic—one of those hours that give hints to the soul, impossible to put in a statement. (Ah, where would be any food for spirituality without night and the stars?) The vacant spaciousness of the air, and the veil'd blue of the heavens, seem'd miracles enough.

As the night advanc'd it changed its spirit and garments to ampler stateliness. I was almost conscious of a definite presence, Nature silently near. The great constellation of the Water-Serpent stretch'd its coils over more than half the heavens. The Swan with outspread wings was flying down the Milky Way. The northern Crown, the Eagle, Lyra, all up there in their places. From the whole dome shot down points of light, rapport with me, through the clear blue-black. All the usual sense of motion, all animal life, seem'd discarded, seem'd a fiction; a curious power, like the placid rest of Egyptian gods, took possession, none the less potent for being impalpable. Earlier I had seen many bats, balancing in the luminous twilight, darting their black forms hither and yon over the river; but now they altogether disappear'd. The evening star and the moon had gone. Alertness and peace lay calmly couching together through the fluid universal shadows.

Aug. 26.—Bright has the day been, and my spirits an equal *forzando*. Then comes the night, different, inexpressibly pensive, with its own tender and temper'd splendor. Venus lingers in the west with a voluptuous dazzle unshown hitherto this summer. Mars rises early, and the red sulky moon, two days past her full; Jupiter at night's meridian, and the long curling-slanted Scorpion stretching full view in the south, Aretus-neck'd. Mars walks the heavens lord-paramount now; all through this month I go out after supper and watch for him; sometimes getting up at midnight to take another look at his unparallel'd lustre. (I see lately an astronomer has made out through the new Washington telescope that Mars has certainly one moon, perhaps two.) Pale and distant, but near in the heavens, Saturn precedes him.

MULLEINS AND MULLEINS

LARGE, placid mulleins, as summer advances, velvety in texture, of a light greenish-drab color, growing everywhere in the fields—at first earth's big rosettes in their broad-leav'd low cluster-plants, eight, ten, twenty leaves to a plant—plentiful on the fallow twenty-acre lot, at the end of the lane, and especially by the ridge-sides of the fences—then close to the ground, but soon springing up—leaves as broad as my hand, and the lower ones twice as long—so fresh and dewy in the morning—stalks now four or five, even seven or eight feet high. The farmers, I find, think the mullein a mean unworthy weed, but I have grown to a fondness for it. Every object has its lesson, enclosing the suggestion of everything else—and lately I sometimes think all is concentrated for me in these hardy, yellow-flower'd weeds. As I come down the lane early in the morning, I pause before their soft wool-like fleece and stem and broad leaves, glittering with countless diamonds. Annually for three summers now, they and I have silently return'd together; at such long intervals I stand or sit among them, musing—and woven with the rest, of so many hours and moods of partial rehabilitation—of my sane or sick spirit, here as near at peace as it can be.

DISTANT SOUNDS

THE axe of the wood-cutter, the measured thud of a single threshing-flail, the crowing of chanticleer in the barn-yard, (with invariable responses from other barn-yards,) and the lowing of cattle—but most of all, or far or near, the wind— through the high tree-tops, or through low bushes, laving one's face and hands so gently, this balmy-bright noon, the coolest for a long time, (Sept. 2)—I will not call it *sighing*, for to me it is always a firm, sane, cheery expression, though a monotone, giving many varieties, or swift or slow, or dense or delicate. The wind in the patch of pine woods off there— how sibilant. Or at sea, I can imagine it this moment, tossing the waves, with spirits of foam flying far, and the free whistle, and the scent of the salt—and that vast paradox somehow with all its action and restlessness conveying a sense of eternal rest.

Other adjuncts.—But the sun and moon here and these times. As never more wonderful by day, the gorgeous orb imperial, so vast, so ardently, lovingly hot—so never a more glorious moon of nights, especially the last three or four. The great planets too—Mars never before so flaming bright, so flashing-large, with slight yellow tinge, (the astronomers say —is it true?—nearer to us than any time the past century)— and well up, lord Jupiter, (a little while since close by the moon)—and in the west, after the sun sinks, voluptuous Venus, now languid and shorn of her beams, as if from some divine excess.

A SUN-BATH—NAKEDNESS

Sunday, Aug. 27.—Another day quite free from mark'd prostration and pain. It seems indeed as if peace and nutriment from heaven subtly filter into me as I slowly hobble down these country lanes and across fields, in the good air—as I sit here in solitude with Nature—open, voiceless, mystic, far removed, yet palpable, eloquent Nature. I merge myself in the scene, in the perfect day. Hovering over the clear brook-water, I am sooth'd by its soft gurgle in one place, and the hoarser murmurs of its three-foot fall in another. Come, ye disconsolate, in whom any latent eligibility is left—come get the sure virtues of creek-shore, and wood and field. Two months (July and August, '77,) have I absorb'd them, and they begin to make a new man of me. Every day, seclusion—every day at least two or three hours of freedom, bathing, no talk, no bonds, no dress, no books, no *manners*.

Shall I tell you, reader, to what I attribute my already much-restored health? That I have been almost two years, off and on, without drugs and medicines, and daily in the open air. Last summer I found a particularly secluded little dell off one side by my creek, originally a large dug-out marl-pit, now abandon'd, fill'd with bushes, trees, grass, a group of willows, a straggling bank, and a spring of delicious water running right through the middle of it, with two or three little cascades. Here I retreated every hot day, and follow it up this summer. Here I realize the meaning of that old fellow who said he was seldom less alone than when alone. Never before did I get so close to Nature; never before did she come so close to me. By old habit, I pencill'd down from time to time, almost automatically, moods, sights, hours, tints and outlines, on the spot. Let me specially record the satisfaction of this current forenoon, so serene and primitive, so conventionally exceptional, natural.

An hour or so after breakfast I wended my way down to the recesses of the aforesaid dell, which I and certain thrushes, catbirds, &c., had all to ourselves. A light southwest wind was blowing through the tree-tops. It was just the place and time for my Adamic air-bath and flesh-brushing from head to foot. So hanging clothes on a rail near by, keeping old broadbrim straw on head and easy shoes on feet, haven't I had a good time the last two hours! First with the stiff-elastic bristles rasping arms, breast, sides, till they turn'd scarlet—then partially bathing in the clear waters of the running brook—taking everything very leisurely, with many rests and pauses—stepping about bare-footed every few minutes now and then in some neighboring black ooze, for unctuous mud-bath to my feet—a brief second and third rinsing in the crystal running waters—rubbing with the fragrant towel—slow negligent promenades on the turf up and down in the sun, varied with occasional rests, and further frictions of the bristle-brush—sometimes carrying my portable chair with me from place to place, as my range is quite extensive here, nearly a hundred rods, feeling quite secure from intrusion, (and that indeed I am not at all nervous about, if it accidentally happens.)

As I walk'd slowly over the grass, the sun shone out enough to show the shadow moving with me. Somehow I seem'd to get identity with each and every thing around me, in its condition. Nature was naked, and I was also. It was too lazy, soothing, and joyous-equable to speculate about. Yet I might have thought somehow in this vein: Perhaps the inner never lost rapport we hold with earth, light, air, trees, &c., is not to be realized through eyes and mind only, but through the whole corporeal body, which I will not have blinded or bandaged any more than the eyes. Sweet, sane, still Nakedness in Nature!—ah if poor, sick, prurient humanity in cities might really know you once more! Is not nakedness then indecent? No, not inherently. It is your thought, your sophistication, your fear, your respectability, that is indecent. There come moods when these clothes of ours are not only too irksome to wear, but are themselves indecent. Perhaps indeed he or she to whom the free exhilarating extasy of nakedness in Nature has never been eligible (and how many thousands there are!) has not really known what purity is—nor what faith or art or health really is. (Probably the whole curriculum of first-class philosophy, beauty, heroism, form, illustrated by the old Hellenic race—the highest height and deepest depth known to civilization in those departments—came from their natural and religious idea of Nakedness.)

Many such hours, from time to time, the last two summers—I attribute my partial rehabilitation largely to them. Some good people may think it a feeble or half-crack'd way of spending one's time and thinking. May-be it is.

DEATH OF WILLIAM CULLEN
BRYANT

New York City.—Came on from West Philadelphia, June 13, in the 2 P.M. train to Jersey city, and so across and to my friends, Mr. and Mrs. J. H. J., and their large house, large family (and large hearts,) amid which I feel at home, at peace—away up on Fifth avenue, near Eighty-sixth street, quiet, breezy, overlooking the dense woody fringe of the park —plenty of space and sky, birds chirping, and air comparatively fresh and odorless. Two hours before starting, saw the announcement of William Cullen Bryant's funeral, and felt a strong desire to attend. I had known Mr. Bryant over thirty years ago, and he had been markedly kind to me. Off and on, along that time for years as they pass'd, we met and chatted together. I thought him very sociable in his way, and a man to become attach'd to. We were both walkers, and when I work'd in Brooklyn he several times came over, middle of afternoons, and we took rambles miles long, till dark, out towards Bedford or Flatbush, in company. On these occasions he gave me clear accounts of scenes in Europe—the cities, looks, architecture, art, especially Italy—where he had travel'd a good deal.

June 14.—The Funeral.—And so the good, stainless, noble old citizen and poet lies in the closed coffin there—and this is his funeral. A solemn, impressive, simple scene, to spirit and senses. The remarkable gathering of gray heads, celebrities— the finely render'd anthem, and other music—the church, dim even now at approaching noon, in its light from the mellow-stain'd windows—the pronounc'd eulogy on the bard who loved Nature so fondly, and sung so well her shows and seasons—ending with these appropriate well-known lines:

> *I gazed upon the glorious sky,*
> *And the green mountains round,*

And thought that when I came to lie
　　At rest within the ground,
'Twere pleasant that in flowery June,
When brooks send up a joyous tune,
　　And groves a cheerful sound,
The sexton's hand, my grave to make,
The rich green mountain turf should break.

JAUNT UP THE HUDSON

June 20th.—On the "Mary Powell," enjoy'd everything beyond precedent. The delicious tender summer day, just warm enough—the constantly changing but ever beautiful panorama on both sides of the river—(went up near a hundred miles)—the high straight walls of the stony Palisades—beautiful Yonkers, and beautiful Irvington—the never-ending hills, mostly in rounded lines, swathed with verdure,—the distant turns, like great shoulders in blue veils—the frequent gray and brown of the tall-rising rocks—the river itself, now narrowing, now expanding—the white sails of the many sloops, yachts, &c., some near, some in the distance—the rapid succession of handsome villages and cities, (our boat is a swift traveler, and makes few stops)—the Race—picturesque West Point, and indeed all along—the costly and often turreted mansions forever showing in some cheery light color, through the woods —make up the scene.

TWO CITY AREAS, CERTAIN HOURS

NEW YORK, *May 24, '79.*—Perhaps no quarters of this city (I have return'd again for awhile,) make more brilliant, animated, crowded, spectacular human presentations these fine May afternoons than the two I am now going to describe from personal observation. First: that area comprising Fourteenth street (especially the short range between Broadway and Fifth avenue) with Union square, its adjacencies, and so retrostretching down Broadway for half a mile. All the walks here are wide, and the spaces ample and free—now flooded with liquid gold from the last two hours of powerful sunshine. The whole area at 5 o'clock, the days of my observations, must have contain'd from thirty to forty thousand finely-dress'd people, all in motion, plenty of them good-looking, many beautiful women, often youths and children, the latter in groups with their nurses—the trottoirs everywhere close-spread, thick-tangled, (yet no collision, no trouble,) with masses of bright color, action, and tasty toilets; (surely the women dress better than ever before, and the men do too.) As if New York would show these afternoons what it can do in its humanity, its choicest physique and physiognomy, and its countless prodigality of locomotion, dry goods, glitter, magnetism, and happiness.

Second: also from 5 to 7 P.M. the stretch of Fifth avenue, all the way from the Central Park exits at Fifty-ninth street, down to Fourteenth, especially along the high grade by Fortieth street, and down the hill. A Mississippi of horses and rich vehicles, not by dozens and scores, but hundreds and thousands—the broad avenue filled and cramm'd with them—a moving, sparkling, hurrying crush, for more than two miles. (I wonder they don't get block'd, but I believe they never do.) Altogether it is to me the marvel sight of New York. I like to get in one of the Fifth avenue stages and ride up, stemming the swift-moving procession. I doubt if London or Paris or any city in the world can show such a carriage carnival as I have seen here five or six times these beautiful May afternoons.

CENTRAL PARK WALKS AND TALKS

May 16 to 22.—I visit Central Park now almost every day, sitting, or slowly rambling, or riding around. The whole place presents its very best appearance this current month—the full lush of the trees, the plentiful white and pink of the flowering shrubs, the emerald green of the grass spreading everywhere, yellow dotted still with dandelions—the specialty of the plentiful gray rocks, peculiar to these grounds, cropping out, miles and miles—and over all the beauty and purity, three days out of four, of our summer skies. As I sit, placidly, early afternoon, off against Ninetieth street, the policeman, C. C., a well-form'd sandy-complexion'd young fellow, comes over and stands near me. We grow quite friendly and chatty forthwith. He is a New Yorker born and raised, and in answer to my questions tells me about the life of a New York Park policeman, (while he talks keeping his eyes and ears vigilantly open, occasionally pausing and moving where he can get full views of the vistas of the road, up and down, and the spaces around.) The pay is $2.40 a day (seven days to a week)—the men come on and work eight hours straight ahead, which is all that is required of them out of the twenty-four. The position has more risks than one might suppose—for instance if a team or horse runs away (which happens daily) each man is expected not only to be prompt, but to waive safety and stop wildest nag or nags—(*do it,* and don't be thinking of your bones or face)—give the alarm-whistle too, so that other guards may repeat, and the vehicles up and down the tracks be warn'd. Injuries to the men are continually happening. There is much alertness and quiet strength. (Few appreciate, I have often thought, the Ulyssean capacity, derring-do, quick readiness in emergencies, practicality, unwitting devotion and heroism, among our American young men and working-people—the firemen, the railroad employés, the steamer and ferry men, the police, the conductors and drivers—the whole splendid average of native stock, city and country.) It is good work, though; and upon the whole the Park force members like it. They see life, and the excitement keeps them up. There is not so much difficulty as might be supposed from tramps, roughs, or in keeping people "off the grass." The worst trouble of the regular Park employé is from malarial fever, chills, and the like.

A FINE AFTERNOON, 4 TO 6

TEN thousand vehicles careering through the Park this perfect afternoon. Such a show! and I have seen all—watch'd it narrowly, and at my leisure. Private barouches, cabs and coupés, some fine horseflesh—lapdogs, footmen, fashions, foreigners, cockades on hats, crests on panels—the full oceanic tide of New York's wealth and "gentility." It was an impressive, rich, interminable circus on a grand scale, full of action and color in the beauty of the day, under the clear sun and moderate breeze. Family groups, couples, single drivers—of course dresses generally elegant—much "style," (yet perhaps little or nothing, even in that direction, that fully justified itself.) Through the windows of two or three of the richest carriages I saw faces almost corpse-like, so ashy and listless. Indeed the whole affair exhibited less of sterling America, either in spirit or countenance, than I had counted on from such a select mass-spectacle. I suppose, as a proof of limitless wealth, leisure, and the aforesaid "gentility," it was tremendous. Yet what I saw those hours (I took two other occasions, two other afternoons to watch the same scene,) confirms a thought that haunts me every additional glimpse I get of our top-loftical general or rather exceptional phases of wealth and fashion in this country—namely, that they are ill at ease, much too conscious, cased in too many cerements, and far from happy—that there is nothing in them which we who are poor and plain need at all envy, and that instead of the perennial smell of the grass and woods and shores, their typical redolence is of soaps and essences, very rare may be, but suggesting the barber shop—something that turns stale and musty in a few hours anyhow.

Perhaps the show on the horseback road was prettiest. Many groups (threes a favorite number,) some couples, some singly—many ladies—frequently horses or parties dashing along on a full run—fine riding the rule—a few really first-class animals. As the afternoon waned, the wheel'd carriages grew less, but the saddle-riders seemed to increase. They linger'd long—and I saw some charming forms and faces.

DEPARTING OF THE BIG STEAMERS

May 15.—A three hours' bay-trip from 12 to 3 this afternoon, accompanying "the City of Brussels" down as far as the Narrows, in behoof of some Europe-bound friends, to give them a good send off. Our spirited little tug, the "Seth Low," kept close to the great black "Brussels," sometimes one side, sometimes the other, always up to her, or even pressing ahead, (like the blooded pony accompanying the royal elephant.) The whole affair, from the first, was an animated, quick-passing, characteristic New York scene; the large, good-looking, well-dress'd crowd on the wharf-end—men and women come to see their friends depart, and bid them God-speed—the ship's sides swarming with passengers—groups of bronze-faced sailors, with uniform'd officers at their posts—the quiet directions, as she quickly unfastens and moves out, prompt to a minute—the emotional faces, adieus and fluttering handkerchiefs, and many smiles and some tears on the wharf—the answering faces, smiles, tears and fluttering handkerchiefs, from the ship—(what can be subtler and finer than this play of faces on such occasions in these responding crowds?—what go more to one's heart?)—the proud, steady, noiseless cleaving of the grand oceaner down the bay—we speeding by her side a few miles, and then turning, wheeling, amid a babel of wild hurrahs, shouted partings, ear-splitting steam whistles, kissing of hands and waving of handkerchiefs.

This departing of the big steamers, noons or afternoons—there is no better medicine when one is listless or vapory. I am fond of going down Wednesdays and Saturdays—their more special days—to watch them and the crowds on the wharves, the arriving passengers, the general bustle and activity, the eager looks from the faces, the clear-toned voices, (a travel'd foreigner, a musician, told me the other day she thinks an American crowd has the finest voices in the world,) the whole look of the great, shapely black ships themselves, and their groups and lined sides—in the setting of our bay with the blue sky overhead. Two days after the above I saw the "Britannic," the "Donau," the "Helvetia" and the "Schiedam" steam out, all off for Europe—a magnificent sight.

BEGIN A LONG JAUNT WEST

THE following three or four months (Sept. to Dec. '79) I made quite a western journey, fetching up at Denver, Colorado, and penetrating the Rocky Mountain region enough to get a good notion of it all. Left West Philadelphia after 9 o'clock one night, middle of September, in a comfortable sleeper. Oblivious of the two or three hundred miles across Pennsylvania; at Pittsburgh in the morning to breakfast. Pretty good view of the city and Birmingham—fog and damp, smoke; coke-furnaces, flames, discolor'd wooden houses, and vast collections of coal-barges. Presently a bit of fine region, West Virginia, the Panhandle, and crossing the river, the Ohio. By day through the latter State—then Indiana—and so rock'd to slumber for a second night, flying like lightning through Illinois.

IN THE SLEEPER

WHAT a fierce weird pleasure to lie in my berth at night in the luxurious palace-car, drawn by the mighty Baldwin—embodying, and filling me, too, full of the swiftest motion, and most resistless strength! It is late, perhaps midnight or after—distances join'd like magic—as we speed through Harrisburg, Columbus, Indianapolis. The element of danger adds zest to it all. On we go, rumbling and flashing, with our loud whinnies thrown out from time to time, or trumpet-blasts, into the darkness. Passing the homes of men, the farms, barns, cattle—the silent villages. And the car itself, the sleeper, with curtains drawn and lights turn'd down—in the berths the slumberers, many of them women and children—as on, on, on, we fly like lightning through the night—how strangely sound and sweet they sleep! (They say the French Voltaire in his time designated the grand opera and a ship of war the most signal illustrations of the growth of humanity's and art's advance beyond primitive barbarism. Perhaps if the witty philosopher were here these days, and went in the same car with perfect bedding and feed from New York to San Francisco, he would shift his type and sample to one of our American sleepers.)

MISSOURI STATE

WE SHOULD have made the run of 960 miles from Philadelphia to St. Louis in thirty-six hours, but we had a collision and bad locomotive smash about two-thirds of the way, which set us back. So merely stopping over night that time in St. Louis, I sped on westward. As I cross'd Missouri State the whole distance by the St. Louis and Kansas City Northern Railroad, a fine early autumn day, I thought my eyes had never looked on scenes of greater pastoral beauty. For over two hundred miles successive rolling prairies, agriculturally perfect view'd by Pennsylvania and New Jersey eyes, and dotted here and there with fine timber. Yet fine as the land is, it isn't the finest portion; (there is a bed of impervious clay and hardpan beneath this section that holds water too firmly, "drowns the land in wet weather, and bakes it in dry," as a cynical farmer told me.) South are some richer tracts, though perhaps the beauty-spots of the State are the northwestern counties. Altogether, I am clear, (now, and from what I have seen and learn'd since,) that Missouri, in climate, soil, relative situation, wheat, grass, mines, railroads, and every important materialistic respect, stands in the front rank of the Union. Of Missouri averaged politically and socially I have heard all sorts of talk, some pretty severe—but I should have no fear myself of getting along safely and comfortably anywhere among the Missourians. They raise a good deal of tobacco. You see at this time quantities of the light greenish-gray leaves pulled and hanging out to dry on temporary frame-works or rows of sticks. Looks much like the mullein familiar to eastern eyes.

LAWRENCE AND TOPEKA, KANSAS

WE THOUGHT of stopping in Kansas City, but when we got there we found a train ready and a crowd of hospitable Kansians to take us on to Lawrence, to which I proceeded. I shall not soon forget my good days in L., in company with Judge Usher and his sons, (especially John and Linton,) true westerners of the noblest type. Nor the similar days in Topeka. Nor the brotherly kindness of my RR. friends there, and the city and State officials. Lawrence and Topeka are large, bustling, half-rural, handsome cities. I took two or three long drives about the latter, drawn by a spirited team over smooth roads.

ON TO DENVER—A FRONTIER INCIDENT

THE jaunt of five or six hundred miles from Topeka to Denver took me through a variety of country, but all unmistakably prolific, western, American, and on the largest scale. For a long distance we follow the line of the Kansas river, (I like better the old name, Kaw,) a stretch of very rich, dark soil, famed for its wheat, and call'd the Golden Belt—then plains and plains, hour after hour—Ellsworth county, the centre of the State—where I must stop a moment to tell a characteristic story of early days—scene the very spot where I am passing—time 1868. In a scrimmage at some public gathering in the town, A. had shot B. quite badly, but had not kill'd him. The sober men of Ellsworth conferr'd with one another and decided that A. deserv'd punishment. As they wished to set a good example and establish their reputation the reverse of a lynching town, they open an informal court and bring both men before them for deliberate trial. Soon as this trial begins the wounded man is led forward to give his testimony. Seeing his enemy in durance and unarm'd, B. walks suddenly up in a fury and shoots A. through the head—shoots him dead. The court is instantly adjourn'd, and its unanimous members, without a word of debate, walk the murderer B. out, wounded as he is, and hang him.

In due time we reach Denver, which city I fall in love with from the first, and have that feeling confirm'd, the longer I stay there. One of my pleasantest days was a jaunt, via Platte cañon, to Leadville.

AN HOUR ON KENOSHA SUMMIT

JOTTINGS from the Rocky Mountains, mostly pencill'd during a day's trip over the South Park RR., returning from Leadville, and especially the hour we were detain'd, (much to my satisfaction,) at Kenosha summit. As afternoon advances, novelties, far-reaching splendors, accumulate under the bright sun in this pure air. But I had better commence with the day.

The confronting of Platte cañon just at dawn, after a ten miles' ride in early darkness on the rail from Denver—the seasonable stoppage at the entrance of the cañon, and good breakfast of eggs, trout, and nice griddle-cakes—then as we travel on, and get well in the gorge, all the wonders, beauty, savage power of the scene—the wild stream of water, from sources of snows, brawling continually in sight one side—the dazzling sun, and the morning lights on the rocks—such turns and grades in the track, squirming around corners, or up and down hills—far glimpses of a hundred peaks, titanic necklaces, stretching north and south—the huge rightly-named Dome-rock—and as we dash along, others similar, simple, monolithic, elephantine.

AN EGOTISTICAL "FIND"

"I HAVE found the law of my own poems," was the unspoken but more-and-more decided feeling that came to me as I pass'd, hour after hour, amid all this grim yet joyous elemental abandon—this plenitude of material, entire absence of art, untrammel'd play of primitive Nature—the chasm, the gorge, the crystal mountain stream, repeated scores, hundreds of miles—the broad handling and absolute uncrampedness—the fantastic forms, bathed in transparent browns, faint reds and grays, towering sometimes a thousand, sometimes two or three thousand feet high—at their tops now and then huge masses pois'd, and mixing with the clouds, with only their outlines, hazed in misty lilac, visible. ("In Nature's grandest shows," says an old Dutch writer, an ecclesiastic, "amid the ocean's depth, if so might be, or countless worlds rolling above at night, a man thinks of them, weighs all, not for themselves or the abstract, but with reference to his own personality, and how they may affect him or color his destinies.")

NEW SENSES—NEW JOYS

WE FOLLOW the stream of amber and bronze brawling along its bed, with its frequent cascades and snow-white foam. Through the cañon we fly—mountains not only each side, but seemingly, till we get near right in front of us—every rood a new view flashing, and each flash defying description—on the almost perpendicular sides, clinging pines, cedars, spruces, crimson sumach bushes, spots of wild grass—but dominating all, those towering rocks, rocks, rocks, bathed in delicate varicolors, with the clear sky of autumn overhead. New senses, new joys, seem develop'd. Talk as you like, a typical Rocky Mountain cañon, or a limitless sea-like stretch of the great Kansas or Colorado plains, under favoring circumstances, tallies, perhaps expresses, certainly awakes, those grandest and subtlest element-emotions in the human soul, that all the marble temples and sculptures from Phidias to Thorwaldsen—all paintings, poems, reminiscences, or even music, probably never can.

STEAM-POWER, TELEGRAPHS, &c.

I GET out on a ten minutes' stoppage at Deer creek, to enjoy the unequal'd combination of hill, stone and wood. As we speed again, the yellow granite in the sunshine, with natural spires, minarets, castellated perches far aloft—then long stretches of straight-upright palisades, rhinoceros color—then gamboge and tinted chromos. Ever the best of my pleasures the cool-fresh Colorado atmosphere, yet sufficiently warm. Signs of man's restless advent and pioneerage, hard as Nature's face is—deserted dug-outs by dozens in the side-hills—the scantling-hut, the telegraph-pole, the smoke of some impromptu chimney or outdoor fire—at intervals little settlements of log-houses, or parties of surveyors or telegraph builders, with their comfortable tents. Once, a canvas office where you could send a message by electricity anywhere around the world! Yes, pronounc'd signs of the man of latest dates, dauntlessly grappling with these grisliest shows of the old kosmos. At several places steam saw-mills, with their piles of logs and boards, and the pipes puffing. Occasionally Platte cañon expanding into a grassy flat of a few acres. At one such place, toward the end, where we stop, and I get out to stretch my legs, as I look skyward, or rather mountain-top-ward, a huge hawk or eagle (a rare sight here) is idly soaring, balancing along the ether, now sinking low and coming quite near, and then up again in stately-languid circles—then higher, higher, slanting to the north, and gradually out of sight.

AMERICA'S BACK-BONE

I JOT these lines literally at Kenosha summit, where we return, afternoon, and take a long rest, 10,000 feet above sea-

level. At this immense height the South Park stretches fifty
miles before me. Mountainous chains and peaks in every variety of perspective, every hue of vista, fringe the view, in
nearer, or middle, or far-dim distance, or fade on the horizon.
We have now reach'd, penetrated the Rockies, (Hayden calls
it the Front Range,) for a hundred miles or so; and though
these chains spread away in every direction, specially north
and south, thousands and thousands farther, I have seen
specimens of the utmost of them, and know henceforth at
least what they are, and what they look like. Not themselves
alone, for they typify stretches and areas of half the globe—
are, in fact, the vertebræ or back-bone of our hemisphere. As
the anatomists say a man is only a spine, topp'd, footed,
breasted and radiated, so the whole Western world is, in a
sense, but an expansion of these mountains. In South America they are the Andes, in Central America and Mexico the
Cordilleras, and in our States they go under different names—
in California the Coast and Cascade ranges—thence more
eastwardly the Sierra Nevadas—but mainly and more cen-
trally here the Rocky Mountains proper, with many an elevation such as Lincoln's, Grey's, Harvard's, Yale's, Long's and
Pike's peaks, all over 14,000 feet high. (East, the highest
peaks of the Alleghanies, the Adirondacks, the Catskills, and
the White Mountains, range from 2000 to 5500 feet—only
Mount Washington, in the latter, 6300 feet.)

THE PARKS

In the midst of all here, lie such beautiful contrasts as the
sunken basins of the North, Middle, and South Parks, (the
latter I am now on one side of, and overlooking,) each the
size of a large, level, almost quadrangular, grassy, western
county, wall'd in by walls of hills, and each park the source
of a river. The ones I specify are the largest in Colorado, but
the whole of that State, and of Wyoming, Utah, Nevada and
western California, through their sierras and ravines, are

copiously mark'd by similar spreads and openings, many of the small ones of paradisiac loveliness and perfection, with their offsets of mountains, streams, atmosphere and hues beyond compare.

A COUPLE OF OLD FRIENDS—A COLERIDGE BIT

Latter April.—Have run down in my country haunt for a couple of days, and am spending them by the pond. I had already discover'd my kingfisher here (but only one—the mate not here yet.) This fine bright morning, down by the creek, he has come out for a spree, circling, flirting, chirping at a round rate. While I am writing these lines he is disporting himself in scoots and rings over the wider parts of the pond, into whose surface he dashes, once or twice making a loud *souse*—the spray flying in the sun—beautiful! I see his white and dark-gray plumage and peculiar shape plainly, as he has deign'd to come very near me. The noble, graceful bird! Now he is sitting on the limb of an old tree, high up, bending over the water—seems to be looking at me while I memorandize. I almost fancy he knows me. *Three days later.* —My second kingfisher is here with his (or her) mate. I saw the two together flying and whirling around. I had heard, in the distance, what I thought was the clear rasping staccato of the birds several times already—but I couldn't be sure the notes came from both until I saw them together. To-day at noon they appear'd, but apparently either on business, or for a little limited exercise only. No wild frolic now, full of free fun and motion, up and down for an hour. Doubtless, now they have cares, duties, incubation responsibilities. The frolics are deferr'd till summer-close.

I don't know as I can finish to-day's memorandum better than with Coleridge's lines, curiously appropriate in more ways than one:

"*All Nature seems at work—slugs leave their lair,*
The bees are stirring—birds are on the wing,
And winter, slumbering in the open air,
Wears on his smiling face a dream of spring;
And I, the while, the sole unbusy thing,
Nor honey make, nor pair, nor build, nor sing."

A WEEK'S VISIT TO BOSTON

May 1, '81.—Seems as if all the ways and means of American travel to-day had been settled, not only with reference to speed and directness, but for the comfort of women, children, invalids, and old fellows like me. I went on by a through train that runs daily from Washington to the Yankee metropolis without change. You get in a sleeping-car soon after dark in Philadelphia, and after ruminating an hour or two, have your bed made up if you like, draw the curtains, and go to sleep in it—fly on through Jersey to New York—hear in your half-slumbers a dull jolting and bumping sound or two—are unconsciously toted from Jersey city by a midnight steamer around the Battery and under the big bridge to the track of the New Haven road—resume your flight eastward, and early the next morning you wake up in Boston. All of which was my experience. I wanted to go to the Revere house. A tall unknown gentleman, (a fellow-passenger on his way to Newport he told me, I had just chatted a few moments before with him,) assisted me out through the depot crowd, procured a hack, put me in it with my traveling bag, saying smilingly and quietly, "Now I want you to let this be *my* ride," paid the driver, and before I could remonstrate bow'd himself off.

The occasion of my jaunt, I suppose I had better say here, was for a public reading of "the death of Abraham Lincoln" essay, on the sixteenth anniversary of that tragedy; which reading duly came off, night of April 15. Then I linger'd a week in Boston—felt pretty well (the mood propitious, my paralysis lull'd)—went around everywhere, and saw all that was to be seen, especially human beings. Boston's immense material growth—commerce, finance, commission stores, the plethora of goods, the crowded streets and sidewalks—made of course the first surprising show. In my trip out West, last year, I thought the wand of future prosperity, future empire, must soon surely be wielded by St. Louis, Chicago, beautiful Denver, perhaps San Francisco; but I see the said wand stretch'd out just as decidedly in Boston, with just as much certainty of staying; evidences of copious capital—indeed no centre of the New World ahead of it, (half the big railroads in the West are built with Yankees' money, and they take the dividends.) Old Boston with its zigzag streets and multitudinous angles, (crush up a sheet of letter-paper in your hand, throw it down, stamp it flat, and that is a map of old Boston) —new Boston with its miles upon miles of large and costly houses—Beacon street, Commonwealth avenue, and a hundred others. But the best new departures and expansions of Boston, and of all the cities of New England, are in another direction.

THE BOSTON OF TO-DAY

IN THE letters we get from Dr. Schliemann (interesting but fishy) about his excavations there in the far-off Homeric area, I notice cities, ruins, &c., as he digs them out of their graves, are certain to be in layers—that is to say, upon the foundation of an old concern, very far down indeed, is always another city or set of ruins, and upon that another superadded —and sometimes upon that still another—each representing either a long or rapid stage of growth and development, different from its predecessor, but unerringly growing out of and resting on it. In the moral, emotional, heroic, and human growths, (the main of a race in my opinion,) something of this kind has certainly taken place in Boston. The New England metropolis of to-day may be described as sunny, (there is something else that makes warmth, mastering even winds and meteorologies, though those are not to be sneez'd at,) joyous, receptive, full of ardor, sparkle, a certain element of

yearning, magnificently tolerant, yet not to be fool'd; fond of
good eating and drinking—costly in costume as its purse can
buy; and all through its best average of houses, streets, people, that subtle something (generally thought to be climate,
but it is not—it is something indefinable in the *race*, the turn
of its development) which effuses behind the whirl of anima-
tion, study, business, a happy and joyous public spirit, as distinguish'd from a sluggish and saturnine one. Makes me think
of the glints we get (as in Symonds's books) of the jolly old
Greek cities. Indeed there is a good deal of the Hellenic in
B., and the people are getting handsomer too—padded out,
with freer motions, and with color in their faces. I never saw
(although this is not Greek) so many *fine-looking gray hair'd
women.* At my lecture I caught myself pausing more than
once to look at them, plentiful everywhere through the audience—healthy and wifely and motherly, and wonderfully
charming and beautiful—I think such as no time or land but
ours could show.

MY TRIBUTE TO FOUR POETS

April 16.—A short but pleasant visit to Longfellow. I am not
one of the calling kind, but as the author of "Evangeline"
kindly took the trouble to come and see me three years ago in
Camden, where I was ill, I felt not only the impulse of my
own pleasure on that occasion, but a duty. He was the only
particular eminence I called on in Boston, and I shall not
soon forget his lit-up face and glowing warmth and courtesy,
in the modes of what is called the old school.

And now just here I feel the impulse to interpolate something about the mighty four who stamp this first American
century with its birth-marks of poetic literature. In a late
magazine one of my reviewers, who ought to know better,
speaks of my "attitude of contempt and scorn and intoler-
ance" toward the leading poets—of my "deriding" them, and
preaching their "uselessness." If anybody cares to know what
I think—and have long thought and avow'd—about them, I

am entirely willing to propound. I can't imagine any better
luck befalling these States for a poetical beginning and initi-
ation than has come from Emerson, Longfellow, Bryant, and
Whittier. Emerson, to me, stands unmistakably at the head,
but for the others I am at a loss where to give any precedence. Each illustrious, each rounded, each distinctive. Emerson for his sweet, vital-tasting melody, rhym'd philosophy,
and poems as amber-clear as the honey of the wild bee he
loves to sing. Longfellow for rich color, graceful forms and
incidents—all that makes life beautiful and love refined—com-
peting with the singers of Europe on their own ground, and,
with one exception, better and finer work than that of any of
them. Bryant pulsing the first interior verse-throbs of a mighty
world—bard of the river and the wood, ever conveying a taste
of open air, with scents as from hayfields, grapes, birch-bor-
ders—always lurkingly fond of threnodies—beginning and ending his long career with chants of death, with here and there
through all, poems, or passages of poems, touching the highest universal truths, enthusiasms, duties—morals as grim and
eternal, if not as stormy and fateful, as anything in Eschylus.
While in Whittier, with his special themes—(his outcropping
love of heroism and war, for all his Quakerdom, his verses at
times like the measur'd step of Cromwell's old veterans)—in
Whittier lives the zeal, the moral energy, that founded New
England—the splendid rectitude and ardor of Luther, Milton,
George Fox—I must not, dare not, say the wilfulness and narrowness—though doubtless the world needs now, and always
will need, almost above all, just such narrowness and wilfulness.

MILLET'S PICTURES — LAST ITEMS

April 18.—Went out three or four miles to the house of
Quincy Shaw, to see a collection of J. F. Millet's pictures.
Two rapt hours. Never before have I been so penetrated by
this kind of expression. I stood long and long before "the
Sower." I believe what the picture-men designate "the first

Sower," as the artist executed a second copy, and a third, and, some think, improved in each. But I doubt it. There is something in this that could hardly be caught again—a sublime murkiness and original pent fury. Besides this masterpiece, there were many others, (I shall never forget the simple evening scene, "Watering the Cow,") all inimitable, all perfect as pictures, works of mere art; and then it seem'd to me, with that last impalpable ethic purpose from the artist (most likely unconscious to himself) which I am always looking for. To me all of them told the full story of what went before and necessitated the great French revolution—the long precedent crushing of the masses of a heroic people into the earth, in abject poverty, hunger—every right denied, humanity attempted to be put back for generations—yet Nature's force, titanic here, the stronger and hardier for that repression—waiting terribly to break forth, revengeful—the pressure on the dykes, and the bursting at last—the storming of the Bastile—the execution of the king and queen—the tempest of massacres and blood. Yet who can wonder?

> Could we wish humanity different?
> Could we wish the people made of wood or stone?
> Or that there be no justice in destiny or time?

The true France, base of all the rest, is certainly in these pictures. I comprehend "Field-People Reposing," "the Diggers," and "the Angelus" in this opinion. Some folks always think of the French as a small race, five or five and a half feet high, and ever frivolous and smirking. Nothing of the sort. The bulk of the personnel of France, before the revolution, was large-sized, serious, industrious as now, and simple. The revolution and Napoleon's wars dwarf'd the standard of human size, but it will come up again. If for nothing else, I should dwell on my brief Boston visit for opening to me the new world of Millet's pictures. Will America ever have such an artist out of her own gestation, body, soul?

Sunday, April 17.—An hour and a half, late this afternoon, in silence and half light, in the great nave of Memorial hall,

Cambridge, the walls thickly cover'd with mural tablets, bearing the names of students and graduates of the university who fell in the secession war.

April 23.—It was well I got away in fair order, for if I had staid another week I should have been killed with kindness, and with eating and drinking.

A DISCOVERY OF OLD AGE

PERHAPS the best is always cumulative. One's eating and drinking one wants fresh, and for the nonce, right off, and have done with it—but I would not give a straw for that person or poem, or friend, or city, or work of art, that was not more grateful the second time than the first—and more still the third. Nay, I do not believe any grandest eligibility ever comes forth at first. In my own experience, (persons, poems, places, characters,) I discover the best hardly ever at first, (no absolute rule about it, however,) sometimes suddenly bursting forth, or stealthily opening to me, perhaps after years of unwitting familiarity, unappreciation, usage.

A VISIT, AT THE LAST, TO
R. W. EMERSON

Concord, Mass.—Out here on a visit—elastic, mellow, Indian-summery weather. Came to-day from Boston, (a pleasant ride of 40 minutes by steam, through Somerville, Belmont, Waltham, Stony Brook, and other lively towns,) convoy'd by my friend F. B. Sanborn, and to his ample house, and the kindness and hospitality of Mrs. S. and their fine family. Am writing this under the shade of some old hickories and elms, just after 4 P.M., on the porch, within a stone's throw of the Concord river. Off against me, across stream, on a meadow and side-hill, haymakers are gathering and wagoning-in probably their second or third crop. The spread of emerald-green and

brown, the knolls, the score or two of little haycocks dotting
the meadow, the loaded-up wagons, the patient horses, the
slow-strong action of the men and pitchforks—all in the just-
waning afternoon, with patches of yellow sun-sheen, mottled
by long shadows—a cricket shrilly chirping, herald of the dusk
—a boat with two figures noiselessly gliding along the little
river, passing under the stone bridge-arch—the slight settling
haze of aerial moisture, the sky and the peacefulness expanding in all directions and overhead—fill and soothe me.

Same evening.—Never had I a better piece of luck befall
me: a long and blessed evening with Emerson, in a way I
couldn't have wish'd better or different. For nearly two hours
he has been placidly sitting where I could see his face in the
best light, near me. Mrs. S.'s back-parlor well fill'd with people, neighbors, many fresh and charming faces, women, mostly young, but some old. My friend A. B. Alcott and his daughter Louisa were there early. A good deal of talk, the subject
Henry Thoreau—some new glints of his life and fortunes,
with letters to and from him—one of the best by Margaret
Fuller, others by Horace Greeley, Channing, &c.—one from
Thoreau himself, most quaint and interesting. (No doubt I
seem'd very stupid to the room-full of company, taking hardly any part in the conversation; but I had "my own pail to
milk in," as the Swiss proverb puts it.) My seat and the relative arrangement were such that, without being rude, or anything of the kind, I could just look squarely at E., which I
did a good part of the two hours. On entering, he had spoken
very briefly and politely to several of the company, then settled himself in his chair, a trifle push'd back, and, though a
listener and apparently an alert one, remain'd silent through
the whole talk and discussion. A lady friend quietly took a
seat next him, to give special attention. A good color in his
face, eyes clear, with the well-known expression of sweetness,
and the old clear-peering aspect quite the same.

Next Day.—Several hours at E.'s house, and dinner there.
An old familiar house, (he has been in it thirty-five years,)
with surroundings, furnishment, roominess, and plain elegance and fullness, signifying democratic ease, sufficient opu-

lence, and an admirable old-fashioned simplicity—modern luxury, with its mere sumptuousness and affectation, either touch'd lightly upon or ignored altogether. Dinner the same. Of course the best of the occasion (Sunday, September 18, '81) was the sight of E. himself. As just said, a healthy color in the cheeks, and good light in the eyes, cheery expression, and just the amount of talking that best suited, namely, a word or short phrase only were needed, and almost always with a smile. Besides Emerson himself, Mrs. E., with their daughter Ellen, the son Edward and his wife, with my friend F. S. and Mrs. S., and others, relatives and intimates. Mrs. Emerson, resuming the subject of the evening before, (I sat next to her,) gave me further and fuller information about Thoreau, who, years ago, during Mr. E.'s absence in Europe, had lived for some time in the family, by invitation.

OTHER CONCORD NOTATIONS

THOUGH the evening at Mr. and Mrs. Sanborn's, and the memorable family dinner at Mr. and Mrs. Emerson's, have most pleasantly and permanently fill'd my memory, I must not slight other notations of Concord. I went to the old Manse, walk'd through the ancient garden, enter'd the rooms, noted the quaintness, the unkempt grass and bushes, the little panes in the windows, the low ceilings, the spicy smell, the creepers embowering the light. Went to the Concord battle ground, which is close by, scann'd French's statue, "the Minute Man," read Emerson's poetic inscription on the base, linger'd a long while on the bridge, and stopp'd by the grave of the unnamed British soldiers buried there the day after the fight in April '75. Then riding on, (thanks to my friend Miss M. and her spirited white ponies, she driving them,) a half hour at Hawthorne's and Thoreau's graves. I got out and went up of course on foot, and stood a long while and ponder'd. They lie close together in a pleasant wooded spot well up the cemetery hill, "Sleepy Hollow." The flat surface of the first was densely cover'd by myrtle, with a border of arborvitæ, and the other had a brown headstone, moderately elaborate, with inscriptions. By Henry's side lies his brother John, of whom much was expected, but he died young. Then to Walden pond, that beautifully embower'd sheet of water, and spent over an hour there. On the spot in the woods where Thoreau had his solitary house is now quite a cairn of stones, to mark the place; I too carried one and deposited on the heap. As we drove back, saw the "School of Philosophy," but it was shut up, and I would not have it open'd for me. Near by stopp'd at the house of W. T. Harris, the Hegelian, who came out, and we had a pleasant chat while I sat in the wagon. I shall not soon forget those Concord drives, and especially that charming Sunday forenoon one with my friend Miss M., and the white ponies.

BOSTON COMMON—MORE OF
EMERSON

Oct. 10-13.—I spend a good deal of time on the Common, these delicious days and nights—every mid-day from 11.30 to about 1—and almost every sunset another hour. I know all the big trees, especially the old elms along Tremont and Beacon streets, and have come to a sociable-silent understanding with most of them, in the sunlit air, (yet crispy-cool enough,) as I saunter along the wide unpaved walks. Up and down this breadth by Beacon street, between these same old elms, I walk'd for two hours, of a bright sharp February mid-day twenty-one years ago, with Emerson, then in his prime, keen, physically and morally magnetic, arm'd at every point, and when he chose, wielding the emotional just as well as the intellectual. During those two hours he was the talker and I the listener. It was an argument-statement, reconnoitring, review, attack, and pressing home, (like an army corps in order, artillery, cavalry, infantry,) of all that could be said against that part (and a main part) in the construction of my poems, "Children of Adam." More precious than gold to me that dissertation—it afforded me, ever after, this strange and paradoxical lesson; each point of E.'s statement was unanswerable, no judge's charge ever more complete or convincing, I could never hear the points better put— and then I felt down in my soul the clear and unmistakable conviction to disobey all, and pursue my own way. "What have you to say then to such things?" said E., pausing in conclusion. "Only that while I can't answer them at all, I feel more settled than ever to adhere to my own theory, and exemplify it," was my candid response. Whereupon we went and had a good dinner at the American House. And thenceforward I never waver'd or was touch'd with qualms, (as I confess I had been two or three times before).

DEATH OF LONGFELLOW

Camden, April 3, '82.—I have just return'd from an old forest haunt, where I love to go occasionally away from parlors, pavements, and the newspapers and magazines—and where, of a clear forenoon, deep in the shade of pines and cedars and a tangle of old laurel-trees and vines, the news of Longfellow's death first reach'd me. For want of anything better, let me lightly twine a sprig of the sweet ground-ivy trailing so plentifully through the dead leaves at my feet, with reflections of that half hour alone, there in the silence, and lay it as my contribution on the dead bard's grave.

Longfellow in his voluminous works seems to me not only to be eminent in the style and forms of poetical expression that mark the present age, (an idiosyncrasy, almost a sickness, of verbal melody,) but to bring what is always dearest as poetry to the general human heart and taste, and probably must be so in the nature of things. He is certainly the sort of bard and counteractant most needed for our materialistic, self-assertive, money-worshipping, Anglo-Saxon races, and especially for the present age in America—an age tyrannically regulated with reference to the manufacturer, the merchant, the financier, the politician and the day workman—for whom and among whom he comes as the poet of melody, courtesy, deference—poet of the mellow twilight of the past in Italy, Germany, Spain, and in Northern Europe—poet of all sympathetic gentleness—and universal poet of women and young people. I should have to think long if I were ask'd to name the man who has done more, and in more valuable directions, for America.

I doubt if there ever was before such a fine intuitive judge and selecter of poems. His translations of many German and Scandinavian pieces are said to be better than the vernaculars. He does not urge or lash. His influence is like good drink or air. He is not tepid either, but always vital, with flavor, motion, grace. He strikes a splendid average, and does not sing exceptional passions, or humanity's jagged escapades. He is not revolutionary, brings nothing offensive or new, does not deal hard blows. On the contrary, his songs soothe and heal, or if they excite, it is a healthy and agreeable excitement. His very anger is gentle, is at second hand, (as in the "Quadroon Girl" and the "Witnesses.")

There is no undue element of pensiveness in Longfellow's strains. Even in the early translation, the Manrique, the movement is as of strong and steady wind or tide, holding up and buoying. Death is not avoided through his many themes, but there is something almost winning in his original verses and renderings on that dread subject—as, closing "the Happiest Land" dispute,

> *And then the landlord's daughter*
> *Up to heaven rais'd her hand,*
> *And said, "Ye may no more contend,*
> *There lies the happiest land."*

To the ungracious complaint-charge of his want of racy nativity and special originality, I shall only say that America and the world may well be reverently thankful—can never be thankful enough—for any such singing-bird vouchsafed out of the centuries, without asking that the notes be different from those of other songsters; adding what I have heard

Longfellow himself say, that ere the New World can be worthily original, and announce herself and her own heroes, she must be well saturated with the originality of others, and respectfully consider the heroes that lived before Agamemnon.

THE GREAT UNREST OF WHICH WE ARE PART

MY THOUGHTS went floating on vast and mystic currents as I sat to-day in solitude and half-shade by the creek—returning mainly to two principle centres. One of my cherish'd themes for a never-achiev'd poem has been the two impetuses of man and the universe—in the latter, creation's incessant unrest, exfoliation. (Darwin's evolution, I suppose.) Indeed, what is Nature but change, in all its visible, and still more its invisible processes? Or what is humanity in its faith, love, heroism, poetry, even morals, but *emotion?*

BY EMERSON'S GRAVE

May 6, '82.—We stand by Emerson's new-made grave without sadness—indeed a solemn joy and faith, almost hauteur—our soul-benison no mere

> *"Warrior, rest, thy task is done,"*

for one beyond the warriors of the world lies surely symboll'd here. A just man, poised on himself, all-loving, all-inclosing, and sane and clear as the sun. Nor does it seem so much Emerson himself we are here to honor—it is conscience, simplicity, culture, humanity's attributes at their best, yet applicable if need be to average affairs, and eligible to all. So used are we to suppose a heroic death can only come from out of battle or storm, or mighty personal contest, or amid dramatic incidents or danger, (have we not been taught so for ages by all the plays and poems?) that few even of those who most sympathizingly mourn Emerson's late departure will fully appreciate the ripen'd grandeur of that event, with its play of calm and fitness, like evening light on the sea.

How I shall henceforth dwell on the blessed hours when, not long since, I saw that benignant face, the clear eyes, the silently smiling mouth, the form yet upright in its great age —to the very last, with so much spring and cheeriness, and such an absence of decrepitude, that even the term *venerable* hardly seem'd fitting.

Perhaps the life now rounded and completed in its mortal development, and which nothing can change or harm more, has it most illustrious halo, not in its splendid intellectual or esthetic products, but as forming in its entirety one of the few, (alas! how few!) perfect and flawless excuses for being, of the entire literary class.

We can say, as Abraham Lincoln at Gettysburg, It is not we who come to consecrate the dead—we reverently come to receive, if so it may be, some consecration to ourselves and daily work from him.

AT PRESENT WRITING — PERSONAL

A letter to a German friend—extract

May 31, '82.—"From to-day I enter upon my 64th year. The paralysis that first affected me nearly ten years ago, has since remain'd, with varying course—seems to have settled quietly down, and will probably continue. I easily tire, am very clumsy, cannot walk far; but my spirits are first-rate. I go around in public almost every day—now and then take long trips, by railroad or boat, hundreds of miles—live largely in the open air—am sun-burnt and stout, (weigh 190)—keep up my activity and interest in life, people, progress, and the questions of the day. About two-thirds of the time I am quite comfortable. What mentality I ever had remains entirely un-affected; though physically I am a half-paralytic, and likely to be so, long as I live. But the principal object of my life seems to have been accomplish'd—I have the most devoted and ardent of friends, and affectionate relatives—and of ene-mies I really make no account."

AFTER TRYING A CERTAIN BOOK

I TRIED to read a beautifully printed and scholarly volume on "the Theory of Poetry," received by mail this morning from England—but gave it up at last for a bad job. Here are some capricious pencillings that follow'd, as I find them in my notes:

In youth and maturity Poems are charged with sunshine and varied pomp of day; but as the soul more and more takes precedence, (the sensuous still included,) the Dusk becomes the poet's atmosphere. I too have sought, and ever seek, the brilliant sun, and make my songs according. But as I grow old, the half-lights of evening are far more to me.

The play of Imagination, with the sensuous objects of Nature for symbols, and Faith—with Love and Pride as the unseen impetus and moving-power of all, make up the curious chess-game of a poem.

Common teachers or critics are always asking "What does it mean?" Symphony of fine musician, or sunset, or sea-waves rolling up the beach—what do they mean? Undoubtedly in the most subtle-elusive sense they mean something—as love does, and religion does, and the best poems;—but who shall fathom and define those meanings? (I do not intend this as a war-rant for wildness and frantic escapades—but to justify the soul's frequent joy in what cannot be defined to the intel-lectual part, or to calculation.)

At its best, poetic lore is like what may be heard of con-versation in the dusk, from speakers far or hid, of which we get only a few broken murmurs. What is not gather'd is far more—perhaps the main thing.

Grandest poetic passages are only to be taken at free removes, as we sometimes look for stars at night, not by gazing directly toward them, but off one side.

(To a poetic student and friend.)—I only seek to put you in rapport. Your own brain, heart, evolution, must not only understand the matter, but largely supply it.

FINAL CONFESSIONS — LITERARY TESTS

So DRAW near their end these garrulous notes. There have doubtless occurr'd some repetitions, technical errors in the consecutiveness of dates, in the minutiæ of botanical, astronomical, &c., exactness, and perhaps elsewhere;—for in gathering up, writing, peremptorily dispatching copy, this hot weather, (last of July and through August, '82,) and delaying not the printers, I have had to hurry along, no time to spare. But in the deepest veracity of all—in reflections of objects, scenes, Nature's outpourings, to my senses and receptivity, as they seem'd to me—in the work of giving those who care for it, some authentic glints, specimen-days of my life—and in the *bona fide* spirit and relations, from author to reader, on all the subjects design'd, and as far as they go, I feel to make unmitigated claims.

The synopsis of my early life, Long Island, New York city, and so forth, and the diary-jottings in the Secession war, tell their own story. My plan in starting what constitutes most of the middle of the book, was originally for hints and data of a Nature-poem that should carry one's experiences a few hours, commencing at noon-flush, and so through the after-part of the day—I suppose led to such idea by my own life-afternoon now arrived. But I soon found I could move at more ease, by giving the narrative at first hand. (Then there is a humiliating lesson one learns, in serene hours, of a fine day or night. Nature seems to look on all fixed-up poetry and art as something almost impertinent.)

Thus I went on, years following, various seasons and areas, spinning forth my thought beneath the night and stars, (or as I was confined to my room by half-sickness,) or at midday looking out upon the sea, or far north steaming over the Saguenay's black breast, jotting all down in the loosest sort of chronological order, and here printing from my impromptu notes, hardly even the seasons group'd together, or anything corrected—so afraid of dropping what smack of outdoors or sun or starlight might cling to the lines, I dared not try to meddle with or smooth them. Every now and then, (not often, but for a foil,) I carried a book in my pocket—or perhaps tore out from some broken or cheap edition a bunch of loose leaves; most always had something of the sort ready, but only took it out when the mood demanded. In that way, utterly out of reach of literary conventions, I re-read many authors.

I cannot divest my appetite of literature, yet I find myself eventually trying it all by Nature—*first premises* many call it, but really the crowning results of all, laws, tallies and proofs. (Has it never occurr'd to any one how the last deciding tests applicable to a book are entirely outside of technical and grammatical ones, and that any truly first-class production has little or nothing to do with the rules and calibres of ordinary critics? or the bloodless chalk of Allibone's Dictionary? I have fancied the ocean and the daylight, the mountain and the forest, putting their spirit in a judgment on our books. I have fancied some disembodied human soul giving its verdict.)

NATURE AND DEMOCRACY —
MORALITY

DEMOCRACY most of all affiliates with the open air, is sunny and hardy and sane only with Nature—just as much as Art is. Something is required to temper both—to check them, restrain them from excess, morbidity. I have wanted, before departure, to bear special testimony to a very old lesson and requisite. American Democracy, in its myriad personalities, in factories, work-shops, stores, offices—through the dense streets and houses of cities, and all their manifold sophisticated life—must either be fibred, vitalized, by regular contact with out-door light and air and growths, farm-scenes, animals, fields, trees, birds, sun-warmth and free skies, or it will certainly dwindle and pale. We cannot have grand races of mechanics, work people, and commonalty, (the only specific purpose of America,) on any less terms. I conceive of no flourishing and heroic elements of Democracy in the United States, or of Democracy maintaining itself at all, without the Nature-element forming a main part—to be its health-element and beauty-element—to really underlie the whole politics, sanity, religion and art of the New World.

Finally, the morality: "Virtue," said Marcus Aurelius, "what is it, only a living and enthusiastic sympathy with Nature?" Perhaps indeed the efforts of the true poets, founders, religions, literatures, all ages, have been, and ever will be, our time and times to come, essentially the same—to bring people back from their persistent strayings and sickly abstractions, to the costless average, divine, original concrete.

DEMOCRATIC VISTAS

[Selections]

* * *

. . . Out of such considerations, such truths, arises for treatment in these Vistas the important question of character, of an American stock-personality, with literatures and arts for outlets and return-expressions, and, of course, to correspond, within outlines common to all. To these, the main affair, the thinkers of the United States, in general so acute, have either given feeblest attention, or have remain'd, and remain, in a state of somnolence.

For my part, I would alarm and caution even the political and business reader, and to the utmost extent, against the prevailing delusion that the establishment of free political institutions, and plentiful intellectual smartness, with general good order, physical plenty, industry, &c., (desirable and precious advantages as they all are,) do, of themselves, determine and yield to our experiment of democracy the fruitage of success. With such advantages at present fully, or almost fully, possess'd—the Union just issued, victorious, from the struggle with the only foes it need ever fear, (namely, those within itself, the interior ones,) and with unprecedented materialistic advancement—society, in these States, is canker'd, crude, superstitious, and rotten. Political, or law-made society is, and private, or voluntary society, is also. In any vigor, the element of the moral conscience, the most important, the verteber to State or man, seems to me either entirely lacking, or seriously enfeebled or ungrown.

I say we had best look our times and lands searchingly in

he face, like a physician diagnosing some deep disease. Never
vas there, perhaps, more hollowness at heart than at present,
nd here in the United States. Genuine belief seems to have
eft us. The underlying principles of the States are not hon-
stly believ'd in, (for all this hectic glow, and these melo-
lramatic screamings,) nor is humanity itself believ'd in. What
•enetrating eye does not everywhere see through the mask?
.he spectacle is appaling. We live in an atmosphere of hy-
•ocrisy throughout. The men believe not in the women, nor
he women in the men. A scornful superciliousness rules
1 literature. The aim of all the *littérateurs* is to find some-
hing to make fun of. A lot of churches, sects, &c., the most
ismal phantasms I know, usurp the name of religion. Con-
ersation is a mass of badinage. From deceit in the spirit,
he mother of all false deeds, the offspring is already in-
alculable. An acute and candid person, in the revenue de-
•artment in Washington, who is led by the course of his
mployment to regularly visit the cities, north, south and
vest, to investigate frauds, has talk'd much with me about his
iscoveries. The depravity of the business classes of our
ountry is not less than has been supposed, but infinitely
reater. The official services of America, national, state, and
nunicipal, in all their branches and departments, except the
idiciary, are saturated in corruption, bribery, falsehood, mal-
dministration; and the judiciary is tainted. The great cities
eek with respectable as much as non-respectable robbery
id scoundrelism. In fashionable life, flippancy, tepid amours,
veak infidelism, small aims, or no aims at all, only to kill
me. In business, (this all-devouring modern word, business,)
ie one sole object is, by any means, pecuniary gain. The
nagician's serpent in the fable ate up all the other serpents;
nd money-making is our magician's serpent, remaining to-day
•le master of the field. The best class we show, is but a mob
f fashionably dress'd speculators and vulgarians. True, in-
eed, behind this fantastic farce, enacted on the visible stage
f society, solid things and stupendous labors are to be dis-
over'd, existing crudely and going on in the background, to
dvance and tell themselves in time. Yet the truths are none

the less terrible. I say that our New World democracy, however great a success in uplifting the masses out of their
sloughs, in materialistic development, products, and in a certain highly-deceptive superficial popular intellectuality, is,
so far, an almost complete failure in its social aspects, and in
really grand religious, moral, literary, and esthetic results. In
vain do we march with unprecedented strides to empire so
colossal, outvying the antique, beyond Alexander's, beyond
the proudest sway of Rome. In vain have we annex'd Texas,
California, Alaska, and reach north for Canada and south
for Cuba. It is as if we were somehow being endow'd with a
vast and more and more thoroughly-appointed body, and then
left with little or no soul.

Let me illustrate further, as I write, with current observations, localities, &c. The subject is important, and will bear repetition. After an absence, I am now again (Septem, 1870)
in New York city and Brooklyn, on a few weeks' vacation.
The splendor, picturesqueness, and oceanic amplitude and
rush of these great cities, the unsurpass'd situation, rivers and
bay, sparkling sea-tides, costly and lofty new buildings, façades of marble and iron, of original grandeur and elegance
of design, with the masses of gay color, the preponderance of
white and blue, the flags flying, the endless ships, the tumultuous streets, Broadway, the heavy, low, musical roar
hardly ever intermitted, even at night; the jobber's houses,
the rich shops, the wharves, the great Central Park, and the
Brooklyn Park of hills, (as I wander among them this beautiful fall weather, musing, watching, absorbing)—the assem-
blages of the citizens in their groups, conversations, trades,
evening amusements, or along the by-quarters—these, I say,
and the like of these, completely satisfy my senses of power,
fulness, motion, &c., and give me, through such senses and
appetites, and through my esthetic conscience, a continued
exaltation and absolute fulfilment. Always and more and
more, as I cross the East and North rivers, the ferries, or with
the pilots in their pilot-houses, or pass an hour in Wall street,

the gold exchange, I realize, (if we must admit such artialisms,) that not Nature alone is great in her fields of eedom and the open air, in her storms, the shows of night ad day, the mountains, forests, seas—but in the artificial, ae work of man too is equally great—in this profusion of eming humanity—in these ingenuities, streets, goods, houses, aips—these hurrying, feverish, electric crowds of men, their omplicated business genius, (not least among the geniuses,) ad all this mighty, many-threaded wealth and industry con-ntrated here.

But sternly discarding, shutting our eyes to the glow and andeur of the general superficial effect, coming down to hat is of the only real importance, Personalities, and ex-nining minutely, we question, we ask, Are there, indeed, en here worthy the name? Are there athletes? Are there rfect women, to match the generous material luxuriance? there a pervading atmosphere of beautiful manners? Are ere crops of fine youths, and majestic old persons? Are ere arts worthy freedom and a rich people? Is there a great oral and religious civilization—the only justification of a eat material one? Confess that to severe eyes, using the oral microscope upon humanity, a sort of dry and flat hara appears, these cities, crowded with petty grotesques, alformations, phantoms, playing meaningless antics. Con-ss that everywhere, in shop, street, church, theatre, bar-om, official chair, are pervading flippancy and vulgarity, w cunning, infidelity—everywhere the youth puny, impu-nt, foppish, prematurely ripe—everywhere an abnormal idinousness, unhealthy forms, male, female, painted, pad-d, dyed, chignon'd, muddy complexions, bad blood, the ca-city for good motherhood deceasing or deceas'd, shallow tions of beauty, with a range of manners, or rather lack of anners, (considering the advantages enjoy'd,) probably the eanest to be seen in the world.

Of all this, and these lamentable conditions, to breathe into em the breath recuperative of sane and heroic life, I say a w founded literature, not merely to copy and reflect exist-

ing surfaces, or pander to what is called taste—not only t
amuse, pass away time, celebrate the beautiful, the refined
the past, or exhibit technical, rhythmic, or grammatical dex
terity—but a literature underlying life, religious, consisten
with science, handling the elements and forces with compe
tent power, teaching and training men—and, as perhaps th
most precious of its results, achieving the entire redemptio
of woman out of these incredible holds and webs of silliness
millinery, and every kind of dyspeptic depletion—and thu
insuring to the States a strong and sweet Female Race, a rac
of perfect Mothers—is what is needed.

And now, in the full conception of these facts and point
and all that they infer, pro and con—with yet unshaken fait
in the elements of the American masses, the composites, o
both sexes, and even consider'd as individuals—and eve
recognizing in them the broadest bases of the best literar
and esthetic appreciation—I proceed with my speculation
Vistas. . . .

* * *

As to the political section of Democracy, which introduce
and breaks ground for further and vaster sections, fev
probably are the minds, even in these republican States, tha
fully comprehend the aptness of that phrase, "THE GOVERN
MENT OF THE PEOPLE, BY THE PEOPLE, FOR THE PEOPLE
which we inherit from the lips of Abraham Lincoln; a for
mula whose verbal shape is homely wit, but whose scope i
cludes both the totality and all minutiæ of the lesson.

The People! Like our huge earth itself, which, to ordinar
scansion, is full of vulgar contradictions and offence, ma
viewed in the lump, displeases, and is a constant puzzle an
affront to the merely educated classes. The rare, cosmical, ar
ist-mind, lit with the Infinite, alone confronts his manifold an
oceanic qualities—but taste, intelligence and culture, (so
called,) have been against the masses, and remain so. Ther
is plenty of glamour about the most damnable crimes an
hoggish meannesses, special and general, of the feuda
and dynastic world over there, with its *personnel* of lords an

ueens and courts, so well-dress'd and so handsome. But the
eople are ungrammatical, untidy, and their sins gaunt and
l-bred.

Literature, strictly consider'd, has never recognized the
eople, and, whatever may be said, does not to-day. Speak-
ig generally, the tendencies of literature, as hitherto pur-
ied, have been to make mostly critical and querulous men.
t seems as if, so far, there were some natural repugnance be-
veen a literary and professional life, and the rude rank spirit
f the democracies. There is, in later literature, a treatment
f benevolence, a charity business, rife enough it is true; but
know nothing more rare, even in this country, than a fit
cientific estimate and reverent appreciation of the People—
f their measureless wealth of latent power and capacity,
ieir vast, artistic contrasts of lights and shades—with, in
merica, their entire reliability in emergencies, and a certain
readth of historic grandeur, of peace or war, far surpassing
ll the vaunted samples of book-heroes, or any *haut ton*
)teries, in all the records of the world.

The movements of the late secession war, and their results,
a any sense that studies well and comprehends them, show
iat popular democracy, whatever its faults and dangers,
:actically justifies itself beyond the proudest claims and wild-
t hopes of its enthusiasts. Probably no future age can know,
it I well know, how the gist of this fiercest and most reso-
te of the world's war-like contentions resided exclusively in
ie unnamed, unknown rank and file; and how the brunt of
s labor of death was, to all essential purposes, volunteer'd.
he People, of their own choice, fighting, dying for their own
ea, insolently attack'd by the secession-slave-power, and its
ry existence imperil'd. Descending to detail, entering any
 the armies, and mixing with the private soldiers, we see
id have seen august spectacles. We have seen the alacrity
ith which the American born populace, the peaceablest and
ost good-natured race in the world, and the most personally
dependent and intelligent, and the least fitted to submit to
ie irksomeness and exasperation of regimental discipline,

sprang, at the first tap of the drum, to arms—not for gain, no
even glory, nor to repel invasion—but for an emblem, a mer
abstraction—for the life, *the safety of the flag*. We have see
the unequal'd docility and obedience of these soldiers. W
have seen them tried long and long by hopelessness, mismar
agement, and by defeat; have seen the incredible slaughte
toward or through which the armies, (as at first Fredericks
burg, and afterward at the Wilderness,) still unhesitating
obey'd orders to advance. We have seen them in trench, o
crouching behind breastwork, or tramping in deep mud, o
amid pouring rain or thick-falling snow, or under force
marches in hottest summer (as on the road to get to Getty
burg)—vast suffocating swarms, divisions, corps, with ever
single man so grimed and black with sweat and dust, his ow
mother would not have known him—his clothes all dirty
stain'd and torn, with sour, accumulated sweat for perfume
many a comrade, perhaps a brother, sun-struck, staggerin
out, dying, by the roadside, of exhaustion—yet the great bul
bearing steadily on, cheery enough, hollow-bellied from hur
ger, but sinewy with unconquerable resolution.

We have seen this race proved by wholesale by drearie
yet more fearful tests—the wound, the amputation, the sha
ter'd face or limb, the slow hot fever, long impatient ancho
age in bed, and all the forms of maiming, operation and di
ease. Alas! America have we seen, though only in her earl
youth, already to hospital brought. There have we watch'
these soldiers, many of them only boys in years—mark'd the
decorum, their religious nature and fortitude, and their swee
affection. Wholesale, truly. For at the front, and through th
camps, in countless tents, stood the regimental, brigade an
division hospitals; while everywhere amid the land, in or nea
cities, rose clusters of huge, white-wash'd, crowded, one-stor
wooden barracks; and there ruled agony with bitter scourg
yet seldom brought a cry; and there stalk'd death by day an
night along the narrow aisles between the rows of cots, or b
the blankets on the ground, and touch'd lightly many a poo
sufferer, often with blessed, welcome touch.

I know not whether I shall be understood, but I realiz

that it is finally from what I learn'd personally mixing in such scenes that I am now penning these pages. One night in the gloomiest period of the war, in the Patent office hospital in Washington city, as I stood by the bedside of a Pennsylvania soldier, who lay, conscious of quick approaching death, yet perfectly calm, and with noble, spiritual manner, the veteran surgeon, turning aside, said to me, that though he had witness'd many, many deaths of soldiers, and had been a worker at Bull Run, Antietam, Fredericksburg, &c., he had not seen yet the first case of man or boy that met the approach of dissolution with cowardly qualms or terror. My own observation fully bears out the remarks.

What have we here, if not, towering above all talk and argument, the plentifully-supplied, last-needed proof of democracy, in its personalities? Curiously enough, too, the proof on his point comes, I should say, every bit as much from the south, as from the north. Although I have spoken only of the latter, yet I deliberately include all. Grand, common stock! to me the accomplish'd and convincing growth, prophetic of the future; proof undeniable to sharpest sense, of perfect beauty, tenderness and pluck, that never feudal lord, nor Greek, nor Roman breed, yet rival'd. Let no tongue ever speak in disparagement of the American races, north or south, to one who has been through the war in the great army hospitals.

Meantime, general humanity, (for to that we return, as, for our purposes, what it really is, to bear in mind,) has always, in every department, been full of perverse maleficence, and is so yet. In downcast hours the soul thinks it always will be—but soon recovers from such sickly moods. I myself see clearly enough the crude, defective streaks in all the strata of the common people; the specimens and vast collections of the ignorant, the credulous, the unfit and uncouth, the incapable, and the very low and poor. The eminent person just mention'd sneeringly asks whether we expect to elevate and improve a nation's politics by absorbing such morbid collections and qualities therein. The point is a formidable one, and there will doubtless always be numbers of solid and reflective citizens who will never get over it. Our answer is general, and is involved in the scope and letter of this essay. We believe the ulterior project of political and all other government, (having, of course, provided for the police, the safety of life, property, and for the basic statute and common law, and their administration, always first in order,) to be among the rest, not merely to rule, to repress disorder, &c., but to develop, to open up to cultivation, to encourage the possibilities of all beneficent and manly outcroppage, and of that aspiration for independence, and the pride and self-respect latent in all characters. (Or, if there be exceptions, we cannot, fixing our eyes on them alone, make theirs the rule for all.)

I say the mission of government, henceforth, in civilized lands, is not repression alone, and not authority alone, not even of law, nor by that favorite standard of the eminent writer, the rule of the best men, the born heroes and captains of the race, (as if such ever, or one time out of a hundred, get into the big places, elective or dynastic)—but higher than the highest arbitrary rule, to train communities through all their grades, beginning with individuals and ending there again, to rule themselves. What Christ appear'd for in the moral-spiritual field for human-kind, namely, that in respect to the absolute soul, there is in the possession of such by each single individual, something so transcendent, so incapable of gradations, (like life,) that, to that extent, it places all beings on a common level, utterly regardless of the distinctions of intellect, virtue, station, or any height or lowliness whatever—is tallied in like manner, in this other field, by democracy's rule that men, the nation, as a common aggregate of living identities, affording in each a separate and complete subject for freedom, worldly thrift and happiness, and for a fair chance for growth, and for protection in citizenship, &c., must, to the political extent of the suffrage or vote, if no further, be placed, in each and in the whole, on one broad, primary, universal, common platform.

The purpose is not altogether direct; perhaps it is more indirect. For it is not that democracy is of exhaustive account, in itself. Perhaps, indeed, it is, (like Nature,) of no account in itself. It is that, as we see, it is the best, perhaps only, fit and full means, formulater, general caller-forth, trainer, for the million, not for grand material personalities only, but for immortal souls. To be a voter with the rest is not so much; and this, like every institute, will have its imperfections. But to become an enfranchised man, and now, impediments removed, to stand and start without humiliation, and equal with the rest; to commence, or have the road clear'd to commence, the grand experiment of development, whose end, (perhaps requiring several generations,) may be the forming of a full-grown man or woman—that *is* something. To ballast the State is also secured, and in our times is to be secured, in no other way.

We do not, (at any rate I do not,) put it either on the ground that the People, the masses, even the best of them, are, in their latent or exhibited qualities, essentially sensible and good—nor on the ground of their rights; but that good or bad, rights or no rights, the democratic formula is the only safe and preservative one for coming times. We endow the masses with the suffrage for their own sake, no doubt; then, perhaps still more, from another point of view, for community's sake. Leaving the rest to the sentimentalists, we present freedom as sufficient in its scientific aspect, cold as ice, reasoning, deductive, clear and passionless as crystal.

Democracy too is law, and of the strictest, amplest kind. Many suppose, (and often in its own ranks the error,) that it means a throwing aside of law, and running riot. But, briefly, it is the superior law, not alone that of physical force, the body, which, adding to, it supersedes with that of the spirit. Law is the unshakable order of the universe forever; and the law over all, and law of laws, is the law of successions; that of the superior law, in time, gradually supplanting and overwhelming the inferior one. (While, for myself, I would cheerfully agree—first covenanting that the formative tendencies shall be administer'd in favor, or at least not against it, and that this reservation be closely construed—that until the individual or community show due signs, or be so minor and fractional as not to endanger the State, the condition of authoritative tutelage may continue, and self-government must abide its time.) Nor is the esthetic point, always an important one, without fascination for highest aiming souls. The common ambition strains for elevations, to become some privileged exclusive. The master sees greatness and health in being part of the mass; nothing will do as well as common ground. Would you have in yourself the divine, vast, general law? Then merge yourself in it.

And, topping democracy, this most alluring record, that it alone can bind, and ever seeks to bind, all nations, all men, of however various and distant lands, into a brotherhood, a family. It is the old, yet ever-modern dream of earth, out of her eldest and her youngest, her fond philosophers and poets. Not that half only, individualism, which isolates. There is another half, which is adhesiveness or love, that fuses, ties and aggregates, making the races comrades, and fraternizing all. Both are to be vitalized by religion, (sole worthiest elevator of man or State,) breathing into the proud, material tissues, the breath of life. For I say at the core of democracy, finally, is the religious element. All the religions, old and new, are there. Nor may the scheme step forth, clothed, in resplendent beauty and command, till these, bearing the best, the latest fruit, the spiritual, shall fully appear.

A portion of our pages we might indite with reference toward Europe, especially the British part of it, more than our own land, perhaps not absolutely needed for the home reader. But the whole question hangs together, and fastens and links all peoples. The liberalist of to-day has this advantage over antique or medieval times, that his doctrine seeks not only to individualize but to universalize. The great word Solidarity has arisen. Of all dangers to a nation, as things exist in our day, there can be no greater one than having certain portions of the people set off from the rest by a line drawn—they not privileged as others, but degraded, humiliated, made of no account. Much quackery teems, of course, even on democracy's side, yet does not really affect the orbic quality of the matter. To work in, if we may so term it, and justify God, his divine aggregate, the People, (or, the veritable horn'd and sharp-tail'd Devil, *his* aggregate, if there be who convulsively insist upon it)—this, I say, is what democracy is for; and this is what our America means, and is doing—may I not say, has done? If not, she means nothing more, and does nothing more, than any other land. And as, by virtue of its kosmical, antiseptic power, Nature's stomach is fully strong enough not only to digest the morbific matter always presented, not to be turn'd aside, and perhaps, indeed, intuitively gravitating thither—but even to change such contributions into nutriment for highest use and life—so American democracy's. That is the lesson we, these days, send over to European lands by every western breeze.

And, truly, whatever may be said in the way of abstract argument, for or against the theory of a wider democratizing of institutions in any civilized country, much trouble might well be saved to all European lands by recognizing this palpable fact, (for a palpable fact it is,) that some form of such democratizing is about the only resource now left. *That,* or chronic dissatisfaction continued, mutterings which grow annually louder and louder, till, in due course, and pretty swiftly in most cases, the inevitable crisis, crash, dynastic ruin. Anything worthy to be call'd statesmanship in the Old World, I should say, among the advanced students, adepts, or men of any brains, does not debate to-day whether to hold on, attempting to lean back and monarchize, or to look forward and democratize—but *how,* and in what degree and part, most prudently to democratize.

The eager and often inconsiderate appeals of reformers and revolutionists are indispensable, to counterbalance the inertness and fossilism making so large a part of human institutions. The latter will always take care of themselves—the danger being that they rapidly tend to ossify us. The former is to be treated with indulgence, and even with respect. As circulation to air, so is agitation and a plentiful degree of speculative license to political and moral sanity. Indirectly, but surely, goodness, virtue, law, (of the very best,) follow freedom. These, to democracy, are what the keel is to the ship, or saltness to the ocean.

The true gravitation-hold of liberalism in the United States will be a more universal ownership of property, general homesteads, general comfort—a vast, intertwining reticulation of wealth. As the human frame, or, indeed, any object in this manifold universe, is best kept together by the simple miracle of its own cohesion, and the necessity, exercise and profit thereof, so a great and varied nationality, occupying millions of square miles, were firmest held and knit by the principle of the safety and endurance of the aggregate of its middling property owners. So that, from another point of view, ungracious as it may sound, and a paradox after what we have been saying, democracy looks with suspicious, ill-satisfied eye upon the very poor, the ignorant, and on those out of business. She asks for men and women with occupations, well-off, owners of houses and acres, and with cash in the bank—and with some cravings for literature, too; and must have them, and hastens to make them. Luckily, the seed is already well-sown, and has taken ineradicable root.

Huge and mighty are our days, our republican lands—and most in their rapid shiftings, their changes, all in the interest of the cause. As I write this particular passage, (November, 1868,) the din of disputation rages around me. Acrid the temper of the parties, vital the pending questions. Congress convenes; the President sends his message; reconstruction is still in abeyance; the nomination and the contest for the twenty-first Presidentiad draw close, with loudest threat and bustle. Of these, and all the like of these, the eventuations I know not; but well I know that behind them, and whatever their eventuations, the vital things remain safe and certain, and all the needed work goes on. Time, with soon or later superciliousness, disposes of Presidents, Congressmen, party platforms, and such. Anon, it clears the stage of each and any mortal shred that thinks itself so potent to its day; and at and after which, (with precious, golden exceptions once or twice in a century,) all that relates to sir potency is flung to moulder in a burial-vault, and no one bothers himself the least bit about it afterward. But the People ever remain, tendencies continue, and all the idiocratic transfers in unbroken chain go on.

In a few years the dominion-heart of America will be far inland, toward the West. Our future national capital may not be where the present one is. It is possible, nay likely, that in less than fifty years, it will migrate a thousand or two miles, will be re-founded, and every thing belonging to it made on a different plan, original, far more superb. The main social, political, spine-character of the States will probably run along the Ohio, Missouri and Mississippi rivers, and west and north of them, including Canada. Those regions, with the group of powerful brothers toward the Pacific, (destined to the mastership of that sea and its countless paradises of islands,) will compact and settle the traits of America, with all the old retain'd, but more expanded, grafted on newer, hardier, purely native stock. A giant growth, composite from the rest, getting their contribution, absorbing it, to make it more illustrious. From the north, intellect, the sun of things, also the idea of unswayable justice, anchor amid the last, the wildest tempests. From the south the living soul, the animus of good and bad, haughtily admitting no demonstration but its own. While from the west itself comes solid personality, with blood and brawn, and the deep quality of all-accepting fusion.

Political democracy, as it exists and practically works in America, with all its threatening evils, supplies a training-school for making first-class men. It is life's gymnasium, not of good only, but of all. We try often, though we fall back often. A brave delight, fit for freedom's athletes, fills these arenas, and fully satisfies, out of the action in them, irrespective of success. Whatever we do not attain, we at any rate attain the experiences of the fight, the hardening of the strong campaign, and throb with currents of attempt at least. Time is ample. Let the victors come after us. Not for nothing does evil play its part among us. Judging from the main portions of the history of the world, so far, justice is always in jeopardy, peace walks amid hourly pitfalls, and of slavery, misery, meanness, the craft of tyrants and the credulity of the populace, in some of their protean forms, no voice can at any time say, They are not. The clouds break a little, and the sun shines out—but soon and certain the lowering darkness falls again, as if to last forever. Yet is there an immortal courage and prophecy in every sane soul that cannot, must not, under any circumstances, capitulate. *Vive,* the attack—the perennial assault! *Vive,* the unpopular cause—the spirit that audaciously aims—the never-abandon'd efforts, pursued the same amid opposing proofs and precedents.

Once, before the war, (Alas! I dare not say how many times the mood has come!) I, too, was fill'd with doubt and gloom. A foreigner, an acute and good man, had impressively said to me, that day—putting in form, indeed, my own observations: "I have travel'd much in the United States, and watch'd their politicians, and listen'd to the speeches of the candidates, and read the journals, and gone into the public houses, and heard the unguarded talk of men. And I have found your vaunted America honeycomb'd from top to toe with infidelism, even to itself and its own programme. I have mark'd the brazen hell-faces of secession and slavery gazing defiantly from all the windows and doorways. I have everywhere found, primarily, thieves and scalliwags arranging the nominations to offices, and sometimes filling the offices themselves. I have found the north just as full of bad stuff as the south. Of the holders of public office in the Nation or the States or their municipalities, I have found that not one in a hundred has been chosen by any spontaneous selection of the outsiders, the people, but all have been nominated and put through by little or large caucuses of the politicians, and have got in by corrupt rings and electioneering, not capacity or desert. I have noticed how the millions of sturdy farmers and mechanics are thus the helpless supple-jacks of comparatively few politicians. And I have noticed more and more, the alarming spectacle of parties usurping the government, and openly and shamelessly wielding it for party purposes."

Sad, serious, deep truths. Yet are there other, still deeper, amply confronting, dominating truths. Over those politicians and great and little rings, and over all their insolence and wiles, and over the powerfulest parties, looms a power, too sluggish maybe, but ever holding decisions and decrees in hand, ready, with stern process, to execute them as soon as plainly needed—and at times, indeed, summarily crushing to atoms the mightiest parties, even in the hour of their pride.

In saner hours far different are the amounts of these things from what, at first sight, they appear. Though it is no doubt important who is elected governor, mayor, or legislator, (and full of dismay when incompetent or vile ones get elected, as they sometimes do,) there are other, quieter contingencies, infinitely more important. Shams, &c., will always be the show, like ocean's scum; enough, if waters deep and clear make up the rest. Enough, that while the piled embroider'd shoddy gaud and fraud spreads to the superficial eye, the hidden warp and weft are genuine, and will wear forever. Enough, in short, that the race, the land which could raise such as the late rebellion, could also put it down.

The average man of a land at last only is important. He, in these States, remains immortal owner and boss, deriving good uses, somehow, out of any sort of servant in office, even the basest; (certain universal requisites, and their settled regularity and protection, being first secured,) a nation like ours, in a sort of geological formation state, trying continually new experiments, choosing new delegations, is not served by the best men only, but sometimes more by those that provoke it —by the combats they arouse. Thus national rage, fury, discussion, &c., better than content. Thus, also, the warning signals, invaluable for after times.

What is more dramatic than the spectacle we have seen repeated, and doubtless long shall see—the popular judgment taking the successful candidates on trial in the offices—standing off, as it were, and observing them and their doings for a while, and always giving, finally, the fit, exactly due reward? I think, after all, the sublimest part of political history, and its culmination, is currently issuing from the American people. I know nothing grander, better exercise, better digestion, more positive proof of the past, the triumphant result of faith in human kind, than a well-contested American national election.

Then still the thought returns, (like the thread-passage in overtures,) giving the key and echo to these pages. When I pass to and fro, different latitudes, different seasons, beholding the crowds of the great cities, New York, Boston, Philadelphia, Cincinnati, Chicago, St. Louis, San Francisco, New Orleans, Baltimore—when I mix with these interminable swarms of alert, turbulent, good-natured, independent citizens, mechanics, clerks, young persons—at the idea of this mass of men, so fresh and free, so loving and so proud, a singular awe falls upon me. I feel, with dejection and amazement, that among our geniuses and talented writers or speakers, few or none have yet really spoken to this people, created a single image-making work for them, or absorb'd the central spirit and the idiosyncrasies which are theirs—and which, thus, in highest ranges, so far remain entirely uncelebrated, unexpress'd.

Dominion strong is the body's; dominion stronger is the mind's. What has fill'd, and fills to-day our intellect, our fancy, furnishing the standards therein, is yet foreign. The great poems, Shakspere included, are poisonous to the idea of the pride and dignity of the common people, the life-blood of democracy. The models of our literature, as we get it from other lands, ultra-marine, have had their birth in courts, and bask'd and grown in castle sunshine; all smells of princes' favors. Of workers of a certain sort, we have, indeed, plenty, contributing after their kind; many elegant, many learn'd, all complacent. But touch'd by the national test, or tried by the standards of democratic personality, they wither to ashes. I say I have not seen a single writer, artist, lecturer, or what not, that has confronted the voiceless but ever erect and active, pervading, underlying will and typic aspiration of the and, in a spirit kindred to itself. Do you call those genteel little creatures American poets? Do you term that perpetual, pistareen, paste-pot work, American art, American drama, taste, verse? I think I hear, echoed as from some mountain-top afar in the west, the scornful laugh of the Genius of these States.

Democracy, in silence, biding its time, ponders its own ideals, not of literature and art only—not of men only, but of women. The idea of the women of America, (extricated from this daze, this fossil and unhealthy air which hangs about the word *lady*,) develop'd, raised to become the robust equals, workers, and, it may be, even practical and political deciders with the men—greater than man, we may admit, through their divine maternity, always their towering, emblematical attribute—but great, at any rate, as man, in all departments; or, rather, capable of being so, soon as they realize it, and can bring themselves to give up toys and fictions, and launch forth, as men do, amid real, independent, stormy life. . . .

* * *

To practically enter into politics is an important part of American personalism. To every young man, north and south, earnestly studying these things, I should here, as an offset to what I have said in former pages, now also say, that may-be to views of very largest scope, after all, perhaps the political, perhaps the literary and sociological,) America goes best about its development its own way—sometimes, to temporary sight, appalling enough. It is the fashion among dillettants and fops (perhaps I myself am not guiltless,) to decry the whole formulation of the active politics of America, as beyond redemption, and to be carefully kept away from. See you that you do not fall into this error. America, it may be, is doing very well upon the whole, notwithstanding these antics of the parties and their leaders, these half-brain'd nominees, the many ignorant ballots, and many elected failures and blatherers. It is the dillettants, and all who shirk their duty, who are not doing well. As for you, I advise you to enter more strongly yet into politics. I advise every young man to do so. Always inform yourself; always do the best you can; always vote. Disengage yourself from parties. They have been useful, and to some extent remain so; but the floating, uncommitted electors, farmers, clerks, mechanics, the masters of parties— watching aloof, inclining victory this side or that side—such are the ones most needed, present and future. For America, if eligible at all to downfall and ruin, is eligible within herself, not without; for I see clearly that the combined foreign world could not beat her down. But these savage, wolfish parties alarm me. Owning no law but their own will, more and more combative, less and less tolerant of the idea of ensemble and of equal brotherhood, the perfect equality of the States, the ever-overarching American ideas, it behooves you to convey yourself implicitly to no party, nor submit blindly to their dictators, but steadily hold yourself judge and master over all of them.

So much, (hastily toss'd together, and leaving far more unsaid,) for an ideal, or intimations of an ideal, toward American manhood. But the other sex, in our land, requires at least a basis of suggestion.

I have seen a young American woman, one of a large family of daughters, who, some years since, migrated from her meagre country home to one of the northern cities, to gain her own support. She soon became an expert seamstress, but finding the employment too confining for health and comfort she went boldly to work for others, to house-keep, cook, clean &c. After trying several places, she fell upon one where she was suited. She has told me that she finds nothing degrading in her position; it is not inconsistent with personal dignity, self-respect, and the respect of others. She confers benefits and receives them. She has good health; her presence itself is healthy and bracing; her character is unstain'd; she has made herself understood, and preserves her independence, and has been able to help her parents, and educate and get place

or her sisters; and her course of life is not without oppor-
unities for mental improvement, and of much quiet, uncost-
ng happiness and love.

I have seen another woman who, from taste and necessity
onjoin'd, has gone into practical affairs, carries on a mechani-
al business, partly works at it herself, dashes out more and
nore into real hardy life, is not abash'd by the coarseness of
he contact, knows how to be firm and silent at the same time,
olds her own with unvarying coolness and decorum, and will
ompare, any day, with superior carpenters, farmers, and even
oatmen and drivers. For all that, she has not lost the charm
f the womanly nature, but preserves and bears it fully, though
hrough such rugged presentation.

Then there is the wife of a mechanic, mother of two chil-
ren, a woman of merely passable English education, but of
ne wit, with all her sex's grace and intuitions, who exhibits,
ndeed, such a noble female personality, that I am fain to
ecord it here. Never abnegating her own proper independ-
nce, but always genially preserving it, and what belongs to it
-cooking, washing, child-nursing, house-tending—she beams
nshine out of all these duties, and makes them illustrious.
hysiologically sweet and sound, loving work, practical, she
et knows that there are intervals, however few, devoted to
ecreation, music, leisure, hospitality—and affords such inter-
als. Whatever she does, and wherever she is, that charm, that
ndescribable perfume of genuine womanhood attends her,
oes with her, exhales from her, which belongs of right to all
ne sex, and is, or ought to be, the invariable atmosphere and
ommon aureola of old as well as young.

My dear mother once described to me a resplendent person,
own on Long Island, whom she knew in early days. She was
nown by the name of the Peacemaker. She was well toward
ghty years old, of happy and sunny temperament, had al-
ays lived on a farm, and was very neighborly, sensible and
iscreet, an invariable and welcom'd favorite, especially with
oung married women. She had numerous children and grand-
hildren. She was uneducated, but possess'd a native dignity.
he had come to be a tacitly agreed upon domestic regulator,

judge, settler of difficulties, shepherdess, and reconciler in the land. She was a sight to draw near and look upon, with her large figure, her profuse snow-white hair, (uncoif'd by any head-dress or cap,) dark eyes, clear complexion, sweet breath, and peculiar personal magnetism.

The foregoing portraits, I admit, are frightfully out of line from these imported models of womanly personality—the stock feminine characters of the current novelists, or of the foreign court poems, (Ophelias, Enids, princesses, or ladies of one thing or another,) which fill the envying dreams of so many poor girls, and are accepted by our men, too, as supreme ideals of feminine excellence to be sought after. But I present mine just for a change.

Then there are mutterings, (we will not now stop to heed them here, but they must be heeded,) of something more revolutionary. The day is coming when the deep questions of woman's entrance amid the arenas of practical life, politics, the suffrage, &c., will not only be argued all around us, but may be put to decision, and real experiment.

Of course, in these States, for both man and woman, we must entirely recast the types of highest personality from what the oriental, feudal, ecclesiastical worlds bequeath us, and which yet possess the imaginative and esthetic fields of the United States, pictorial and melodramatic, not without use as studies, but making sad work, and forming a strange anachronism upon the scenes and exigencies around us. Of course, the old undying elements remain. The task is, to successfully adjust them to new combinations, our own days. Nor is this so incredible. I can conceive a community, to-day and here, in which, on a sufficient scale, the perfect personalities, without noise meet; say in some pleasant western settlement or town, where a couple of hundred best men and women, of ordinary worldly status, have by luck been drawn together, with nothing extra of genius or wealth, but virtuous, chaste, industrious, cheerful, resolute, friendly and devout. I can conceive such a community organized in running order, powers judiciously delegated—farming, building, trade, courts, mails, schools, elections, all attended to; and then the rest of life, the main hing, freely branching and blossoming in each individual, and bearing golden fruit. I can see there, in every young and old man, after his kind, and in every woman after hers, a true personality, develop'd, exercised proportionately in body, mind, and spirit. I can imagine this case as one not necessarily are or difficult, but in buoyant accordance with the municipal and general requirements of our times. And I can realize in it he culmination of something better than any stereotyped *eclat* of history or poems. Perhaps, unsung, undramatized, unput in essays or biographies—perhaps even some such community already exists, in Ohio, Illinois, Missouri, or somewhere, practically fulfilling itself, and thus outvying, in cheapest vulgar life, all that has been hitherto shown in best ideal pictures. . . .

* * *

By points like these we, in reflection, token what we mean by any land's or people's genuine literature. And thus compared and tested, judging amid the influence of loftiest products only, what do our current copious fields of print, covering in manifold forms, the United States, better, for an analogy, present, than, as in certain regions of the sea, those spreading, undulating masses of squid, through which the whale swimming, with head half out, feeds?

Not but that doubtless our current so-called literature, (like an endless supply of small coin,) performs a certain service, and may-be, too, the service needed for the time (the preparation-service, as children learn to spell.) Everybody reads, and truly nearly everybody writes, either books, or for the magazines or journals. The matter has magnitude, too, after a sort. But is it really advancing? or, has it advanced for a long while? There is something impressive about the huge editions of the dailies and weeklies, the mountain-stacks of white paper piled in the press-vaults, and the proud, crashing, ten-cylinder presses, which I can stand and watch any time by the half hour. Then, (though the States in the field of imagination present not a single first-class work, not a single great literatus,) the main objects, to amuse, to titillate, to pass away time, to circulate the news, and rumors of news, to rhyme and read rhyme, are yet attain'd, and on a scale of infinity. To-day, in books, in the rivalry of writers, especially novelists, success, (so-call'd,) is for him or her who strikes the mean flat average, the sensational appetite for stimulus, incident, persiflage, &c., and depicts, to the common calibre, sensual, exterior life. To such, or the luckiest of them, as we see, the audiences are limitless and profitable; but they cease presently. While this day, or any day, to workmen portraying interior or spiritual life, the audiences were limited, and often laggard—but they last forever.

Compared with the past, our modern science soars, and our journals serve—but ideal and even ordinary romantic literature does not, I think, substantially advance. Behold the prolific brood of the contemporary novel, magazine-tale, theatre-play, &c. The same endless thread of tangled and superlative love-story, inherited, apparently from the Amadises and Palmerins of the 13th, 14th, and 15th centuries over there in Europe. The costumes and associations brought down to date, the seasoning hotter and more varied, the dragons and ogres left out —but the *thing*, I should say, has not advanced—is just as sensational, just as strain'd—remains about the same, nor more nor less.

What is the reason our time, our lands, that we see no fresh local courage, sanity, of our own—the Mississippi, stalwart Western men, real mental and physical facts, Southerners, &c. in the body of our literature? especially the poetic part of it. But always, instead, a parcel of dandies and ennuyees, dapper little gentlemen from abroad, who flood us with their thin sentiment of parlors, parasols, piano-songs, tinkling rhymes, the five-hundredth importation—or whimpering and crying about something, chasing one aborted conceit after another, and forever occupied in dyspeptic amours with dyspeptic women. While, current and novel, the grandest events and revolutions, and stormiest passions of history, are crossing to-day with unparallel'd rapidity and magnificence over the stages of our own and all the continents, offering new materials, opening new vistas, with largest needs, inviting the daring launching forth of conceptions in literature, inspired by them, soaring in highest regions, serving art in its highest, (which is only the other name for serving God, and serving humanity,) where is the man of letters, where is the book, with any nobler aim than to follow in the old track, repeat what has been said before—and, as its utmost triumph, sell well, and be erudite or elegant?

Mark the roads, the processes, through which these States have arrived, standing easy, henceforth ever-equal, ever-compact, in their range to-day. European adventures? the most antique? Asiatic or African? old history—miracles—romances? Rather, our own unquestion'd facts. They hasten, incredible, blazing bright as fire. From the deeds and days of Columbus down to the present, and including the present—and especially the late Secession war—when I con them, I feel, every leaf, like stopping to see if I have not made a mistake, and fall'n on the splendid figments of some dream. But it is no dream. We stand, live, move, in the huge flow of our age's materialism —in its spirituality. We have had founded for us the most positive of lands. The founders have pass'd to other spheres —but what are these terrible duties they have left us?

Their politics the United States have, in my opinion, with all their faults, already substantially establish'd, for good, on their own native, sound, long-vista'd principles, never to be overturn'd, offering a sure basis for all the rest. With that, their future religious forms, sociology, literature, teachers, schools, costumes, &c., are of course to make a compact whole, uniform, on tallying principles. For how can we remain, divided, contradicting ourselves, this way? I say we can only attain harmony and stability by consulting ensemble and the ethic purports, and faithfully building upon them. For the New World, indeed, after two grand stages of preparation-strata, I perceive that now a third stage, being ready for, (and without which the other two were useless,) with unmistakable signs appears. The First stage was the planning and putting on record the political foundation rights of immense masses of people—indeed all people—in the organization of republican National, State, and municipal governments, all constructed with reference to each, and each to all. This is the American programme, not for classes, but for universal man, and is embodied in the compacts of the Declaration of Independence, and, as it began and has now grown, with its amendments, the Federal Constitution—and in the State governments, with all their interiors, and with general suffrage; those having the sense not only of what is in themselves, but that their certain several things started, planted, hundreds of others in the same direction duly arise and follow. The Second stage relates to material prosperity, wealth, produce, labor-saving machines, iron, cotton, local, State and continental railways, intercommunication and trade with all lands, steamships, mining, general employment, organization of great cities, cheap appliances for comfort, numberless technical schools, books, newspapers, a currency for money circulation, &c. The Third stage, rising out of the previous ones, to make them and all illustrious, I, now, for one, promulge, announcing a native expression-spirit, getting into form, adult, and through mentality, for these States, self-contain'd, different from others, more expansive, more rich and free, to be evidenced by original authors and poets to come, by American personalities, plenty of them, male and female, traversing the States, none excepted—and by native superber tableaux and growths of language, songs, operas, orations, lectures, architecture—and by a sublime and serious Religious Democracy sternly taking command, dissolving the old, sloughing off surfaces, and from its own interior and vital principles, reconstructing, democratizing society.

For America, type of progress, and of essential faith in man, above all his errors and wickedness—few suspect how deep, how deep it really strikes. The world evidently supposes, and we have evidently supposed so too, that the States are merely to achieve the equal franchise, an elective government—to inaugurate the respectability of labor, and become a nation of practical operatives, law-abiding, orderly and well-off. Yes, those are indeed parts of the task of America; but they not only do not exhaust the progressive conception, but rather arise, teeming with it, as the mediums of deeper, higher progress. Daughter of a physical revolution—mother of the true revolutions, which are of the interior life, and of the arts. For so long as the spirit is not changed, any change of appearance is of no avail.

The old men, I remember as a boy, were always talking of American independence. What is independence? Freedom from all laws or bonds except those of one's own being, control'd by the universal ones. To lands, to man, to woman, what is there at last to each, but the inherent soul, nativity, idiocrasy, free, highest-poised, soaring its own flight, following out itself?

At present, these States, in their theology and social standards, (of greater importance than their political institutions,) are entirely held possession of by foreign lands. We see the sons and daughters of the New World, ignorant of its genius, not yet inaugurating the native, the universal, and the near, still importing the distant, the partial, and the dead. We see London, Paris, Italy—not original, superb, as where they belong—but second-hand here, where they do not belong. We see the shreds of Hebrews, Romans, Greeks; but where, on her own soil, do we see, in any faithful, highest, proud expression, America herself? I sometimes question whether she has a corner in her own house.

Not but that in one sense, and a very grand one, good theology, good art, or good literature, has certain features shared in common. The combination fraternizes, ties the races —is, in many particulars, under laws applicable indifferently to all, irrespective of climate or date, and, from whatever source, appeals to emotions, pride, love, spirituality, common to humankind. Nevertheless, they touch a man closest, (perhaps only actually touch him,) even in these, in their expression through autochthonic lights and shades, flavors, fondnesses, aversions, specific incidents, illustrations, out of his own nationality, geography, surroundings, antecedents, &c.

The spirit and the form are one, and depend far more on association, identity and place, than is supposed. Subtly interwoven with the materiality and personality of a land, a race —Teuton, Turk, Californian, or what not—there is always something—I can hardly tell what it is—history but describes the results of it—it is the same as the untellable look of some human faces. Nature, too, in her stolid forms, is full of it—but to most it is there a secret. This something is rooted in the invisible roots, the profoundest meanings of that place, race, or nationality; and to absorb and again effuse it, uttering words and products as from its midst, and carrying it into highest regions, is the work, or a main part of the work, of any country's true author, poet, historian, lecturer, and perhaps even priest and philosoph. Here, and here only, are the foundations for our really valuable and permanent verse, drama, &c.

But at present, (judged by any higher scale than that which finds the chief ends of existence to be to feverishly make money during one-half of it, and by some "amusement," or perhaps foreign travel, flippantly kill time, the other half,) and consider'd with reference to purposes of patriotism, health, a noble personality, religion, and the democratic adjustments, all these swarms of poems, literary magazines, dramatic plays, resultant so far from American intellect, and the formation of our best ideas, are useless and a mockery. They strengthen and nourish no one, express nothing characteristic, give decision and purpose to no one, and suffice only the lowest level of vacant minds.

Of what is called the drama, or dramatic presentation in the United States, as now put forth at the theatres, I should say it deserves to be treated with the same gravity, and on a par with the questions of ornamental confectionery at public dinners, or the arrangement of curtains and hangings in a ball room—nor more, nor less. Of the other, I will not insult the reader's intelligence, (once really entering into the atmosphere of these Vistas,) by supposing it necessary to show, in detail, why the copious dribble, either of our little or well-known rhymesters, does not fulfil, in any respect, the needs and august occasions of this land. America demands a poetry that is bold, modern, and all-surrounding and kosmical, as she is herself. It must in no respect ignore science or the modern, but inspire itself with science and the modern. It must bend its vision toward the future, more than the past. Like America, it must extricate itself from even the greatest models of the past, and, while courteous to them, must have entire faith in itself, and the products of its own democratic spirit only. Like her, it must place in the van, and hold up at all hazards, the banner of the divine pride of man in himself, (the radical foundation of the new religion.) Long enough have the People been listening to poems in which common humanity, deferential, bends low, humiliated, acknowledging superiors. But America listens to no such poems. Erect, inflated, and fully self-esteeming be the chant; and then America will listen with pleased ears. . .

* * *

. . . I hail with joy the oceanic, variegated, intense practical energy, the demand for facts, even the business materialism of the current age, our States. But woe to the age or land in which these things, movements, stopping at themselves, do not tend to ideas. As fuel to flame, and flame to the heavens, so must wealth, science, materialism—even this democracy of which we make so much—unerringly feed the highest mind, the soul. Infinitude the flight: fathomless the mystery. Man, so diminutive, dilates beyond the sensible universe, competes with, outcopes space and time, meditating even one great idea. Thus, and thus only, does a human being, his spirit, ascend above, and justify, objective Nature, which, probably nothing in itself, is incredibly and divinely serviceable, indispensable, real, here. And as the purport of objective Nature is doubtless folded, hidden, somewhere here—as somewhere here is what this globe and its manifold forms, and the light of day, and night's darkness, and life itself, with all its experiences, are for—it is here the great literature, especially verse, must get its inspiration and throbbing blood. Then may we attain to a poetry worthy the immortal soul of man, and which, while absorbing materials, and, in their own sense, the shows of Nature, will, above all, have, both directly and indirectly, a freeing, fluidizing, expanding, religious character, exulting with science, fructifying the moral elements, and stimulating aspirations, and meditations on the unknown.

The process, so far, is indirect and peculiar, and though it may be suggested, cannot be defined. Observing, rapport, and with intuition, the shows and forms presented by Nature, the sensuous luxuriance, the beautiful in living men and women, the actual play of passions, in history and life—and, above all, from those developments either in Nature or human personality in which power, (dearest of all to the sense of the artist,) transacts itself—out of these, and seizing what is in them, the poet, the esthetic worker in any field, by the divine magic of his genius, projects them, their analogies, by curious removes, indirections, in literature and art. (No useless attempt to repeat the material creation, by daguerreotyping the exact likeness by mortal mental means.) This is the image-making faculty, coping with material creation, and rivaling, almost triumphing over it. This alone, when all the other parts of a specimen of literature or art are ready and waiting, can breathe into it the breath of life, and endow it with identity.

"The true question to ask," says the librarian of Congress in a paper read before the Social Science Convention at New York, October, 1869, "The true question to ask respecting a book, is, *has it help'd any human soul?*" This is the hint, statement, not only of the great literatus, his book, but of every great artist. It may be that all works of art are to be first tried by their art qualities, their image-forming talent, and their dramatic, pictorial, plot-constructing, euphonious and other talents. Then, whenever claiming to be first-class works, they are to be strictly and sternly tried by their foundation in, and radiation, in the highest sense, and always indirectly, of the ethic principles, and eligibility to free, arouse, dilate.

As, within the purposes of the Kosmos, and vivifying all meteorology, and all the congeries of the mineral, vegetable and animal worlds—all the physical growth and development of man, and all the history of the race in politics, religions, wars, &c., there is a moral purpose, a visible or invisible intention, certainly underlying all—its results and proof needing to be patiently waited for—needing intuition, faith, idiosyncrasy, to its realization, which many, and especially the intellectual, do not have—so in the product, or congeries of the product, of the greatest literatus. This is the last, profoundest measure and test of a first-class literary or esthetic achievement, and when understood and put in force must fain, I say, lead to works, books, nobler than any hitherto known. Lo! Nature, (the only complete, actual poem,) existing calmly in the divine scheme, containing all, content, careless of the criticisms of a day, or these endless and wordy chatterers. And lo! to the consciousness of the soul, the permanent identity, the thought, the something, before which the magnitude even of democracy, art, literature, &c., dwindles, becomes partial, measurable—something that fully satisfies, (which those do not.) That something is the All, and the idea of All, with the accompanying idea of eternity, and of itself, the soul, buoyant, indestructible, sailing space forever, visiting every region, as a ship the sea. And again lo! the pulsations in all matter, all spirit, throbbing forever—the eternal beats, eternal systole and diastole of life in things—wherefrom I feel and know that death is not the ending, as was thought, but rather the real beginning—and that nothing ever is or can be lost, nor ever die, nor soul, nor matter.

In the future of these States must arise poets immenser far, and make great poems of death. The poems of life are great, but there must be the poems of the purports of life, not only in itself, but beyond itself. I have eulogized Homer, the sacred bards of Jewry, Eschylus, Juvenal, Shakespere, &c., and acknowledged their inestimable value. But, (with perhaps the exception, in some, not all respects, of the second-mention'd,) I say there must, for future and democratic purposes, appear poets, (dare I to say so?) of higher class even than any of those—poets not only possess'd of the religious fire and abandon of Isaiah, luxuriant in the epic talent of Homer, or for proud characters as in Shakespere, but consistent with the

Hegelian formulas, and consistent with modern science. America needs, and the world needs, a class of bards who will, now and ever, so link and tally the rational physical being of man, with the ensembles of time and space, and with this vast and multiform show, Nature, surrounding him, ever tantalizing him, equally a part, and yet not a part of him, as to essentially harmonize, satisfy, and put at rest. Faith, very old, now scared away by science, must be restored, brought back by the same power that caused her departure—restored with new sway, deeper, wider, higher than ever. Surely, this universal ennui, this coward fear, this shuddering at death, these low, degrading views, are not always to rule the spirit pervading future society, as it has the past, and does the present. What the Roman Lucretius sought most nobly, yet all too blindly, negatively to do for his age and its successors, must be done positively by some great coming literatus, especially poet, who, while remaining fully poet, will absorb whatever science indicates, with spiritualism, and out of them, and out of his own genius, will compose the great poem of death. Then will man indeed confront Nature, and confront time and space, both with science, and *con amore,* and take his right place, prepared for life, master of fortune and misfortune. And then that which was long wanted will be supplied, and the ship that had it not before in all her voyages, will have an anchor.

There are still other standards, suggestions, for products of high literatuses. That which really balances and conserves the social and political world is not so much legislation, police, treaties, and dread of punishment, as the latent eternal intuitional sense, in humanity, of fairness, manliness, decorum, &c. Indeed, this perennial regulation, control, and oversight, by self-suppliance, is *sine qua non* to democracy; and a highest widest aim of democratic literature may well be to bring forth, cultivate, brace, and strengthen this sense, in individuals and society. A strong mastership of the general inferior self by the superior self, is to be aided, secured, indirectly, but surely, by the literatus, in his works, shaping, for individual or aggregate democracy, a great passionate body, in and along with which goes a great masterful spirit.

And still, providing for contingencies, I fain confront the fact, the need of powerful native philosophs and orators and bards, these States, as rallying points to come, in time of danger, and to fend off ruin and defection. For history is long, long, long. Shift and turn the combinations of the statement as we may, the problem of the future of America is in certain respects as dark as it is vast. Pride, competition, segregation, vicious wilfulness, and license beyond example, brood already upon us. Unwieldy and immense, who shall hold in behemoth? who bridle leviathan? Flaunt it as we choose, athwart and over the roads of our progress loom huge uncertainty, and dreadful, threatening gloom. It is useless to deny it: Democracy grows rankly up the thickest, noxious, deadliest plants and fruits of all—brings worse and worse invaders— needs newer, larger, stronger, keener compensations and compellers.

Our lands, embracing so much, (embracing indeed the whole, rejecting none,) hold in their breast that flame also, capable of consuming themselves, consuming us all. Short as the span of our national life has been, already have death and downfall crowded close upon us—and will again crowd close, no doubt, even if warded off. Ages to come may never know, but I know, how narrowly during the late secession war— and more than once, and more than twice or thrice—our Nationality, (wherein bound up, as in a ship in a storm, depended, and yet depend, all our best life, all hope, all value,) just grazed, just by a hair escaped destruction. Alas! to think of them! the agony and bloody sweat of certain of those hours! those cruel, sharp, suspended crises!

Even to-day, amid these whirls, incredible flippancy, and blind fury of parties, infidelity, entire lack of first-class captains and leaders, added to the plentiful meanness and vulgarity of the ostensible masses—that problem, the labor question, beginning to open like a yawning gulf, rapidly widening every year—what prospect have we? We sail a dangerous sea of seething currents, cross and undercurrents, vortices—all so dark, untried—and whither shall we turn? It seems as if the Almighty had spread before this nation charts of imperial destinies, dazzling as the sun, yet with many a deep intestine difficulty, and human aggregate of cankerous imperfection,—saying, lo! the roads, the only plans of development, long and varied with all terrible balks and ebullitions. You said in your soul, I will be empire of empires, overshadowing all else, past and present, putting the history of old-world dynasties, conquests behind me, as of no account—making a new history, a history of democracy, making old history a dwarf—I alone inaugurating largeness, culminating time. If these, O lands of America, are indeed the prizes, the determinations of your soul, be it so. But behold the cost, and already specimens of the cost. Thought you greatness was to ripen for you like a pear? If you would have greatness, know that you must conquer it through ages, centuries—must pay for it with a proportionate price. For you too, as for all lands, the struggle, the traitor, the wily person in office, scrofulous wealth, the surfeit of prosperity, the demonism of greed, the hell of passion, the decay of faith, the long postponement, the fossil-like lethargy, the ceaseless need of revolutions, prophets, thunderstorms, deaths, births, new projections and invigorations of ideas and men.

Yet I have dream'd, merged in that hidden-tangled problem of our fate, whose long unraveling stretches mysteriously through time—dream'd out, portray'd, hinted already—a little or a larger band—a band of brave and true, unprecedented yet—arm'd and equipt at every point—the members separated, it may be, by different dates and States, or south, or north, or east, or west—Pacific, Atlantic, Southern, Canadian—a year, a century here, and other centuries there—but always one, compact in soul, conscience-conserving, God-inculcating, inspired achievers, not only in literature, the greatest art, but achievers in all art—a new, undying order, dynasty, from age to age transmitted—a band, a class, at least as fit to cope with current years, our dangers, needs, as those who, for their times, so long, so well, in armor or in cowl, upheld and made illustrious, that far-back feudal, priestly world. To offset chivalry, indeed, those vanish'd countless knights, old altars, abbeys, priests, ages and strings of ages, a knightlier and more sacred cause to-day demands, and shall supply, in a New World, to larger, grander work, more than the counterpart and tally of them.

Arrived now, definitely, at an apex for these Vistas, I confess that the promulgation and belief in such a class or institution—a new and greater literatus order—its possibility, (nay certainty,) underlies these entire speculations—and that the rest, the other parts, as superstructures, are all founded upon it. It really seems to me the condition, not only of our future national and democratic development, but of our perpetuation. In the highly artificial and materialistic bases of modern civilization, with the corresponding arrangements and methods of living, the force-infusion of intellect alone, the depraving influences of riches just as much as poverty, the absence of all high ideals in character—with the long series of tendencies, shapings, which few are strong enough to resist, and which now seem, with steam-engine speed, to be everywhere turning out the generations of humanity like uniform iron castings—all of which, as compared with the feudal ages, we can yet do nothing better than accept, make the best of, and even welcome, upon the whole, for their oceanic practical grandeur, and their restless wholesale kneading of the masses—I say of all this tremendous and dominant play of solely materialistic bearings upon current life in the United States, with the results as already seen, accumulating, and reaching far into the future, that they must either be confronted and met by at least an equally subtle and tremendous force-infusion for purposes of spiritualization, for the pure conscience, for genuine esthetics, and for absolute and primal manliness and womanliness—or else our modern civilization, with all its improvements, is in vain, and we are on the road to a destiny, a status, equivalent, in its real world, to that of the fabled damned.

Prospecting thus the coming unsped days, and that new order in them—marking the endless train of exercise, development, unwind, in nation as in man, which life is for—we see, fore-indicated, amid these prospects and hopes, new law-forces of spoken and written language—not merely the pedagogue-forms, correct, regular, familiar with precedents, made for matters of outside propriety, fine words, thoughts definitely told out—but a language fann'd by the breath of Nature, which leaps overhead, cares mostly for impetus and effects, and for what it plants and invigorates to grow—tallies life and character, and seldomer tells a thing than suggests or necessitates it. In fact, a new theory of literary composition for imaginative works of the very first class, and especially for highest poems, is the sole course open to these States. Books are to be call'd for, and supplied, on the assumption that the process of reading is not a half-sleep, but, in highest sense, an exercise, a gymnast's struggle; that the reader is to do something for himself, must be on the alert, must himself or herself construct indeed the poem, argument, history, metaphysical essay—the text furnishing the hints, the clue, the start or frame-work. Not the book needs so much to be the complete thing, but the reader of the book does. That were to make a nation of supple and athletic minds, well-train'd, intuitive, used to depend on themselves, and not on a few coteries of writers.

Investigating here, we see, not that it is a little thing we have, in having the bequeath'd libraries, countless shelves of volumes, records, &c.; yet how serious the danger, depending entirely on them, of the bloodless vein, the nerveless arm, the false application, at second or third hand. We see that the real interest of this people of ours in the theology, history, poetry, politics, and personal models of the past, (the British islands, for instance, and indeed all the past,) is not necessarily to mould ourselves or our literature upon them, but to attain fuller, more definite comparisons, warnings, and the insight to ourselves, our own present, and our own far grander, different, future history, religion, social customs, &c. We see that almost everything that has been written, sung, or stated, of old, with reference to humanity under the feudal and oriental institutes, religions, and for other lands, needs to be re-written, re-sung, re-stated, in terms consistent with the institution of these States, and to come in range and obedient uniformity with them.

We see, as in the universes of the material kosmos, after meteorological, vegetable, and animal cycles, man at last arises, born through them, to prove them, concentrate them, to turn upon them with wonder and love—to command them, adorn them, and carry them upward into superior realms—so, out of the series of the preceding social and political universes, now arise these States. We see that while many were supposing things established and completed, really the grandest things always remain; and discover that the work of the New World is not ended, but only fairly begun.

We see our land, America, her literature, esthetics, &c., as, substantially, the getting in form, or effusement and statement, of deepest basic elements and loftiest final meanings, of history and man—and the portrayal, (under the eternal laws and conditions of beauty,) of our own physiognomy, the subjective tie and expression of the objective, as from our own combination, continuation, and points of view—and the deposit and record of the national mentality, character, appeals, heroism, wars, and even liberties—where these, and all, culminate in native literary and artistic formulation, to be perpetuated; and not having which native, first-class formulation, she will flounder about, and her other, however imposing, eminent greatness, prove merely a passing gleam; but truly having which, she will understand herself, live nobly, nobly contribute, emanate, and, swinging, poised safely on herself, illumin'd and illuming, become a full-form'd world, and divine Mother not only of material but spiritual worlds, in ceaseless succession through time—the main thing being the average, the bodily, the concrete, the democratic, the popular, on which all the superstructures of the future are to permanently rest.

ORIGINS *of* ATTEMPTED SECESSION

*Not the whole matter, but some side facts worth conning
to-day and any day*

I CONSIDER the war of attempted secession, 1860–65, not as
a struggle of two distinct and separate peoples, but a conflict
(often happening, and very fierce) between the passions and
paradoxes of one and the same identity—perhaps the only
terms on which that identity could really become fused, homogeneous and lasting. The origin and conditions out of
which it arose, are full of lessons, full of warnings yet to the
Republic—and always will be. The underlying and principal
of those origins are yet singularly ignored. The Northern
States were really just as responsible for that war, (in its
precedents, foundations, instigations,) as the South. Let me
try to give my view. From the age of 21 to 40, (1840–'60,) I
was interested in the political movements of the land, not so
much as a participant, but as an observer, and a regular voter
at the elections. I think I was conversant with the springs of
action, and their workings, not only in New York city and
Brooklyn, but understood them in the whole country, as I
have made leisurely tours through all the middle States, and
partially through the western and southern, and down to New
Orleans, in which city I resided for some time. (I was there
at the close of the Mexican war—saw and talk'd with General
Taylor, and the other generals and officers, who were fêted
and detain'd several days on their return victorious from that
expedition.)

Of course many and very contradictory things, specialties,
developments, constitutional views, &c., went to make up the

origin of the war—but the most significant general fact can be best indicated and stated as follows: For twenty-five years previous to the outbreak, the controlling "Democratic" nominating conventions of our Republic—starting from their primaries in wards or districts, and so expanding to counties, powerful cities, States, and to the great Presidential nominating conventions—were getting to represent and be composed of more and more putrid and dangerous materials. Let me give a schedule, or list, of one of these representative conventions for a long time before, and inclusive of, that which nominated Buchanan. (Remember they had come to be the fountains and tissues of the American body politic, forming, as it were, the whole blood, legislation, office-holding, &c.) One of these conventions, from 1840 to '60, exhibited a spectacle such as could never be seen except in our own age and in these States. The members who composed it were, seven-eighths of them, the meanest kind of bawling and blowing office-holders, office-seekers, pimps, malignants, conspirators, murderers, fancy-men, custom-house clerks, contractors, kept-editors, spaniels well-train'd to carry and fetch, jobbers, infidels, disunionists, terrorists, mail-riflers, slave-catchers, pushers of slavery, creatures of the President, creatures of would-be Presidents, spies, bribers, compromisers, lobbyers, sponges, ruin'd sports, expell'd gamblers, policy-backers, monte-dealers, duellists, carriers of conceal'd weapons, deaf men, pimpled men, scarr'd inside with vile disease, gaudy outside with gold chains made from the people's money and harlots' money twisted together; crawling, serpentine men, the lousy combings and born freedom-sellers of the earth. And whence came they? From back-yards and bar-rooms; from out of the custom-houses, marshals' offices, post-offices, and gambling-hells; from the President's house, the jail, the station-house; from unnamed by-places, where devilish disunion was hatch'd at midnight; from political hearses, and from the coffins inside, and from the shrouds inside of the coffins; from the tumors and abscesses of the land; from the skeletons and skulls in the vaults of the federal alms-houses; and from the running sores of the great cities. Such, I say, form'd, or absolutely control'd the forming of, the entire personnel, the atmosphere, nutriment and chyle, of our municipal, State, and National politics—substantially permeating, handling, deciding, and wielding everything—legislation, nominations, elections, "public sentiment," &c.—while the great masses of the people, farmers, mechanics, and traders, were helpless in their gripe. These conditions were mostly prevalent in the north and west, and especially in New York and Philadelphia cities; and the southern leaders, (bad enough, but of a far higher order,) struck hands and affiliated with, and used them. Is it strange that a thunder-storm follow'd such morbid and stifling cloud-strata?

I say then, that what, as just outlined, heralded, and made the ground ready for secession revolt, ought to be held up, through all the future, as the most instructive lesson in American political history—the most significant warning and beacon-light to coming generations. I say that the sixteenth, seventeenth and eighteenth terms of the American Presidency have shown that the villainy and shallowness of rulers (back'd by the machinery of great parties) are just as eligible to these States as to any foreign despotism, kingdom, or empire—there is not a bit of difference. History is to record those three Presidentiads, and especially the administrations of Fillmore and Buchanan, as so far our topmost warning and shame. Never were publicly display'd more deform'd, mediocre, snivelling, unreliable, false-hearted men. Never were these States so insulted, and attempted to be betray'd. All the main purposes for which the government was establish'd were openly denied. The perfect equality of slavery with freedom was flauntingly preach'd in the north—nay, the superiority of slavery. The slave trade was proposed to be renew'd. Everywhere frowns and misunderstandings—everywhere exasperations and humiliations. (The slavery contest is settled—and the war is long over—yet do not those putrid conditions, too many of them, still exist? still result in diseases, fevers, wounds—not of war and army hospitals—but the wounds and diseases of peace?)

Out of those generic influences, mainly in New York, Pennsylvania, Ohio, &c., arose the attempt at disunion. To philosophical examination, the malignant fever of that war shows its embryonic sources, and the original nourishment of its life and growth, in the north. I say secession, below the surface, originated and was brought to maturity in the free States. I allude to the score of years preceding 1860. My deliberate opinion is now, that if at the opening of the contest the abstract duality-question of *slavery and quiet* could have been submitted to a direct popular vote, as against their opposite, they would have triumphantly carried the day in a majority of the northern States—in the large cities, leading off with New York and Philadelphia, by tremendous majorities. The events of '61 amazed everybody north and south, and burst all prophecies and calculations like bubbles. But even then, and during the whole war, the stern fact remains that (not only did the north put it down, but) *the secession cause had numerically just as many sympathizers in the free as in the rebel States.*

As to slavery, abstractly and practically, (its idea, and the determination to establish and expand it, especially in the new territories, the future America,) it is too common, I repeat, to identify it exclusively with the south. In fact down to the opening of the war, the whole country had about an equal hand in it. The north had at least been just as guilty, if not more guilty; and the east and west had. The former Presidents and Congresses had been guilty—the governors and legislatures of every northern State had been guilty, and the mayors of New York and other northern cities had all been guilty—their hands were all stain'd. And as the conflict took decided shape, it is hard to tell which class, the leading southern or northern disunionists, was more stunn'd and disappointed at the non-action of the free-state secession element, so largely existing and counted on by those leaders, both sections.

So much for that point, and for the north. As to the inception and direct instigation of the war, in the south itself, I shall not attempt interiors or complications. Behind all, the idea that it was from a resolute and arrogant determination on the part of the extreme slaveholders, the Calhounites, to carry the states rights' portion of the constitutional compact to its farthest verge, and nationalize slavery, or else disrupt the Union, and found a new empire, with slavery for its corner-stone, was and is undoubtedly the true theory. (If successful, this attempt might—I am not sure, but it might—have destroy'd not only our American republic, in anything like first-class proportions, in itself and its prestige, but for ages at least, the cause of Liberty and Equality everywhere—and would have been the greatest triumph of reaction, and the severest blow to political and every other freedom, possible to conceive. Its worst result would have inured to the southern States themselves.) That our national democratic experiment, principle, and machinery, could triumphantly sustain such a shock, and that the Constitution could weather it, like a ship a storm, and come out of it as sound and whole as before, is by far the most signal proof yet of the stability of that experiment, Democracy, and of those principles, and that Constitution.

Of the war itself, we know in the ostent what has been done. The numbers of the dead and wounded can be told or approximated, the debt posted and put on record, the material events narrated, &c. Meantime, elections go on, laws are pass'd, political parties struggle, issue their platforms, &c., just the same as before. But immensest results, not only in politics, but in literature, poems, and sociology, are doubtless waiting yet unform'd in the future. How long they will wait I cannot tell. The pageant of history's retrospect shows us, ages since, all Europe marching on the crusades, those arm'd uprisings of the people, stirr'd by a mere idea, to grandest attempt—and, when once baffled in it, returning at intervals, twice, thrice, and again. An unsurpass'd series of revolutionary events, influences. Yet it took over two hundred years for the seeds of the crusades to germinate, before beginning even to sprout. Two hundred years they lay, sleeping, not dead, but dormant in the ground. Then, out of them, unerringly, arts, travel, navigation, politics, literature, freedom, the spirit of adventure, inquiry, all arose, grew, and steadily sped on to what we see at present. Far back there, that huge agitation-struggle of the crusades stands, as undoubtedly the embryo, the start, of the high preëminence of experiment, civilization and enterprise which the European nations have since sustain'd, and of which these States are the heirs.

Another illustration—(history is full of them, although the war itself, the victory of the Union, and the relations of our equal States, present features of which there are no precedents in the past.) The conquest of England eight centuries ago, by the Franco-Normans—the obliteration of the old, (in many respects so needing obliteration)—the Domesday Book, and the repartition of the land—the old impedimenta removed, even by blood and ruthless violence, and a new, progressive genesis establish'd, new seeds sown—time has proved plain enough that, bitter as they were, all these were the most salutary series of revolutions that could possibly have happen'd. Out of them, and by them mainly, have come, out of Albic, Roman and Saxon England—and without them could not have come—not only the England of the 500 years down to the present, and of the present—but these States. Nor, except for that terrible dislocation and overturn, would these States, as they are, exist to-day.

It is certain to me that the United States, by virtue of that war and its results, and through that and them only, are now ready to enter, and most certainly enter, upon their genuine career in history, as no more torn and divided in their spinal requisites, but a great homogeneous Nation—free states all—a moral and political unity in variety, such as Nature shows in her grandest physical works, and as much greater than any mere work of Nature, as the moral and political, the work of man, his mind, his soul, are, in their loftiest sense, greater than the merely physical. Out of that war not only has the nationality of the States escaped from being strangled, but more than any of the rest, and, in my opinion, more than the north itself, the vital heart and breath of the south have escaped us from the pressure of a general nightmare, and are henceforth to enter on a life, development, and active freedom, whose realities are certain in the future, notwithstanding all the southern vexations of the hour—a development which could not possibly have been achiev'd on any less terms, or by any other means than that grim lesson, or something equivalent to it. And I predict that the south is yet to outstrip the north.

PREFACE, 1855

to first issue OF "Leaves of Grass"

Brooklyn, N. Y.

America does not repel the past, or what the past has produced under its forms, or amid other politics, or the idea of castes, or the old religions—accepts the lessons with calmness —is not impatient because the slough still sticks to opinions and manners and literature, while the life which served its requirements has passed into the new life of the new forms— perceives that the corpse is slowly borne from the eating and sleeping rooms of the house—perceives that it waits a little while in the door—that it was fittest for its days—that its action has descended to the stalwart and well-shaped heir who approaches—and that he shall be fittest for his days.

The Americans of all nations at any time upon the earth, have probably the fullest poetical nature. The United States themselves are essentially the greatest poem. In the history of the earth hitherto, the largest and most stirring appear tame and orderly to their ampler largeness and stir. Here at last is something in the doings of man that corresponds with the broadcast doings of the day and night. Here is action untied from strings, necessarily blind to particulars and details, magnificently moving in masses. Here is the hospitality which for ever indicates heroes. Here the performance, disdaining the trivial, unapproach'd in the tremendous audacity of its crowds and groupings, and the push of its perspective, spreads with crampless and flowing breadth, and showers its prolific and splendid extravagance. One sees it must indeed own the riches of the summer and winter, and need never be bankrupt while corn grows from the ground, or the orchards drop apples, or the bays contain fish, or men beget children upon women.

Other states indicate themselves in their deputies—but the genius of the United States is not best or most in its executives or legislatures, nor in its ambassadors or authors, or colleges or churches or parlors, nor even in its newspapers or inventors—but always most in the common people, south, north, west, east, in all its States, through all its mighty amplitude. The largeness of the nation, however, were monstrous without a corresponding largeness and generosity of the spirit of the citizen. Not swarming states, nor streets and steamships, nor prosperous business, nor farms, nor capital, nor learning, may suffice for the ideal of man—nor suffice the poet. No reminiscences may suffice either. A live nation can always cut a deep mark, and can have the best authority the cheapest—namely, from its own soul. This is the sum of the profitable uses of individuals or states, and of present action and grandeur, and of the subjects of poets. (As if it were necessary to trot back generation after generation to the eastern records! As if the beauty and sacredness of the demonstrable must fall behind that of the mythical! As if men do not make their mark out of any times! As if the opening of the western continent by discovery, and what has transpired in North and South America, were less than the small theatre of the antique, or the aimless sleep-walking of the middle ages!) The pride of the United States leaves the wealth and finesse of the cities, and all returns of commerce and agriculture, and all the magnitude of geography or shows of exterior victory, to enjoy the sight and realization of full-sized men, or one full-sized man unconquerable and simple.

The American poets are to enclose old and new, for

America is the race of races. The expression of the American poet is to be transcendent and new. It is to be indirect, and not direct or descriptive or epic. Its quality goes through these to much more. Let the age and wars of other nations be chanted, and their eras and characters be illustrated, and that finish the verse. Not so the great psalm of the republic. Here the theme is creative, and has vista. Whatever stagnates in the fiat of custom or obedience or legislation, the great poet never stagnates. Obedience does not master him, he masters it. High up out of reach he stands, turning a concentrated light—he turns the pivot with his finger—he baffles the swiftest runners as he stands, and easily overtakes and envelopes them. The time straying toward infidelity and confections and persiflage he withholds by steady faith. Faith is the antiseptic of the soul—it pervades the common people and preserves them—they never give up believing and expecting and trusting. There is that indescribable freshness and unconsciousness about an illiterate person, that humbles and mocks the power of the noblest expressive genius. The poet sees for a certainty how one not a great artist may be just as sacred and perfect as the greatest artist.

The power to destroy or remould is freely used by the greatest poet, but seldom the power of attack. What is past is past. If he does not expose superior models, and prove himself by every step he takes, he is not what is wanted. The presence of the great poet conquers—not parleying, or struggling, or any prepared attempts. Now he has passed that way, see after him! There is not left any vestige of despair, or misanthropy, or cunning, or exclusiveness, or the ignominy of a nativity or color, or delusion of hell or the necessity of hell—and no man thenceforward shall be degraded for ignorance or weakness or sin. The greatest poet hardly knows pettiness or triviality. If he breathes into anything that was before thought small, it dilates with the grandeur and life of the universe. He is a seer—he is individual—he is complete in himself—the others are as good as he, only he sees it, and they do not. He is not one of the chorus—he does not stop for any regulation—he is the president of regulation. What the eyesight does to the rest, he does to the rest. Who knows the curious mystery of the eyesight? The other senses corroborate themselves, but this is removed from any proof but its own, and foreruns the identities of the spiritual world. A single glance of it mocks all the investigations of man, and all the instruments and books of the earth, and all reasoning. What is marvellous? what is unlikely? what is impossible or baseless or vague—after you have once just open'd the space of a peach-pit, and given audience to far and near, and to the sunset, and had all things enter with electric swiftness, softly and duly, without confusion or jostling or jam?

The land and sea, the animals, fishes and birds, the sky of heaven and the orbs, the forests, mountains and rivers, are not small themes—but folks expect of the poet to indicate more than the beauty and dignity which always attach to dumb real objects—they expect him to indicate the path between reality and their souls. Men and women perceive the beauty well enough—probably as well as he. The passionate tenacity of hunters, woodmen, early risers, cultivators of gardens and orchards and fields, the love of healthy women for the manly form, seafaring persons, drivers of horses, the passion for light and the open air, all is an old varied sign of the unfailing perception of beauty, and of a residence of the poetic in out-door people. They can never be assisted by poets to perceive—some may, but they never can. The poetic quality is not marshal'd in rhyme or uniformity, or abstract addresses to things, nor in melancholy complaints or good precepts, but is the life of these and much else, and is in the soul. The profit of rhyme is that it drops seeds of a sweeter and more luxuriant rhyme, and of uniformity that it conveys itself into its own roots in the ground out of sight. The rhyme and uniformity of perfect poems show the free growth of metrical laws, and bud from them as unerringly and loosely as lilacs and roses on a bush, and take shapes as compact as the shapes of chestnuts and oranges, and melons and pears, and shed the perfume impalpable to form. The fluency and ornaments of the finest poems or music or orations or recitations, are not independent but dependent. All beauty comes from beautiful blood and a beautiful brain. If the greatnesses are in conjunction in a man or woman, it is enough —the fact will prevail through the universe; but the gaggery and gilt of a million years will not prevail. Who troubles himself about his ornaments or fluency is lost. This is what you shall do: Love the earth and sun and the animals, despise riches, give alms to every one that asks, stand up for the stupid and crazy, devote your income and labor to others, hate tyrants, argue not concerning God, have patience and indulgence toward the people, take off your hat to nothing known or unknown, or to any man or number of men—go freely with powerful uneducated persons, and with the young, and with the mothers of families—re-examine all you have been told in school or church or in any book, and dismiss whatever insults your own soul; and your very flesh shall be a great poem, and have the richest fluency, not only in its words, but in the silent lines of its lips and face, and between the lashes of your eyes, and in every motion and joint of your body. The poet shall not spend his time in unneeded work. He shall know that the ground is already plough'd and manured; others may not know it, but he shall. He shall go directly to the creation. His trust shall master the trust of everything he touches—and shall master all attachment.

The known universe has one complete lover, and that is the greatest poet. He consumes an eternal passion, and is indifferent which chance happens, and which possible contingency of fortune or misfortune, and persuades daily and hourly his delicious pay. What baulks or breaks others is fuel for his burning progress to contact and amorous joy. Other proportions of the reception of pleasure dwindle to nothing to his proportions. All expected from heaven or from the highest, he is rapport with in the sight of the daybreak, or the scenes of the winter woods, or the presence of children playing, or with his arm around the neck of a man or woman. His love above all love has leisure and expanse—he leaves room ahead of himself. He is no irresolute or suspicious lover—he is sure—he scorns intervals. His experience and the showers and thrills are not for nothing. Nothing can jar him —suffering and darkness cannot—death and fear cannot. To him complaint and jealousy and envy are corpses buried and rotten in the earth—he saw them buried. The sea is not surer of the shore, or the shore of the sea, than he is the fruition of his love, and of all perfection and beauty.

The fruition of beauty is no chance of miss or hit—it is as inevitable as life—it is exact and plumb as gravitation. From the eyesight proceeds another eyesight, and from the hearing proceeds another hearing, and from the voice proceeds another voice, eternally curious of the harmony of things with man. These understand the law of perfection in masses and floods —that it is profuse and impartial—that there is not a minute of the light or dark, nor an acre of the earth and sea, without it—nor any direction of the sky, nor any trade or employment, nor any turn of events. This is the reason that about the proper expression of beauty there is precision and balance. One part does not need to be thrust above another. The best singer is not the one who has the most lithe and powerful organ. The pleasure of poems is not in them that take the handsomest measure and sound.

Without effort, and without exposing in the least how it is done, the greatest poet brings the spirit of any or all events and passions and scenes and persons, some more and some less, to bear on your individual character as you hear or read. To do this well is to compete with the laws that pursue and follow Time. What is the purpose must surely be there, and the clue of it must be there—and the faintest indication is the indication of the best, and then becomes the clearest indication. Past and present and future are not disjoin'd but join'd. The greatest poet forms the consistence of what is to be, from what has been and is. He drags the dead out of their coffins and stands them again on their feet. He says to the past, Rise and walk before me that I may realize you. He learns the lesson—he places himself where the future becomes present. The greatest poet does not only dazzle his rays over character and scenes and passions—he finally ascends, and finishes all—he exhibits the pinnacles that no man can tell what they are for, or what is beyond—he glows a moment on the extremest verge. He is most wonderful in his last half-hidden smile or frown; by that flash of the moment of parting the one that sees it shall be encouraged or terrified afterward for many years. The greatest poet does not moralize or make applications of morals—he knows the soul. The soul has that measureless pride which consists in never acknowledging any lessons or deductions but its own. But it has sympathy as measureless as its pride, and the one balances the other, and neither can stretch too far while it stretches in company with the other. The inmost secrets of art sleep with the twain. The greatest poet has lain close betwixt both, and they are vital in his style and thoughts.

The art of art, the glory of expression and the sunshine of the light of letters, is simplicity. Nothing is better than simplicity—nothing can make up for excess, or for the lack of definiteness. To carry on the heave of impulse and pierce intellectual depths and give all subjects their articulations, are powers neither common nor very uncommon. But to speak in literature with the perfect rectitude and insouciance of the movements of animals, and the unimpeachableness of the sentiment of trees in the woods and grass by the roadside, is the flawless triumph of art. If you have look'd on him who has achiev'd it you have look'd on one of the masters of the artists of all nations and times. You shall not contemplate the flight of the gray gull over the bay, or the mettlesome action of the blood horse, or the tall leaning of sunflowers on their stalk, or the appearance of the sun journeying through heaven, or the appearance of the moon afterward, with any more satisfaction than you shall contemplate him. The great poet has less a mark'd style, and is more the channel of thoughts and things without increase or diminution, and is the free channel of himself. He swears to his art, I will not be meddlesome, I will not have in my writing any elegance, or effect, or originality, to hang in the way between me and the rest like curtains. I will have nothing hang in the way, not the richest curtains. What I tell I tell for precisely what it is. Let who may exalt or startle or fascinate or soothe, I will have purposes as health or heat or snow has, and be as regardless of observation. What I experience or portray shall go from my composition without a shred of my composition. You shall stand by my side and look in the mirror with me.

The old red blood and stainless gentility of great poets will be proved by their unconstraint. A heroic person walks at his ease through and out of that custom or precedent or authority that suits him not. Of the traits of the brotherhood of first-class writers, savants, musicians, inventors and artists, nothing is finer than silent defiance advancing from new free forms. In the need of poems, philosophy, politics, mechanism, science, behavior, the craft of art, an appropriate native grand opera, shipcraft, or any craft, he is greatest for ever and ever who contributes the greatest original practical example. The cleanest expression is that which finds no sphere worthy of itself, and makes one.

The messages of great poems to each man and woman are, Come to us on equal terms, only then can you understand us. We are no better than you, what we inclose you inclose, what we enjoy you may enjoy. Did you suppose there could be only one Supreme? We affirm there can be unnumber'd Supremes, and that one does not countervail another any more than one eyesight countervails another—and that men can be good or grand only of the consciousness of their supremacy within them. What do you think is the grandeur of storms and dismemberments, and the deadliest battles and wrecks, and the wildest fury of the elements, and the power of the sea, and the motion of nature, and the throes of human desires, and dignity and hate and love? It is that something in the soul which says, Rage on, whirl on, I tread master here and everywhere—Master of the spasms of the sky and of the shatter of the sea, Master of nature and passion and death, and of all terror and all pain.

The American bards shall be mark'd for generosity and affection, and for encouraging competitors. They shall be Kosmos, without monopoly or secrecy, glad to pass anything to any one—hungry for equals night and day. They shall not be careful of riches and privilege—they shall be riches and privilege—they shall perceive who the most affluent man is. The most affluent man is he that confronts all the shows he sees by equivalents out of the stronger wealth of himself. The American bard shall delineate no class of persons, nor one or two out of the strata of interests, nor love most nor truth most, nor the soul most, nor the body most—and not be for the Eastern states more than the Western, or the Northern states more than the Southern.

Exact science and its practical movements are no checks on the greatest poet, but always his encouragement and support. The outset and remembrance are there—there the arms that lifted him first, and braced him best—there he returns after all his goings and comings. The sailor and traveler—the anatomist, chemist, astronomer, geologist, phrenologist, spiritualist, mathematician, historian, and lexicographer, are not poets, but they are the lawgivers of poets, and their construction underlies the structure of every perfect poem. No matter what rises or is utter'd, they sent the seed of the conception of it—of them and by them stand the visible proofs of souls. If there shall be love and content between the father and the son, and if the greatness of the son is the exuding of the greatness of the father, there shall be love between the poet and the man of demonstrable science. In the beauty of poems are henceforth the tuft and final applause of science.

Great is the faith of the flush of knowledge, and of the investigation of the depths of qualities and things. Cleaving and circling here swells the soul of the poet, yet is president of itself always. The depths are fathomless, and therefore calm. The innocence and nakedness are resumed—they are neither modest nor immodest. The whole theory of the supernatural, and all that was twined with it or educed out of it, departs as a dream. What has ever happen'd—what happens, and whatever may or shall happen, the vital laws inclose all. They are sufficient for any case and for all cases—none to be hurried or retarded—any special miracle of affairs or persons inadmissible in the vast clear scheme where every motion and every spear of grass, and the frames and spirits of men and women and all that concerns them, are unspeakably perfect miracles, all referring to all, and each distinct and in its place. It is also not consistent with the reality of the soul to admit that there is anything in the known universe more divine than men and women.

Men and women, and the earth and all upon it, are to be taken as they are, and the investigation of their past and present and future shall be unintermitted, and shall be done with perfect candor. Upon this basis philosophy speculates, ever looking toward the poet, even regarding the eternal tendencies of all toward happiness, never inconsistent with what is clear to the senses and to the soul. For the eternal tendencies of all toward happiness make the only point of sane philosophy. Whatever comprehends less than that—whatever is less than the laws of light and of astronomical motion—or less than the laws that follow the thief, the liar, the glutton and the drunkard, through this life and doubtless afterward—or less than vast stretches of time, or the slow formation of density, or the patient upheaving of strata—is of no account. Whatever would put God in a poem or system of philosophy as contending against some being or influence, is also of no account. Sanity and ensemble characterize the great master—spoilt in one principle, all is spoilt. The great master has nothing to do with miracles. He sees health for himself in being one of the mass—he sees the hiatus in singular eminence. To the perfect shape comes common ground. To be under the general law is great, for that is to correspond with it. The master knows that he is unspeakably great, and that all are unspeakably great—that nothing, for instance, is greater than to conceive children, and bring them up well—that to *be* is just as great as to perceive or tell.

In the make of the great masters the idea of political liberty is indispensable. Liberty takes the adherence of heroes wherever man and woman exist—but never takes any adherence or welcome from the rest more than from poets. They are the voice and exposition of liberty. They out of ages are worthy the grand idea—to them it is confided, and they must sustain it. Nothing has precedence of it, and nothing can warp or degrade it.

As the attributes of the poets of the kosmos concentre in the real body, and in the pleasure of things, they possess the superiority of genuineness over all fiction and romance. As they emit themselves, facts are shower'd over with light—the daylight is lit with more volatile light—the deep between the setting and rising sun goes deeper many fold. Each precise object or condition or combination or process exhibits a beauty—the multiplication table its—old age its—the carpenter's trade its—the grand opera its—the huge-hull'd clean-shap'd New York clipper at sea under steam or full sail gleams with unmatch'd beauty—the American circles and large harmonies of government gleam with theirs—and the commonest definite intentions and actions with theirs. The poets of the kosmos advance through all interpositions and coverings and turmoils and stratagems to first principles. They are of use—they dissolve poverty from its need, and riches from its conceit. You large proprietor, they say, shall not realize or perceive more than any one else. The owner of the library is not he who holds a legal title to it, having bought and paid for it. Any one and every one is owner of the library, (indeed he or she alone is owner,) who can read the same through all the varieties of tongues and subjects and styles, and in whom they enter with ease, and make supple and powerful and rich and large.

These American States, strong and healthy and accomplish'd, shall receive no pleasure from violations of natural models, and must not permit them. In paintings or mouldings or carvings in mineral or wood, or in the illustrations of books or newspapers, or in the patterns of woven stuffs, or anything to beautify rooms or furniture or costumes, or to put upon cornices or monuments, or on the prows or sterns of ships, or to put anywhere before the human eye indoors or out, that which distorts honest shapes, or which creates unearthly beings or places or contingencies, is a nuisance and revolt. Of the human form especially, it is so great it must never be made ridiculous. Of ornaments to a work nothing outre can be allow'd—but those ornaments can be allow'd that conform to the perfect facts of the open air, and that flow out of the nature of the work, and come irrepressibly from it, and are necessary to the completion of the work. Most works are most beautiful without ornament. Exaggerations will be revenged in human physiology. Clean and vigorous children are jetted and conceiv'd only in those communities where the models of natural forms are public every day. Great genius and the people of these States must never be demean'd to romances. As soon as histories are properly told, no more need of romances.

The great poets are to be known by the absence in them of tricks, and by the justification of perfect personal candor. All faults may be forgiven of him who has perfect candor. Henceforth let no man of us lie, for we have seen that openness wins the inner and outer world, and that there is no single exception, and that never since our earth gather'd itself in a mass have deceit or subterfuge or prevarication attracted its smallest particle or the faintest tinge of a shade— and that through the enveloping wealth and rank of a state, or the whole republic of states, a sneak or sly person shall be discover'd and despised—and that the soul has never once been fool'd and never can be fool'd—and thrift without the loving nod of the soul is only a fœtid puff—and there never grew up in any of the continents of the globe, nor upon any planet or satellite, nor in that condition which precedes the birth of babes, nor at any time during the changes of life, nor in any stretch of abeyance or action of vitality, nor in any process of formation or reformation anywhere, a being whose instinct hated the truth.

Extreme caution or prudence, the soundest organic health, large hope and comparison and fondness for women and children, large alimentiveness and destructiveness and causality, with a perfect sense of the oneness of nature, and the propriety of the same spirit applied to human affairs, are called up of the float of the brain of the world to be parts of the greatest poet from his birth out of his mother's womb, and from her birth out of her mother's. Caution seldom goes far enough. It has been thought that the prudent citizen was the citizen who applied himself to solid gains, and did well for himself and for his family, and completed a lawful life without debt or crime. The greatest poet sees and admits these economies as he sees the economies of food and sleep, but has higher notions of prudence than to think he gives much when he gives a few slight attentions at the latch of the gate. The premises of the prudence of life are not the hospitality of it, or the ripeness and harvest of it. Beyond the independence of a little sum laid aside for burial-money, and of a few clapboards around and shingles overhead on a lot of American soil own'd, and the easy dollars that supply the year's plain clothing and meals, the melancholy prudence of the abandonment of such a great being as a man is, to the toss and pallor of years of money-making, with all their scorching days and icy night, and all their stifling deceits and underhand dodgings, or infinitesimals of parlors, or shameless stuffing while others starve, and all the loss of the bloom and odor of the earth, and of the flowers and atmosphere, and of the sea, and of the true taste of the women and men you pass or have to do with in youth or middle age, and the issuing sickness and desperate revolt at the close of a life without elevation or naïveté, (even if you have achiev'd a secure 10,000 a year, or election to Congress or the Governorship,) and the ghastly chatter of a death without serenity or majesty, is the great fraud upon modern civilization and forethought, blotching the surface and system which civilization undeniably drafts, and moistening with tears the immense features it spreads and spreads with such velocity before the reach'd kisses of the soul.

Ever the right explanation remains to be made about prudence. The prudence of the mere wealth and respectability of the most esteem'd life appears too faint for the eye to observe at all, when little and large alike drop quietly aside at the thought of the prudence suitable for immortality. What is the wisdom that fills the thinness of a year, or seventy or eighty years—to the wisdom spaced out by ages, and coming back at a certain time with strong reinforcements and rich presents, and the clear faces of wedding-guests as far as you can look, in every direction, running gaily toward you? Only the soul is of itself—all else has reference to what ensues. All that a person does or thinks is of consequence. Nor can the push of charity or personal force ever be anything else than the profoundest reason, whether it brings argument to hand or no. No specification is necessary—to add or subtract or divide is in vain. Little or big, learn'd or unlearn'd, white or black, legal or illegal, sick or well, from the first inspiration down the windpipe to the last expiration out of it, all that a male or female does that is vigorous and benevolent and clean is so much sure profit to him or her in the unshakable order of the universe, and through the whole scope of it forever. The prudence of the greatest poet answers at last the craving and glut of the soul, puts off nothing, permits no let-up for its own case or any case, has no particular sabbath or judgment day, divides not the living from the dead, or the righteous from the unrighteous, is satisfied with the present, matches every thought or act by its correlative, and knows no possible forgiveness or deputed atonement.

The direct trial of him who would be the greatest poet is to-day. If he does not flood himself with the immediate age as with vast oceanic tides—if he be not himself the age transfigur'd, and if to him is not open'd the eternity which gives similitude to all periods and locations and processes, and animate and inanimate forms, and which is the bond of time, and rises up from its inconceivable vagueness and infiniteness in the swimming shapes of to-day, and is held by the ductile anchors of life, and makes the present spot the passage from what was to what shall be, and commits itself to the representation of this wave of an hour, and this one of the sixty beautiful children of the wave—let him merge in the general run, and wait his development.

Still the final test of poems, or any character or work, remains. The prescient poet projects himself centuries ahead, and judges performer or performance after the changes of time. Does it live through them? Does it still hold on untried? Will the same style, and the direction of genius to similar points, be satisfactory now? Have the marches of tens and hundreds and thousands of years made willing detours to the right hand and the left hand for his sake? Is he beloved long and long after he is buried? Does the young man think often of him? and the young woman think often of him? and do the middle-aged and the old think of him?

A great poem is for ages and ages in common, and for all degrees and complexions, and all departments and sects, and for a woman as much as a man, and a man as much as a woman. A great poem is no finish to a man or woman, but rather a beginning. Has any one fancied he could sit at last under some due authority, and rest satisfied with explanations, and realize, and be content and full? To no such terminus does the greatest poet bring—he brings neither cessation nor shelter'd fatness and ease. The touch of him, like Nature, tells in action. Whom he takes he takes with firm sure grasp into live regions previously unattain'd—thenceforward is no rest—they see the space and ineffable sheen that turn the old spots and lights into dead vacuums. Now there shall be a man cohered out of tumult and chaos—the elder encourages the younger and shows him how—they two shall launch off fearlessly together till the new world fits an orbit for itself, and looks unabash'd on the lesser orbits of the stars, and sweeps through the ceaseless rings, and shall never be quiet again.

There will soon be no more priests. Their work is done. A new order shall arise, and they shall be the priests of man, and every man shall be his own priest. They shall find their inspiration in real objects to-day, symptoms of the past and future. They shall not deign to defend immortality or God, or the perfection of things, or liberty, or the exquisite beauty and reality of the soul. They shall arise in America, and be responded to from the remainder of the earth.

The English language befriends the grand American expression—it is brawny enough, and limber and full enough. On the tough stock of a race who through all change of circumstance was never without the idea of political liberty, which is the animus of all liberty, it has attracted the terms of daintier and gayer and subtler and more elegant tongues. It is the powerful language of resistance—it is the dialect of common sense. It is the speech of the proud and melancholy races, and of all who aspire. It is the chosen tongue to express growth, faith, self-esteem, freedom, justice, equality, friendliness, amplitude, prudence, decision, and courage. It is the medium that shall wellnigh express the inexpressible.

No great literature, nor any like style of behavior or oratory, or social intercourse or household arrangements, or public institutions, or the treatment by bosses of employ'd people, nor executive detail, or detail of the army and navy, nor spirit of legislation or courts, or police or tuition or architecture, or songs or amusements, can long elude the jealous and passionate instinct of American standards. Whether or no the sign appears from the mouths of the people, it throbs a live interrogation in every freeman's and freewoman's heart, after that which passes by, or this built to remain. Is it uniform with my country? Are its disposals without ignominious distinctions? Is it for the ever-growing communes of brothers and lovers, large, well united, proud, beyond the old models, generous beyond all models? Is it something grown fresh out of the fields, or drawn from the sea for use to me to-day here? I know that what answers for me, an American, in Texas, Ohio, Canada, must answer for any individual or nation that serves for a part of my materials. Does this answer? Is it for the nursing of the young of the republic? Does it solve readily with the sweet milk of the nipples of the breasts of the Mother of Many Children?

America prepares with composure and good-will for the visitors that have sent word. It is not intellect that is to be their warrant and welcome. The talented, the artist, the ingenious, the editor, the statesman, the erudite, are not unappreciated—they fall in their place and do their work. The soul of the nation also does its work. It rejects none, it permits all. Only toward the like of itself will it advance half way. An individual is as superb as a nation when he has the qualities which make a superb nation. The soul of the largest and wealthiest and proudest nation may well go half-way to meet that of its poets.

DEATH of ABRAHAM LINCOLN

Lecture *deliver'd in New York, April 14, 1879—in Philadelphia, '80—in Boston, '81*

How often since that dark and dripping Saturday—that chilly April day, now fifteen years bygone—my heart has entertain'd the dream, the wish, to give of Abraham Lincoln's death, its own special thought and memorial. Yet now the sought-for opportunity offers, I find my notes incompetent, (why, for truly profound themes, is statement so idle? why does the right phrase never offer?) and the fit tribute I dream'd of, waits unprepared as ever. My talk here indeed is less because of itself or anything in it, and nearly altogether because I feel a desire, apart from any talk, to specify the day, the martyrdom. It is for this, my friends, I have call'd you together. Oft as the rolling years bring back this hour, let it again, however briefly, be dwelt upon. For my own part, I hope and desire, till my own dying day, whenever the 14th or 15th of April comes, to annually gather a few friends, and hold its tragic reminiscence. No narrow or sectional reminiscence. It belongs to these States in their entirety—not the North only, but the South—perhaps belongs most tenderly and devoutly to the South, of all; for there, really, this man's birth-stock. There and thence his antecedent stamp. Why should I not say that thence his manliest traits—his universality—his canny, easy ways and words upon the surface—his inflexible determination and courage at heart? Have you never realized it, my friends, that Lincoln, though grafted on the West, is essentially, in personnel and character, a Southern contribution?

And though by no means proposing to resume the Secession war to-night, I would briefly remind you of the public conditions preceding that contest. For twenty years, and especially during the four or five before the war actually began, the aspect of affairs in the United States, though without the flash of military excitement, presents more than the survey of a battle, or any extended campaign, or series, even of Nature's convulsions. The hot passions of the South—the strange mixture at the North of inertia, incredulity, and conscious power—the incendiarism of the abolitionists—the rascality and *grip* of the politicians, unparallel'd in any land, any age. To these I must not omit adding the honesty of the essential bulk of the people everywhere—yet with all the seething fury and contradiction of their natures more arous'd than the Atlantic's waves in wildest equinox. In politics, what can be more ominous, (though generally unappreciated then)—what more significant than the Presidentiads of Fillmore and Buchanan? proving conclusively that the weakness and wickedness of elected rulers are just as likely to afflict us here, as in the countries of the Old World, under their monarchies, emperors, and aristocracies. In that Old World were everywhere heard underground rumblings, that died out, only to again surely return. While in America the volcano, though civic yet, continued to grow more and more convulsive—more and more stormy and threatening.

In the height of all this excitement and chaos, hovering on the edge at first, and then merged in its very midst, and destined to play a leading part, appears a strange and awkward figure. I shall not easily forget the first time I ever saw Abraham Lincoln. It must have been about the 18th or 19th of February, 1861. It was rather a pleasant afternoon, in New York city, as he arrived there from the West, to remain a few hours, and then pass on to Washington, to prepare for his inauguration. I saw him in Broadway, near the site of the present Post-office. He came down, I think from Canal street, to stop at the Astor House. The broad spaces, sidewalks, and streets in the neighborhood, and for some distance, were crowded with solid masses of people, many thousands. The omnibuses and other vehicles had all been turn'd off, leaving an unusual hush in that busy part of the city. Presently two or three shabby hack barouches made their way with some difficulty through the crowd, and drew up at the Astor House entrance. A tall figure step'd out of the centre of these barouches, paus'd leisurely on the sidewalk, look'd up at the granite walls and looming architecture of the grand old hotel —then, after a relieving stretch of arms and legs, turn'd round for over a minute to slowly and good-humoredly scan the appearance of the vast and silent crowds. There were no speeches—no compliments—no welcome—as far as I could hear, not a word said. Still much anxiety was conceal'd in that quiet. Cautious persons had fear'd some mark'd insult or indignity to the President-elect—for he possess'd no personal popularity at all in New York city, and very little political. But it was evidently tacitly agreed that if the few political supporters of Mr. Lincoln present would entirely abstain from any demonstration on their side, the immense majority, who were any thing but supporters, would abstain on their side also. The result was a sulky, unbroken silence, such as certainly never before characterized so great a New York crowd.

Almost in the same neighborhood I distinctly remember'd seeing Lafayette on his visit to America in 1825. I had also personally seen and heard, various years afterward, how Andrew Jackson, Clay, Webster, Hungarian Kossuth, Filibuster Walker, the Prince of Wales on his visit, and other celebres, native and foreign, had been welcom'd there—all that indescribable human roar and magnetism, unlike any other sound in the universe—the glad exulting thunder-shouts of countless unloos'd throats of men! But on this occasion, not a voice— not a sound. From the top of an omnibus, (driven up one side, close by, and block'd by the curbstone and the crowds,) I had, I say, a capital view of it all, and especially of Mr. Lincoln, his look and gait—his perfect composure and coolness— his unusual and uncouth height, his dress of complete black, stovepipe hat push'd back on the head, dark-brown complexion, seam'd and wrinkled yet canny-looking face, black, bushy head of hair, disproportionately long neck, and his hands held behind as he stood observing the people. He look'd with curiosity upon that immense sea of faces, and the sea of faces return'd the look with similar curiosity. In both there was a dash of comedy, almost farce, such as Shakspere puts in his blackest tragedies. The crowd that hemm'd around consisted I should think of thirty to forty thousand men, not a single one his personal friend—while I have no doubt, (so frenzied were the ferments of the time,) many an assassin's knife and pistol lurk'd in hip or breast-pocket there, ready, soon as break and riot came.

But no break or riot came. The tall figure gave another relieving stretch or two of arms and legs; then with moderate pace, and accompanied by a few unknown looking persons, ascended the portico-steps of the Astor House, disappear'd through its broad entrance—and the dumb-show ended.

I saw Abraham Lincoln often the four years following that date. He changed rapidly and much during his Presidency—but this scene, and him in it, are indelibly stamped upon my recollection. As I sat on the top of my omnibus, and had a good view of him, the thought, dim and inchoate then, has since come out clear enough, that four sorts of genius, four mighty and primal hands, will be needed to the complete limning of this man's future portrait—the eyes and brains and finger-touch of Plutarch and Eschylus and Michel Angelo, assisted by Rabelais.

And now—(Mr. Lincoln passing on from this scene to Washington, where he was inaugurated, amid armed cavalry, and sharpshooters at every point—the first instance of the kind in our history—and I hope it will be the last)—now the rapid succession of well-known events, (too well known—I believe, these days, we almost hate to hear them mention'd)—the national flag fired on at Sumter—the uprising of the North, in paroxysms of astonishment and rage—the chaos of divided councils—the call for troops—the first Bull Run—the stunning cast-down, shock, and dismay of the North—and so in full flood the Secession war. Four years of lurid, bleeding, murky, murderous war. Who paint those years, with all their scenes?—the hard-fought engagements—the defeats, plans, failures—the gloomy hours, days, when our Nationality seem'd hung in pall of doubt, perhaps death—the Mephistophelean sneers of foreign lands and attachés—the dreaded Scylla of European interference, and the Charybdis of the tremendously dangerous latent strata of secession sympathizers throughout the free States, (far more numerous than is supposed)—the long marches in summer—the hot sweat, and many a sunstroke, as on the rush to Gettysburg in '63—the night battles in the woods, as under Hooker at Chancellorsville—the camps in winter—the military prisons—the hospitals—(alas! alas! the hospitals.)

The Secession war? Nay, let me call it the Union war. Though whatever call'd, it is even yet too near us—too vast and too closely overshadowing—its branches unform'd yet, (but certain,) shooting too far into the future—and the most indicative and mightiest of them yet ungrown. A great literature will yet arise out of the era of those four years, those scenes—era compressing centuries of native passion, first-class pictures, tempests of life and death—an inexhaustible mine for the histories, drama, romance, and even philosophy, of peoples to come—indeed the verteber of poetry and art, (of personal character too,) for all future America—far more grand, in my opinion, to the hands capable of it, than Homer's siege of Troy, or the French wars to Shakspere.

But I must leave these speculations, and come to the theme I have assign'd and limited myself to. Of the actual murder of President Lincoln, though so much has been written, probably the facts are yet very indefinite in most persons' minds. I read from my memoranda, written at the time, and revised frequently and finally since.

The day, April 14, 1865, seems to have been a pleasant one throughout the whole land—the moral atmosphere pleasant too—the long storm, so dark, so fratricidal, full of blood and doubt and gloom, over and ended at last by the sun-rise of such an absolute National victory, and utter break-down of Secessionism—we almost doubted our own senses! Lee had capitulated beneath the apple-tree of Appomattox. The other armies, the flanges of the revolt, swiftly follow'd. And could

it really be, then? Out of all the affairs of this world of woe
and failure and disorder, was there really come the confirm'd,
unerring sign of plan, like a shaft of pure light—of rightful
rule—of God? So the day, as I say, was propitious. Early
herbage, early flowers, were out. (I remember where I was
stopping at the time, the season being advanced, there were
many lilacs in full bloom. By one of those caprices that enter
and give tinge to events without being at all a part of them, I
find myself always reminded of the great tragedy of that day
by the sight and odor of these blossoms. It never fails.)

But I must not dwell on accessories. The deed hastens. The
popular afternoon paper of Washington, the little "Evening
Star," had spatter'd all over its third page, divided among the
advertisements in a sensational manner, in a hundred different places, *The President and his Lady will be at the Theatre
this evening.* . . . (Lincoln was fond of the theatre. I have
myself seen him there several times. I remember thinking
how funny it was that he, in some respects the leading actor
in the stormiest drama known to real history's stage through
centuries, should sit there and be so completely interested and
absorb'd in those human jack-straws, moving about with their
silly little gestures, foreign spirit, and flatulent text.)

On this occasion the theatre was crowded, many ladies in
rich and gay costumes, officers in their uniforms, many well-
known citizens, young folks, the usual clusters of gas-lights,
the usual magnetism of so many people, cheerful, with perfumes, music of violins and flutes—(and over all, and saturat-
ing all, that vast, vague wonder, *Victory,* the nation's victory, the triumph of the Union, filling the air, the thought,
the sense, with exhilaration more than all music and perfumes.)

The President came betimes, and, with his wife, witness'd
the play from the large stage-boxes of the second tier, two
thrown into one, and profusely draped with the national flag.
The acts and scenes of the piece—one of those singularly written compositions which have at least the merit of giving entire relief to an audience engaged in mental action or busi-

ness excitements and cares during the day, as it makes not the slightest call on either the moral, emotional, esthetic, or spiritual nature—a piece, ("Our American Cousin,") in which, among other characters, so call'd, a Yankee, certainly such a one as was never seen, or the least like it ever seen, in North America, is introduced in England, with a varied fol-de-rol of talk, plot, scenery, and such phantasmagoria as goes to make up a modern popular drama—had progress'd through perhaps a couple of its acts, when in the midst of this comedy, or non-such, or whatever it is to be call'd, and to offset it, or finish it out, as if in Nature's and the great Muse's mockery of those poor mimes, came interpolated that scene, not really or exact-ly to be described at all, (for on the many hundreds who were there it seems to this hour to have left a passing blur, a dream, a blotch)—and yet partially to be described as I now proceed to give it. There is a scene in the play representing a modern parlor, in which two unprecedented English ladies are inform'd by the impossible Yankee that he is not a man of fortune, and therefore undesirable for marriage-catching pur-poses; after which, the comments being finish'd, the dramatic trio make exit, leaving the stage clear for a moment. At this period came the murder of Abraham Lincoln. Great as all its manifold train, circling round it, and stretching into the fu-ture for many a century, in the politics, history, art, &c., of the New World, in point of fact the main thing, the actual murder, transpired with the quiet and simplicity of any com-monest occurrence—the bursting of a bud or pod in the growth of vegetation, for instance. Through the general hum following the stage pause, with the change of positions, came the muffled sound of a pistol-shot, which not one-hundredth part of the audience heard at the time—and yet a moment's hush—somehow, surely, a vague startled thrill—and then, through the ornamented, draperied, starr'd and striped space-way of the President's box, a sudden figure, a man, raises himself with hands and feet, stands a moment on the railing, leaps below to the stage, (a distance of perhaps fourteen or fifteen feet,) falls out of position, catching his boot-heel in the copious drapery, (the American flag,) falls on one knee, quickly recovers himself, rises as if nothing had happen'd, (he really sprains his ankle, but unfelt then)—and so the figure, Booth, the murderer, dress'd in plain black broadcloth, bare-headed, with full, glossy, raven hair, and his eyes like some mad animal's flashing with light and resolution, yet with a certain strange calmness, holds aloft in one hand a large knife—walks along not much back from the footlights—turns fully toward the audience his face of statuesque beauty, lit by those basilisk eyes, flashing with desperation, perhaps insanity—launches out in a firm and steady voice the words *Sic semper tyrannis*—and then walks with neither slow nor very rapid pace diagonally across to the back of the stage, and disappears. (Had not all this terrible scene—making the mimic ones preposterous—had it not all been rehears'd, in blank, by Booth, beforehand?)

A moment's hush—a scream—the cry of *murder*—Mrs. Lincoln leaning out of the box, with ashy cheeks and lips, with involuntary cry, pointing to the retreating figure, *He has kill'd the President*. And still a moment's strange, incredulous suspense—and then the deluge!—then that mixture of horror, noises, uncertainty—(the sound, somewhere back, of a horse's hoofs clattering with speed)—the people burst through chairs and railings, and break them up—there is inextricable confusion and terror—women faint—quite feeble persons fall, and are trampled on—many cries of agony are heard—the broad stage suddenly fills to suffocation with a dense and motley crowd, like some horrible carnival—the audience rush generally upon it, at least the strong men do—the actors and actresses are all there in their play-costumes and painted faces, with mortal fright showing through the rouge—the screams and calls, confused talk—redoubled, trebled—two or three manage to pass up water from the stage to the President's box—others try to clamber up—&c., &c.

In the midst of all this, the soldiers of the President's guard, with others, suddenly drawn to the scene, burst in— (some two hundred altogether)—they storm the house, through all the tiers, especially the upper ones, inflamed with fury, literally charging the audience with fix'd bayonets, muskets and pistols, shouting *Clear out! clear out! you sons of——* . . . . Such the wild scene, or a suggestion of it rather, inside the play-house that night.

Outside, too, in the atmosphere of shock and craze, crowds of people, fill'd with frenzy, ready to seize any outlet for it, come near committing murder several times on innocent individuals. One such case was especially exciting. The infuriated crowd, through some chance, got started against one man, either for words he utter'd, or perhaps without any cause at all, and were proceeding at once to actually hang him on a neighboring lamp-post, when he was rescued by a few heroic policemen, who placed him in their midst, and fought their way slowly and amid great peril toward the station house. It was a fitting episode of the whole affair. The crowd rushing and eddying to and fro—the night, the yells, the pale faces, many frighten'd people trying in vain to extricate themselves—the attack'd man, not yet freed from the jaws of death, looking like a corpse—the silent, resolute, half-dozen policemen, with no weapons but their little clubs, yet stern and steady through all those eddying swarms—made a fitting side-scene to the grand tragedy of the murder. They gain'd the station house with the protected man, whom they placed in security for the night, and discharged him in the morning.

And in the midst of that pandemonium, infuriated soldiers, the audience and the crowd, the stage, and all its actors and actresses, its paint-pots, spangles, and gas-lights—the life blood from those veins, the best and sweetest of the land, drips slowly down, and death's ooze already begins its little bubbles on the lips.

Thus the visible incidents and surroundings of Abraham Lincoln's murder, as they really occur'd. Thus ended the attempted secession of these States; thus the four years' war. But the main things come subtly and invisibly afterward, perhaps long afterward—neither military, political, nor (great as those are,) historical. I say, certain secondary and indirect results, out of the tragedy of this death, are, in my opinion, greatest. Not the event of the murder itself. Not that Mr. Lincoln strings the principal points and personages of the period, like beads, upon the single string of his career. Not that his idiosyncrasy, in its sudden appearance and disappearance, stamps this Republic with a stamp more mark'd and enduring than any yet given by any one man—(more even than Washington's;)—but, join'd with these, the immeasurable value and meaning of that whole tragedy lies, to me, in senses finally dearest to a nation, (and here all our own)—the imaginative and artistic senses—the literary and dramatic ones. Not in any common or low meaning of those terms, but a meaning precious to the race, and to every age. A long and varied series of contradictory events arrives at last at its highest poetic, single, central, pictorial denouement. The whole involved, baffling, multiform whirl of the secession period comes to a head, and is gather'd in one brief flash of lightning-illumination—one simple, fierce deed. Its sharp culmination, and as it were solution, of so many bloody and angry problems, illustrates those climax-moments on the stage of universal Time, where the historic Muse at one entrance, and the tragic Muse at the other, suddenly ringing down the curtain, close an immense act in the long drama of creative thought, and give it radiation, tableau, stranger than fiction. Fit radiation—fit close! How the imagination—how the student loves these things! America, too, is to have them. For not in all great deaths, nor far or near—not Cæsar in the Roman senate-house, or Napoleon passing away in the wild night-storm at St. Helena—not Paleologus, falling, desperately fighting, piled over dozens deep with Grecian corpses—not calm old Socrates, drinking the hemlock—outvies that terminus of the secession war, in one man's life, here in our midst, in our own time—that seal of the emancipation of three million slaves—that parturition and delivery of our at last really free Republic, born again, henceforth to commence its career of genuine homogeneous Union, compact, consistent with itself.

Nor will ever future American Patriots and Unionists, indifferently over the whole land, or North or South, find a better moral to their lesson. The final use of the greatest men of a Nation is, after all, not with reference to their deeds in themselves, or their direct bearing on their times or lands. The final use of a heroic-eminent life—especially of a heroic-eminent death—is its indirect filtering into the nation and the race, and to give, often at many removes, but unerringly, age after age, color and fibre to the personalism of the youth and maturity of that age, and of mankind. Then there is a cement to the whole people, subtler, more underlying, than any thing in written constitution, or courts or armies—namely, the cement of a death identified thoroughly with that people, at its head, and for its sake. Strange, (is it not?) that battles, martyrs, agonies, blood, even assassination, should so condense—perhaps only really, lastingly condense—a Nationality.

I repeat it—the grand deaths of the race—the dramatic deaths of every nationality—are its most important inheritance-value—in some respects beyond its literature and art—(as the hero is beyond his finest portrait, and the battle itself beyond its choicest song or epic.) Is not here indeed the point underlying all tragedy? the famous pieces of the Grecian masters—and all masters? Why, if the old Greeks had had this man, what trilogies of plays—what epics—would have been made out of him! How the rhapsodes would have recited him! How quickly that quaint tall form would have enter'd into the region where men vitalize gods, and gods divinify men! But Lincoln, his times, his death—great as any, any age—belong altogether to our own, and are autochthonic. (Sometimes indeed I think our American days, our own stage —the actors we know and have shaken hands, or talk'd with —more fateful than any thing in Eschylus—more heroic than the fighters around Troy—afford kings of men for our Democracy prouder than Agamemnon—models of character cute and hardy as Ulysses—deaths more pitiful than Priam's.)

When, centuries hence, (as it must, in my opinion, be centuries hence before the life of these States, or of Democracy, can be really written and illustrated,) the leading historians and dramatists seek for some personage, some special event, incisive enough to mark with deepest cut, and mnemonize, this turbulent Nineteenth century of ours, (not only these States, but all over the political and social world)—something, perhaps, to close that gorgeous procession of European feudalism, with all its pomp and caste-prejudices, (of whose long train we in America are yet so inextricably the heirs)—something to identify with terrible identification, by far the greatest revolutionary step in the history of the United States, (perhaps the greatest of the world, our century)—the absolute extirpation and erasure of slavery from the States—those historians will seek in vain for any point to serve more thoroughly their purpose, than Abraham Lincoln's death.

Dear to the Muse—thrice dear to Nationality—to the whole human race—precious to this Union—precious to Democracy—unspeakably and forever precious—their first great Martyr Chief.

COLLECT: NOTES LEFT OVER

NATIONALITY (AND YET)

It is more and more clear to me that the main sustenance for highest separate personality, these States, is to come from that general sustenance of the aggregate, (as air, earth, rains, give sustenance to a tree)—and that such personality, by democratic standards, will only be fully coherent, grand and free, through the cohesion, grandeur and freedom of the common aggregate, the Union. Thus the existence of the true American continental solidarity of the future, depending on myriads of superb, large-sized, emotional and physically perfect individualities, of one sex just as much as the other, the supply of such individualities, in my opinion, wholly depends on a compacted imperial ensemble. The theory and practice of both sovereignties, contradictory as they are, are necessary. As the centripetal law were fatal alone, or the centrifugal law deadly and destructive alone, but together forming the law of eternal kosmical action, evolution, preservation, and life—so, by itself alone, the fullness of individuality, even the sanest, would surely destroy itself. This is what makes the importance to the identities of these States of the thoroughly fused, relentless, dominating Union—a moral and spiritual idea, subjecting all the parts with remorseless power, more needed by American democracy than by any of history's hitherto empires or feudalities and the *sine qua non* of carrying out the republican principle to develop itself in the New World through hundreds, thousands of years to come.

Indeed, what most needs fostering through the hundred years to come, in all parts of the United States, north, south, Mississippi valley, and Atlantic and Pacific coasts, is this fused and fervent identity of the individual, whoever he or she may be, and wherever the place, with the idea and fact of AMERICAN TOTALITY, and with what is meant by the Flag, the stars and stripes. We need this conviction of nationality as a faith, to be absorb'd in the blood and belief of the people everywhere, south, north, west, east, to emanate in their life, and in native literature and art. We want the germinal idea that America, inheritor of the past, is the custodian of the future of humanity. Judging from history, it is some such moral and spiritual ideas appropriate to them, (and such ideas only,) that have made the profoundest glory and endurance of nations in the past. The races of Judea, the classic clusters of Greece and Rome, and the feudal and ecclesiastical clusters of the Middle Ages, were each and all vitalized by their separate distinctive ideas, ingrain'd in them, redeeming many sins, and indeed, in a sense, the principal reason-why for their whole career.

Then, in the thought of nationality especially for the United States, and making them original, and different from all other countries, another point ever remains to be considered. There are two distinct principles—aye, paradoxes—at the life-fountain and life-continuation of the States; one, the sacred principle of the Union, the right of ensemble, at whatever sacrifice—and yet another, an equally sacred principle, the right of each State, consider'd as a separate sovereign individual, in its own sphere. Some go zealously for one set of these rights, and some as zealously for the other set. We must have both; or rather, bred out of them, as out of mother and father, a third set, the perennial result and combination of both, and neither jeopardized. I say the loss or abdication of one set, in the future, will be ruin to democracy just as much as the loss of the other set. The problem is, to harmoniously adjust the two, and the play of the two. [Observe the lesson of the divinity of Nature, ever checking the excess of one law, by an opposite, or seemingly opposite law—generally the other side of the same law.] For the theory of this Republic is, not that the General government is the fountain of all life and power, dispensing it forth, around, and to the remotest portions of our territory, but that THE PEOPLE are, represented in both, underlying both the General and State governments, and consider'd just as well in their individualities and in their separate aggregates, or States, as consider'd in one vast aggregate, the Union. This was the original dual theory and foundation of the United States, as distinguish'd from the feudal and ecclesiastical single idea of monarchies and papacies, and the divine right of kings. (Kings have been of use, hitherto, as representing the idea of the identity of nations. But, to American democracy, *both* ideas must be fulfill'd, and in my opinion the loss of vitality of either one will indeed be the loss of vitality of the other.)

EMERSON'S BOOKS
(THE SHADOWS OF THEM)

IN THE regions we call Nature, towering beyond all measurement, with infinite spread, infinite depth and height—in those regions, including Man, socially and historically, with his moral-emotional influences—how small a part, (it came in my mind to-day,) has literature really depicted—even summing up all of it, all ages. Seems at its best some little fleet of boats, hugging the shores of a boundless sea, and never venturing, exploring the unmapp'd—never, Columbus-like, sailing out for New Worlds, and to complete the orb's rondure. Emerson writes frequently in the atmosphere of this thought, and his books report one or two things from that very ocean and air, and more legibly address'd to our age and American polity than by any man yet. But I will begin by scarifying him— thus proving that I am not insensible to his deepest lessons. I will consider his books from a democratic and western point of view. I will specify the shadows on these sunny expanses. Somebody has said of heroic character that "wherever the tallest peaks are present, must inevitably be deep chasms and valleys." Mine be the ungracious task (for reasons) of leaving unmention'd both sunny expanses and sky-reaching heights, to dwell on the bare spots and darknesses. I have a theory that no artist or work of the very first class may be or can be without them.

First, then, these pages are perhaps too perfect, too concentrated. (How good, for instance, is good butter, good sugar. But to be eating nothing but sugar and butter all the time! even if ever so good.) And though the author has much to say of freedom and wildness and simplicity and spontaneity, no performance was ever more based on artificial scholarships and decorums at third or fourth removes, (he calls it culture,) and built up from them. It is always a *make*, never an unconscious *growth*. It is the porcelain figure or statuette of lion, or stag, or Indian hunter—and a very choice

statuette too—appropriate for the rosewood or marble bracket
of parlor or library; never the animal itself, or the hunter
himself. Indeed, who wants the real animal or hunter? What
would that do amid astral and bric-a-brac and tapestry, and
ladies and gentlemen talking in subdued tones of Browning
and Longfellow and all? The least suspicion of such actual
bull, or Indian, or of Nature carrying out itself, would put all
those good people to instant terror and flight.

Emerson, in my opinion, is not most eminent as poet or
artist or teacher, though valuable in all those. He is best as
critic, or diagnoser. Not passion or imagination or warp or
weakness, or any pronounced cause or specialty, dominates
him. Cold and bloodless intellectuality dominates him. (I
know the fires, emotions, love, egotisms, glow deep, perennial, as in all New Englanders—but the façade hides them well
—they give no sign.) He does not see or take one side, one
presentation only or mainly, (as all the poets, or most of the
fine writers anyhow)—he sees all sides. His final influence is
to make his students cease to worship anything—almost cease
to believe in anything, outside of themselves. These books
will fill, and well fill, certain stretches of life, certain stages of
development—are, (like the tenets or theology the author of
them preach'd when a young man,) unspeakably serviceable
and precious as a stage. But in old or nervous or solemnest or
dying hours, when one needs the impalpably soothing and
vitalizing influences of abysmic Nature, or its affinities in literature or human society, and the soul resents the keenest mere
intellection, they will not be sought for.

For a philosopher, Emerson possesses a singularly dandi-
fied theory of manners. He seems to have no notion at all
that manners are simply the signs by which the chemist or
metallurgist knows his metals. To the profound scientist,
all metals are profound, as they really are. The little one, like
the conventional world, will make much of gold and silver
only. Then to the real artist in humanity, what are called bad
manners are often the most picturesque and significant of all.
Suppose these books becoming absorb'd, the permanent chyle
of American general and particular character—what a well-

wash'd and grammatical, but bloodless and helpless, race we should turn out! No, no, dear friend; though the States want scholars, undoubtedly, and perhaps want ladies and gentlemen who use the bath frequently, and never laugh loud, or talk wrong, they don't want scholars, or ladies and gentlemen, at the expense of all the rest. They want good farmers, sailors, mechanics, clerks, citizens—perfect business and social relations—perfect fathers and mothers. If we could only have these, or their approximations, plenty of them, fine and large and sane and generous and patriotic, they might make their verbs disagree from their nominatives, and laugh like volleys of musketeers, if they should please. Of course these are not all America wants, but they are first of all to be provided on a large scale. And, with tremendous errors and escapades, this, substantially, is what the States seem to have an intuition of, and to be mainly aiming at. The plan of a select class, superfined, (demarcated from the rest,) the plan of Old World lands and literatures, is not so objectionable in itself, but because it chokes the true plan for us, and indeed is death to it. As to such special class, the United States can never produce any equal to the splendid show, (far, far beyond comparison or competition here,) of the principal European nations, both in the past and at the present day. But an immense and distinctive commonalty over our vast and varied area, west and east, south and north—in fact, for the first time in history, a great, aggregated, real PEOPLE, worthy the name, and made of develop'd heroic individuals, both sexes—is America's principal, perhaps only, reason for being. If ever accomplish'd, it will be at least as much, (I lately think, doubly as much,) the result of fitting and democratic sociologies, literatures and arts—if we ever get them—as of our democratic politics.

At times it has been doubtful to me if Emerson really knows or feels what Poetry is at its highest, as in the Bible, for instance, or Homer or Shakspere. I see he covertly or plainly likes best superb verbal polish, or something old or odd—Waller's "Go, lovely rose," or Lovelace's lines "to Lucasta"—the quaint conceits of the old French bards, and the like. Of *power* he seems to have a gentleman's admiration—but in his inmost heart the grandest attribute of God and Poets is always subordinate to the octaves, conceits, polite kinks, and verbs.

The reminiscence that years ago I began like most young-sters to have a touch (though it came late, and was only on the surface) of Emerson-on-the-brain—that I read his writings reverently, and address'd him in print as "Master," and for a month or so thought of him as such—I retain not only with composure, but positive satisfaction. I have noticed that most young people of eager minds pass through this stage of exercise.

The best part of Emersonianism is, it breeds the giant that destroys itself. Who wants to be any man's mere follower? lurks behind every page. No teacher ever taught, that has so provided for his pupil's setting up independently—no truer evolutionist.

VENTURES, ON AN OLD THEME

A DIALOGUE—*One party says*—We arrange our lives—even the best and boldest men and women that exist, just as much as the most limited—with reference to what society conventionally rules and makes right. We retire to our rooms for freedom; to undress, bathe, unloose everything in freedom. These, and much else, would not be proper in society.

Other party answers—Such is the rule of society. Not always so, and considerable exceptions still exist. However, it must be called the general rule, sanction'd by immemorial usage, and will probably always remain so.

First party—Why not, then, respect it in your poems?

Answer—One reason, and to me a profound one, is that the soul of a man or woman demands, enjoys compensation in the highest directions for this very restraint of himself or herself, level'd to the average, or rather mean, low, however eternally practical, requirements of society's intercourse. To balance this indispensable abnegation, the free minds of poets relieve themselves, and strengthen and enrich mankind with free flights in all the directions not tolerated by ordinary society.

First party—But must not outrage or give offence to it.

Answer—No, not in the deepest sense—and do not, and cannot. The vast averages of time and the race *en masse* settle these things. Only understand that the conventional standards and laws proper enough for ordinary society apply neither to the action of the soul, nor its poets. In fact the latter know no laws but the laws of themselves, planted in them by God, and are themselves the last standards of the law, and its final exponents—responsible to Him directly, and not at all to mere etiquette. Often the best service that can be done to the race, is to lift the veil, at least for a time, from these rules and fossil-etiquettes.

NEW POETRY—*California, Canada, Texas*—In my opinion the time has arrived to essentially break down the barriers of form between prose and poetry. I say the latter is henceforth to win and maintain its character regardless of rhyme, and the measurement-rules of iambic, spondee, dactyl, &c., and that even if rhyme and those measurements continue to furnish the medium for inferior writers and themes, (especially for persiflage and the comic, as there seems henceforward, to the perfect taste, something inevitably comic in rhyme, merely in itself, and anyhow,) the truest and greatest *Poetry*, (while subtly and necessarily always rhythmic, and distinguishable easily enough,) can never again, in the English language, be express'd in arbitrary and rhyming metre, any more than the greatest eloquence, or the truest power and passion. While admitting that the venerable and heavenly forms of chiming versification have in their time play'd great and fitting parts—that the pensive complaint, the ballads, wars, amours, legends of Europe, &c., have, many of them, been inimitably render'd in rhyming verse—that there have been very illustrious poets whose shapes the mantle of such verse has beautifully and appropriately envelopt—and though the mantle has fallen, with perhaps added beauty, on some of our own age—it is notwithstanding, certain to me, that the day of such conventional rhyme is ended. In America, at any rate, and as a medium of highest æsthetic practical or spiritual expression, present or future, it palpably fails, and must fail, to serve. The Muse of the Prairies, of California, Canada, Texas, and of the peaks of Colorado, dismissing the literary, as well as social etiquette of over-sea feudalism and caste, joyfully enlarging, adapting itself to comprehend the size of the whole people, with the free play, emotions, pride, passions, experiences, that belong to them, body and soul—to the general globe, and all its relations in astronomy, as the savants portray them to us—to the modern, the busy Nineteenth century, (as grandly poetic as any, only different,) with steamships, railroads, factories, electric telegraphs, cylinder presses —to the thought of the solidarity of nations, the brotherhood and sisterhood of the entire earth—to the dignity and heroism of the practical labor of farms, factories, foundries, workshops, mines, or on shipboard, or on lakes and rivers—resumes that other medium of expression, more flexible, more eligible— soars to the freer, vast, diviner heaven of prose.

Of poems of the third or fourth class, (perhaps even some of the second,) it makes little or no difference who writes them—they are good enough for what they are; nor is it necessary that they should be actual emanations from the personality and life of the writers. The very reverse sometimes gives piquancy. But poems of the first class, (poems of the depth, as distinguished from those of the surface,) are to be sternly tallied with the poets themselves, and tried by them and their lives. Who wants a glorification of courage and manly defiance from a coward or a sneak?—a ballad of benevolence or chastity from some rhyming hunks, or lascivious, glib *roué?*

In these States, beyond all precedent, poetry will have to do with actual facts, with the concrete States, and—for we have not much more than begun—with the definitive getting into shape of the Union. Indeed I sometimes think *it* alone is to define the Union, (namely, to give it artistic character, spirituality, dignity.) What American humanity is most in danger of is an overwhelming prosperity, "business" worldliness, materialism: what is most lacking, east, west, north, south, is a fervid and glowing Nationality and patriotism, cohering all the parts into one. Who may fend that danger, and fill that lack in the future, but a class of loftiest poets?

If the United States haven't grown poets, on any scale of grandeur, it is certain they import, print, and read more poetry than any equal number of people elsewhere—probably more than all the rest of the world combined.

Poetry (like a grand personality) is a growth of many generations—many rare combinations.

To have great poets, there must be great audiences, too.

BRITISH LITERATURE

To AVOID mistake, I would say that I not only commend the study of this literature, but wish our sources of supply and comparison vastly enlarged. American students may well derive from all former lands—from forenoon Greece and Rome, down to the perturb'd medieval times, the Crusades, and so to Italy, the German intellect—all the older literatures, and all the newer ones—from witty and warlike France, and markedly, and in many ways, and at many different periods, from the enterprise and soul of the great Spanish race—bearing ourselves always courteous, always deferential, indebted beyond measure to the mother-world, to all its nations dead, as all its nations living—the offspring, this America of ours, the daughter, not by any means of the British isles exclusively, but of the continent, and all continents. Indeed, it is time we should realize and fully fructify those germs we also hold from Italy, France, Spain, especially in the best imaginative productions of those lands, which are, in many ways, loftier and subtler than the English, or British, and indispensable to complete our service, proportions, educations, reminiscences, &c. . . . The British element these States hold, and have always held, enormously beyond its fit proportions. I have already spoken of Shakspere. He seems to me of astral genius, first class, entirely fit for feudalism. His contributions, especially to the literature of the passions, are immense, forever dear to humanity—and his name is always to be reverenced in America. But there is much in him ever offensive to democracy. He is not only the tally of feudalism, but I should say Shakspere is incarnated, uncompromising feudalism in literature. Then one seems to detect something in him—I hardly know how to describe it—even amid the dazzle of his genius; and, in inferior manifestations, it is found in nearly all leading British authors. (Perhaps we will have to import the words Snob, Snobbish, &c., after all.) While of the great poems of Asian antiquity, the Indian epics, the book of Job, the Ionian Iliad, the unsurpassedly simple, loving, perfect idyls of the life and death of Christ, in the New Testament, (indeed Homer and the Biblical utterances intertwine familiarly with us, in the main,) and along down, of most of the characteristic, imaginative or romantic relics of the continent, as the Cid, Cervantes' Don Quixote, &c., I should say they substantially adjust themselves to us, and, far off as they are, accord curiously with our bed and board to-day, in New York, Washington, Canada, Ohio, Texas, California—and with our notions, both of seriousness and of fun, and our standards of heroism, manliness, and even the democratic requirements —those requirements are not only not fulfilled in the Shaksperean productions, but are insulted on every page.

I add that—while England is among the greatest of lands in political freedom, or the idea of it, and in stalwart personal character, &c.—the spirit of English literature is not great, at least is not greatest—and its products are no models for us. With the exception of Shakspere, there is no first-class genius in that literature—which, with a truly vast amount of value, and of artificial beauty, (largely from the classics,) is almost always material, sensual, not spiritual—almost always congests, makes plethoric, not frees, expands, dilates—is cold, anti-democratic, loves to be sluggish and stately, and shows much of that characteristic of vulgar persons, the dread of saying or doing something not at all improper in itself, but unconventional, and that may be laugh'd at. In its best, the sombre pervades it; it is moody, melancholy, and, to give it its due, expresses, in characters and plots, those qualities, in an un-rival'd manner. Yet not as the black thunderstorms, and in great normal, crashing passions, of the Greek dramatists—clearing the air, refreshing afterward, bracing with power; but as in Hamlet, moping, sick, uncertain, and leaving ever after a secret taste for the blues, the morbid fascination, the luxury of woe. . . .

I strongly recommend all the young men and young women of the United States to whom it may be eligible, to overhaul the well-freighted fleets, the literatures of Italy, Spain, France, Germany, so full of those elements of freedom, self-possession, gay-heartedness, subtlety, dilation, needed in preparations for the future of the States. I only wish we could have really good translations. I rejoice at the feeling for Oriental re-searches and poetry, and hope it will go on.

DARWINISM—
(THEN FURTHERMORE)

RUNNING through prehistoric ages—coming down from them into the daybreak of our records, founding theology, suffusing literature, and so brought onward—(a sort of verteber and marrow to all the antique races and lands, Egypt, India, Greece, Rome, the Chinese, the Jews, &c., and giving cast and complexion to their art, poems, and their politics as well as ecclesiasticism, all of which we more or less inherit,) appear those venerable claims to origin from God himself, or from gods and goddesses—ancestry from divine beings of vaster beauty, size, and power than ours. But in current and latest times, the theory of human origin that seems to have most made its mark, (curiously reversing the antique,) is that we have come on, originated, develop, from monkeys, baboons—a theory more significant perhaps in its indirections, or what it necessitates, than it is even in itself. (Of the twain, far apart as they seem, and angrily as their conflicting ad-vocates to-day oppose each other, are not both theories to be possibly reconciled, and even blended? Can we, indeed, spare either of them? Better still, out of them is not a third theory, the real one, or suggesting the real one, to arise?)

Of this old theory, evolution, as broach'd anew, trebled, with indeed all-devouring claims, by Darwin, it has so much in it, and is so needed as a counterpoise to yet widely prevailing and unspeakably tenacious, enfeebling superstitions—is fused, by the new man, into such grand, modest, truly scientific accompaniments—that the world of erudition, both moral and physical, cannot but be eventually better'd and broaden'd in its speculations, from the advent of Darwinism. Nevertheless, the problem of origins, human and other, is not the least whit nearer its solution. In due time the Evolution theory will have to abate its vehemence, cannot be allow'd to dominate every thing else, and will have to take its place as a segment of the circle, the cluster—as but one of many theories, many thoughts, of profoundest value—and re-adjusting and differentiating much, yet leaving the divine secrets just as inexplicable and unreachable as before—may-be more so.

Then furthermore—What is finally to be done by priest or poet—and by priest or poet only—amid all the stupendous and dazzling novelties of our century, with the advent of America, and of science and democracy—remains just as indispensable, after all the work of the grand astronomers, chemists, linguists, historians, and explorers of the last hundred years—and the wondrous German and other metaphysicians of that time—and will continue to remain, needed, America and here, just the same as in the world of Europe, or Asia, of a hundred, or a thousand, or several thousand years ago. I think indeed *more* needed, to furnish statements from the present points, the added arriere, and the unspeakably immenser vistas of to-day. Only the priests and poets of the modern, at least as exalted as any in the past, fully absorbing and appreciating the results of the past, in the commonalty of all humanity, all time, (the main results already, for there is perhaps nothing more, or at any rate not much, strictly new, only more important modern combinations, and new relative adjustments,) must indeed recast the old metal, the already achiev'd material, into and through new moulds, current forms.

Meantime, the highest and subtlest and broadest truths of modern science wait for their true assignment and last vivid flashes of light—as Democracy waits for its—through first-class metaphysicians and speculative philosophs—laying the basements and foundations for those new, more expanded, more harmonious, more melodious, freer American poems.

"SOCIETY"

I HAVE myself little or no hope from what is technically called "Society" in our American cities. New York, of which place I have spoken so sharply, still promises something, in time, out of its tremendous and varied materials, with a certain superiority of intuitions, and the advantage of constant agitation, and ever new and rapid dealings of the cards. Of Boston, with its circles of social mummies, swathed in cerements harder than brass—its bloodless religion, (Unitarianism,) its complacent vanity of scientism and literature, lots of grammatical correctness, mere knowledge, (always wearisome, in itself)—its zealous abstractions, ghosts of reforms—I should say, (ever admitting its business powers, its sharp, almost demoniac, intellect, and no lack, in its own way, of courage and generosity)—there is, at present, little of cheering, satisfying sign. In the West, California, &c., "society" is yet unform'd, puerile, seemingly unconscious of anything above a driving business, or to liberally spend the money made by it, in the usual rounds and shows.

Then there is, to the humorous observer of American attempts at fashion, according to the models of foreign courts and saloons, quite a comic side—particularly visible at Washington city—a sort of high-life-below-stairs business. As if any farce could be funnier, for instance, than the scenes of the crowds, winter nights, meandering around our Presidents and their wives, cabinet officers, western or other Senators, Representatives, &c.; born of good laboring mechanic or farming stock and antecedents, attempting those full-dress receptions, finesse of parlors, foreign ceremonies, etiquettes, &c.

Indeed, consider'd with any sense of propriety, or any sense at all, the whole of this illy-play'd fashionable play and display, with their absorption of the best part of our wealthier citizens' time, money, energies, &c., is ridiculously out of place in the United States. As if our proper man and woman, (far, far greater words than "gentleman" and "lady,") could still fail to see, and presently achieve, not this spectral business, but something truly noble, active, sane, American—by modes, perfections of character, manners, costumes, social relations, &c., adjusted to standards, far, far different from those.

Eminent and liberal foreigners, British or continental, must at times have their faith fearfully tried by what they see of our New World personalities. The shallowest and least American persons seem surest to push abroad, and call without fail on well-known foreigners, who are doubtless affected with indescribable qualms by these queer ones. Then, more than half of our authors and writers evidently think it a great thing to be "aristocratic," and sneer at progress, democracy, revolution, &c. If some international literary snobs' gallery were establish'd, it is certain that America could contribute at least her full share of the portraits, and some very distinguish'd ones. Observe that the most impudent slanders, low insults, &c., on the great revolutionary authors, leaders, poets, &c., of Europe, have their origin and main circulation in certain circles here. The treatment of Victor Hugo living, and Byron dead, are samples. Both deserving so well of America, and both persistently attempted to be soil'd here by unclean birds, male and female.

Meanwhile I must still offset the like of the foregoing, and all it infers, by the recognition of the fact, that while the surfaces of current society here show so much that is dismal, noisome, and vapory, there are, beyond question, inexhaustible supplies, as of true gold ore, in the mines of America's general humanity. Let us, not ignoring the dross, give fit stress to these precious immortal values also. Let it be distinctly admitted, that—whatever may be said of our fashionable society, and of any foul fractions and episodes—only here in America, out of the long history and manifold presentations of the ages, has at last arisen, and now stands, what never before took positive form and sway, *the People*—and that view'd en-masse, and while fully acknowledging deficiencies, dangers, faults, this people, inchoate, latent, not yet come to majority, nor to its own religious, literary, or æsthetic expression, yet affords, to-day, an exultant justification of all the faith, all the hopes and prayers and prophecies of good men through the past—the stablest, solidest-based government of the world—the most assured in a future—the beaming Pharos to whose perennial light all earnest eyes, the world over, are tending—and that already, in and from it, the democratic principle, having been mortally tried by severest tests, fatalities of war and peace, now issues from the trial, unharm'd, trebly-invigorated, perhaps to commence forthwith its finally triumphant march around the globe.

THE TRAMP AND STRIKE QUESTIONS

Part of a Lecture proposed, (never deliver'd)

Two grim and spectral dangers—dangerous to peace, to health, to social security, to progress—long known in concrete to the governments of the Old World, and there eventuating, more than once or twice, in dynastic overturns, bloodshed, days, months, of terror—seem of late years to be nearing the New World, nay, to be gradually establishing themselves among us. What mean these phantoms here? (I personify them in fictitious shapes, but they are very real.) Is the fresh and broad demesne of America destined also to give them foothold and lodgment, permanent domicile?

Beneath the whole political world, what most presses and perplexes to-day, sending vastest results affecting the future, is not the abstract question of democracy, but of social and economic organization, the treatment of working-people by employers, and all that goes along with it—not only the wages-payment part, but a certain spirit and principle, to vivify anew these relations; all the questions of progress, strength, tariffs, finance, &c., really evolving themselves more or less directly out of the Poverty Question, ("the Science of Wealth," and a dozen other names are given it, but I prefer the severe one just used.) I will begin by calling the reader's attention to a thought upon the matter which may not have struck you before—the wealth of the civilized world, as contrasted with its poverty—what does it derivatively stand for, and represent? A rich person ought to have a strong stomach. As in Europe the wealth of to-day mainly results from, and represents, the rapine, murder, outrages, treachery, hoggishness, of hundreds of years ago, and onward, later, so in America, after the same token—(not yet so bad, perhaps, or at any rate not so palpable —we have not existed long enough—but we seem to be doing our best to make it up.)

Curious as it may seem, it is in what are call'd the poorest, lowest characters you will sometimes, nay generally, find glints of the most sublime virtues, eligibilities, heroisms. Then it is doubtful whether the State is to be saved, either in the monotonous long run, or in tremendous special crises, by its good people only. When the storm is deadliest, and the disease most imminent, help often comes from strange quarters—(the homœopathic motto, you remember, *cure the bite with a hair of the same dog.*)

The American Revolution of 1776 was simply a great strike, successful for its immediate object—but whether a real success judged by the scale of the centuries, and the long-striking balance of Time, yet remains to be settled. The French Revolution was absolutely a strike, and a very terrible and relentless one, against ages of bad pay, unjust division of wealth-products, and the hoggish monopoly of a few, rolling in superfluity, against the vast bulk of the work-people, living in squalor.

If the United States, like the countries of the Old World, are also to grow vast crops of poor, desperate, dissatisfied, nomadic, miserably-waged populations, such as we see looming upon us of late years—steadily, even if slowly, eating into them like a cancer of lungs or stomach—then our republican experiment, notwithstanding all its surface-successes, is at heart an unhealthy failure.

Feb., '79.—I saw to-day a sight I had never seen before—and it amazed, and made me serious; three quite good-looking American men, of respectable personal presence, two of them young, carrying chiffonier-bags on their shoulders, and the usual long iron hooks in their hands, plodding along, their eyes cast down, spying for scraps, rags, bones, &c.

DEMOCRACY IN THE NEW WORLD,

estimated and summ'd-up to-day, having thoroughly justified itself the past hundred years, (as far as growth, vitality and power are concern'd,) by severest and most varied trials of peace and war, and having establish'd itself for good, with all its necessities and benefits, for time to come, is now to be seriously consider'd also in its pronounc'd and already de-velopt dangers. While the battle was raging, and the result suspended, all defections and criticisms were to be hush'd, and everything bent with vehemence unmitigated toward the urge of victory. But that victory settled, new responsibil-ities advance. I can conceive of no better service in the United States, henceforth, by democrats of thorough and heart-felt faith, than boldly exposing the weakness, liabilities and infinite corruptions of democracy. By the unprecedented opening-up of humanity en-masse in the United States, the last hundred years, under our institutions, not only the good qualities of the race, but just as much the bad ones, are prominently brought forward. Man is about the same, in the main, whether with despotism, or whether with freedom.

"The ideal form of human society," Canon Kingsley de-clares, "is democracy. A nation—and were it even possible, a whole world—of free men, lifting free foreheads to God and Nature; calling no man master, for One is their master, even God; knowing and doing their duties toward the Maker of the universe, and therefore to each other; not from fear, nor calculation of profit or loss, but because they have seen the beauty of righteousness, and trust, and peace; because the law of God is in their hearts. Such a nation—such a society—what nobler conception of moral existence can we form? Would not that, indeed, be the kingdom of God come on earth?"

To this faith, founded in the ideal, let us hold—and never abandon or lose it. Then what a spectacle is *practically* exhibited by our American democracy to-day!

FOUNDATION STAGES—THEN OTHERS

THOUGH I think I fully comprehend the absence of moral tone in our current politics and business, and the almost entire futility of absolute and simple honor as a counterpoise against the enormous greed for worldly wealth, with the trickeries of gaining it, all through society our day, I still do not share the depression and despair on the subject which I find possessing many good people. The advent of America, the history of the past century, has been the first general aperture and opening-up to the average human commonalty, on the broadest scale, of the eligibilities to wealth and worldly success and eminence, and has been fully taken advantage of; and the example has spread hence, in ripples, to all nations. To these eligibilities—to this limitless aperture, the race has tended, en-masse, roaring and rushing and crude, and fiercely, turbidly hastening—and we have seen the first stages, and are now in the midst of the result of it all, so far. But there will certainly ensue other stages, and entirely different ones. In nothing is there more evolution than the American mind. Soon, it will be fully realized that ostensible wealth and money-making, show, luxury, &c., imperatively necessitate something beyond—namely, the sane, eternal moral and spiritual-esthetic attributes, elements. (We cannot have even that realization on any less terms than the price we are now paying for it.) Soon, it will be understood clearly, that the State cannot flourish, (nay, cannot exist,) without those elements. They will gradually enter into the chyle of sociology and literature. They will finally make the blood and brawn of the best American individualities of both sexes—and thus, with them, to a certainty, (through these very processes of to-day,) dominate the New World.

GENERAL SUFFRAGE, ELECTIONS, &c.

IT STILL remains doubtful to me whether these will ever secure, officially, the best wit and capacity—whether, through them, the first-class genius of America will ever personally appear in the high political stations, the Presidency, Congress, the leading State offices, &c. Those offices, or the candidacy for them, arranged, won, by caucusing, money, the favoritism or pecuniary interest of rings, the superior manipulation of the ins over the outs, or the outs over the ins, are, indeed, at best, the mere business agencies of the people, are useful as formulating, neither the best and highest, but the average of the public judgment, sense, justice, (or sometimes want of judgment, sense, justice.) We elect Presidents, Congressmen, &c., not so much to have them consider and decide for us, but as surest practical means of expressing the will of majorities on mooted questions, measures, &c.

As to general suffrage, after all, since we have gone so far, the more general it is, the better. I favor the widest opening of the doors. Let the ventilation and area be wide enough, and all is safe. We can never have a born penitentiary-bird, or panel-thief, or lowest gambling-hell or groggery keeper, for President—though such may not only emulate, but get, high offices from localities—even from the proud and wealthy city of New York.

WHO GETS THE PLUNDER?

THE protectionists are fond of flashing to the public eye the glittering delusion of great money-results from manufactures, mines, artificial exports—so many millions from this source, and so many from that—such a seductive, unanswerable show —an immense revenue of annual cash from iron, cotton, woollen, leather goods, and a hundred other things, all bolstered up by "protection." But the really important point of all is, *into whose pockets does this plunder really go?* It would be some excuse and satisfaction if even a fair proportion of it went to the masses of laboring-men—resulting in homesteads to such, men, women, children—myriads of actual homes in fee simple, in every State, (not the false glamour of the stunning wealth reported in the census, in the statistics, or tables in the newspapers,) but a fair division and generous average to those workmen and workwomen—*that* would be something. But the fact itself is nothing of the kind. The profits of "protection" go altogether to a few score select persons—who, by favors of Congress, State legislatures, the banks, and other special advantages, are forming a vulgar aristocracy, full as bad as anything in the British or European castes, of blood, or the dynasties there of the past. As Sismondi pointed out, the true prosperity of a nation is not in the great wealth of a special class, but is only to be really attain'd in having the bulk of the people provided with homes or land in fee simple. This may not be the best show, but it is the best reality.

FRIENDSHIP (THE REAL ARTICLE)

THOUGH Nature maintains, and must prevail, there will always be plenty of people, and good people, who cannot, or think they cannot, see anything in that last, wisest, most envelop'd of proverbs, "Friendship rules the World." Modern society, in its largest vein, is essentially intellectual, infidelistic —secretly admires, and depends most on, pure compulsion or science, its rule and sovereignty—is, in short, in "cultivated" quarters, deeply Napoleonic.

"Friendship," said Bonaparte, in one of his lightning-flashes of candid garrulity, "Friendship is but a name. I love no one —not even my brothers; Joseph perhaps a little. Still, if I do love him, it is from habit, because he is the eldest of us. Duroc? Ay, him, if any one, I love in a sort—but why? He suits me; he is cool, undemonstrative, unfeeling—has no weak affections—never embraces any one—never weeps."

I am not sure but the same analogy is to be applied, in cases, often seen, where, with an extra devolopment and acuteness of the intellectual faculties, there is a mark'd absence of the spiritual, affectional, and sometimes, though more rarely, the highest æsthetic and moral elements of cognition.

LACKS AND WANTS YET

OF MOST foreign countries, small or large, from the remotest times known, down to our own, each has contributed after its kind, directly or indirectly, at least one great undying song, to help vitalize and increase the valor, wisdom, and elegance of humanity, from the points of view attain'd by it up to date. The stupendous epics of India, the holy Bible itself, the Homeric canticles, the Nibelungen, the Cid Campeador, the Inferno, Shakspere's dramas of the passions and of the feudal lords, Burns's songs, Goethe's in Germany, Tennyson's poems in England, Victor Hugo's in France, and many more, are the widely various yet integral signs or landmarks, (in certain respects the highest set up by the human mind and soul, beyond science, invention, political amelioration, &c.,) narrating in subtlest, best ways, the long, long routes of history, and giving identity to the stages arrived at by aggregate humanity, and the conclusions assumed in its progressive and varied civilizations. . . . Where is America's art-rendering, in any thing like the spirit worthy of herself and the modern, to these characteristic immortal monuments?

So far, our Democratic society, (estimating its various strata, in the mass, as one,) possesses nothing—nor have we contributed any characteristic music, the finest tie of nationality —to make up for that glowing, blood-throbbing, religious, social, emotional, artistic, indefinable, indescribably beautiful charm and hold which fused the separate parts of the old feudal societies together, in their wonderful interpenetration, in Europe and Asia, of love, belief, and loyalty, running one way like a living weft—and picturesque responsibility, duty, and blessedness, running like a warp the other way. (In the Southern States, under slavery, much of the same.) . . . In coincidence, and as things now exist in the States, what is more terrible, more alarming, than the total want of any such fusion and mutuality of love, belief, and rapport of interest, between the comparatively few successful rich, and the great masses of the unsuccessful, the poor? As a mixed political and social question, is not this full of dark significance? Is it not worth considering as a problem and puzzle in our democracy—an indispensable want to be supplied?

RULERS STRICTLY OUT OF THE MASSES

In the talk (which I welcome) about the need of men of training, thoroughly school'd and experienced men, for statesmen, I would present the following as an offset. It was written by me twenty years ago—and has been curiously verified since:

I say no body of men are fit to make Presidents, Judges, and Generals, unless they themselves supply the best specimens of the same; and that supplying one or two such specimens illuminates the whole body for a thousand years. I expect to see the day when the like of the present personnel of the governments, Federal, State, municipal, military, and naval, will be look'd upon with derision, and when qualified mechanics and young men will reach Congress and other official stations, sent in their working costumes, fresh from their benches and tools, and returning to them again with dignity. The young fellows must prepare to do credit to this destiny, for the stuff is in them. Nothing gives place, recollect, and never ought to give place, except to its clean superiors. There is more rude and undevelopt bravery, friendship, conscientiousness, clear-sightedness, and practical genius for any scope of action, even the broadest and highest, now among the American mechanics and young men, than in all the official persons in these States, legislative, executive, judicial, military, and naval, and more than among all the literary persons. I would be much pleased to see some heroic, shrewd, fully-inform'd, healthy-bodied, middle-aged, beard-faced American blacksmith or boatman come down from the West across the Alleghenies, and walk into the Presidency, dress'd in a clean suit of working attire, and with the tan all over his face, breast, and arms; I would certainly vote for that sort of man, possessing the due requirements, before any other candidate.

(The facts of rank-and-file workingmen, mechanics, Lincoln, Johnson, Grant, Garfield, brought forward from the masses and placed in the Presidency, and swaying its mighty powers with firm hand—really with more sway than any king in history, and with better capacity in using that sway—can we not see that these facts have bearings far, far beyond their political or party ones?)

MONUMENTS—THE PAST AND PRESENT

IF YOU go to Europe, (to say nothing of Asia, more ancient and massive still,) you cannot stir without meeting venerable mementos—cathedrals, ruins of temples, castles, monuments of the great, statues and paintings, (far, far beyond anything America can ever expect to produce,) haunts of heroes long saints, poets, divinities, with deepest associations of ages. But here in the New World, while *those* we can never emulate, we have *more* than those to build, and far more greatly to build. (I am not sure but the day for conventional monuments, statues, memorials, &c., has pass'd away—and that they are henceforth superfluous and vulgar.) An enlarged general superior humanity, (partly indeed resulting from those,) we are to build. European, Asiatic greatness are in the past. Vaster and subtler, America, combining, justifying the past, yet works for a grander future, in living democratic forms. (Here too are indicated the paths for our national bards.) Other times, other lands, have had their missions— Art, War, Ecclesiasticism, Literature, Discovery, Trade, Architecture, &c., &c.—but that grand future is the enclosing purport of the United States.

LITTLE OR NOTHING NEW,
AFTER ALL

How small were the best thoughts, poems, conclusions, except for a certain invariable resemblance and uniform standard in the final thoughts, theology, poems, &c., of all nations, all civilizations, all centuries and times. Those precious legacies— accumulations! They come to us from the far-off—from all eras, and all lands—from Egypt, and India, and Greece, and Rome—and along through the middle and later ages, in the grand monarchies of Europe—born under far different institutes and conditions from ours—but out of the insight and inspiration of the same old humanity—the same old heart and brain—the same old countenance yearningly, pensively, looking forth. What we have to do to-day is to receive them cheerfully, and to give them ensemble, and a modern American and democratic physiognomy.

A LINCOLN REMINISCENCE

As is well known, story-telling was often with President Lincoln a weapon which he employ'd with great skill. Very often he could not give a point-blank reply or comment—and these indirections, (sometimes funny, but not always so,) were probably the best responses possible. In the gloomiest period of the war, he had a call from a large delegation of bank presidents. In the talk after business was settled, one of the big Dons asked Mr. Lincoln if his confidence in the permanency of the Union was not beginning to be shaken—whereupon the homely President told a little story: "When I was a young man in Illinois," said he, "I boarded for a time with a deacon of the Presbyterian church. One night I was roused from my sleep by a rap at the door, and I heard the deacon's voice exclaiming, 'Arise, Abraham! the day of judgment has come!' I sprang from my bed and rushed to the window, and saw the stars falling in great showers; but looking back of them in the heavens I saw the grand old constellations, with which I was so well acquainted, fixed and true in their places. Gentlemen, the world did not come to an end then, nor will the Union now."

FREEDOM

It is not only true that most people entirely misunderstand Freedom, but I sometimes think I have not yet met one person who rightly understands it. The whole Universe is absolute Law. Freedom only opens entire activity and license *under the law*. To the degraded or undevelopt—and even to too many others—the thought of freedom is a thought of escaping from law—which, of course, is impossible. More precious than all worldly riches is Freedom—freedom from the painful constipation and poor narrowness of ecclesiasticism —freedom in manners, habiliments, furniture, from the silliness and tyranny of local fashions—entire freedom from party rings and mere conventions in Politics—and better than all, a general Freedom of One's-Self from the tyrannic domination of vices, habits, appetites, under which nearly every man of us, (often the greatest brawler for freedom,) is enslaved. Can we attain such enfranchisement—the true Democracy, and the height of it? While we are from birth to death the subjects of irresistible law, enclosing every movement and minute, we yet escape, by a paradox, into true free will. Strange as it may seem, we only attain to freedom by a knowledge of, and implicit obedience to, Law. Great—unspeakably great—is the Will! the free Soul of man! At its greatest, understanding and obeying the laws, it can then, and then only, maintain true liberty. For there is to the highest, that law as absolute as any—more absolute than any —the Law of Liberty. The shallow, as intimated, consider liberty a release from all law, from every constraint. The wise see in it, on the contrary, the potent Law of Laws, namely, the fusion and combination of the conscious will, or partial individual law, with those universal, eternal, unconscious ones, which run through all Time, pervade history, prove immortality, give moral purpose to the entire objective world, and the last dignity to human life.

BOOK-CLASSES—AMERICA'S
LITERATURE

FOR certain purposes, literary productions through all the recorded ages may be roughly divided into two classes. The first consisting of only a score or two, perhaps less, of typical, primal, representative works, different from any before, and embodying in themselves their own main laws and reasons for being. Then the second class, books and writings innumerable, incessant—to be briefly described as radiations or offshoots, or more or less imitations of the first. The works of the first class, as said, have their own laws, and may indeed be described as making those laws, and amenable only to them. The sharp warning of Margaret Fuller, unquell'd for thirty years, yet sounds in the air; "It does not follow that because the United States print and read more books, magazines, and newspapers than all the rest of the world, that they really have, therefore, a literature."

OUR REAL CULMINATION

THE final culmination of this vast and varied Republic will be the production and perennial establishment of millions of comfortable city homesteads and moderate-sized farms, healthy and independent, single separate ownership, fee simple, life in them complete but cheap, within reach of all. Exceptional wealth, splendor, countless manufactures, excess of exports, immense capital and capitalists, the five-dollar-a-day hotels well fill'd, artificial improvements, even books, colleges, and the suffrage—all, in many respects, in themselves, (hard as it is to say so, and sharp as a surgeon's lance,) from, more or less, a sort of anti-democratic disease and monstrosity, except as they contribute by curious indirections to that culmination—seem to me mainly of value, or worth consideration, only with reference to it.

There is a subtle something in the common earth, crops, cattle, air, trees, &c., and in having to do at first hand with them, that forms the only purifying and perennial element for individuals and for society. I must confess I want to see the agricultural occupation of America at first hand permanently broaden'd. Its gains are the only ones on which God seems to smile. What others—what business, profit, wealth, without a taint? What fortune else—what dollar—does not stand for, and come from, more or less imposition, lying, unnaturalness?

AN AMERICAN PROBLEM

ONE of the problems presented in America these times is, how to combine one's duty and policy as a member of associations, societies, brotherhoods or what not, and one's obligations to the State and Nation, with essential freedom as an individual personality, without which freedom a man cannot grow or expand, or be full, modern, heroic, democratic, American. With all the necessities and benefits of association, (and the world cannot get along without it,) the true nobility and satisfaction of a man consist in his thinking and acting for himself. The problem, I say, is to combine the two, so as not to ignore either.

THE LAST COLLECTIVE
COMPACTION

I LIKE well our polyglot construction-stamp, and the retention thereof, in the broad, the tolerating, the many-sided, the collective. All nations here—a home for every race on earth. British, German, Scandinavian, Spanish, French, Italian— papers published, plays acted, speeches made, in all languages—on our shores the crowning resultant of those distillations, decantations, compactions of humanity, that have been going on, on trial, over the earth so long.

GOOD-BYE MY FANCY

[SELECTIONS]

INSCRIPTION FOR A LITTLE BOOK ON GIORDANO BRUNO

As America's mental courage (the thought comes to me to-day) is so indebted, above all current lands and peoples, to the noble army of Old-World martyrs past, how incumbent on us that we clear those martyrs' lives and names, and hold them up for reverent admiration, as well as beacons. And typical of this, and standing for it and all perhaps, Giordano Bruno may well be put, to-day and to come, in our New World's thankfulest heart and memory.   W. W.

February 24th, 1890.
        Camden, N. J.

SPLINTERS

WHILE I stand in reverence before the fact of Humanity, the People, I will confess, in writing my L of G, the least consideration out of all that has had to do with it has been the consideration of "the public"—at any rate as it now exists. Strange as it may sound for a democrat to say so, I am clear that no free and original and lofty-soaring poem, or one ambitious of those achievements, can possibly be fulfill'd by any writer who has largely in his thought *the public*—or the question, What will establish'd literature—What will the current authorities say about it?

As far as I have sought any, not the best laid out garden or parterre has been my model—but Nature has been. I know

478

that in a sense the garden is nature too, but I had to choose —I could not give both. Besides the gardens are well represented in poetry; while Nature (in letter and in spirit, in the divine essence,) little if at all.

Certainly, (while I have not hit it by a long shot,) I have aim'd at the most ambitious, the best—and sometimes feel to advance that aim (even with all its arrogance) as the most redeeming part of my books. I have never so much cared to feed the esthetic or intellectual palates—but if I could arouse from its slumbers that eligibility in every soul for its own true exercise! if I could only wield that lever!

Out from the well-tended concrete and the physical—and in them and from them only—radiate the spiritual and heroic.

Undoubtedly many points belonging to this essay—perhaps of the greatest necessity, fitness and importance to it—have been left out or forgotten. But the amount of the whole matter —poems, preface and everything—is merely to make one of those little punctures or eye-lets the actors possess in the theatre-curtains to look out upon "the house"—one brief, honest, living glance.

GAY-HEARTEDNESS

WALKING on the old Navy Yard bridge, Washington, D. C., once with a companion, Mr. Marshall, from England, a great traveler and observer, as a squad of laughing young black girls pass'd us—then two copper-color'd boys, one good-looking lad 15 or 16, barefoot, running after—"What *gay creatures* they all appear to be," said Mr. M. Then we fell to talking about the general lack of buoyant animal spirits. "I think," said Mr. M., "that in all my travels, and all my intercourse with people of every and any class, especially the cultivated ones, (the literary and fashionable folks,) I have never yet come across what I should call a really GAY-HEARTED MAN."

It was a terrible criticism—cut into me like a surgeon's lance. Made me silent the whole walk home.

AS IN A SWOON

As IN a swoon, one instant,
Another sun, ineffable, full-dazzles me,
And all the orbs I knew—and brighter, unknown orbs;
One instant of the future land, Heaven's land.

L OF G

THOUGHTS, suggestions, aspirations, pictures,
Cities and farms—by day and night—book of peace and war,
Of platitudes and of the commonplace.

For out-door health, the land and sea—for good will,
For America—for all the earth, all nations, the common
     people,
(Not of one nation only—not America only.)

In it each claim, ideal, line, by all lines, claims, ideals, tem-
     per'd;
Each right and wish by other wishes, rights.

AFTER THE ARGUMENT

A GROUP of little children with their ways and chatter flow in,
Like welcome rippling water o'er my heated nerves and flesh.

FOR US TWO, READER DEAR

SIMPLE, spontaneous, curious, two souls interchanging,
With the original testimony for us continued to the last.

A SICK SPELL

Christmas Day, 25th Dec., 1888.—Am somewhat easier and freer to-day and the last three days—sit up most of the time—read and write, and receive my visitors. Have now been indoors sick for seven months—half of the time bad, bad, vertigo, indigestion, bladder, gastric, head trouble, inertia—Dr. Bucke, Dr. Osler, Drs. Wharton and Walsh—now Edward Wilkins my help and nurse. A fine, splendid, sunny day. My "November Boughs" is printed and out; and my "Complete Works, Poems and Prose," a big volume, 900 pages, also. It is ab't noon, and I sit here pretty comfortable.

TO BE PRESENT ONLY

At the Complimentary Dinner, Camden, New Jersey, May 31, 1889.—Walt Whitman said:

My friends, though announced to give an address, there is no such intention. Following the impulse of spirit, (for I am at least half of Quaker stock) I have obeyed the command to come and look at you, for a minute, and show myself, face to face; which is probably the best I can do. But I have felt no command to make a speech; and shall not therefore attempt any. All I have felt the imperative conviction to say I have already printed in my books of poems or prose; to which I refer any who may be curious. And so, hail and farewell. Deeply acknowledging this deep compliment, with my best respects and love to you personally—to Camden—to New Jersey, and to all represented here—you must excuse me from any word further.

F'm Pall-Mall Gazette, London, England, Feb. 8, 1890

"INTESTINAL AGITATION"

MR. ERNEST RHYS has just receiv'd an interesting letter from Walt Whitman, dated "Camden, January 22, 1890." The following is an extract from it:

I am still here—no very mark'd or significant change or happening—fairly buoyant spirits, &c.—but surely, slowly ebbing. At this moment sitting here, in my den, Mickle Street, by the oakwood fire, in the same big strong old chair with wolf-skin spread over back—bright sun, cold, dry winter day. America continues—is generally busy enough all over her vast demesnes (intestinal agitation I call it,) talking, plodding, making money, every one trying to get on—perhaps to get towards the top—but no special individual signalism—(just as well, I guess.)

FEELING FAIRLY

Friday, July 27, 1890.—Feeling fairly these days, and even jovial—sleep and appetite good enough to be thankful for—had a dish of Maryland blackberries, some good rye bread and a cup of tea, for my breakfast—relish'd all—fine weather—bright sun to-day—pleasant north-west breeze blowing in the open window as I sit here in my big rattan chair—two great fine roses (white and red, blooming, fragrant, sent by mail by W. S. K. and wife, Mass.) are in a glass of water on the table before me.

Am now in my 72d year.

TWO QUESTIONS

An editor of (or in) a leading monthly magazine (Harper's Monthly, July, 1890,) asks: "A hundred years from now will W. W. be popularly rated a great poet—or will he be forgotten?" . . . A mighty ticklish question—which can only be left for a hundred years hence—perhaps more than that. But whether W. W. has been mainly rejected by his own times is an easier question to answer.

All along from 1860 to '91, many of the pieces in L of G, and its annexes, were first sent to publishers or magazine editors before being printed in the L, and were peremptorily rejected by them, and sent back to their author. The "Eidolons" was sent back by Dr. H., of "Scribner's Monthly" with a lengthy, very insulting and contemptuous letter. "To the Sun-Set Breeze," was rejected by the editor of "Harper's Monthly" as being "an improvisation" only. "On, on ye jocund twain" was rejected by the "Century" editor as being personal merely. Several of the pieces went the rounds of all the monthlies, to be thus summarily rejected.

June, '90.—The ———— rejects and sends back my little poem, so I am now set out in the cold by every big magazine and publisher, and may as well understand and admit it—which is just as well, for I find I am palpably losing my sight and ratiocination.

From the Camden Post, April 16, '91

OUT IN THE OPEN AGAIN

Walt Whitman got out in the mid-April sun and warmth of yesterday, propelled in his wheel chair, the first time after four months of imprisonment in his sick room. He has had the worst winter yet, mainly from grippe and gastric troubles, and threaten'd blindness; but keeps good spirits, and has a new little forthcoming book in the printer's hands.

LAST SAVED ITEMS

f'm a vast batch left to oblivion

In its highest aspect, and striking its grandest average, essential Poetry expresses and goes along with essential Religion—has been and is more the adjunct, and more serviceable to that true religion (for of course there is a false one and plenty of it,) than all the priests and creeds and churches that now exist or have ever existed—Even while the temporary prevalent theory and practice of poetry is merely one-side and ornamental and dainty—a love-sigh, a bit of jewelry, a feudal conceit, an ingenious tale or intellectual *finesse,* adjusted to the low taste and calibre that will always sufficiently generally prevail—(ranges of stairs necessary to ascend the higher.)

The sectarian, church and doctrinal, follies, crimes, fanaticisms, aggregate and individual, so rife all thro' history, are proofs of the radicalness and universality of the indestructible element of humanity's Religion, just as much as any, and are the other side of it. Just as disease proves health, and is the other side of it. . . . The philosophy of Greece taught normality and the beauty of life. Christianity teaches how to endure illness and death. I have wonder'd whether a third philosophy fusing both, and doing full justice to both, might not be outlined.

It will not be enough to say that no Nation ever achiev'd materialistic, political and money-making successes, with general physical comfort, as fully as the United States of America are to-day achieving them. I know very well that those are the indispensable foundations—the *sine qua non* of moral and heroic (poetic) fruitions to come. For if those pre-successes were all—if they ended at that—if nothing more were yielded than so far appears—a gross materialistic prosperity only—America, tried by subtlest tests, were a failure—has not advanced the standard of humanity a bit further than other nations. Or, in plain terms, has but inherited and enjoy'd the results of ordinary claims and preceding ages.

Nature seem'd to use me a long while—myself all well, able, strong and happy—to portray power, freedom, health. But after a while she seems to fancy, may-be I can see and understand it all better by being deprived of most of those.

How difficult it is to add anything more to literature—and how unsatisfactory for any earnest spirit to serve merely the amusement of the multitude! (It even seems to me, said H. Heine, more invigorating to accomplish something bad than something empty.)

The Highest said: Don't let us begin so low—isn't our range too coarse—too gross? . . . The Soul answer'd: No, not when we consider what it is all for—the end involved in Time and Space.

Essentially my own printed records, all my volumes, are doubtless but off-hand utterances f'm Personality, spontaneous, following implicitly the inscrutable command, dominated by that Personality, vaguely even if decidedly, and with little or nothing of plan, art, erudition, &c. If I have chosen to hold the reins, the mastery, it has mainly been to give the way, the power, the road, to the invisible steeds. (I wanted to see how a Person of America, the last half of the 19th century, w'd appear, put quite freely and fairly in honest type.)

Haven't I given specimen clues, if no more? At any rate I have written enough to weary myself—and I will dispatch it to the printers, and cease. But how much—how many topics, of the greatest point and cogency, I am leaving untouch'd!

Walt Whitman:
Biographical Note

Walt Whitman: Biographical Note

THE CHRONOLOGY of the poet's life is curiously meagre, even after the excellent work of recent biographers such as Emory Holloway. To reverse Whitman's dictum, we might say that this was no man, but a book. As in the ancient bards of nature and fertility with whom Whitman allied himself, the essential facts are that he was born, he loved, and he died; and despite the ten volumes of Whitman's complete writings, the author appears almost deliberately anonymous.

He was born May 31, 1819, on Long Island: the "Paumanok" from which he started. When his family moved to Brooklyn, he attended elementary school there, and, at the age of twelve, he began his literary career as a printer's devil. After this, in his teens, he was a schoolteacher for a while, an editor of a Long Island paper, a casual journalist. In 1846, he became editor of the Brooklyn *Daily Eagle*, while continuing to publish rather florid prose, propaganda verses, and some blood-curdling thrillers which showed the benefits of a moral life. In 1848 he took a trip to Orleans which was almost surely the beginning of his sexual, emotional, and artistic liberation; and the true nature of which he tried afterwards to disguise by attributing to himself, though unmarried, six southern children. "Circumstances (connected with their fortune and benefit)," he wrote to John Addington Symonds, "have separated me from intimate relations."

These circumstances also became a highly controversial issue among Whitman scholars. Meanwhile, during the seven years before the publication of *Leaves of Grass*, on July 4th, 1855, Whitman edited another paper and, moving on from this too, outwardly a complete failure, he worked as a carpenter in Brooklyn. During the Civil War years, his second crucial emotional experience, he was a government clerk and then a nurse in the Washington hospitals. In 1865 he was dismissed from his post in the Indian Bureau because of the immorality of his poetry. He was then writing the only great verses of the Civil War produced by an American poet.

In 1871 he published *Democratic Vistas* and the fifth edition of *Leaves of Grass*. He was ill from the war experiences; his mother died; and he suffered a paralytic stroke. (The connection between these events may be significant in the true inward history of Whitman's emotional life.) He partially recovered the use of his physical faculties; he turned to nature for solace, as he recorded in the touching and beautiful passages of *Specimen Days*. From the experience of his age, sickness and solitude, and from the memories of the social cataclysm he had witnessed, came this great diary of the war between the states.

It was published in 1882, when Whitman was sixty-three, and dependent on the generosity of friends and admirers for a living of any sort. "The paralysis that first affected me nearly ten years ago, has since remain'd, with varying course," he wrote. "I easily tire, am very clumsy, cannot walk far; but my spirits are first-rate." Aside from the trips he took, his whole activity was devoted to writing and maintaining his interest in "life, people, progress, and the questions of the day." The successive editions of *Leaves of Grass*, ten by the date of his death, contained new poems and ceaseless revisions of the older ones. In 1884 he settled down in Camden, New Jersey; in 1888 he suffered another attack of paralysis. In 1890 he had time to offer, for Queen Victoria's birthday—

"A bunch of white and pink arbutus, silent, spicy, shy,
    From Hudson's, Delaware's, or Potomac's woody banks."

During the same year, meditating on the question put by *Harper's Monthly*: "A hundred years from now will W.W. be popularly rated a great poet—or will he be forgotten?"— Whitman jotted down in his notes: "A mighty ticklish question—which can only be left for a hundred years hence."

In 1891, ill with pneumonia, he had his last birthday dinner. In March, 1892, preparing another edition of *Leaves of Grass,* he died in Camden. . . . Wearying of his own verses at last, so he had proclaimed earlier, he wished to emerge personally for his readers from behind the screen where he had hid. But the screen nevertheless stood there to the very end: which was only fitting for this descendant of the ancient race of orphic and gnomic bards who traced themselves back to Kronos, Zeus, Hercules, as Whitman said, while "buying drafts" of Osiris and Isis.

It is interesting to compare the standard accounts of Whitman's life today with his own brief summary, jotted down towards the close of his career. This autobiographical statement follows.

Walt Whitman:
Autobiographical Note

Walt Whitman: Autobiographical Note

ANYTHING like unmitigated acceptance of my *Leaves of Grass* book, and heart-felt response to it, in a popular however faint degree, bubbled forth as a fresh spring from the ground in England in 1876. The time was a critical and turning point in my personal and literary life. Let me revert to my memorandum book, Camden, New Jersey, that year, fill'd with addresses, receipts, purchase, &c., of the two volumes pub'd then by myself—the *Leaves,* and the *Two Rivulets*—some home customers for them, but mostly from the British Islands. I was seriously paralyzed from the Secession war, poor, in debt, was expecting death, (the doctors put four chances out of five against me,)—and I had the books printed during the lingering interim to occupy the tediousness of glum days and nights. Curiously, the sale abroad proved prompt, and what one might call copious: the names came in lists and the money with them, by foreign mail. The price was $10 a set. Both the cash and the emotional cheer were deep medicines; many paid double or treble price, (Tennyson and Ruskin did,) and many sent kind and eulogistic letters; ladies, clergymen, social leaders, persons of rank, and high officials. Those blessed gales from the British Islands probably (certainly) saved me. . . .

Severely scann'd, it was perhaps no very great or vehement success; but the tide had palpably shifted at any rate, and the sluices were turn'd into my own veins and pockets. That emotional, audacious, open-handed, friendly-mouth'd just-opportune English action, I say, pluck'd me like a brand from the burning, and gave me life again, to finish my book, since ab't completed. I do not forget it, and shall not; and if I ever have a biographer I charge him to put it in the narrative. I have had the noblest friends and backers in America; Wm. O'Connor, Dr. R. M. Bucke, John Burroughs, Geo. W. Childs, good ones in Boston, and Carnegie and R. G. Ingersoll in New York; and yet perhaps the tenderest and gratefulest breath of my heart has gone, and ever goes, over the sea-gales across the big pond.

About myself at present. I will soon enter upon my 73d year, if I live—have pass'd an active life, as country schoolteacher, gardener, printer, carpenter, author and journalist, domicil'd in nearly all the United States and principal cities, North and South—went to the front (moving about and occupied as army nurse and missionary) during the Secession war, 1861 to '65, and in the Virginia hospitals and after the battles of that time, tending the Northern and Southern wounded alike—work'd down South and in Washington city arduously three years—contracted the paralysis which I have suffer'd ever since—and now live in a little cottage of my own, near the Delaware in New Jersey. My chief book, unrhym'd and unmetrical (it has taken thirty years, peace and war, "a borning") has its aim as once said, "to utter the same old human *critter*—but now in Democratic American modern and scientific conditions." Then I have publish'd two prose works "Specimen Days," and a late one "November Boughs." (A little volume "Good-Bye my Fancy" is soon to be out, wh' will finish the matter.) I do not propose here to enter the much-fought field of the literary criticism of any of those works.

But for a few portraiture or descriptive bits. To-day in the upper of a little wooden house of two stories near the Delaware river, east shore, sixty miles up from the sea, is a rather large 20-by-20 low ceiling'd room something like a big old ship's cabin. The floor, three quarters of it with an ingrain carpet, is half cover'd by a deep litter of books, papers, magazines, thrown-down letters and circulars, rejected manuscripts, memoranda, bits of light or strong twine, a bundle to be "express'd," and two or three venerable scrap books. In the room stand two large tables (one of ancient St. Domingo mahogany with immense leaves) cover'd by a jumble of more papers, a varied and copious array of writing materials, several glass and china vessels or jars, some with cologne-water, others with real honey, granulated sugar, a large bunch of beautiful fresh yellow chrysanthemums, some letters and envelope papers ready for the post office, many photographs, and a hundred indescribable things besides. There are all around many books, some quite handsome editions, some half cover'd by dust, some within reach, evidently used, (good-sized print, no type less than long primer,) some maps, the Bible, (the strong cheap edition of the English crown,) Homer, Shakespere, Walter Scott, Emerson, Ticknor's "Spanish Literature," John Carlyle's Dante, Felton's Greece, George Sand's Consuelo, a very choice little Epictetus, some novels, the latest foreign and American monthlies, quarterlies, and so on. There being quite a strew of printer's proofs and slips, and the daily papers, the place with its quaint old fashion'd calmness has also a smack of something alert and of current work. There are several trunks and depositaries back'd up at the walls; (one well-bound and big box came by express lately from Washington city, after storage there for nearly twenty years.) Indeed the whole room is a sort of result and storage collection of my own past life. I have here various editions of my own writings, and sell them upon request; one is a big volume of complete poems and prose, 1000 pages, autograph, essays, speeches, portraits from life, &c. Another is a little *Leaves of Grass*, latest date, six portraits, morocco bound, in pocket-book form.

Fortunately the apartment is quite roomy. There are three windows in front. At one side is the stove, with a cheerful fire of oak wood, near by a good supply of fresh sticks, whose faint aroma is plain. On another side is the bed with white coverlid and woollen blankets. Toward the windows is a huge arm-chair, (a Christmas present from Thomas Donaldson's young daughter and son, Philadelphia) timber'd as by some stout ship's spars, yellow polish'd, ample, with rattan-woven seat and back, and over the latter a great wide wolf-skin of hairy black and silver, spread to guard against cold and draught. A time-worn look and scent of old oak attach both to the chair and the person occupying it.

But probably (even at the charge of parrot talk) I cannot give no more authentic brief sketch than "from an old remembrance copy," where I have lately put myself on record as follows: Was born May 31, 1819, in my father's farm-house, at West Hills, L. I., New York State. My parents' folks mostly farmers and sailors—on my father's side, of English—on my mother's, (Van Velsor's) from Hollandic immigration. There was, first and last, a large family of children; (I was the second.) We moved to Brooklyn while I was still a little one in frocks—and there in B. I grew up out of frocks—then as child and boy went to the public schools—then to work in a printing office. When only sixteen or seventeen years old, and for three years afterward, I went to teaching country schools down in Queens and Suffolk counties, Long Island, and "boarded round." Then, returning to New York, work'd as printer and writer, (with an occasional shy at "poetry.")

1848–'9.—About this time—after ten or twelve years of experiences and work and lots of fun in New York and Brooklyn—went off on a leisurely journey and working expedition (my brother Jeff with me) through all the Middle States, and down the Ohio and Mississippi rivers. Lived a while in New Orleans, and work'd there. (Have lived quite a good deal in the Southern States.) After a time, plodded back northward, up the Mississippi, the Missouri, &c., and around to, and by way of, the great lakes, Michigan, Huron and Erie, to Niagara Falls and Lower Canada—finally returning through Central New York, and down the Hudson. 1852–'54—Occupied in house-building in Brooklyn. (For a little while of the first part of that time in printing a daily and weekly paper.)

1855.—Lost my dear father this year by death. . . . Commenced putting *Leaves of Grass* to press, for good—after many MSS. doings and undoings—(I had great trouble in leaving out the stock "poetical" touches—but succeeded at last.) The book has since had some eight hitches or stages of growth, with one annex (and another to come out in 1891, which will complete it.)

1862.—In December of this year went down to the field of war in Virginia. My brother George reported badly wounded in the Fredericksburg fight. (For 1863 and '64, see *Specimen Days.*) 1865 to '71—Had a place as clerk (till well on in '73) in the Attorney General's Office, Washington. (New York and Brooklyn seem more like *home*, as I was born near, and brought up in them, and lived, man and boy, for 30 years. But I lived some years in Washington, and have visited, and partially lived, in most of the Western and Eastern cities.)

1873.—This year lost, by death, my dear dear mother—and, just before, my sister Martha—the two best and sweetest women I have ever seen or known, or ever expect to see. Same year, February, a sudden climax and prostration from paralysis. Had been simmering inside for several years; broke out during those times temporarily, and then went over. But now a serious attack, beyond cure. Dr. Drinkard, my Washington physician, (and a first-rate one,) said it was the result of too extreme bodily and emotional strain continued at Washington and "down in front," in 1863, '4 and '5. I doubt if a heartier, stronger, healthier physique, more balanced upon itself, or more unconscious, more sound, ever lived, from 1835 to '72. My greatest call (Quaker) to go around and do what I could there in those war-scenes where I had fallen, among the sick and wounded, was, that I seem'd to be *so strong and well.* (I consider'd myself invulnerable.) But this last attack shatter'd me completely. Quit work at Washington, and moved to Camden, New Jersey—where I have lived since, receiving many buffets and some precious caresses—and now write these lines. Since then, (1874–'91) a long stretch of illness, or half-illness, with occasional lulls. During these latter, have revised and printed over all my books—Bro't out

"November Boughs"—and at intervals leisurely and exploringly travel'd to the Prairie States, the Rocky Mountains, Canada, to New York, to my birthplace in Long Island, and to Boston. But physical disability and the war-paralysis above alluded to have settled upon me more and more, the last year or so. Am now (1891) domicil'd, and have been for some years, in this little old cottage and lot in Mickle Street, Camden, with a house-keeper and man nurse. Bodily I am completely disabled, but still write for publication. I keep generally buoyant spirits, write often as there comes any lull in physical sufferings, get in the sun and down to the river whenever I can, retain fair appetite, assimilation and digestion, sensibilities acute as ever, the strength and volition of my right arm good, eyesight dimming, but brain normal, and retain my heart's and soul's unmitigated faith not only in their own original literary plans, but in the essential bulk of American humanity east and west, north and south, city and country, through thick and thin, to the last. Nor must I forget, in conclusion, a special, prayerful, thankful God's blessing to my dear firm friends and personal helpers, men and women, home and foreign, old and young.

Walt Whitman:
Selected Bibliography

Walt Whitman: Selected Bibliography

THE BEST recent editions of Whitman's work are the *Inner Sanctum Edition,* edited by Louis Untermeyer; the *Complete Poetry and Prose,* as prepared by Whitman for the Deathbed Edition, with an introduction by Malcolm Cowley; and the *Viking Portable Library Whitman,* edited by Mark Van Doren.

The Untermeyer edition includes an excellent survey of Whitman criticism from the first publication of *Leaves of Grass* in 1855. Notable early comments are those by Emerson, Thoreau and Henry James; in England by Swinburne, W. M. Rossetti and Anne Gilchrist. Add to these William James (*The Varieties of Religious Experience*) for the psychologists; George Santayana (*Interpretations of Poetry and Religion*) for the philosophers; and Edith Wharton (*A Backward Glance*) for the novelists.

D. H. Lawrence's *Studies in Classic American Literature* is an admirable volume of creative interpretation; strictly personal, illuminating even when wrong, as the chapter on Whitman shows. Among the more sober historians, the best accounts are those by Van Wyck Brooks in *America's Coming of Age* and *The Times of Melville and Whitman;* by Vernon Parrington in *Main Currents in American Thought;* and by F. O. Matthiessen in *American Renaissance.*

The history of Whitman scholarship is marked by the extravagance of a cult and the malice of literary opponents; only in the modern period has there been a more objective approach to critical evaluation. A useful summary of these trends is contained in Gay Wilson Allen's *Walt Whitman Handbook,* an excellent reference work. Modern biographies of Whitman include those by Bliss Perry (1906), Emory

Holloway (1926), Newton Arvin (1938), and Henry Seidel Canby (1943). In the field of scholarly research there are interesting studies by Clifton Joseph Furness, Sculley Bradley, Charles Glicksberg and F. I. Carpenter, among others.

The *Complete Writings of Walt Whitman*, in ten volumes, was published in 1902 under the editorial supervision of Richard Bucke, Thomas Harned and Horace Traubel. A variorum edition of *Leaves of Grass*, compiled by Oscar Triggs, was published in 1929. Holloway's *Complete Poetry and Selected Prose* appeared in 1938.

One of the confusing elements in the interpretation of Whitman's work is the difference in time between the original publication of the poems and Whitman's later revisions. The dates for the verses are deceptive, and so are the verses. As for the selections in a popular-priced edition of Whitman, there must be a compromise between the poet, the editor, and the space. In the long run the world will do what it pleases with any book, as Whitman said about his own; and perhaps the more the world pleases, the greater the book.

For the centenary of *Leaves of Grass* there are scheduled to appear a new biography of Whitman by Gay Wilson Allen; an anthology of Whitman criticism outside the United States, edited by Allen; and a volume of new essays on Whitman edited by Milton Hindus. The Library of Congress and the United States Information Service have arranged for centennial lectures, and other Whitman events will be sponsored by libraries and universities.

Index of Titles
and
Dates of Poems

Index of Titles
And Dates of Poems

THESE SYMBOLS GUARANTEE
THE BEST IN READING

POCKET BOOKS, INC. is the largest publisher of books in the world today in terms of the number of copies it has sold and is currently selling. Nearly 500,000,000 copies have carried the symbol of "Gertrude," the little kangaroo which is the colophon of POCKET BOOKS, INC., or the perky bird which is the trademark of CARDINAL EDITIONS, books of exceptional merit and value, priced at 25¢, 35¢ and 50¢.

Only genuine POCKET BOOK and CARDINAL editions carry these symbols. The titles are carefully chosen from the lists of all leading publishers and present the most distinguished and most widely diversified group offered today by any publisher of paper-bound books. Watch for these symbols. They are your guarantee of the best in reading at the lowest possible price.